This is a story about [men].
The women whom [they...]
are seen mainly through their eyes.

**BRIGADIER GENERAL
ANSON McCOOK**
*Led his 2nd Ohio
in six major battles.*

**NAVAL LIEUTENANT
RODERICK McCOOK**
*First naval officer to
capture Rebel Army regiment.*

**CHAPLAIN
HENRY McCOOK**
*Fighting chaplain
of the 41st Illinois.*

**LIEUTENANT
JOHN McCOOK**
*Fought in the first
land battle of the war.*

COLONEL GEORGE McCOOK
*Law partner of Edwin Stanton,
secretary of war.*

**BRIGADIER GENERAL
ROBERT McCOOK**
*Led first successful
bayonet charge of war.*

**MAJOR GENERAL
ALEXANDER McCOOK**
*Youngest general in the
Union volunteer army.*

**BRIGADIER GENERAL
DAN McCOOK JR.**
*Law partner of General
William T. Sherman.*

COLONEL JOHN McCOOK
*Youngest of the clan, fought in
nine major battles east and west.*

PRIVATE CHARLES McCOOK
*Died in his father's
arms at Bull Run.*

**MAJOR GENERAL
EDWIN STANTON McCOOK**
*Namesake of Lincoln's
secretary of war.*

The Fighting McCooks

The Fighting McCooks

The true story of America's famous fighting family.
Seventeen McCooks fought for the North in the Civil War:
three major generals, three brigadier generals,
one naval lieutenant, four surgeons, two colonels,
one major, one lieutenant, one private, and one chaplain.
Four gave their lives to save the Union.

"A record of which the nation may well feel proud,"
Thirty-ninth Congress of the United States, April 13, 1866

By Charles and Barbara Whalen

WESTMORELAND
PRESS

Publisher's Cataloging-in-Publication
(Provided by Quality Books, Inc.)

   Whalen, Charles W.
      The fighting McCooks / by Charles and Barbara Whalen.
      p. cm.
      Includes bibliographical references and index.
      LCCN 2006923900
      ISBN-13: 978-0-9779081-4-1
      ISBN-10: 0-9779081-4-3

      1. McCook family. 2. United States—History—Civil
   War, 1861-1865—Biography. 3. Ohio—History—Civil War,
   1861-1865—Biography.   I. Whalen, Barbara, 1928-
   II. Title.

   E467.W45 2006   973.7'41'0922
                              QBI06-600095

Printed in the United States of America
1 2 3 4 5 6 7 8 9 10 — 12 11 10 09 08 07 06

Book and cover design by Jill Dible

Westmoreland Press
5301 Portsmouth Road
Bethesda, Maryland 20816

*Dedicated to all the descendants
of the Fighting McCooks*

Contents

Prologue

It was the winter of 1860–61 in the Ohio Valley. On a wind-swept bank of the Ohio River, the western border between free and slave states, a bellicose doctor named John McCook stood beside a little brass cannon.

Soon a steamboat hove into view on the broad bosom of the winding river. Downbound, it was rumored to be carrying munitions from the Pittsburgh arsenal to the arming South. When the boat came into range, Dr. McCook fired his cannon furiously, and the startled deckhands dove for cover.

Folklore in the Ohio Valley says it was these artillery salvos, and not those fired a few months later at Fort Sumter, that were the opening shots of the Civil War.

Chapter 1

JUDGE DANIEL MCCOOK
at the White House

Dusk was descending on Washington City as Daniel McCook shouldered his musket in the magnificent East Room of the White House. It was April 18, 1861. The Civil War was six days old.

In the East Room it was a seriocomic scene of swashbuckling adventure as Daniel McCook and sixty assorted Westerners, wearing stovepipe hats and wielding guns with fixed bayonets, marched spiritedly on the thick velvet carpet. They were drilling to the shrill orders of a notorious Kansas gunslinger, clad in a torn shirt and rusty coat, who strutted the ballroom waving a huge sword under the glittering gaslight from three enormous chandeliers. These were the so-called Frontier Guards.

Earlier that afternoon the men had been recruited in the lobby of Willard's Hotel by the gunslinger who led them up Pennsylvania Avenue to the White House, where he announced that they had come to save

President Lincoln from a lynching. This was in response to rumors that an army of fifteen thousand Southerners, flushed with victory after the capture of Fort Sumter, was marching toward the panic-stricken capital to drag Lincoln from his bed and hang him from the nearest tree.

"Is this the 'irrepressible conflict' of which we have heard so much?" Daniel McCook mused dryly.

It was ironic. He, a member of one of Ohio's most prominent Democrat families, had scathingly derided the 1858 prediction of Republican Senator William H. Seward of New York that "an irrepressible conflict" was inevitable between the nineteen free states and the fifteen slave states. Now the odious conflict had come, and McCook, at the age of sixty-two, found himself on the front line.

Daniel McCook, called "Judge" due to his tenure as a probate judge in the Ohio Valley, was a familiar figure in the nation's capital. A tall man, he stood six-feet-two-inches in his stocking feet and had the commanding presence of a Scotch-Irish clan chieftain. A handsome man, he possessed a square jaw and canny blue-gray eyes. A well-liked man, he had a host of friends in high places. A family man, he was proud of his twelve children, including nine sons and three daughters.

Unfortunately, Daniel McCook was also a very ambitious man, with a tendency to cut corners and step on toes. He had once been a prosperous lawyer, merchant, and landowner in the Ohio Valley. But he had taken risks. He had gone broke. So he had come to Washington to remake his fortune.

During the winter of 1860–61, Daniel McCook was working frantically as a lobbyist on Capitol Hill, promoting the passage of the Pacific Railroad Bill. Sponsored by his good friend U.S. Senator Stephen A. Douglas of Illinois, the bill authorized the building of a transcontinental railroad from Chicago to San Francisco.

Coincidentally, Daniel was also promoting the interests of the Mount Carbon Coal Company. The firm, owning twenty-four hundred acres in one of the richest coalfields in southern Illinois, was in an excellent position to make iron for the railroad. Millionaires were being made every day, and Daniel McCook could see no reason that he should not be one of them.

His optimism prevailed even as the nation began to unravel. Abraham Lincoln, elected president the preceding November 6, would not be inaugurated until March 4, 1861. In the meantime Southern states started seceding, one by one . . . South Carolina . . . Mississippi . . . Florida . . . Alabama.

Undaunted, Daniel McCook forged ahead with business as usual. The Mount Carbon Coal Company needed two hundred thousand dollars to develop its iron-making capacity. McCook had commissioned a friend in Connecticut, Richard H. Phelps, to raise the money from wealthy Hartford bankers who had financed many of the nation's canals and railroads.

During January and February, McCook wrote Phelps almost daily. Torn between hopes for his business and fears for his country, Daniel's spirits soared and sank like a cork on the sea.

After rebels seized Federal forts in the Deep South, his spirits sank:

January 12

My Dear Sir,
 I fear the actions of those <u>Southern fools</u>. . . .

Three days later, as the Crittenden Resolutions, designed to appease the South, were being debated in the Senate, Daniel's spirits soared:

January 15

Politically things look like improvement.

But the very next day, after the Senate rejected the resolutions, his spirits sank again:

January 16
. . . many thought the last ray of hope had vanished.

And a week later, in spite of the fact that Georgia and Louisiana had seceded, his spirits soared again:

27th Jany
Politically things are looking better. I now have no doubt of a compromise.

McCook's hopes were pinned on a peace conference to be held in Washington on February 4. It was a last-ditch effort to hold the Union together. However, the six seceded Southern states refused to attend. Four days later, in Montgomery, Alabama, they formed the Confederate States of America.

To add to McCook's woes, Richard Phelps wrote that the Hartford bankers liked the Illinois iron-making venture, but, nervous about loaning money during the national crisis, they preferred to buy the company and develop the land themselves.

McCook's reply was indignant:

February 21

. . . *it is not for sale.*

His reasons were twofold. One was iron. The other was oil. Two years earlier the world's first oil well had been sunk in Pennsylvania. So he cautioned Phelps:

> *Say nothing to the people on the subject of Oil. I have an idea on Oil to communicate to you—. . . keep dark until I see you.*

Confident that he could succeed where Phelps had failed, Daniel McCook hurriedly packed his bag and started for Connecticut. It was a fifteen-hour train trip with seven car changes, a horse-pulled passage through Baltimore, a streetcar ride through Philadelphia, and three ferryboat crossings of the Susquehanna, Delaware, and Hudson rivers.

Arriving in Hartford, McCook used all his considerable charm on the flinty-eyed financiers. While he was there, Texas became the seventh state to secede. On March 3 Congress adjourned.

The next day, amid deep gloom, Abraham Lincoln was inaugurated as the sixteenth president of the United States. For several weeks Lincoln did little, hoping that secession fever would die down. Newspapers called it "masterly inactivity."

With the North on the verge of a nervous breakdown, the Hartford bankers held on to their money. So it was a disappointed, but not yet defeated, Daniel McCook who caught a train to New York City to try

U.S. Capitol at Lincoln's first inauguration,
March 4, 1861

Wall Street financiers. Turned down again, he was forced to resort to high-interest Jersey City moneymen. He wrote Phelps after the deal:

> *April 3*
> *The terms they make are hard, but <u>necessity is a poor man's law</u>. This is a great sacrifice, but the best that I could do.*

Then, politically astute, Daniel predicted:

> *I fear that before Lincoln gets over his "masterly inactivity" that the border states will be gone—and the Southern Republics will be recognized by <u>France</u> and <u>England</u>, when we will all be at sea.*

McCook's fears were well-founded. English aristocrats, worried that democracy might take root in their own country, would be delighted to see their former colonies disintegrate. If England recognized the Confederacy, France was sure to follow.

His letter to Phelps continued:

> *Lincoln must call a Special Session of Congress, when he will be compelled to show his hand.*

McCook returned to Washington as President Lincoln finally did "show his hand" by refusing to give up Fort Sumter, the Federal fort in Charleston's harbor, as South Carolina demanded. On April 12 the Confederates attacked the fort. On April 13 Fort Sumter fell. On April 15 Lincoln asked Northern states to furnish seventy-five thousand volunteers for three months to put down the Southern rebellion.

That day McCook wrote Phelps:

> *April 15*
> *My Dear Sir,*
> *Ere this will reach you will have heard that all the evils of Civil War is upon us.*

The worst evil was that Washington City was ripe for capture. Forty miles south of the Mason-Dixon line, the nation's capital was sandwiched between the slave-owning states of Virginia and Maryland. Most of the sixteen-thousand-man U.S. Army was out west fighting Indians. The little U.S. Navy was scattered to the seven seas. Only a fifteen-hundred-man garrison was on hand to protect the Capitol, and a fifteen-thousand-man Confederate Army was said to be just across the Long Bridge on the other side of the Potomac River.

Terrified, most of Washington's sixty thousand residents and visitors fled. Trains were filled to overflowing. Roads were clogged with carriages. Wagons were heaped with household goods. The poor walked, pushing their things in wheelbarrows.

Those few people remaining in town were mostly Southerners waiting for their army to arrive. No one was trusted. Traitors were everywhere. Even White House servants were suspect. On the afternoon of April 18 rumors raced through town that assassins were going to storm the White House that night and kill Lincoln.

That was when notorious gunslinger U.S. Senator-elect James H. Lane of Kansas recruited Daniel McCook and the other Westerners into the Frontier Guards in the lobby of Willard's Hotel and marched them to the White House. Brushing past "Old Edward," the wizened Irish doorman who had served seven U.S. presidents, Lane and his militia set up camp in the East Room. A crate of ammunition was dumped in the middle of the floor where, a year earlier, America's loveliest belles had been presented to England's Prince of Wales.

In President Thomas Jefferson's day the East Room had been an elegant chamber of gold and white Grecian simplicity. Now, befitting the burgeoning nation, it was a Romanesque mélange of red. Red damask sofas, red fringed draperies, and red wallpaper competed with a mammoth three-thousand-pound Brussels carpet festooned with garlands of bright flowers. It was as ostentatiously overdecorated as any railroad tycoon's Victorian parlor.

Daniel McCook could remember when, in happier times, the East Room was the scene of the famous presidential levees, evening receptions to which everyone in the nation was welcome. Parading the floor on those occasions were members of the president's cabinet, Supreme Court justices, Western frontiersmen in scuffed boots, Broadway swells in patent leather shoes, diamond-bedecked Southern belles, homespun rustics from the territories, foreign diplomats weighted down with medals, and Indian chiefs in towering headdresses from the Far West who had been brought to Washington to be impressed by the awesome power of the federal government.

Now the East Room was a barrack.

President Abraham Lincoln, working in his office upstairs, heard the ringing of rammers in musket barrels and decided to go down and swap stories with the rough-hewn men of the West. The fifty-two-year-old backwoods politician had an inexhaustible fund of earthy jokes that he loved to share. Laughter relieved his all-too-frequent bouts of depression.

Presidential reception in the East Room of the White House

The homeliest man ever to preside at the White House ambled awk-wardly down the Great Staircase. He seemed a giant, loose-limbed skele-ton, with his sinewy six-foot-four-inch frame draped in ill-fitting clothes, with his gray eyes deep-set in a leathery and dark-hued face, and with his shuffling stride propelling him slowly across the marble-floored Grand Foyer to the door of the East Room. There the president was stopped.

"Password?" asked the sentry.

The gunslinging Senator-elect Lane, who once killed a Kansas neigh-bor over a mere fence dispute, had gone out to stalk Pennsylvania Avenue. But he had left word that no one was to enter the East Room without the password.

Lincoln had to admit that he did not know it.

Then, said the sentry, more afraid of Lane than Lincoln, the president could not come in. Raucous laughter ricocheted through the White House as Lincoln, a good-natured and self-confident man who could see humor in everything and needed no pose of importance, beat a hasty retreat back upstairs. The roaring Westerners knew that this was just the sort of rustic comedy that the rail-splitter from Illinois most enjoyed. What a good joke on old Abe!

Southerners, when they read the story the next day in the *Washington Evening Star*, were not amused. They felt that Easterners, with their stiff, self-righteous ways, were bad enough. Westerners, rude and crude, were far worse.

So, as they waited impatiently for their army to arrive and capture the Capitol for the Confederacy, Southern men oiled their pistols and Southern women opened their windows and sat down at their pianos. By day and night the defiant strains of "Dixie" drifted through the deserted streets of the desolate city.

On April 19 the news was dire: The Federal arsenal at Harper's Ferry had fallen. Many of the naval officers at the Norfolk Navy Yard had resigned. Only one telegraph line to the North was working. The first deaths of the war occurred when the Sixth Massachusetts Regiment, fighting its way through Baltimore, had four men killed and thirty-six wounded. The regiment finally made it to Washington and marched up to the Capitol to sleep in the Senate chamber barricaded with flour bar-rels and sandbags.

On April 20 the city was isolated: Maryland rebels had torn up the one railroad track leading north and burned all the bridges. A delegation of Baltimore men came to the White House and demanded that no more Federal troops pass through their city. President Lincoln, trying to keep the border state of Maryland from seceding, agreed. He wired the Seventh New York Volunteer Infantry Regiment to come by sea. The ranks of the Frontier Guards swelled to 120 men, including two senators, three congressmen, several newspaper editors, the chief justice of the Supreme Court, and two of Daniel McCook's nephews, Edward and Henry, who arrived on the last train from Ohio.

On April 21 the city was silent: The last telegraph wire to the North had been cut. All the ships at the Norfolk Navy Yard had been burned to keep them from falling into Rebel hands. President Lincoln climbed to the roof of the White House to look for the ships bringing the Seventh New York. The Potomac River was empty. Rebel campfires burned ominously on the Virginia shore. The two little Lincoln boys had been spirited out of the city, and Mrs. Lincoln sat up all night fully dressed, waiting to be captured.

On April 22 the city was dark and deserted: The *Washington Evening Star* carried the notice—"The Washington Theatre has been closed for the present, the condition of affairs here just now not being favorable to theatricals." There was a flurry of store closings. The jeweler Galt marked his fine things down to "panic prices." The Frontier Guards marched up and down in front of the White House armed with minié rifles, sword bayonets, and navy revolvers.

On April 23 the city was braced for an attack: Gloom was everywhere. Eight miles of railroad track between Annapolis and Washington had been torn up. General-in-Chief of the U.S. Army Winfield Scott came to the White House for dinner and talked of the possibility of famine. Messengers sent out on horseback did not return. A haggard Lincoln scanned the Potomac River with his long field glass, looking for the ships bringing the Seventh New York and muttering, "Why don't they come?"

On April 24 the city was veiled with the melancholy grandeur of impending doom: Under the light of a full moon the townhouses around Lafayette Square were shuttered and dark. The Capitol was barricaded with heaps of iron and marble ten feet high. The eerie silence was broken only by the hammering on the unfinished Capitol dome, which Lincoln had ordered to show that the nation would survive, and the pianos incessantly tinkling "Dixie."

"Dixie" was heard again about noon on April 25: This time it was played by a band, a big band, the magnificent band of the crack Seventh New York Volunteer Infantry Regiment as it marched up Pennsylvania Avenue, one thousand men strong, with the Stars and Stripes flying in the bright sun at the head of the troops.

The hollowed-eyed occupants of the White House ran out on the lawn to cheer. Mrs. Lincoln wept for joy. The president, who had aged visually during the weeklong ordeal, stood at the North Portico to welcome the regiment that had arrived by ship at Annapolis the previous evening and worked all night repairing the railroad by the light of the full moon. The siege was over.

The mission of the Frontier Guards also was over. A grateful President Lincoln thanked them for their loyalty, and they all went out on the South Lawn of the White House to have their picture taken. The men were resplendent in their frock coats, stovepipe hats, and muskets affixed with towering bayonets.

Frontier Guards on the South Lawn of the White House

Two days later ten thousand Northern troops had arrived, and more were coming. Newspaper reporters, sipping brandy toddies at the bar in Willard's Hotel, could not understand why the Confederates had not attacked the city during the seven-day siege. The supremely self-confident Daniel McCook knew why, as he wrote Richard Phelps:

> *May 4*
>
> *My dear Sir,*
> *. . . I belonged to the "Frontier Guards," commanded by James H. Lane of Kansas notoriety. They were a terror to evil doers. After their organization, secession stock depressed in the market. We heard no more of hanging Lincoln. . . .*
>
> *Very Respectfully*
> *Daniel McCook*

After a week in the White House, the ingratiating McCook had a new friend in the highest place of all. For the rest of his life, Daniel McCook would be President Lincoln's ally in the fight to save the Union.

Therein lay another irony. When Lincoln asked for seventy-five thousand volunteers to subdue Southern rebels, his authority rested in a law enacted by Congress on February 28, 1795, requested by President George Washington to subdue Western rebels during the Whiskey Rebellion.

One of those rebels, called the Whiskey Boys, had been Daniel McCook's father.

*Territory trod by the Fighting McCooks
in their quest to save the Union*

Chapter 2

THE WHISKEY BOY
and His Clan in the Ohio River Valley

"A' thought A' was a-comin' til a land of liberty . . . ," ranted the big redheaded rebel who was Daniel McCook's father. The year was 1794.

In the great Ohio River Valley, west of the Appalachian Mountains, immigrant George McCook's thick brogue dripped with sarcasm. He was one of the Whiskey Boys, those Western frontiersmen who refused to pay "unjust" taxes on their whiskey stills.

Fighting for a cause came naturally to a man of Scottish ancestry like McCook.

The Romans discovered in the first century A.D. the fighting spirit of the Scots. Although Roman Legions conquered most of Britain, they never could subdue the fierce tribes in the north, who painted their bodies bright colors before they went gaily into battle. Finally, Roman

Emperor Hadrian just resorted to a great stone wall to keep them at bay. Hadrian's Wall, stretching seventy-three miles across Britain from sea to sea, was the northernmost boundary of the Roman Empire.

Seventeen centuries passed. The Scots, now ruled by England, were encouraged to migrate to northern Ireland to improve their fortunes and civilize the Irish. Neither happened. The land was poor, and the natives refused to be tamed. The only thing that the Presbyterian Scots and Catholic Irish could agree on was their mutual hatred of the English.

During the eighteenth century some two hundred thousand Scots left the unhappy isle and sailed to America where, for lack of a better name, they were called "Scotch-Irish."

George McCook, born in Ballymony in 1752, fled in 1790, just ahead of an English noose. Encouraged by the American Revolution, the thirty-eight-year-old merchant had joined the United Irishmen, a conspiracy of Scots and Irish created to overthrow the English. A revolt failed. McCook was wanted for questioning. The punishment for treason was death. Clearly, it was time to emigrate.

Arriving in America with his wife Mary and nine-year-old daughter Fanny, George McCook discovered that land on the eastern seaboard was expensive. So, like most Scotch-Irish immigrants, he headed west to find cheap acreage. Some of the Scotch-Irish trekked southwest, through Virginia's Shenandoah Valley, to the Carolinas and Georgia. Others trudged due west, over the Appalachian Mountains, to the great Ohio Valley. Beyond it lay the vast riches of the Northwest Territory.

The McCooks took the latter route. After weeks of toiling over the mountains, they arrived at Fort Pitt in western Pennsylvania. Outside the fort was a cluster of cabins called Pittsburgh. George bought several lots at the triangle where the Allegheny and Monongahela rivers met to form the great Ohio River.

Soon, however, the McCooks had to flee again. Shawnee Indians, encouraged by the English, went on the warpath to halt the westward flow of settlers. Fort Pitt braced for an attack. Hearing tales of how the Indians scalped men, ravished women, and carried children into captivity, George McCook hurriedly traded his choice Pittsburgh lots for a crate of Irish sickles and headed south to the little village of Canonsburgh, Pennsylvania, in the gentle Chartiers Valley.

There he became a merchant and a Whiskey Boy.

The Whiskey Rebellion, in full furor, was a fight between east and west. The Whiskey Boys charged that Easterners had encouraged them to go west to expand the nation, but then refused to help when Indians, trying to hold onto their ancestral lands, fought back. Now Easterners were taxing the whiskey stills of Westerners to pay off Revolutionary War debts.

During the summer of 1794 the Whiskey Boys waged a reign of terror in the Ohio Valley. After tarring and feathering tax collectors, they fought a pitched battle with troops from Fort Pitt. George McCook, in the middle of the melee, took a bullet through his wool hat. Next, the rebels stole a U.S. mail pouch from a Philadelphia-to-Pittsburgh stagecoach and opened it in Canonsburgh's Black Horse Tavern. Discovering plans for armed force against them, they designed a flag and began recruiting an army of seven thousand men to seize Fort Pitt and form a Western Republic.

The Whiskey Rebellion was the first test of the power of the young United States of America, under its six-year-old Constitution, to enforce a federal law within a state.

President George Washington sent the Whiskey Boys a warning and an olive branch. When they ignored both, the president raised a twelve-thousand-man Army of the Western Expedition, composed of state militias from Virginia, Maryland, New Jersey, and Pennsylvania. Mounting his charger, Washington led the army west to the Appalachian Mountains, where he turned over the field command to one of his favorite Revolutionary War comrades, General "Light Horse" Harry Lee of Virginia.

George Washington, knowing the Ohio Valley well from his days as a young surveyor, also sent a courier galloping off to General Anthony Wayne in the Northwest Territory. Victorious after defeating the Indians at the Battle of Fallen Timbers, "Mad Anthony" was ordered to turn his three-thousand-man army around and strike the rebels from the rear.

The Whiskey Boys were trapped. The ringleaders were captured and taken to the federal capital of Philadelphia. Two were tried and found guilty of treason, but to the surprise of Europeans, there were no hangings. President Washington, showing the "Old World" the merciful nature of the "New World," pardoned the men, sent them home, and held out a helping hand to the West.

◌

The nation's great westward expansion began in 1795 after the signing of the Treaty of Greenville between General Anthony Wayne and the Indians he had defeated in the Battle of Fallen Timbers. As the tribes gave up vast tracts of land and withdrew further west, white men pushed vigorously into the Northwest Territory.

Peddlers and priests, adventurers and vagabonds, explorers and soldiers of fortune joined thousands of settlers who surged over the Appalachian Mountains. Upon reaching the Ohio River, they boarded flatboats and poled their way down the broad body of water as it turned and twisted its way west for almost a thousand miles into the heart of the great North American continent where it joined the Mississippi.

Travelers, on their way west, often halted at the village of Canonsburgh. By night they reveled at the Black Horse Tavern, where the stolen U.S. Mail pouch had been opened during the Whiskey Rebellion. By day they replenished their supplies at the log cabin store of George McCook. The former Whiskey Boy had become a respectable tax-paying merchant and charter member of the Chartiers Hill Presbyterian Church.

George McCook also became the father of five more children. Proud of his progeny, he had big plans for them. His three daughters were expected to marry well. His three sons were expected to become educated gentlemen in one of the three professions of the day: medicine, law, or ministry. With that in mind, McCook encouraged the founding of Jefferson College in Canonsburgh. It was the first college west of the Appalachian Mountains.

George McCook, a big man with enormous strength, also expected his sons to keep their Scotch-Irish toughness. That was handy in the West, where popular pastimes included knife-throwing, log-rolling, and wrestling—with thumbnails grown long for eye-gouging.

◌

As they grew up, the three clannish McCook brothers were well-known in the Ohio Valley. They were tall, rangy fellows with curly chestnut hair, blue-gray eyes, and the craggy map of Scotland on their faces.

George, the eldest, had been born on June 15, 1795. A brilliant student, fluent in Latin and Greek, he graduated from Jefferson College as valedictorian of his class at the age of sixteen. After briefly studying the law, he turned to medicine and was a licensed physician by the time he was twenty. George was curt.

Daniel, the second son, was born on June 20, 1798. The quintessential young-man-in-a-hurry, he was too impatient to spend much time in college. Instead, he left to read the law with a Canonsburgh attorney. Daniel was crafty.

John, the youngest son, was born on February 22, 1806. He planned to attend Jefferson College and then study with the eminent Dr. Daniel Drake at the Ohio Medical School in Cincinnati. John was convivial.

⟿

Margaret and Martha Latimer were the pretty young daughters of Abraham Latimer, a well-to-do merchant whose fine stone house was across the road from the modest log cabin of the McCooks. The Latimer girls, gently raised and knowing little of work, might have married wealthy older gentlemen.

Instead, they were wooed and won by the young, impecunious, but ambitious McCook brothers. Dr. George McCook and Margaret Latimer were married on January 18, 1816, when he was twenty and she was sixteen.

A year and a half later, Daniel McCook and Martha Latimer were married on August 28, 1817, when he was nineteen and she was fifteen. They were young, but people were marrying young. The country was young. Most of the population was under the age of twenty.

Eventually, the Black Horse Tavern closed, and the entrepreneurial Dr. George McCook bought it at a sheriff's sale. He turned it into a general store with Daniel as the proprietor. Daniel and Martha lived above the store where, at the age of eighteen, she gave birth to her first child. Three more babies followed quickly.

⟿

"Ohio Fever" gripped the nation. Carved out of the Northwest Territory, Ohio had become the seventeenth state in 1803. It soon was a very prosperous one. The National Road, built from Baltimore to the Ohio River, was finished in 1815 and brought hundreds of thousands of settlers swarming into the state to put down roots in the rich Ohio soil.

That included Dr. and Mrs. George McCook. Seeing great opportunities in Ohio, they left Canonsburgh in 1819 and moved to New Lisbon in the northeastern section of the state. It was a bustling market town, known as "The Gateway to the West." Soon Dr. George had a thriving medical practice and a large, impressive brick house.

In 1824 Daniel McCook, Esquire, also caught Ohio Fever. Hiring three wagoners to haul his belongings, Daniel moved Martha and their four small children from Canonsburgh to New Lisbon. However, after Daniel was gone, the town of Canonsburgh discovered that its little brass cannon was also gone.

Purchased during the War of 1812, the little cannon always stood in front of the Black Horse Tavern, where the stolen mail was opened during the Whiskey Rebellion. The town wanted it back. On March 15, 1824, a notice appeared in the *Washington Reporter*, an Ohio Valley newspaper:

$ 5 Reward,

WILL be given for the return of a PIECE OF ARTILLERY, Stolen on or about the *fourth day of February*, from the Subscribers, who, (together with a number of others) contributed for the purchase of the same; and *Ten Dollars* for the apprehension and conviction of the Thief.

JAMES MILLER,
ROBERT BOYCE

Canonsburgh, March 15, 1824.

N.B. The said Piece of Ordnance is suspected to have been conveyed to New Lisbon, Ohio.

Dr. George McCook promptly sent the newspaper a letter, stating that in the winter of 1819, as an investment, he had purchased the Black Horse Tavern

> *and a canon weighing about 140 pounds was on the lot and frozen in the ground. By virtue of this purchase I obtained lawful possession of the . . . canon, for it was immoveably attached to the premises.*

Dr. George, who had studied law, assumed that would end the matter. It did not. Two of the wagoners who hauled Daniel's belongings to Ohio swore under oath that McCook stole the cannon and hid it in one of the wagons. The two men also accused the third wagoner, an illiterate and penniless fellow, of refusing to testify because he feared the hostility of the clannish McCooks.

Daniel McCook was arrested, on the testimony of the two wagoners, and charged with a felony. Dr. George McCook, rushing to the rescue, produced sworn statements from three prominent Ohioans that the cannon had arrived in New Lisbon, not hidden, but fully visible in one of the wagons.

However, it was the testimony of the third wagoner that ended the matter. He revealed that the person behind the charges was Samuel Canon, a son of the late founder of the town. The wagoner's statement, surprisingly well-written for an illiterate fellow, stated:

> *Samuel Canon called upon me and requested me to put my name to a paper relating to the cannon. . . . I replied that I had nothing to do with the cannon . . . nor did I wish to have anything to do with it . . . and that I ever told any person that I did not wish to excite the hostility of the McCooks on account of my pecuniary circumstances is a falsehood.*

> *X*
>
> *John Balentine—His Mark*

According to Ohio Valley lore:

> *A deal was struck. The case was dropped. The two wagoneers were not charged with perjury. There was no record of Daniel McCook's arrest. Samuel Canon dropped out of sight. And the little brass cannon stayed in Ohio.*

ᔕ

The 1820s was the great canal-building era in the nation.

Americans had long dreamed of tying their vast continent together with canals. In upstate New York the 363-mile Erie Canal, linking the Great Lakes to the Hudson River, was finished in 1825. It revolutionized trade. The cost of shipping a ton of wheat from Buffalo to New York City fell from one hundred dollars to ten dollars. New York replaced Philadelphia as the nation's busiest port.

Ohio began digging. Two publicly financed canals were started between Lake Erie and the Ohio River. In 1828 a third canal, a privately financed one, was planned to be the shortest waterway between Pittsburgh and Cleveland.

Called the Sandy and Beaver Canal, it would run through New Lisbon. Not surprisingly, the three McCook brothers had been speculating in land and owned much acreage, including a jointly owned family farm, along the canal route. It promised to make them all wealthy.

A West Point engineer surveyed the land, and a Swiss engineer arrived from Europe to oversee the seventy-three-mile project. Costs for the Sandy and Beaver Canal were estimated at three thousand to five thousand dollars per mile, not including two tunnels, thirty dams, ninety locks, three reservoirs, and a four-hundred-foot aqueduct. Weaving through the picturesque hills and valleys of northeastern Ohio, it was called "The Romantic Canal."

At the same time, in the East, a tiny steam engine named the *Tom Thumb* chugged merrily along on wooden tracks. Laughing people called it the "Iron Horse."

ᔕ

In 1832 Daniel McCook wanted only one thing for Christmas. The ambitious thirty-four-year-old lawyer was not home with Martha and their six children on Christmas morning. Instead, he was at the State Capitol in Columbus, Ohio.

Daniel McCook and his equally shrewd partner, Isaac Atkinson, had been busy for the past year lobbying lawmakers to create a new county along the path of the Sandy and Beaver Canal. By the time the Ohio General Assembly met in December, McCook and Atkinson had almost enough votes to pass their bill. However, one state senator was a holdout. Discovering that the senator had a brother-in-law who kept a tavern in Columbus, Isaac Atkinson dropped in at the tavern for a little chat.

"If this bill becomes law," said Atkinson, "I am going to banquet the members of the Assembly, the government officials, and the prominent men of the state . . . and it is my intention to give that banquet at your tavern."

The bill passed. The banquet was held. The new county was called Carroll. The county seat was Carrollton. They were named for Charles Carroll of Carrollton, Maryland, the oldest living signer of the Declaration of Independence. Isaac Atkinson and Daniel McCook controlled both town and county. It had been a nice piece of legerdemain.

By 1836 Ohio, like the nation, was climbing a dizzying spiral of growth in business, industry, banking, and land speculation. It was sparked by the building of roads and canals and was spurred by the belief that, with hard work, everyone would be wealthy.

Daniel McCook and his two brothers were riding high.

Daniel was the well-to-do squire of Carrollton. He was the clerk of courts, co-owned several mills and a brickyard, and speculated in land. In addition, he was a grain and wool merchant who, when the Sandy and Beaver Canal was finished, would be able to ship his goods by water all the way to New Orleans and New York City.

Intending to build the finest house in town for Martha and their eight children, Daniel bought a choice corner lot on the Carrollton public square. He drew up plans for a Federal-style house with three layers of brick in all exterior and interior walls, a handsome front door with sidelights and a fanlight, a graceful winding stairway, ceilings twelve feet high, fireplaces with hand-carved mantels in every room, and a spacious parlor overlooking the back garden. A large room on the corner would be his law office and general store.

Dr. John McCook was a well-liked family physician in New Lisbon, Ohio. He had married the lovely and talented Catherine Sheldon, from a fine, old Connecticut family. Catherine McCook painted, wrote poetry, and played one of the few pianos in town. Dr. John, active in the political and business life of the community, was planning to build a large four-story woolen mill on the banks of the Sandy and Beaver Canal.

Dr. George McCook, fulfilling the promise of his youth, was a renowned surgeon in New Lisbon. In addition to being the father of two sons and seven daughters, he was an investor in the Sandy and Beaver Canal, an associate judge of the Columbiana County Court, and grand

Daniel McCook's house in Carrollton, Ohio,
with his law office and general store on the left-hand corner

master of the Masonic lodge. On the McCook family farm near New Lisbon he raised Durham cattle, French and Spanish marino sheep, and Chilton and Morgan horses. In addition, at forty years of age, the indefatigable Dr. George had returned to college to study the latest surgery skills, graduating from Jefferson Medical College in Philadelphia in 1836.

As if that were not enough, Dr. George was running for Congress as the Democrat candidate in Ohio's Seventeenth District, comprising Columbiana and Carroll counties. His Whig opponent was Andrew W. Loomis, a popular attorney.

Daniel McCook, as clerk of courts in Carroll County, was in charge of counting election votes. On October 11, 1836, Daniel certified the election thusly:

DR. GEORGE MCCOOK	1,000 VOTES
ANDREW W. LOOMIS	837 VOTES
ANDREW LOOMIS	116 VOTES

The Loomis vote was split. According to Daniel McCook, this was done "in strict accordance with the facts" because Loomis's middle initial was missing on the ballot in two townships. But, in spite of Daniel's brotherly help, Dr. George still lost the election by 33 votes because Loomis was given all of the 953 votes in Carroll County and had an 80-vote margin in Columbiana County.

The victorious Whigs lost no time in bringing charges of impeachment against the highhanded Daniel McCook. In the *Case of Daniel McCook, Esq.*, the Articles of Impeachment charged that McCook

> *falsely and corruptly made and certified, under the official seal of the said Clerk, a certain false, forged and counterfeited paper . . .*

Daniel plotted his defense with friends in the Democrat Party. One was a brilliant twenty-three-year-old attorney named Edwin McMasters Stanton. Since Stanton was running for prosecuting attorney in adjoining Harrison County, it would not have been prudent for him to be known as Daniel's defense attorney. However, Stanton loved intrigue, liked playing double roles, and was learning how to maneuver within the labyrinthian world of politics.

The strategy was clever. The grand jury was packed with Democrats who managed to delay the trial for several sessions until they could uncover some Whig skullduggery. Finally, finding that the Whigs had dipped into public funds to go to a political convention, the Democrats charged them with malfeasance. Amid political squabbling, the case against Daniel McCook was dismissed.

Coincidentally, Daniel's seventh son, born in 1837 as the case was going to the grand jury, was named Edwin Stanton McCook.

Twenty-five years later, Daniel McCook's good friend Edwin Stanton would become one of the most powerful men in the nation and one of the most controversial figures in American history.

⌐

Shrill blasts from the hunter's horn heralded the entry of the stagecoach into Carrollton. From the mail pouch came a letter to Daniel McCook from the chaplain of the U.S.S. *Delaware*. The ship, carrying Daniel's nineteen-year-old midshipman son John, was on a training cruise to South America.

> *United States Ship Delaware*
> *Rio De Janeiro, April 2, 1842*
>
> *Dear Sir,*
> *. . . it is with a sorrowful heart – for I too am a parent – that I beg you to nerve yourself . . . your excellent, and I doubt not, favorite son, is no more.*
> *. . . God comfort you and bless you all.*
> *Charles Henry Allen*

Midshipman John McCook, a handsome and high-spirited lad who was the third of Daniel and Martha's ten children, had been serving his night watch in the tops during a rainstorm when he came down with a cold. Several days later three sick seamen came aboard his ship. John's cold worsened; he suddenly became delirious, lapsed into a coma, and died. He was buried in Rio.

Daniel and Martha were devastated. Martha's great-grandfather had been Admiral George Latimer, R.N., of the British Navy. The McCooks had expected no less of their dashing son, who was eulogized in the diary of the U.S.S. *Delaware's* executive officer, Captain David G. Farragut:

> *Apr. 1st interred the remains of Midshipman McCook in the English burying ground with all the honours due his rank. Thus terminated the short career of a zealous young officer who if he had been spared was likely to prove one of Neptune's worthiest sons.*

᛬

Two and a half years after the death of his son John at sea, Daniel McCook was standing trial again.

On November 25, 1844, three weeks after James K. Polk was elected president of the United States, the elders of the Carrollton Presbyterian Church charged McCook with

> *the unchristian and dishonorable conduct of betting on the result of the election . . . for president and vice president of the United States . . . any amount of money from fifty to a thousand dollars.*

Daniel pleaded guilty, but he was bitter. At forty-six years of age, his life had turned sour. First, there was the loss of his beloved son John at sea. Then, there were the mean-spirited people of Carrollton who, after all he had done for them, had nothing better to do than bring him to trial. Finally, there was the Sandy and Beaver Canal. Although planned in 1828, the digging did not start until 1834, and now, ten years later, the canal still was not finished.

The economic boom of 1836 had burst into the Panic of 1837. The country sank into a deep recession, and all canal building stopped. By the time the economy improved, the "Iron Horse" was galloping into Ohio. The Pennsylvania Railroad wanted to come through the area with its Pittsburgh-to-Cleveland line. But the backers of the Sandy and Beaver Canal, fearing that the railroad would hurt canal business, turned the offer down.

⌒

One bright spot in Daniel McCook's life was the law partnership forged between his good friend Edwin Stanton and George Wythe McCook, Daniel and Martha's second son. The new law firm of Stanton and McCook, formed in 1845, promised to be one of the best in the Ohio Valley.

Edwin Stanton was now nationally famous. His brilliant performance in a celebrated Washington trial brought courtroom spectators to their feet in applause.

George Wythe McCook, his junior partner, was born on November 2, 1821, in Canonsburgh, Pennsylvania. As a toddler, George had ridden in the wagon with the little brass cannon when his father moved the family to Ohio. After graduating from Franklin College in New Athens, Ohio, at the age of nineteen, George studied law with Stanton in Steubenville, a prosperous town of three thousand that hugged the hills on the west bank of the Ohio River.

The two men, now partners, could not have been more different.

Edwin Stanton, short and stocky, had piercing brown eyes and a large head covered with a thatch of wildly disheveled hair. Irascible, cunning, and manipulative, he was famous for browbeating juries and insulting opposing lawyers. Willing to win at any cost, Stanton once swallowed poison and vomited it up to prove that his client did not commit murder.

George McCook, tall and trim, had merry blue eyes that viewed the world with unflagging good cheer. He loved playing cards, smoking cigars, eating good food, drinking good wine, reading the classics, and going to the theatre. Like all the McCooks, George had a reputation for fearless physical prowess. But he was also a born diplomat, priding himself on being able to see both sides of a dispute.

The partners were alike, however, in one respect. Thirty-one-year-old widower Stanton and twenty-four-year-old bachelor McCook were both admirers of a lovely young schoolteacher named Margaret Beatty. Intelligent and spirited, she recently had returned to Steubenville with her wealthy parents from an eight-month grand tour of Europe.

In time-honored tradition, George captured Margaret's heart when, in 1846, he donned a captain's uniform to go to Mexico and fight for his

EDWIN M. STANTON   GEORGE W. McCOOK

Partners in the law firm of Stanton and McCook

country's right to annex Texas. Edwin Stanton, suffering from chronic asthma, was not able to volunteer. However, Stanton generously loaned George his horse to train the men, and he promised to care for Margaret.

During the year that he was in Mexico, convivial George McCook spent his nights making rum punches, singing in chorus with fellow officers, and writing long letters home. Love letters went to Margaret. Family letters went to his father. Political letters went to his law partner.

His law partner, meanwhile, appeared to be playing another double role. Behind Edwin Stanton's brusque exterior was a lonely man longing for friends, as he revealed in his letters to George. Also behind Edwin Stanton's brusque exterior was a lonely man longing for love, as he revealed in his letters to Margaret:

> *Margaret,*
>   *The capacity to excite love belongs to all women . . . in some, highly gifted like yourself, it seems to be independent of the will—an absolute condition of their being, as much as for the rose to bloom and excite by its fragrance and beauty.*

In exciting the love of others, therefore, you but obey a law of your being, independent of your will, and which you could not, if you would, avoid.

To feel love, and desire its return, is the lot of almost every woman, and oftentimes in proportion to their own loveliness, is this desire to be loved.

Of that, hereafter, let me speak.

Edwin M. Stanton

Almost thirteen thousand U.S. soldiers died in Mexico, but George McCook did not. After surviving malaria and a grueling 107-mile nine-day march across burning desert sands, George came home to Steubenville a hero and a colonel, a title he carried for the rest of his life.

Weary of wooing by mail and eager to claim his bride, George persuaded Margaret to elope to Pittsburgh. He went there first by Ohio River steamboat to make arrangements for their marriage, buy himself some new clothes, and write his last letter as her suitor.

> *Monongahela House, Pittsburgh*
> *Sunday morning*
>
> *My dearest,*
> *The hush of the day is on the city whilst I sit down to write to you. So soon we are to be wedded that this is the last letter of my strange wooing, and I scarce can write you anything. My heart beats high at the very thought of you. . . .*
> *Yours ever, with a heart overflowing with love,*
>
> *Geo. W. McCook*

Edwin Stanton loyally escorted Margaret to Pittsburgh and was the best man at the wedding of Colonel George McCook and Margaret Beatty on the evening of August 5, 1847. It was, quite possibly, one of the few suits that Stanton ever lost.

〜

By now, railroad tracks crossed Ohio like a spider's web. But none went through New Lisbon or Carrollton. Smart men were moving away. That included Daniel McCook. It was the biggest gamble of his life.

Mortgaging his Carrollton house and seventeen other properties, Daniel packed up most of his family in 1847 and steamboated down the Ohio River to the wilderness of southern Illinois. There he bought 2,360 acres of ore-laden land to manufacture iron for the railroads chugging west. At Elizabethtown he built a fine ten-thousand-dollar house, and nearby he constructed a large iron-making blast furnace. It was named Martha Furnace in honor of his long-suffering wife, the mother of his twelve children.

In his spare time the enterprising Daniel McCook traveled around the state making friends in high places. One was U.S. Senator Stephen A. Douglas. Another was Illinois Governor Augustus French. These friendships paid off. On December 6, 1849, Governor French commissioned Daniel McCook as the first probate judge of Hardin County, Illinois.

〜

Back in Ohio, things were also going well for newlyweds Colonel and Mrs. George McCook. Financially astute, George was able to buy "Hillside," a Federal-style mansion in Steubenville on several acres of land overlooking the Ohio River. In time, Margaret would present George with seven children born there. Four would survive. The sixteen-room house would become a hospitable haven for all the McCook clan as well as a mecca for social and political gatherings in eastern Ohio.

Hillside was renowned for its furnishings, paintings, and book-lined library, as well as for its fine food and wines. Summertime dinner parties on the lawns were lit by Japanese lanterns that glowed until the wee hours of the morning.

Edwin Stanton, who did not care for socializing, had announced soon after George and Margaret's wedding that Steubenville was dull and that he was moving to Pittsburgh to practice law. However, Edwin retained his partnership with George, and the firm of Stanton and McCook prospered, representing railroads and industries in the rich Ohio Valley.

Hillside

By 1853, Daniel McCook's dream of an Illinois iron-making empire had turned into a nightmare. Vast deposits of iron ore, discovered in Minnesota near Lake Superior, were much richer than southern Illinois ore and sounded the death knell of Martha Furnace.

McCook lost everything, including his fine Carrollton house and seventeen other properties. Broke, he headed for Washington where he had good friends like Senator Stephen Douglas. Through their help, the man who once thought nothing of betting one thousand dollars on an election was forced to settle for work as a bounty land clerk in the Pension Office for sixteen hundred dollars a year.

Daniel's younger brother, Dr. John McCook, also was having a run of bad luck. The Sandy and Beaver Canal was finally finished in 1855. But only one boat made the entire trip, and it had to be towed through mud for the last mile. Investors lost two million dollars.

Dr. John McCook stayed in New Lisbon long after most smart men left. Although he loved the little town, he was financially ruined. Leaving the little brass cannon behind to become the town's artillery piece, Dr. John moved with his wife and six children to Steubenville, a town that wisely had welcomed the railroad.

⌒

It was not entirely his fault that Daniel McCook was fired in 1857 from his job at the Pension Office in Washington. Mainly, it was the result of a bitter political fight between two powerful Democrats, Senator Stephen Douglas and President James Buchanan, over the slavery question in the Kansas territory.

Buchanan, to appease the South, wanted Kansas to be a slave state. Douglas, to appease the North, wanted it to be a free state. Their bitter quarrel divided the Democrat Party, with Buchanan vowing to destroy Douglas politically and purge the government of his friends. Daniel McCook, accused of talking politics in the office, was one of the first to go.

Senator Douglas, coming to the rescue, landed McCook a job as a map clerk in the U.S. House of Representatives at $150 a month. Six months later that too was gone. This time it was due to his son George.

Colonel George McCook had been politically, as well as financially, successful. Rising to power in the Democrat Party, he had been elected Ohio's attorney general in 1853. In the spring of 1858 George came to Washington to do a favor for a boyhood friend, Clement L. Vallandigham.

Vallandigham, an Ohio Democrat, was trying to claim his Third District seat in the U.S. House of Representatives after a contested election. George McCook successfully argued the case before Congress, and Vallandigham was seated on May 25. Unfortunately, this angered Senator Douglas, who knew that Vallandigham would side with President Buchanan in their vicious intraparty fight. Two weeks later Daniel McCook was out of a job again.

George, certain that Douglas was getting even with him, wrote his parents to assure them that he and three of his brothers, who were financially successful, would support the family.

Abraham Lincoln in 1857, a year before debating Stephen Douglas

Steubenville, 29 June, '58

Dear Father and Mother,

You have four sons looking the world in the face with eyes very different and dispositions strangely unlike, but they are the same in one thing. If the roof tree begins to totter, it is a generous race as to who shall be first with a broad shoulder for its support.

Mother need not have sent Judge Douglas' kind letter to assure me that the stab, although coming through one of his friends, was not of his direction. When I strike at the Judge again I will give timely warning. . . .

My tenderest love . . . and dutiful affection of a son who can never repay what he owes you.

George

However, Daniel McCook was too proud to exist on his sons' largesse. He prevailed on Douglas who, to his credit, took pity on the hapless victim of Democrat infighting. Douglas agreed to pay McCook $125 a month out of his own pocket to work in his Washington office while Douglas went home to Illinois to campaign for reelection to the U.S. Senate. His opponent was a backwoods Republican lawyer named Abraham Lincoln.

"A house divided against itself cannot stand," Lincoln had declared on June 16. "I believe this government cannot endure permanently half slave and half free."

Douglas claimed that Lincoln's speech invited civil war, and their ensuing debates on slavery attracted wide attention in the press. Douglas was returned to the Senate, but Lincoln was propelled to national attention.

Unfortunately, Daniel McCook's pay was slow in coming. Douglas was heavily in debt due to spending fifty thousand dollars on his reelection campaign and, rumors said, borrowing one hundred thousand dollars from New York financiers to speculate in western land along the route of the proposed transcontinental railroad.

McCook was forced to plead for a pittance.

Jany 20, 59

Dear Judge,

    I regret exceedingly that my extreme circumstances compel me to draw upon your generosity, and present you with my bill.

    If I had $200, I could get along for a time. I hope you will excuse the apparent importunity of this note, as nothing but dire necessity induced this application.

Very respectfully,
Daniel McCook

᠆᠆

By 1860 Daniel McCook was living alone on the "wrong" side of Pennsylvania Avenue. His family was grown. Martha was back on the family farm near New Lisbon, Ohio. So, until he was successful at hitching the Mount Carbon Coal Company like a caboose onto the end of Douglas's railroad bill, McCook was making ends meet by staying at Mrs. Paris's boarding house at 331 Pennsylvania Avenue. On the south side of the avenue, it was near Central Market and Tiber Creek, the canal into which butchered carcasses were thrown. The stench was overwhelming.

Life had delivered many a hard blow to the weather-worn warrior of sixty-two winters. His face was deeply lined. His curly chestnut hair was now a grizzled gray. But Daniel was not beaten. He still stood six-feet-two-inches in his stocking feet. He still had the commanding presence of a clan chieftain, and he still had friends in high places.

One of them, Senator Stephen A. Douglas, was running for president of the United States.

Most of the McCooks were solid Douglas Democrats. Although opposed to slavery, they believed that the North would have to let the South keep its "peculiar institution" in order to preserve the Union. They also believed that Douglas, who had been vital to the passage of the Compromise of 1850, was the only man who could keep 22 million Northerners and 6 million Southerners united.

To the McCooks' deep dismay, Abraham Lincoln was elected on November 6, 1860. Lincoln would not take office until March 4. In the meantime, South Carolina seceded and demanded that the lame-duck President James Buchanan hand over Fort Sumter in Charleston's harbor.

It did not happen, partly due to another high-placed friend of Daniel McCook.

Edwin Stanton, having remarried and dissolved his law partnership with George McCook, moved to Washington and was now the attorney general in President Buchanan's cabinet. Stanton feared that the old and tired president would give up Fort Sumter, to avoid bloodshed, as he had done with other Federal forts in the South. If he did so, Stanton felt that there would be no Union left by the time Lincoln was inaugurated.

So again, playing a double role, Stanton skillfully maneuvered in the labyrinthian world of politics. While pretending to agree with Buchanan, Stanton worked secretly behind his back with Republicans in Congress to force the Democrat president to stand his ground on Fort Sumter. It was a thin line that the attorney general walked between loyalty to his president and patriotism for his country.

But the ploy was successful, as the satisfied Stanton wrote to his former law partner George McCook:

> *Washington, Feb 4, 1861*
>
> *Dear Sir,*
> *It was very plain that as long as the United States continued to run away there would be no 'bloodshed' and now that the Government has determined to stand its ground there will still be 'no bloodshed'.*

Stanton's letter ended with a mention of another double role he once had played.

> *I hope Mrs. McCook has recovered her health and beg you to give her my compliments.*
>
> *Yours truly,*
> *Edwin M. Stanton*

Five weeks later, the newly inaugurated President Lincoln also tried to stand his ground and hold onto Fort Sumter. When it fell and bloodshed began, the McCooks swiftly changed from Peace Democrats to War Democrats.

Seventeen descendants of the Whiskey Boy volunteered to save the Union. Their patriotism was predicted by the eldest of the clan, Dr. George McCook. Speaking during a war rally at Pittsburgh City Hall to raise troops, Dr. George was rudely interrupted.

"Listen, old fellow," shouted a heckler, "if you're so anxious to get shot, why don't you go to the war?"

"Young man," Dr. George curtly retorted, pointing at the protestor with his long surgeon's finger, "if this war lasts six months, there will be more McCooks in the army than there are Indians in hell!"

Dr. George McCook

The Ohio River Valley

Chapter 3

LIEUTENANT JOHN McCOOK
in the First Land Battle of the Civil War

The eighteen-year-old lad was off to battle in his frock coat, good trousers, and best boots, stumbling along the rutty clay road in the Allegheny Mountains of western Virginia. It was June 1, 1861. The Civil War was seven weeks old. Some of the Northern volunteers did not yet have their uniforms.

Night fell, and the rains came in a drenching downpour. Lieutenant John McCook and the boys in Company D slogged on in the dark, some walking out of their shoes as they struggled through quicksandlike mud up to their ankles. Their colonel urged the new recruits on at a pace expected of veteran troops, and some of them, drenched and cold and dead tired, fell asleep on the twenty-two-mile all-night march. A reporter from the *New York Times*, also drenched and cold and dead tired, was convinced that the feat "was never exceeded in the military history of the country."

Lieutenant John McCook was an excellent student who knew all about Napoleon's great campaigns. He also knew that this clumsy caper bore not the slightest resemblance to the glory of war pictured in his history books. John James McCook, called "Little Johnny" by his family, was smart, handsome, and spoiled. The youngest of Dr. John and Catherine McCook's five sons was born in New Lisbon on February 2, 1843, when hopes were still high for the Sandy and Beaver Canal.

His father was a physician and businessman who was building a large four-story woolen mill on the banks of the canal. The family lived in a big brick home in New Lisbon that also contained Dr. John's medical office. There he practiced all the skills of a family doctor, from performing surgeries to delivering babies to pulling teeth.

Often at night Dr. John had to saddle his horse and ride out to remote farms in the rain or snow to treat his patients. Returning home at dawn, he was plastered with mud from head to foot, and his saddle bags were stuffed with beef, pork, potatoes, and flour that he often received in lieu of money, while from the bulging pockets of his great overcoat came a supply of nuts, cookies, and even kittens.

Dr. John loved life in New Lisbon. He sang with his wife Catherine in the Presbyterian church choir. He was elected Columbiana County treasurer and was captain of the local militia. When General William Henry Harrison came to New Lisbon in 1838, he was escorted into town by the New Lisbon Guards commanded by Dr. John. He only left the town, and then very reluctantly, after it chose the Sandy and Beaver Canal over the railroad.

Little Johnny was twelve when the family moved to Steubenville. After graduating from high school at the age of fifteen, proficient in Latin and Greek, he entered his father's alma mater in Canonsburgh, Pennsylvania.

Jefferson College had grown to be one of the ten largest institutions of higher education in the nation, with an enrollment slightly behind Harvard and Princeton. Little Johnny studied for the ministry and was the editor of the college paper. Unfortunately, at the end of his sophomore year in 1860, he ran an article lampooning the faculty and was promptly expelled.

Dr. John McCook asked his pastor to write the college president and plead for Johnny's readmission. The president finally acquiesced, provid-

Dr. John McCook

ing that the lad sign a petition recanting his deed. But proud Little Johnny, indignant that he had been expelled without an opportunity to appear before the faculty to defend himself, refused to sign. In that case, decided the college president, the boy did not seem to have the right attitude for the ministry and "the end of justice and the cause of religion would not be promoted by acceding to your request."

So Little Johnny took up another profession by which gentlemen advanced in the world. He began studying law with a local Steubenville attorney.

Six months hence, in late winter of 1861, President-elect Lincoln's private train came through town on its way to Washington. A great crowd gathered at the railway station on the banks of the Ohio River. Little Johnny stood at the edge, gazing on the scene with caustic eyes. He had no fondness for Lincoln, considering him a low-bred, lank, slab-sided rail-splitter and dangerously near to an abolitionist to boot.

At length on the rear platform of the train a gaunt form appeared. As it straightened itself out to a seemingly incredible height, it was silhouetted against the Virginia bluffs on the opposite shore. Johnny heard his voice without discerning, or even caring to discern, all that he said. But once Lincoln half-turned and swung his long right arm toward the Virginia shore.

"Our friends over there . . . ," Lincoln said, his high-pitched Illinois drawl drifting back to Johnny's apathetic ears.

Then the train chugged eastward. A few weeks later, after Lincoln was inaugurated, the people of Steubenville waited nervously to see what the South would do. Ohio was divided, as was the entire North, with people endlessly arguing whether to try to keep the Southern states in the Union or to "let the wayward sisters go in peace."

All indecision ended on April 12 when newsboys ran into the streets shouting, "Extra! Extra! Sumter fired on!" Patriotism erupted like steam from a long-covered kettle. Republicans and Democrats alike backed Lincoln in his call for troops. The North was united, finally and at any cost, to save the Union.

Courthouse bells rang loudly throughout Ohio, and men turned out en masse to join the three-month volunteer army. In a holiday spirit, business was suspended and people joined in singing "The Union Forever, Hurrah Boys, Hurrah!" Church chimes played "Yankee Doodle." Ladies started sewing uniforms. Everywhere there were meetings and speeches and flag-raisings. When the Stars and Stripes went down at Fort Sumter, they went up in every town and village in Ohio. There were flags on church spires, flags on taverns, flags on houses and barns and stores and inns and boats on the Ohio River.

Ohio, by now, was third in wealth and population of the nation's thirty-three states. Canals and railroads had brought great prosperity to Ohio's mills and factories. Governor William Dennison, moving quickly to assume leadership in the West, telegraphed the president:

> *What portion of the 75,000 militia you call for do you give to Ohio? We will furnish the largest number you will receive.*

Lincoln wired back:

> *Thirteen regiments.*

Governor Dennison, empowered to appoint generals, offered Little Johnny's cousin, Colonel George McCook, a brigadier general's star and the command of Ohio's first four regiments. Colonel McCook was not only a veteran of the Mexican War, but an influential Democrat; Governor Dennison, a Republican, was anxious to commit Democrats to the fight.

George, hurrying home to Hillside to tell Margaret of the great honor, received a great shock. She was opposed. Her reasons were many. George was almost forty years old. He still suffered chills and fever from the malaria he contracted in Mexico. They had three young children. Margaret's health was fragile. When these arguments failed, she used her most effective weapon. She cried as though her heart would break.

George was devastated. After almost fourteen years of marriage, Margaret was still the great love of his life. Six months earlier, in Europe on a business trip, he had written to her while boating down the Rhine River, reminiscing about how he had loved her passionately from afar before finally winning her hand.

Coblenz, 17 Oct. 60

Love of mine,

. . . Last night I could scarcely get to sleep thinking of you and the dear old time . . . the sleigh ride in the bitter cold. . . .

How tonight I would wrap you in my love, as on that night of the ride when I wished to fold you closely in the robes and yet loved you so much that I dreaded to offend you by touching you. Oh! You never knew, Liebenfranken, how dearly you were loved.

Yours ever and only,

George

Now, torn between his love for his wife and his love for his country, George searched his soul for which was stronger. In the end, Margaret won.

George was aware that many in the McCook clan would be disdainful of the sacrifice he was making. Nevertheless, giving Margaret his word that he would decline the command, George went to Columbus to explain to the governor. But while he was at the State House, an urgent telegram arrived from Washington. The Capitol was in danger of being captured. Troops were needed at once, and George was asked to get them there.

With no time to explain to Margaret, he left that night by train with the First and Second Ohio Regiments. After Maryland rebels tore up the railroad tracks, George was forced to halt his men in Pennsylvania. From there he finally wrote his wife.

Lancaster, 25 April '61

> *My dearest Margaret,*
>
> *I had to run away. There was no other way for it but I expected to get straight through to Washington and immediately return home, having declined the command of the first four regiments as Brigadier General . . . but as the troops found themselves in difficulty . . . it would be such cowardice as to make me unworthy of your love if I were to leave them now.*

Your own,
George

When Washington was safe, George returned home to accept an administration position as Ohio's adjutant general. It would let him keep his promise to Margaret, not to command men in battle, while helping Governor Dennison get the state ready for war.

The Ohio arsenal contained only a few boxes of rusted smooth-bore muskets, some worn-out six-pounder field pieces, and a pile of mildewed harnesses. The governor sent agents to England to buy one hundred thousand dollars worth of Enfield rifles. He installed heavy cannon along the Ohio River, the dividing line between North and South. He also assured the people of western Virginia that if they remained loyal to the Union, Ohio would protect them.

The hardscrabble mountaineers of western Virginia had long felt snubbed by the aristocratic plantation owners of eastern Virginia. They accepted Ohio's offer and its men, too. Since Ohio's thirteen regiments had been quickly filled, the state sent its surplus volunteers across the Ohio River to enlist in Wheeling. That included Little Johnny McCook.

On May 15 Little Johnny was mustered into Company D, First Virginia Foot Volunteers. He was in camp barely two weeks before he wrote home for cigars, tobacco, clothes, and money. Wearily his irritated father replied.

Steubenville, May 30, 1861

Dear John,

*I received your letter and anxious as I am to meet your demands
for money, I find it utterly impossible, nor do I understand why
you demand so much.*

*I sent you $25 . . . and now you only want $40 or $50 more.
If you play the soldier, you must live like one.*

Dr. John McCook knew why his youngest son wanted money. As soon as tents went up in army camps, sutlers appeared with wagons loaded with delectable things, sausages, cheeses, canned goods, and tobacco. The soldiers were allowed to buy on credit, ranging from twenty-five cents to two dollars, until payday.

Dr. John also knew why his dapper son wanted clothes. He did not yet have his uniform, which was still being sewn by the ladies of Steubenville. However,

> *. . . you took with you seven shirts, and as many handkerchiefs.
> What has become of them?*

Dr. John said that he would send Little Johnny the arms he would need as an officer, a treasured family sword, and Dr. John's own pistol, but when he got his uniform,

> *You ought to send home your fine boots and all your clothes that
> is not absolutely necessary, for you will lose them or be com-
> pelled to throw them away, for you cannot take so much bag-
> gage with you.*

I am ever your
father
John McCook

However, before the luxury-loving Beau Brummel received his uniform, he was on his way to battle in the mountains of western Virginia still wearing his frock coat and good trousers.

At 4:00 a.m. on June 2, after the all-night, rain-drenched, twenty-two-mile march, Little Johnny's regiment joined a Union surprise attack on a Confederate camp at Philippi, Virginia. Some two thousand Rebels fled, and the Union recruits gave chase, capturing a few prisoners plus some swords, guns, and a colonel's hat and gold epaulets. Little Johnny and his comrades waved them in the air with a whoop as their trophies of war.

That was the Battle of Philippi, the first land fight of the Civil War. It was hailed in the press as the "Philippi Races" due to the rapid retreat of the enemy. Northerners were sure that the end of the war was in sight. On the heels of this success, citizens of Virginia's thirty-five western counties met in Wheeling on June 11 and voted to remain in the Union.

That day Lieutenant John McCook finally got his uniform. However, no tents had appeared, and the boys slept in the open, rain or shine.

Ten days later Major General George B. McClellan arrived to take command of the Union Army of Occupation. McClellan was a thirty-four-year-old magnetic man who swept into the mountains with all the aplomb of someone who had graduated second in his class at West Point.

Lieutenant John McCook, thanks to his family's political connections, was assigned a position on McClellan's staff as assistant quartermaster. Little Johnny, to his chagrin, discovered that his job was to keep track of everything an army needs, including muskets, tents, ax handles, kettles, stationery, rulers, and bottles of ink. Four days later he quit.

Announcing indignantly that he had not enlisted to do storekeeping, Little Johnny requested a transfer back to his old regiment. His mother was disappointed. His sister Mary was scornful. His furious father sent him a scathing letter:

> *July 6, 1861*
>
> Dear John,
>   . . . *I can assure you I was much astonished at your resigning your position on the General Staff. Mary thinks you a* _____*ass for so doing and I feel disposed to concur.*
>   *In haste your father,*
>   *John McCook*

Major General George B. McClellan

On July 9 General McClellan, with twelve thousand troops, launched an attack on two Rebel-held mountain strongholds. Little Johnny was in a brigade of four thousand men, under the command of Brigadier General Thomas A. Morris, that staged a feigned attack on Laurel Hill. McClellan, with a force of eight thousand men including Little Johnny's cousin, Colonel Robert McCook, made the real assault on Rich Mountain.

The Battle of Rich Mountain was a Union victory, due mainly to the flanking strategy of McClellan's subordinate, Brigadier General William S. Rosecrans. Although McClellan hesitated to attack, failing to carry out his part of the operation, he took credit for the success and wired Washington triumphantly:

We have annihilated the enemy in Western Virginia.

The North was elated. McClellan was hailed in the press as a young Napoleon. Receiving the thanks of Congress, he issued a congratulatory message to his troops:

Soldiers of the Army of the West! You have annihilated two armies! I have confidence in you!

McClellan's "Soldiers of the Army of the West" were praised in poetry and prose. However, the glory of war seemed elusive to Lieutenant John McCook, who found himself doing dull garrison duty in the mountains. He discovered, like thousands of soldiers before him, that war consisted of weeks of idle camp life notable for card playing, profanity, stealing, and consorting with women of easy virtue, interspersed with bursts of forced marching, spirited skirmishes, and occasional hand-to-hand battles.

Little Johnny's comrades, hastily recruited and never having had the time to be adequately trained in soldierly skills, complained about the food, the weather, the uniforms, and the officers. Unused to communal life, twelve to twenty men registered sick each day, the most prevalent illness being acute diarrhea, a common ailment among new recruits. Their pay was poor and usually late. Food supplies included flour, corn, pork, and beans, but since most army cooks were novices, many soldiers preferred to fry or boil their own food. On the march they ate salt pork and cementlike biscuits called hardtack which they carried in their knapsacks. The recruits drank gallons of coffee and also jugs of moonshine whenever they could get their hands on it. Poorly made clothing of shoddy or rewoven wool often fell apart in the first storm. If it lasted for ninety days they were lucky.

In spite of the hardships, some of the boys planned to sign up for three years. On May 3 President Lincoln had asked for forty-two thousand three-year volunteers. The boys heard that, as an inducement, the government would put them on the same footing as the regular U.S. Army: thirteen dollars a month and, with an honorable discharge, one hundred dollars and 160 acres of land.

Little Johnny, tempted to reenlist, had asked his father for advice. Dr. John, convinced that his youngest son had no aptitude for military life, replied,

> *I cannot advise you to accept the offer.*

Johnny's mother, writing to say that she looked forward to his coming home on August 15, received a petulant letter in reply:

> *August 10, 1861*
>
> *Dear Father and Mother,*
>
> *You could not wish any more than I do that I were home. Here I am in a dirty tent, doing nothing all day but sleep and write passes and orders on the Sutler, at night sleeping on a straw bed—not a bed of roses by any means—*
>
> *I hope you won't forget . . . that your dear youngest is away from the enjoyments of home, pestered by flies, sweltering under the rays of a red hot sun, and soaked with rain by turns and so needs comfort and consolation from you. . . .*
>
> *I think it was real mean of you not to send us those good things which we so politely asked for. But all right, just wait until you go out soldiering and I stay at home. Then see who'll send you anything good to eat. But enough . . . My love to everybody who cares anything about me.*
>
> *Your affectionate,*
> *John*

By now all of his clan, four brothers and eight cousins, were in the fight to save the Union. But Little Johnny had enough. Not for him was the glory of war as he found it. Not for him was the glory of war found three weeks earlier by his cousin Charlie at the Battle of Bull Run.

*Territory trod by the Fighting McCooks
in their quest to save the Union*

Chapter 4

PRIVATE CHARLES McCOOK
at the Battle of Bull Run

His black felt slouch hat, jauntily decorated with colorful ornaments, shaded his eyes from the scorching afternoon sun as eighteen-year-old Private Charles McCook marched to battle. He was Daniel and Martha's eighth son.

The temperature stood at ninety-five degrees on July 16, 1861, as Brigadier General Irvin McDowell's thirty-thousand-man Union Army of Northeastern Virginia, the largest force ever commanded on the North American continent, began its long-awaited and widely heralded attack on a Rebel Army at Manassas Junction, Virginia. The railroad junction, thirty-seven miles south of Washington, was held by some twenty thousand Confederates under the command of General Pierre G. T. Beauregard, the victor of Fort Sumter.

Union spirits were high. The Northern boys hoped that the Southern scoundrels would stand and fight, but feared they would run again as they did in western Virginia. So far the Civil War had been a series of minor fights and skirmishes. Most were Northern victories. Manassas was to be the great battle to end it all.

General-in-Chief of the U.S. Army Winfield Scott doubted it. Predicting that the Civil War was going to be a long one, and knowing that most of the Northern three-month enlistments were almost up, General Scott urged President Lincoln to wait until a well-trained army of forty-two thousand three-year men, called for on May 3, was ready for battle.

But Lincoln was pressured by Congress and the Northern press to capture the Confederate capital. It had been moved from Montgomery, Alabama, to Richmond, Virginia, one hundred miles south of Washington. On June 26 Horace Greeley's *New York Tribune*, with a million readers weekly, began printing a terse demand and repeating it day after day:

> *Forward to Richmond. The Rebel Congress must not be allowed to meet there on the 20th of July. By that date the place must be held by the national army.*

Bowing to pressure, Lincoln ordered General McDowell to attack Manassas and then continue "On to Richmond."

Overjoyed to be on the march, the Northern volunteers were as eager as if going on a picnic. Cocky and self-confident, they strode with a swaggering gait, bragging of their prowess and itching for a fight.

Private Charles McCook, Company I, Second Ohio, Second Brigade, First Division, trudged the dusty road in his Ohio militia uniform of black pilot coat, red flannel blouse, gray doeskin pantaloons, wool knit stockings, and heavy brogan shoes. Strapped to his stalwart frame was his Springfield rifle, cartridge belt and box, cap box, bayonet, scabbard, knapsack, canteen, and haversack filled with three days' rations. He was in what the army called "light marching order."

It was a spectacular sight as the Union Army surged southward under silken banners. Most of the soldiers were members of state militias, as in 1794 during the Whiskey Rebellion. Their uniforms were as diverse and colorful as the Northern states from which they came.

Some New Englanders sported Revolutionary War tricorn hats. Others wore gray forage caps with red pompons. Pennsylvania boys pinned deer tails on their hats. Massachusetts men were in blue. Regiments from New Hampshire wore gray. Vermont mountaineers marched in green.

New Yorkers were the most flamboyant. Their Fire Zouaves were garbed in costumes similar to those worn by French troops in North Africa, baggy red breeches, short blue coats, yellow cummerbunds, and red fezzes with yellow tassels. They were armed with rifles and huge bowie knives. The Fourteenth Brooklyn was resplendent in snow-white gaiters and bright red breeches, modeled on the French Chasseurs. Colonel Blenker of the Eighth New York sported a magnificent red-lined cape. The glorious New York Garibaldi Guards, patterned on Italian bersagliere sharpshooters, wore red blouses and magnificent black hats with sweeping green feathers.

Fanciful and picturesque, much of the Union Army resembled a traveling theatrical troupe.

Behind them came the baggage of war. There were miles of artillery caissons, ammunition carts, ambulances, and white-topped supply wagons driven by wagoners thrashing their six-mule teams and shouting colorful oaths. In their wake plodded a herd of 150 beef cattle to be slaughtered for the victory dinner.

Off in the dusty distance, racing to catch up, careened a carriage driven by the commanding figure of Judge Daniel McCook. With him were four members of Congress, a large hamper of food, and his loaded Colt revolving rifle.

The Democrat congressmen, all good friends of McCook, were John McClernand, John Logan, and John Richardson of Illinois, and John Noell of Missouri. They planned to fight as civilian volunteers beside their constituents. Daniel McCook planned to fight beside his young son Charlie.

The boy was in Brigadier General Daniel Tyler's First Division, which had the honor of leading the army south. Actually, there were three McCooks in Tyler's division. Charlie's older brother Alex was colonel of the First Ohio regiment, and Charlie's cousin Anson was a captain in the Second Ohio. They could take care of themselves.

Catching up to Tyler's division near Centreville, three miles from Manassas, Daniel McCook and his congressional comrades got their first taste of battle when a reconnaissance probe at Blackburn's Ford over Bull Run Creek turned into a full-fledged fight.

Daniel McCook leaped into action. Congressmen McClernand and Logan, soon to be generals in the western theatre of war, joined him. Slinging their rifles over their shoulders, the three men dashed onto the field in their frock coats and top hats to carry wounded men to safety. Dodging bullets and covered with blood, they turned their blazing eyes and soaring oaths on those recruits who ran at the first sight of death.

Not all the members of Congress, however, participated in the battle-field bravado. John Richardson, for one, thought his companions were much too rash. "I shall never go with McCook again," he vowed.

Nineteen Union soldiers were killed, thirty-eight were wounded, and twenty-six were missing. General McDowell's scouts told him that the Confederates were heavily fortified behind Bull Run. The stream was too deep to wade except for a few fords. The stone bridge on the main road, the Warrenton Turnpike, was barricaded with a mountainous abatis of felled trees with sharpened branches, so McDowell ordered his army to bivouac while he drew up a plan for crossing Bull Run.

Private Charles McCook encamped with the Second Ohio on a hillside near the village of Centreville. The nights were quiet, and the boys could hear rumbling trains, tooting engines, and cheering men. It was clear that the Southern boys were reinforcing. The Northern boys, however, were not concerned. They felt that was the concern of the generals, not the foot soldiers like Charlie.

Charles Morris McCook had been born in Carrollton, Ohio, on November 15, 1842, seven and a half months after his midshipman brother John died at sea. Charlie was named for Commodore Charles A. Morris, under whose flag John had been serving.

When the Civil War started, Charlie was a student at Milnor Hall, the preparatory school for Kenyon College in Gambier, Ohio. Ignoring orders from his headmaster to stay in school, Charlie ran away and enlisted in the Second Ohio Volunteer Infantry Regiment on April 17. By now his three-month enlistment was up, but Charlie refused to go home and miss this great battle to end the war.

On Saturday night, July 20, General McDowell held a council of war. In spite of warnings that evil would come from fighting on the Sabbath, he announced to his generals that they would march at 2:00 a.m. The news, spreading quickly through the camps, was followed by the aroma of fresh coffee, frying bacon, whiskey, and cigars. Congressmen arrived to fight beside their constituents. Body servants of officers hurriedly packed their trunks. Mounted orderlies galloped up and down the Warrenton Turnpike with dispatches. Artillery and cavalry horses, sensing the tension, were restless and neighing.

Toward midnight quiet settled on the camps. The sky was clear. The moon was full. The stars were brilliant. Only the plaintive notes of the katydids and whippoorwills broke the silence.

Then, about a mile or so ahead, rifle shots on the picket line set off all the farm dogs for miles around, who barked and howled incessantly all night. This made it hard for some of the older men to fall asleep. But boys like Charlie, with the ease of youth, dropped off quickly to get in a few winks before being nudged awake at 2:00 a.m.

General Tyler's First Division led the way down the Warrenton Turnpike. His three brigades were to stage a feigned attack at the stone bridge over Bull Run. The real attack, however, was to be made by the

Stone bridge over Bull Run

Second and Third Divisions, led by Brigadier Generals David Hunter and Samuel P. Heintzelman. After crossing Bull Run at undefended fords two miles upstream, they were to surprise and strike the Confederate left flank. Tyler, after clearing the abatis from the bridge, would join the fight.

Charlie spied the graceful little double-arched stone bridge over Bull Run just after daylight. He and his comrades took position on a hillside overlooking the stream. Then a thirty-pounder Parrott gun, pulled by its six-horse team, lumbered up and sent the first shot screaming over Bull Run at 6:30 a.m., shattering the stillness of the Sabbath. Confederate artillery, choosing not to reveal their hidden positions in the woods beyond the stream, did not respond.

Tyler kept up his cannonading until about 10:00 a.m., when Hunter's division appeared on the other side of Bull Run. Then the Rebels charged out of the woods with infantry and cavalry toward the advancing Union lines. So the battle began.

Daniel McCook, on the hillside, had a front-row seat. He alternated between taking potshots at enemy cavalry with his rifle and trading bon mots with several European observers and a half-dozen reporters who accompanied the division. Another lively companion on the hillside was Father Bernard O'Reilly, S.J., Catholic chaplain of the Sixty-ninth New York. In the battle of wits, the judge was a good match for the Jesuit.

Shortly, General Tyler sent his First and Third Brigades, commanded by Colonels Erasmus E. Keyes and William T. Sherman, across the stream to join the fight. Father O'Reilly, seated at the foot of an old oak tree, heard the confessions of the "Fighting Irish" Catholics of the Sixty-ninth New York before they splashed across Bull Run with fixed bayonets.

Charlie, to his disappointment, had to remain behind. His brigade, made up of the First Ohio, Second Ohio, and Second New York, was commanded by Brigadier General Robert C. Schenck, a political general who had no battlefield experience. He was ordered to remain in reserve at the bridge.

By noon it appeared to Daniel McCook and the others on the hillside that the battle was won. The Federals held the Warrenton Turnpike on the other side of Bull Run. The Confederates had retreated to a wooded plateau and disappeared amid tall grass and trees.

"Victory! Victory! The day is ours!" shouted General McDowell to his troops as he rode the battlefield, ordering up his artillery for a grand Napoleonic charge.

"Victory!" echoed his courier as he galloped off to send a telegram to the president.

A lull settled over the land. Union soldiers, exhausted after fighting for two hours in wool uniforms under the blazing sun, dropped to the ground and gulped down cornpone and bacon from their haversacks. Daniel McCook seized the opportunity to give the good news to Charlie. The boy had been assigned guard duty at a field hospital set up in Mrs. Spindle's farmhouse about a quarter mile in the rear.

Mrs. Spindle's house, 1861

It was a sickening sight. The yard was filled with wounded and bleeding soldiers. Inside the house, the parlor was the operating room, where it took several strong men to hold a soldier down on a table to be anesthetized so that a surgeon could cut off his shattered arm or leg. The severed limbs were thrown out a window, and there was a large pile of them, bloody and ghostly white, on the lawn.

Leaving these stomach-turning realities of war, Daniel McCook took his son back to his carriage to give him some lunch. There, a short distance away on a hillside, was an incongruous scene.

Gay and lively luncheon parties were being enjoyed by Washington civilians who had come out to watch the battle. Sitting under parasols to protect themselves from the noontime sun, ladies in hoop-skirted dresses and large garden hats nibbled on picnics packed by caterers. Gentlemen sported silk top hats and long white linen dusters. Braced with pistols and brandy flasks, they followed the fighting through field glasses.

Every carriage, wagon, gig, and riding horse in Washington had been leased for the day, and the scene resembled a steeplechase race. There were senators and congressmen, reporters, foreign diplomats, the secretary of war, a Supreme Court justice peering through his opera glasses, and photographer Mathew Brady lugging his heavy camera. Regimental bands played national airs. Artists sketched. Journalists interviewed members of Congress. Entrepreneur camp sutlers sold roast chicken, biscuits, and sherry while children pestered them for extra pieces of pie.

After lunch Daniel McCook, anxious to see General McDowell's artillery charge, left Charlie at the hospital and hurried back to his vantage spot on the hillside.

About 1:00 p.m. McDowell sent eleven cannon of the crack regular U.S. Army artillery, pulled by six-horse teams, in a sweeping charge up to the wooded plateau where the enemy had retreated. In Napoleonic style, Union artillery would silence Confederate guns, then Union infantry would pierce holes in Confederate lines, and finally Union cavalry would gallop through to scatter and defeat the Confederate Army.

The charge might have been successful except for two factors. First, the Rebels had been reinforced. Second, there was mass confusion about uniforms. Some Confederate officers still wore their old blue regular U.S. Army uniforms. Many soldiers on both sides wore gray. In the smoke and confusion of battle, terrible mistakes were made. Friends fired on friends. Foes went unscathed.

Instead of a quick Union victory, the battle raged savagely on. The two Union batteries were destroyed. Forty men and seventy-five horses were killed or disabled. Enemies fought hand-to-hand, clubbing each other with rifles and slashing with knives. The fierce fight seesawed back and forth most of the afternoon under the broiling sun.

"The cannonade and discharge of musketry far excelled that of Waterloo," the European observers told Daniel McCook, comparing this battle to Napoleon's last one.

Finally, however, a hard-won Union victory seemed certain about 4:00 p.m. to Daniel McCook and the other observers on the hillside. The abatis had been cleared from the bridge. General Schenck's brigade, preparing to march, was forming ranks in the road. Regimental bands were playing triumphant tunes. Civilians were looking around for unexploded shells to take home as trophies, and reporters were debating whether to go "On to Richmond" with McDowell's army.

No one realized that the tide was about to turn.

Just then a sentry up in a tall pine tree shouted down that he could see fresh enemy troops running onto the battlefield. They were the last of

Confusion of uniforms at the Battle of Bull Run

twelve thousand reinforcements that had arrived by train from the Shenandoah Valley to increase the Confederate Army to some thirty-two thousand. Charging across the fields, the Southerners were screaming like nothing the Northerners had ever heard before.

It was like a screech of excruciating pain or a wild animal's triumphant cry at the kill. It was the Rebel yell.

Union soldiers looked for their own reinforcements and found none. Schenck's three-thousand-man brigade had been held too long at the bridge. Had it been sent in, the brigade might have stanched the flood-tide that now swept back over the battlefield.

Union soldiers, who had been marching and fighting for fourteen hours, felt betrayed and quit the battlefield in disgust. At first it was just a trickle. Then it was a stream. Then it was a torrent of bitter men surging back over the bridge and through the ranks of Schenck's brigade, formed in the road and ready to march.

Covered with mud and sweat, the faces of the retreating men were haggard and from their parched mouths came terrible tales. In the confusion of battle, they had been fired on by their own men. Their regiments had been cut to pieces. Their officers were dead. Nothing could stop the Union deluge, not even General McDowell himself, galloping the battle-field on horseback and shouting at his men to turn around.

Daniel McCook, running back to the field hospital to tell Charlie of the rout, discovered a Confederate infantry attack on the Union left flank. Calling for a battery, McCook climbed a fence to direct the artillery fire. His older son, Colonel Alexander McCook, ordered him to get down, but the incorrigible Daniel McCook ignored his son and stayed on the fence until the attack was repelled.

Then Daniel ran to warn Charlie, but he was too late.

A Confederate cavalry attack had charged the Union field hospital with all the whirling fury of a hurricane. Charlie, trying to rejoin his regiment, was cut off. As a cavalryman pursued him, the boy attempted to keep the horse at bay with his bayonet.

"Surrender!" shouted the Confederate.

"No!" cried Charlie, "never to a Rebel."

Circling behind him, the horseman shot him in the back.

"Now, damn you," he demanded, "will you surrender?"

"No, never," cried the boy again.

Daniel McCook ran up as the cavalryman was beating Charlie with the flat of his sword. McCook raised his rifle, but before he could fire, a shot rang out and the Confederate fell from his horse. The devastated father picked up his son and carried him into the field hospital where he was told by the surgeon that the wound was not fatal and the boy could be moved. Fashioning a bed for him in his carriage, Daniel McCook started for Washington.

There was no panic in the Union retreat until a shell fired by pursuing Confederates hit a small bridge over Cub Run, blocking the road. People shouted that the Black Horse Cavalry was coming to take them all prisoners, and a wild stampede began.

Artillery wagons fought for space with private carriages. Galloping six-horse teams crashed into each other. Ambulance drivers, hired for the battle, turned their wagons around empty and abandoned hundreds of wounded men. Teamsters dumped their ammunition over the side in order to flee faster. Baggage trains tossed trunks aside. Soldiers cut horses loose and mounted two to a steed. A U.S. senator flung himself on an army mule. The herd of beef cattle, intended for the victory dinner, turned tail and fled.

Retreat of the Union Army and general stampede

Daniel McCook, driving fast over rough roads, found that this gave Charlie great pain. The boy said that he could feel the points of his backbone cutting his entrails and asked to be laid down by the side of the road.

"I can die one place as well as another," Charlie said.

But Daniel, anxious to get him to a doctor, kept going. At Fairfax Court House almost all the inns, taverns, and houses had been turned into hospitals. Charlie was carried into one. An army surgeon, after removing the bullet, said that it had severed the rectum, cut off the bladder, and torn up the intestines. The wound was fatal. After the anguished father told his son, he made him some tea and bathed his wound.

By midnight the retreating Union Army had passed through Fairfax Court House on its way back to Washington. The doctors and nurses also had gone. Daniel McCook was left alone with a house full of wounded soldiers and his dying son. As Charlie neared death, he asked his father to give a message to his mother.

"Tell her that I refused to surrender, that I am not afraid of death, that I am glad to die for my country," he murmured.

Then Charlie quoted a Latin verse from Horace that he had learned at Milnor Hall, the preparatory school for Kenyon College: "*Dulce et decorum est pro patria mori*" (It is sweet and glorious to die for one's country).

Daniel McCook lay on the bed beside his son. About 2:30 a.m. Charlie raised his head onto his father's pillow and, his breathing short and quick, died without a struggle or moan. Daniel, in writing of that moment, confessed:

This was the most gloomy hour of my life.

He rolled Charlie's body up in his blankets, covered him with canvas, and strapped him to the lid of a musket box. Then, swapping his carriage for a small wagon, Daniel placed the body of his dead son in it and started for Washington.

A light rain was falling, and the roadside was lined with hundreds of soldiers sleeping in the mud. Others sat huddled against fences, nursing their wounds. Written on some hats were the words "Richmond or hell." Occasionally an officer was seen riding horseback sound asleep. The colorful uniforms that had caused such confusion on the battlefield now all looked alike, covered with mud.

Long Bridge over the Potomac River

Reaching the Long Bridge over the Potomac River, Daniel McCook walked his horse slowly across the lengthy wooden span. As the first fingers of dawn groped over the unfinished dome of the Capitol, they fell on the judge driving the little wagon with the shrouded body of his son strapped to the lid of a musket box.

On the Washington side of the river, a company of Zouaves formed an escort. Dressed in their bright crimson breeches with short blue jackets and red fezzes with yellow tassels, the Zouaves walked on either side of the mud-splattered wagon as the little procession slowly crossed the Mall in front of the Capitol, turned onto Pennsylvania Avenue, and came to a stop at Mrs. Paris's boarding house.

Martha McCook, who had come to Washington to be near her boys in uniform, took her dead son in her arms. Her tears mingled with the rain that fell sullenly on the cobblestones of Pennsylvania Avenue.

Union casualties at the Battle of Bull Run were some 460 killed, 1,124 wounded, and more than 1,200 captured or missing. Confederate casualties were almost 400 killed and some 1,600 wounded.

Private Charles Morris McCook was the only soldier killed in

Company I, Second Ohio Volunteer Infantry Regiment. The first body brought back to Washington, he was buried in the Congressional Cemetery on Capitol Hill with his messmates as his pallbearers.

The next morning, in the lobby of Willard's Hotel, a listening crowd heard the story of the boy who refused to surrender. His brother Edwin held up the bullet that had killed him and swore that the entire McCook clan—brothers and cousins and fathers and uncles—would pick up Charlie's fallen banner and carry it forward to save the Union.

And so the legend was born. From that day forward they were called "the Fighting McCooks."

The Battle of Bull Run, named by the North for the nearest body of water, or Manassas, named by the South for the nearest town, had immediate consequences. Although General McDowell had been assured that twelve thousand Confederate soldiers in the Shenandoah Valley would be prevented from reinforcing Beauregard, the Rebels managed to slip away and come by rail. Three brigades had arrived by Sunday morning, and the fourth came during the battle.

However, there must be a scapegoat, and it was General McDowell. He was removed from command, and President Lincoln summoned General George McClellan, fresh from his victories in western Virginia, to take command of the shattered army.

Congress authorized the enlistment of 1 million men, and the North girded itself for war.

Daniel McCook girded himself for revenge. In the ancient Scottish tradition, he vowed to avenge Charlie's death, as he wrote an old friend in Ohio:

> *I leave on tomorrow for the bank of the upper Potomac with my rifle in search of game. I am determined to pay the boys across the river for Bull Run.*
>
> *Very Respectfully*
> *Daniel McCook*

*Territory trod by the Fighting McCooks
in their quest to save the Union*

Chapter 5

Colonel Alexander McCook
and the War in the West

"Father, get down!" Colonel Alexander McCook had shouted when he saw Daniel McCook climb a fence to direct artillery fire during the Battle of Bull Run. "Your life is not paid for!"

It was a typical cavalier comment from Daniel and Martha's fifth son. Four months before Fort Sumter fell, the thirty-year-old U.S. Army lieutenant had made a prediction about Southern secession.

"There's going to be a war out of this," Alex said, "and before it's through, I'll ride a horse!"

Nine months later he was the youngest brigadier general in the Union volunteer army. To some he was the most colorful. To others he was the most controversial.

Alexander McDowell McCook was born on the family farm outside New Lisbon on April 22, 1831, and used his full name his whole life. His close friends called him "McD." His brother Dan called him "the happi-est man alive." Undeniably happy, Alex was also undeniably headstrong.

Daniel McCook, ambitious for all his sons, used his political connections with Ohio Congressman John D. Cummin to secure an appointment for Alex to the United States Military Academy at West Point. The stocky sixteen-year-old lad arrived at the formidable gray battlements above the Hudson River on July 1, 1847.

Irrepressible Alex was a carefree cadet, earning demerits for laughing in ranks, swinging his arms while marching, late at drill, hair not cut, asleep in bed before Taps, and shouting at cavalry exercises. He was not a partic-ularly studious cadet. Failing a course in mathematics during his second year, Alex was required to repeat the entire year. Graduating in 1852, he ranked thirtieth in a class of forty-two.

An oil portrait, painted in honor of his graduation, depicted a handsome young man with bright china-blue eyes, a Roman nose with an upward curve at the tip, a firm jaw, and a self-confident mien.

Second Lieutenant Alexander McDowell McCook, like many young U.S. Army officers, was sent west to fight Indians. He and his father cor-responded often, as the clannish McCooks were avid letter writers. On January 3, 1855, Alex wrote him from Fort Union, New Mexico:

> *Dear Father,*
>> *We all anticipate a long campaign against the Apaches next spring—or as soon as the grass will be sufficiently good to subsist our animals. I thought sometime ago that the Indians would remain quiet, but as fast as we quiet one band a new one breaks out. . . .*

Alex had a favor to ask. Since General Washington's day, Southerners had headed the army. Northerners frequently were passed over for promo-tion. Discouraged, many Northern officers resigned to enter business. But Alex loved the army and was not above pulling a few political strings. He asked his father, who was working in Washington and had friends in high places, if he could

> *succeed to get me up a little. A Captaincy would give me twelve years promotion and a First Lieutenancy about six or seven.*

Colonel William J. Hardee

Daniel McCook rarely failed his sons. After Alex had proven himself a good officer—fighting in the Battles of Sauwatchie Pass and Arkansas River, serving with Fauntleroy's expedition against the Apaches, and commanding a squad of 150 Pueblo and Navajo Indians in the Gila River Expedition—he received a commendation from Army General-in-Chief Winfield Scott.

After five years on the frontier, Alex was ordered to return to West Point on February 16, 1858, as assistant instructor of infantry tactics and the art of war. It was a plum post.

His superior was Colonel William Joseph Hardee, commandant of cadets. Hardee was a dynamic man, one of the most distinguished officers in the U.S. Army, highly regarded for his 1855 manual *Rifle and Light*

Infantry Tactics. It was popularly known as *Hardee's Tactics*. Alex McCook, like all Hardee's assistants, idolized him.

Hardee, a stern drillmaster and disciplinarian, had improved the training of cadets by emphasizing precision and speed in maneuvering masses of men on the battlefield. It was the European style of warfare that he had learned in France at the Royal Academy School. Alex McCook, emulating Hardee's discipline, enforced it with his own brand of humor. The cadets responded well. Hardee was pleased, and McCook was promoted to first lieutenant.

Colonel Hardee also improved the social life at West Point by hosting balls three nights a week during the summer season. Belles flocked to the academy, and no one enjoyed their company more than Hardee. A charming widower of forty-three, he loved teasing the ladies and feigning jealousy when they flirted with his assistants.

In the summer of 1860 Hardee wrote to a young lady from Schenectady, New York, who had taken a fancy to Alex McCook. Alex, with his buoyant high spirits and boundless self-confidence, was always the life of the party and a fine raconteur who could keep everyone amused and laughing. But Hardee could not resist a Shakespearean poke at the broad-shouldered and large-framed bon vivant whose waist had expanded greatly since his cadet days:

> *So McCook . . . saw you off—did McCook say unutterable things? I should like to see him making love! Sir Jno Falstaff must be a fool to him. However, he is a clever fellow and would make a good husband. Tell me if you are engaged to him. Is the coast clear? It is well to know one's rivals.*

The "rivals" parted at the end of the summer. In two and a half years, they had become good friends. Hardee and McCook shared a love of repartee, lovely ladies, and holidays in New York City. Although neither had excelled academically as cadets, they shared a deep love of the army.

Hardee was assigned to go west with the First U.S. Cavalry. The next winter, when Georgia seceded, he was one of the first Southerners to resign from the U.S. Army and offer his services to his native state. Of the 600 commissioned U.S. Army officers on active duty before the war, 179 transferred their allegiance to the Confederacy.

First Lieutenant Alexander McCook was the first Northern U.S. Army officer to join the Union volunteer army. On April 15, 1861, when President Lincoln called for Northern states to furnish troops, Alex immediately telegraphed Ohio Governor William Dennison. The next day he was sworn into the service of the state, and on April 22 he was elected colonel of the First Ohio Volunteer Infantry Regiment. Under Ohio law, three-month militias elected their own officers.

After training his regiment, Alex led it across the Potomac River into Virginia where it was assigned to the Second Brigade, First Division, Army of Northeastern Virginia. He discovered that his camp was near Arlington House, a handsome Grecian-style plantation mansion that had been appropriated by the army. Overlooking Washington, it was the vacated home of Confederate General Robert E. Lee.

Arlington House, vacated home of Confederate General Robert E. Lee, being used as headquarters for the Union Army

Lee, a fifty-four-year-old U.S. Army colonel who had declined the command of the Union Army to fight for Virginia, was the son of General "Light Horse" Harry Lee, who had led the Army of the Western Expedition against Alex's grandfather during the Whiskey Rebellion of 1794.

Alex next discovered that the brigadier general commanding his brigade was as green as the new recruits. He was one of Lincoln's first political generals.

Robert Cumming Schenck, a former congressman and diplomat, had campaigned for Lincoln's election to the presidency. Hurrying to the White House to offer his services during the hectic early days of war, Schenck found the new president harassed and abrupt. Lincoln, who had not expected nor anticipated war, suddenly found himself the commander-in-chief of the army, as specified in the Constitution.

Many of the top U.S. Army officers, like Robert E. Lee, Albert Sidney Johnston, and Joseph E. Johnston, were Southerners who had resigned to fight for the Confederacy. Northern generals were in short supply.

"Schenck," asked Lincoln, "can you fight?"

"I don't know, sir," replied Schenck, "but I can try."

"Well," said Lincoln, "I'll give you a chance to try. You shall be made a brigadier general."

The fifty-two-year-old Schenck, not lacking in self-confidence, secretly had hoped to be a two-star major general. But he accepted the brigadier's single star with good grace, taking command of the Second Brigade with aplomb. It was not long before the political general and the professional colonel clashed.

On June 17 Schenck took command of McCook's First Ohio Regiment while McCook was away from camp. Embarking on a railroad reconnaissance mission, Schenck ignored orders to advance with caution. With the whistle tooting loudly, the train rode straight into a Rebel artillery ambush at the village of Vienna. Eight men were killed, four were wounded, and the train was wrecked.

Alex McCook, having returned to camp and learning of the mission, galloped hard to reach the train and climbed aboard shortly before the attack. He saved the regiment from capture by fighting a rear guard action as they escaped down the railroad tracks, carrying their dead and wounded in blankets.

Village of Centreville, Virginia

Lincoln loyally defended Schenck, but there was an uproar in the Northern press. A *New York Times* editorial said that exposing volunteers to the experiments of "incompetent commanders does not greatly strengthen confidence in eventual success."

The second clash between the two men came after the disastrous Battle of Bull Run. Schenck, due to the Vienna escapade, had not been sent into battle but had been held in reserve at the stone bridge. When the tide turned and the demoralized Union soldiers retreated, General McDowell ordered Schenck to serve as rear guard at Centreville. Schenck, after issuing orders to his regimental commanders, promptly retired to his tent and went to sleep.

By sundown the last dregs of the disintegrated Union Army had straggled through the village. The rains came, and with them, reports that the victorious Confederates were advancing on Centreville from several directions. Colonel McCook and the other colonels of the brigade, judging that their position was not only indefensible but no longer necessary, went to Schenck's tent to awaken him and tell him that if he did not wish to suffer the ignominy of being captured in bed, it was time to leave.

"We deem it absolutely necessary for the safety of our troops to abandon this point at once," McCook urged.

"That you shall never do with my consent!" replied Schenck with outraged indignation. "I have been ordered to hold this position, and in turn I order you to hold it with me."

The two men faced each other angrily. McCook knew that, in the absence of the commanding general, Schenck did not have to follow blind obedience to an outdated order. He had the battlefield authority to countermand the order to save his men. Schenck, not knowing this well-settled principle of military law, threatened to court martial the headstrong young colonel.

McCook was fully aware of the seriousness of his action, but, confident that the facts would justify his course, he turned on his heel to lead the First Ohio back to defend Washington. After the Union rout at Bull Run, the U.S. Capitol could easily be captured. The colonels of the Second Ohio and Second New York followed his lead. General Schenck was left standing alone with his staff in the rain at the deserted village of Centreville.

Shortly after his brigade abandoned him, Schenck got an order from General McDowell to fall back on Washington. In light of the recent newspaper furor about his qualifications to be a general, Schenck did not file court martial charges. Instead, he credited McCook with anticipating McDowell's decision and recommended the colonel for promotion to brigadier general. But the humiliating incident was not forgotten by Schenck nor his chief of staff, Major Donn Piatt.

Colonel Alexander McCook, meanwhile, went to Ohio to train troops to fight in the West.

⌒

The nation, in its struggle for survival, was divided into two main theatres of war. The east lay between the Appalachian Mountains and the sea. The west lay between the Appalachians and the Mississippi River.

In the proposed Union volunteer army of 1 million men, Ohio was to recruit thirty-three infantry regiments, seven artillery companies, and twelve cavalry companies. Gone were the colorful state militia uniforms that had caused such confusion at Bull Run. Now all Union volunteers were to wear the standard light blue trousers and dark blue blouses of the regular U.S. Army.

Alex McCook, after being recommended by the president and confirmed by the Senate, received his general's star on September 3 while he was training his new three-year First Ohio Regiment in Dayton.

The third largest city in Ohio, Dayton was a prosperous place of some twenty thousand people in the agriculturally rich Miami Valley of southwestern Ohio. It boasted six railroads, the 266-mile Miami and Erie Canal, the most luxurious hotel between Cincinnati and Cleveland, and a classical Grecian-style courthouse patterned after the Theseum of Athens.

Dominating Dayton economically, as the McCooks had once dominated Carrollton, was the wealthy and aristocratic Phillips family. They claimed as their ancestors Revolutionary War hero General Nathanael Greene, who wintered with Washington at Valley Forge; Jonathan Dickinson, who founded Princeton College; and William the Conqueror, who defeated Britain at the Battle of Hastings in 1066.

Dominating Dayton socially was the belle of the family, the beautiful Kate Phillips. An artist, passing through the city, saw her at the theater and asked if he might paint her portrait. Her rosy-cheeked oval face, framed by auburn hair, was graced with large and gentle eyes.

But Kate's eyes could change from angelic to mischievous, as the good ladies of Dayton knew. Few forgot her fashion coup at the Hard Times ball given by her parents during an economic recession in 1857. On the morning of the ball, eighteen-year-old Kate impulsively sent her father to the dressmaker with a bolt of cheap cloth. That evening, when guests arrived in their silks and satins at the elegant Phillips home, on the corner of First and Ludlow streets, Kate greeted them dressed as a poor country girl in pink and white striped calico. One upstaged matron wrote peevishly to her daughter that Kate's dress was "a piece of affectation."

Alex McCook was intrigued. Soon he was calling at the Phillips home, making Kate laugh with his merry wit, singing ballads in his deep, rich voice, escorting her to his camp to review his troops, waltzing with her at the weekly balls that he gave for his men, and discovering that although he had fancied other lovely ladies in other lovely towns, this time it was different. The general was in love.

But time for courting was short. At the end of September he was ordered to assume his field command in Kentucky. After he left Kate and his troops and Dayton, one of his soldiers wrote home:

> *We hated to part with McCook for we all liked him.*

On October 14 Brigadier General Alexander McDowell McCook reported to Brigadier General William Tecumseh Sherman at Louisville, Kentucky. Sherman, commanding the Army of the Cumberland, was an old friend. Both he and Alex had been in Tyler's division at Bull Run.

Wealthy Kentucky, the home of thoroughbred racehorses and fine bourbon whiskey, had hoped to stay out of the bloody fight. The Ohio River formed her northern border, and she had strong economic, political, and social ties to both North and South.

Kentucky Governor Beriah Magoffin, in response to Lincoln's first call for seventy-five thousand troops, had replied:

> *Kentucky will furnish no troops for the wicked purpose of subduing her sister Southern states.*

Ohio Governor William Dennison had countered:

> *If Kentucky will not fill her quota of troops, then Ohio will fill it for her.*

President Lincoln considered Kentucky, his birthplace, crucial. It was one of the four slave-owning border states, with Maryland, Delaware, and Missouri, that he desperately wanted to keep in the Union. Lincoln explained his concern in a letter to Senator Orville Browning of Illinois:

> *I think to lose Kentucky is nearly the same as to lose the whole game. Kentucky gone, we cannot hold Missouri, nor as I think, Maryland.*

Lincoln promised not to send Union troops into Kentucky as long as the Confederates stayed out. But on September 3 Rebel troops marched in and took possession of the vital Mississippi River town of Columbus, "The Gibraltar of the West."

The North responded by sending Union troops into the state. Soon there was a "long Kentucky line" dividing the state horizontally from the Mississippi River in the west to the Cumberland Gap in the east. The Confederates were south of the line, and the Federals north of it.

Sherman gave McCook command of his largest division, the Second Division covering central Kentucky, and sent him a warning message that the enemy

> *awaits us on the other side of Green River . . . you must be pre-*
> *pared for anything.*

Alex knew the truth of that statement when he found that the enemy was his former West Point superior, good friend and "rival," Major General William J. Hardee.

Hardee commanded the First Division of the Confederate Central Army of Kentucky. Flying over his headquarters at Bowling Green was a flag he had designed, a blue field with a full silver moon crossed by two cannon. This was the only Confederate division flag allowed to be carried into battle. Wary foes watched for it.

Officers in both armies used his manual, *Hardee's Tactics*, as their bible.

Alex McCook, knowing his enemy only too well, rigorously drilled the thirteen thousand newly recruited men in his division from Ohio, Indiana, Illinois, Michigan, Wisconsin, Minnesota, Kentucky, Tennessee, and Missouri. He followed Napoleon's dictum: a highly disciplined army that can march twenty miles a day can cope with an army twice as large that can march only ten miles a day. McCook also knew that good infantry could march horses and mules to death. So he marched his men relentlessly until his Second Division was one of the best in the west.

From Hardee, McCook had learned to be a strict disciplinarian. Alex did it with typically good humor. His punishments of those who violated military regulations, while neither cruel nor harsh, were whimsical. One day while riding on an inspection tour, McCook came upon some of his soldiers whom he had ordered to march back and forth with railroad ties instead of guns. As the general rode up, the men were ordered to "present arms" with the wooden ties. McCook returned the salute gravely, but after he was out of their sight he broke into a hearty laugh.

However, Alex's irrepressible spirits and witty asides irritated some of the older and more somber Union generals. Their views were close to those of newspaper reporter William Shanks of the *New York Herald*, who wrote disapprovingly that McCook was "an overgrown schoolboy without dignity."

The power of the press was a deep concern to many in the military. Hundreds of reporters began covering the movements of both armies. For the first time in warfare, the speed of the telegraph made it possible for newspapers to receive information within hours of its being announced at army headquarters. People at home, as well as the enemy, often knew more about the army's marching orders than the soldiers in the field. Alex McCook, angry at the unauthorized snooping of reporter Whitelaw Reid of the *Cincinnati Gazette*, had him arrested and thrown out of camp.

While McCook regarded reporters as pests, General Sherman considered them spies and lying dogs. After Northern newspapers reported Sherman

New York Herald reporters with their wagon headquarters

crazy for insisting that he would need two hundred thousand men to push the Confederates down to the Gulf of Mexico, the War Department relieved him of his command on November 9. This confirmed Sherman's belief that the press "has the power to destroy us as they please."

On the other hand, Alex McCook's father found that the press also had the power to promote. Daniel McCook, with his customary ease of making friends in high places, saw to it that the exploits of the Fighting McCooks got front-page coverage.

The indefatigable Daniel McCook also donned a uniform. On November 9 he was enrolled as a captain in the Ohio Militia, after having fought in three battles in civilian garb, more than once narrowly escaping with his life.

On October 16, as a volunteer with the Twenty-eighth Pennsylvania, McCook had fought at Bolivar Heights, Maryland, earning mention in the official report of Colonel John Geary:

> *It affords me pleasure to mention that Honorable Daniel McCook, father of General McCook, as an amateur soldier, gun in hand, volunteered and rendered much service during the engagement.*

Daniel McCook's battlefield bravado continued to be a worry to his son Alex. But Alex had more pressing concerns. He was warily watching the movements of his old friend Hardee across the middle of the long Kentucky line.

They were soon to meet on the bloodiest battlefields of the west.

*Territory trod by the Fighting McCooks
in their quest to save the Union*

Chapter 6

CHAPLAIN HENRY MCCOOK
and the Holy War

While Alex McCook was holding the middle of the long Kentucky line, his cousin Henry was marching to battle on the western end of the line.

Twenty-four-year-old Chaplain Henry McCook could not have been happier. The honor of the McCook clan as well as the will of God called him to battle. A muscular five-feet-ten-inches tall, the clergyman was dark complexioned with black hair, bushy side-whiskers, and a firm jaw. He was a man who knew how to fight as well as pray.

In Henry's mind this was a holy war. An abolitionist, he saw the struggle between North and South as God's way of ending slavery, and he longed to do battle to atone for the sins of the nation. A true Celt, an idealist, a writer, and a brawler, Henry McCook had the syntax of a poet and the sinews of a pugilist.

The loud booming of the little brass cannon was one of the first sounds heard by Henry Christopher McCook. The third son of Dr. John and Catherine was born in New Lisbon on July 3, 1837, and the next morning the McCook clan fired off their cannon as usual to celebrate Independence Day.

Nicknamed "Dutch" by his schoolmates because he was tough and stubborn, Henry was the leader of one of the town gangs, called Dutch McCook's Crowd. A rival group, called the Sheep Hill Gang, was led by Henry's schoolmate Mark Hanna, a son of the prominent Quaker family who were big investors, along with the McCooks, in the Sandy and Beaver Canal.

Skirmishes between the street gangs were frequent until one boy, wielding an ancestral sword, badly hacked the arm of a rival. Weeping mothers implored the boys to stop. But it took the six-foot-two-inch Dr. John McCook, using his red rawhide strap, "mighty as the sword of Gideon," to end the gang wars for good.

The boys were steered, instead, into a debating club called the Polydelphian Society of New Lisbon. The first question debated, "Was the Mexican War justifiable?" brought the answer "no." Other issues— "Should flogging be abolished in the navy?" "Should Canada be annexed to the United States?" "Should women be allowed to vote?" and "Have the Negroes more cause for complaint against the Whites than the Indians?"—all were answered "yes."

Henry graduated from the New Lisbon High School at fourteen, was principal of the high school and superintendent of the Columbiana County schools at seventeen, graduated from Jefferson College in 1859 at the age of twenty-one, and began to study law. Suddenly, he found himself in another fight. This time it was a battle for his soul.

Henry had felt that he was suited for the law because he liked to debate and write and fight. But slowly another idea crept into a corner of his mind. It was the preposterous notion that he give his talents to the ministry. He rejected the idea outright, but it would not go away. He refused to go to Sunday services so that he would not be tempted. Still, the idea stuck. And so it went, back and forth, all summer. Finally, summer ended and so did the battle. Henry gave himself to the church and never looked back.

That fall he entered the Western Theological Seminary in Allegheny, Pennsylvania, to become a Presbyterian minister. He also became an abolitionist. It should not have been surprising to his family.

Henry's first schoolteacher was an abolitionist. New Lisbon, founded by Quakers in 1803, was an early center of opposition to slavery and an important station on the Underground Railroad. The Hanna family, staunch Quakers, had a trap door to their cellar concealed under a rug. There they hid escaped slaves until dark when they were taken in wagons with false bottoms to the next station on their way to freedom in Canada.

Abolitionists William Lloyd Garrison, Frederick Douglass, Parker Pillsbury, and Wendell Phillips all spoke in Columbiana County. A New Lisbon boy was with John Brown when, in trying to start a slave rebellion, he made his raid on the U.S. arsenal at Harper's Ferry on October 16, 1859.

In the winter of 1859–60 Henry was sent to serve as a lay preacher in Missouri. It was his first experience in a slave state, and he described the shock in a letter to his brother, Little Johnny.

Jany 13, 1860

Dear Johnny,

    On the Monday after New Year's, I went out 15 miles to witness the humane and Christian spectacle of a slave auction. The place of the auction stands in the midst of a colony of "old Virginians" and when I arrived I found the village thronged with men, mules and horses. A grog-shop in the vicinity was doing a thriving business; I stuck my head into the door, and could just catch a view of the busy bar-tenders, through the boisterous crowd that filled the room. An old black-smith shop had been appropriated to the "niggers", and in the center of this on the floor a fire was burning, around which an ebon group of brothers, sisters, sons, fathers, mothers, wives, husbands and little ones were huddled, stretching their trembling limbs (it was intensely cold) over the faint blaze, their sad faces looking sadder and darker through the cloud of blue smoke that enveloped them.

    About 11 o'clock the scene began and, oh Heavens, what a scene! There, beneath the bright blue sky of a new-year's morn, on the soil of this boasted "land of the free and the home of the brave", under the proud and protecting folds of the "Star Spangled banner", sixty men, women and children . . . were put up before a large crowd of men, many rude, vulgar and intoxicated, and publicly sold into perpetual slavery.

Yet Henry did not have an answer for the evil.

Since my sojourn here I have been trying to study the "peculiar institution". My convictions of its heinous wickedness are unabated, but how to remedy the wrong I cannot see. I am persuaded that immediate abolition is impossible; a mad and dangerous scheme. It will take centuries to emancipate the slaves and Emancipation when it does come must come from the hands of the masters themselves.

Your aff. brother

Hen

I hope you will not read these remarks to any one. They might travel this way and do me harm.

But Henry's fears for himself disappeared after he saw a pile of ashes, all that remained of a runaway slave who had been caught and burned to death as a lesson to the others.

When Henry came home on vacation the next summer, he was invited to preach at the Steubenville Presbyterian Church. His sermon was a moving plea for the abolition of slavery. But abolitionism was not approved widely in Northern churches, by any means. The parishioners were shocked at his radical views and his impassioned defense of John Brown, who had been hanged six months earlier. Many in the congregation were openly contemptuous. His fiancée was embarrassed. His family was furious.

The McCooks did not approve of slavery nor its spread to the western territories. But, as firm Douglas Democrats, they agreed with Senator Douglas that the North would have to allow the South to keep its "peculiar institution" in order to preserve the Union.

Henry's four brothers and his father, Dr. John, were waiting for him when he came home from church. How he did catch it! The verbal scuffling was like a dog fight, with Dr. John and the older boys aiming like big hounds at his neck, while Little Johnny sailed in like a terrier to snap at his heels.

But Henry, who had seen the "peculiar institution" in all its ugliness, was firm. He deserted the Democrats, became a Republican, and rejoiced when Lincoln was elected. The people had spoken.

When the war began, Henry was serving as a curate at the Presbyterian church in Clinton, Illinois. Hurrying to Washington, he arrived on the last train to reach the capital and joined his Uncle Daniel in the Frontier Guards. Then, when the siege was lifted, Henry went to Ohio to become a chaplain in the volunteer army. He was doomed to disappointment.

Each regiment was permitted to have one chaplain, with a captain's rank and pay of twelve hundred dollars. However, the War Department, remembering that during the Mexican War some scoundrels had pretended to be ministers in order to get the salary, decreed that a chaplain must be an ordained minister of some Christian denomination. Henry, not yet ordained, was crestfallen. Returning to his parish in Clinton, Illinois, he salved his conscience by stumping the county to raise troops.

However, when his cousin Charlie was killed at Bull Run, Henry could stay out no longer. Enlisting in the Forty-first Illinois Volunteer Infantry Regiment, he was elected a first lieutenant and assured that he would be made chaplain after his ordination in the fall.

On July 27, 1861, before leaving for camp, Henry climbed to the top of his church's belfry tower and hung the Stars and Stripes. He hoped the flag would remind the congregation to pray for the boys in blue. Also, he hoped it would remind the boys in blue that God was on their side in this holy war.

It was a war that was commanded, at the western end of the long Kentucky line, by one of the nation's great explorers. To Henry he was also a great hero.

Major General John Charles Frémont was known as the "Pathfinder" for his surveys of a route from the Mississippi River to the Pacific Ocean. He had been the first presidential candidate of the Republican Party in 1856, and he was a fervent abolitionist.

The forty-eight-year-old Frémont, with his headquarters at St. Louis, was a strong and arbitrary figure. After a Union defeat at Wilson's Creek,

Presbyterian church in Clinton, Illinois, where Henry McCook hung the U.S. flag from the belfry tower

Missouri, on August 10, 1861, Frémont declared martial law throughout Missouri, issued a proclamation calling for the confiscation of property belonging to those "who shall take up arms against the United States," and announced that slaves owned by Southern sympathizers "are hereby declared freemen."

Henry McCook was delighted. President Lincoln was not.

Trying to keep the border states in the Union, Lincoln had assured them that the aim of the war was the preservation of the Union and not the abolition of slavery.

Since Frémont's "emancipation proclamation" threatened to drive the border states into the Confederacy, Lincoln asked him to revoke it. When Frémont refused, Lincoln ordered him to do so.

Henry McCook, trying to forget his deep disappointment in Lincoln, immersed himself in his work. Ordained a Presbyterian minister on October 1, 1861, Henry assumed his duties as regimental chaplain of the Forty-first Illinois.

By the fall of 1861 there were 472 chaplains in the Union Army, 450 Protestant ministers and 22 Catholic priests. There were no rabbis, as the secretary of war had specified that chaplains must be Christians. Jewish soldiers protested, but in the wisdom of the War Department, the order stood.

Many soldiers carried Bibles, given to them by their families and communities in hopes that the Good Book and the chaplain would save their generally irreverent and wayward youths. Sunday services consisted of scripture readings, a sermon, and hymns. The soldiers' favorites were "Rock of Ages," "Blest Be the Tie That Binds," "Sweet Hour of Prayer," and "There Is a Fountain Filled with Blood."

Sermons warned about the evils of whiskey, tobacco, and women camp followers. Attendance was spotty. Soldiers were encouraged to go to services, but they noted that not many of their officers did, apparently assuming that their rank alone would open the gates to heaven.

Sunday religious services in the Union Army

On November 6, after months of itching for a fight, Captain Henry McCook got his marching orders. The Forty-first Illinois, assigned to Brigadier General Eleazer A. Paine's Third Brigade at Paducah, Kentucky, was ordered to support a movement on the Mississippi River by Brigadier General Ulysses S. Grant. Grant was making a probe, or demonstration, on a Confederate camp at Belmont, Missouri. It was the western end of the long Kentucky line.

With great anticipation Henry marched to his first fight. But one week later he wrote, with great disappointment, to his cousin Mary in Hartford, Connecticut.

Mary Sheldon, lively and outgoing, was a niece of Henry's mother. Mary lived with her half-sister Eliza Butler, a shy heiress whom the McCook boys called the "quiet little mouse." Both young ladies had just returned from a grand tour of Europe and, as part of their war effort, began knitting gloves and scarves. In addition, Mary promised to correspond faithfully with all of her McCook cousins in uniform.

Henry, in his letter, told her of the Battle of Belmont.

> *Paducah, Ky. Nov. 12, 1861*
>
> *My Dear Cousin,*
>> *Last week I had a little experience in forced marching. Wednesday morn our Brigade—Genl. Paine commanding— received orders to march at 2 pm with three days rations in haversacks. . . . We made 12 miles by night and encamped on the bank of a creek. The bridge across it had been cut down obstructing our progress. I kindled a rousing fire and around it the Colonel, Adjutant and one or two others besides myself stretched ourselves for sleep. The night was damp and chilly and I slept but little. We were off by daybreak, I with a headache. All day we could hear the roaring of the guns at Belmont, and our boys pressed on eager to join in the contest. We passed over 24 miles by dark and halted . . . to await orders. The firing of the guns had ceased and we saw evidently that we were just a day too late.*

General Grant, instead of demonstrating against Belmont, had launched a full-scale attack without waiting for General Paine. Defeated with heavy loss of life, Grant had been forced to retreat, leaving behind many of his dead and wounded.

> *Judge of my disappointment and sorrow when the orders came to return to Paducah—and with them the sad tidings—brought in by a spy—of the dreadful slaughter and repulse of our poor boys at Belmont.*

To add to Henry's woes, he heard that President Lincoln had relieved General Frémont of his command. The nation's ministers and the anti-slavery press were overwhelmingly on Frémont's side in the emancipation dispute. But the president, firmly in command, felt that the autocratic Frémont was out of control and must go.

> *The news of Frémont's removal, which we first learned on our arrival, set us all into a rage from which many of us—I at least—have scarcely yet recovered.*
> *Good-bye! Write again & soon.*
> *Your affectionate cousin*
> *Henry*

During the next few weeks Henry's spirits sank even lower when he discovered that officers in his regiment were selling runaway slaves back to their owners after the Negroes had sought sanctuary in the Union camp.

The question of what to do with runaway slaves in the border states had puzzled the federal government since the start of the war. In August Congress had passed the Confiscation Act, freeing slaves who came into Union camps, unless they had served in the Confederate Army. But two days later, Secretary of War Simon Cameron insisted that the Union Army must abide by an 1850 law imposing heavy penalties on anyone interfering with the recovery of runaway slaves.

In October General Sherman, commanding the Army of the Cumberland, had written about runaway slaves to Henry's cousin, General Alexander McCook:

Major General John Charles Frémont

> *The laws of the United States and of Kentucky, all of which are binding on us, compel us to surrender a runaway negro on application of negro's owner or agent.*

Chaplain Henry McCook was angry. While some officers were making money by selling slaves, he had not been paid a cent for his three months' service.

The day after Thanksgiving he received a box from his brother, Little Johnny. The lad, after being mustered out of the army, had entered Trinity College in Hartford and accepted an invitation to live with cousin Mary and her half-sister Eliza at the commodious Butler house. From their well-staffed kitchen had come a box of homemade goodies for Henry.

His letter of thanks was tinged with bitterness.

Paducah, Ky., Nov. 29, 1861

Dear Johnny,

Your "Thanksgiving Present" arrived just a day too late. Many thanks, however. As I am quite a moderate eater, I expect it to last me a long time. I suppose you celebrated the day in regular Yankee style. I should have loved dearly to have sat around the bountiful board of our good cousins to enjoy their New England cheer. My Thanksgiving dinner consisted of Hard Crackers (you have heard of them, I dare say) and tea!

Indulging in heavy sarcasm, Henry enclosed a sketch he had made of a slave being sold at auction.

As some mark of appreciation for your kindness in remembering me, I send you the accompanying gift. It is peculiar to this soil—indigenous, the inhabitants say; quite as much so as "pumpkin pies" and "Thanksgivings" are to New England. It is the chief production of this region and the great source of wealth. It is deemed of exceeding value. Men have been known to sacrifice their honor, their humanity, their country, their souls for its possession. It has one strong characteristic—peculiar to this kind of property—it reasons and runs away.

Ichabod (the darkey's name) has a mate and six young ones here (he calls them his "wife am' chillen"! —ha, ha) and they all made a great ado when he left, crying and sighing very much like human beings in distress. (Indeed, these creatures bear a striking resemblance to mankind in some of their ways.) I really thought the parting hurt their feelings vastly; but la! the people here say they don't mind it one bit; that they really haven't any feelings; it's only a way they have on such occasions, and the "fuss" is all "put on". (I must say they are excellent mimics, their tears and sorrow were so nearly like nature that one who wasn't acquainted with the habits of the deceitful creatures would have been deceived.) I hope you will be pleased with my gift.

Your aff. brother

Hen

Thanksgiving day, November 1861, in the Union Army

Captain Henry McCook was fighting another battle within himself. Firm in his convictions, he would not bend. Unlike Lincoln, a politician who understood the necessity of compromise, Henry would not compromise. If the Union Army was in the slave-trading business, then the holy war was a sham. God could not possibly be on their side.

There was only one thing for Henry to do. And shortly before Christmas he sat down in his tent to do it.

Paducah, Ky. Dec. 21st, 1861

To J. C. Kelton
Asst. Adj. Genl.
Dept. Mo.
Sir:

I hereby most respectfully tender my resignation as Chaplain of the 41st Regiment Ills. Vols.

My reasons are as follows. It is well and publicly known throughout the Regiment that certain of its officers, Lieutenants, brought into camp fugitive slaves who had placed themselves under their protection at the Pickets, and afterwards delivered them over to their masters receiving therefore sums varying from fifty to twenty dollars each. Believing such trading in slaves to be a gross prostitution of the honor of officers and of the good name of the Regiment, I endeavored to secure the co-operation of the Colonel in a plan to obtain the dismissal of the offenders from the service. The Colonel declines acting. This course paralyzes any effort to be rid of the obnoxious parties. Therefore I cannot submit to share the disgrace which doubtless will fall upon the whole Regiment as well as upon the guilty.

I cannot comfortably associate with officers and feel bound to treat as gentlemen those whom I believe to have forfeited every claim to consideration as either officers or gentlemen.

I cannot consent to leave unexposed and unpunished such outrages upon our Soldiery, our Country, our Humanity, and yet I feel unwilling, with myself an officer, to rebuke in the Press and from the Pulpit, in such terms as I feel are deserved, men who still hold offices in our Regiment, and who have the command of many of those to whom I minister.

I do not desire to be one of a Regiment where slave-trading officers, if deemed dishonorable, are not dealt with as such.

I have received no pay, and have no public property in my possession. The above resignation to be immediate and unconditional.

Very Respectfully
Henry McCook

*Territory trod by the Fighting McCooks
in their quest to save the Union*

Chapter 7

Colonel Robert McCook
at the Battle of Mill Springs

"Charge, my bully Dutchmen!" shouted Colonel Robert McCook to the men of his all-German Ninth Ohio Regiment, as he stood tall in the saddle and lifted his sword high.

It was the bitterly cold morning of January 19, 1862, at the eastern end of the long Kentucky line, three weeks after his cousin Henry had resigned at the western end of the line.

As Colonel McCook led his men in a furious bayonet attack against the Confederates in a fallow cornfield near Mill Springs, a thousand Germans swept around the corner of a stable wielding their gleaming sabers and screaming their savage Teutonic "Hurrah" battle cries and hurling themselves like demons on the startled Rebels who scattered like chaff in the wind.

It was the first successful bayonet charge of the war, the first significant Union victory in the west, and the first break in the long Kentucky line.

Colonel Robert McCook, Daniel and Martha's fourth son, was recommended for promotion to brigadier general.

The hero of Mill Springs was a warrior who charged into battle with the devil-may-care dash of the ancient Scots. He was a magnetic man, muscular and of medium height. Half-veiled steel-gray eyes glinted from a taut face chiseled with high cheekbones and a slash of a mouth, while an unruly shock of coarse brown hair was thrown back carelessly, covering half his ears.

Colonel McCook took pride in only one thing—his Ninth Ohio—the first all-German regiment in the west. Drilled to perfection and proclaimed by General George McClellan as the finest regiment he had seen in either Europe or America, the Ninth Ohio Volunteer Infantry Regiment always had more clothing, ammunition, and food than any other unit, and their thirty-four-year-old commander never deigned to explain where he got them. Abrupt and brusque, Colonel Robert Latimer McCook was a rough-hewn gem with neither the time nor the temper to be polished.

Born on December 28, 1827, in New Lisbon, he was known as "an old-fashioned child, sober beyond his years." A rough-and-tumble boyhood was spent tramping the woods of eastern Ohio to bring home wild game—quail, rabbit, and venison—for the family table. After finishing school at fifteen and caring not for college, he worked for two years as his father's deputy in the Carroll County courthouse. Then he began the study of law with the firm of Stanton and McCook in Steubenville.

The rough-and-tumble side of the law, learned from Edwin Stanton, came naturally to Bob McCook. He was always ready to fight when provoked. No one prized the privilege of self-defense more or resorted to it with greater alacrity. In 1847 he was charged with assault and battery, entered a plea of nolo contendere, and paid a fine of ten dollars.

Robert L. McCook, Esquire, gained early admission to argue before the U.S. Supreme Court. By 1858 he was the law partner of the Honorable Johann B. Stallo, judge of the superior court in Cincinnati. They had a large and lucrative practice among the German immigrants who formed one-third of the city's population. McCook, one of their most enthusiastic defenders, earned a reputation as "Fighting Bob McCook."

Financially successful, Bob was able to buy a house at 260 Walnut Street, hire a free Negro as a manservant, and make the grand tour of Europe in the summer of 1860.

Observing the armies of France, Austria, Italy, and Prussia, McCook preferred the Prussians for their innate discipline and unwavering obedience to authority. Convinced that war between the states was inevitable, he began reading *Hardee's Tactics,* the bible of infantry warfare, when he returned home to Cincinnati.

Known as the "Gateway to the South," Cincinnati was one of the nation's largest manufacturing centers and the most prosperous city in the west. A metropolis of 161,000 people on the Ohio River, it sent some thirty-five hundred steamboats and three thousand flatboats annually up and down southern rivers with the North's machinery and textiles to trade for the South's sugar and cotton.

Cincinnati also had strong social links with the South. Wealthy plantation owners often sent their sons and daughters to its academies to be educated, leading to marriage between the two cultures. Cincinnati, known as the "Athens of the West" for its interest in literature and the arts, considered itself just as cultured and refined as Richmond or Charleston.

However, when war broke out, Cincinnatians overwhelmingly sided with the North. Men rushed to enlist. Bob McCook, remembering the martial skills of the Prussians, proposed an all-German regiment. In less than two days there were more than a thousand names on the list, names like Sondershoff and Kammerling and Hermannsdorfer. Although Ohio's quota of troops was filled, McCook had enough political clout to get the regiment accepted by the governor. In gratitude the men voted unanimously for him as their colonel. That was how a Scotch-Irishman, who knew little German, became the commander of a regiment whose men spoke broken English.

Stepping smartly to the music of their twenty-piece band, the Ninth Ohio left for Camp Harrison, thirteen miles north of Cincinnati, on April 24. They were clad in the short, white linen jackets of the Turnverein Society. Bob McCook, leading them on horseback, wore civilian clothing with a stovepipe hat and a sword strapped to his side.

Major August Willich, a former Prussian officer who had commanded a corps in the 1849 German revolution, drilled and disciplined the regiment, and Colonel McCook organized it, discovering in the process that there was more to war than fighting. A friend found him in camp sitting on the sill of a wooden shanty, his knee serving as a desk, immersed in the paperwork of approving requisitions and signing documents.

"I have just found out what it is to be a colonel," McCook laughed ruefully, "and that is to be head clerk to a thousand Dutchmen!"

He was a most solicitous head clerk, promising the German immigrants, who often felt discriminated against, that if they fought for their new country, he would fight for them. And so he did. McCook made sure that they had the best of everything. The German quarters at camp were the liveliest of all as the men, with beer steins held high, filled the nights with as much gemütlich singing as any Bavarian beer hall.

Never was a father more concerned for the welfare of his sons than Colonel McCook was for his men. He was rewarded by their willingness to follow him even, as he said, "to hell itself."

On May 3 President Lincoln, realizing that seventy-five thousand three-month volunteers would not be enough to put down the rebellion, asked for forty-two thousand three-year volunteers. The Ninth Ohio was the first regiment in the state to change from a three-month to a three-year regiment.

By mid-June they were in western Virginia with General McClellan's Army of Occupation. After a hard march through the mountains, covering fifteen miles in three hours, Colonel McCook set up camp in the Tygart Valley against the advice of other Union officers who thought the valley position too vulnerable. McCook stubbornly refused to move to a safer spot.

"We came to fight," he said, "and if the Rebels think they can drive my Dutchmen out of the hollow, let them try it."

They did not try it. Soon the Rebels were calling the Ninth Ohio the "Dutch devils," commanded by a colonel who was brave to the point of being foolhardy. By early July, although Bob McCook had been in the field only three weeks, he had established a reputation for daring and was reported by the *Cincinnati Daily Commercial* to be the most valuable reconnaissance officer in the Army of Occupation.

As General McClellan launched his campaign to drive the Confederates out of western Virginia, he gave McCook the command of the lead brigade, dispatching the War Department on July 6:

> *My advance guard, consisting of the Fourth and Ninth Ohio,*
> *Loomis' Michigan battery, and Burdsal's Ohio dragoons, under*
> *the command of Colonel R. L. McCook, moves at 4 a.m.*
> *tomorrow to seize the Middle Fork Bridge. . . .*

Skirmishing with the enemy, reconnoitering the forest, and pushing through the mountain passes, McCook enjoyed the campaign as something of a rare sport. Riding at the head of his brigade, he ignored those who urged him to remain in the rear, insisting that he would not ask his men to go where he feared to lead.

By July 11 the Rebels had been routed from western Virginia. Ten days later the North suffered its defeat at Bull Run, and McClellan was summoned to Washington to build a new three-year Army of the Potomac. He offered Bob McCook the opportunity to go with him, including a promotion to brigadier general, but McCook turned it down. He had given his word to the Germans of the Ninth Ohio that he would stay with them until the war was over and they would all return to Cincinnati together.

Remaining in the Appalachians during that rainy summer, McCook led the Second Brigade of the Army of Occupation, under the command of General William S. Rosecrans. The approach of fall brought beautiful weather, but it also brought the Confederates. General Robert E. Lee entered the mountains with an army of ten thousand to recapture western Virginia.

Marching through the Great Kanawha Valley in search of Lee, Bob McCook loved the mountainous land that his cousin Little Johnny had loathed. Western Virginia was a blue haze wilderness with deep purple valleys and brilliant crimson sunsets. At dusk they camped by clear streams under great pine trees, with all the tents sparkling bright and the Germans of the Ninth Ohio singing their Teutonic battle songs.

Around the campfire, McCook renewed his friendship with Major Rutherford B. Hayes of the Twenty-third Ohio. The two attorneys, who had been good friends in Cincinnati before the war, now became as close as brothers. Talking long into the night, they both relished outdoor life and the camaraderie of soldering.

By late September Rosecrans and Lee were on two mountaintops, several miles apart, glaring at each other. Lee had been reinforced to twenty-thousand men, the weather had changed, and the mountains were rainy and cold. Much of the Union Army was wet and shivering, but McCook's men, as usual, were high and dry. Major Hayes, sharing a tent with McCook, wrote his wife Lucy about life on their mountain perch.

Major Rutherford B. Hayes

Sept. 27th, 1861

Dear L:

We are in the midst of a very cold rain storm. Rain for fifteen hours—getting colder and colder, and still raining. In leaky tents, with worn out blankets, insufficient socks and shoes, many without overcoats. This is no joke. I am living with McCook in a good tent, as well provided as anybody in camp, better than either Gen. Cox or Rosecrans.

I write this in Gen. Cox's tent. He sits on one cot reading, or trying to read, or pretending to read, Dickens' new novel "Great Expectations". McCook and Gen. Rosecrans are in the opposite tent over a smoke trying to think they are warmed by the fire under it. Our enemy, far worse provided than we are, are no doubt shivering on the opposite hill now hidden by the driving rain and fog.

Good-bye dearest.
Affectionately,
R

Hayes had learned in a letter from Lucy that there was much discouragement about the war at home. Newspaper reporters reported misery and shortages at camps everywhere, with some regiments sending their officers back home to go door-to-door begging for funds and supplies. But, as Hayes wrote his wife on October 19, troops with resourceful officers did not need to beg:

McCook can feed, clothe, blanket half a regiment more any time while alongside of him is a regiment ragged, hungry and blanketless, full of correspondents writing home complaints about somebody. It is here as elsewhere. The thrifty and energetic get along, and the lazy and thoughtless send emissaries to the cities to beg.

Colonel McCook frequently had all the field officers in the army protesting against his determined and successful efforts to provide for the comfort of his men. When the complaints reached General Rosecrans, he

General Robert E. Lee

ordered all regiments to turn in their extra wagons. McCook always obeyed promptly. However, the next day the Ninth Ohio again had twice as many wagons as any other regiment. Their colonel, characteristically, never explained where he got them.

By mid-October Rosecrans, with eighty-five hundred men, had out-maneuvered Lee with twenty thousand. Lee returned to Richmond amid taunts of "Granny Lee" for having been outgeneraled. By mid-November

Rosecrans had forced the Confederates from the vital Kanawha Valley and reported to the War Department that western Virginia was pacified. On November 26 delegates from forty-eight counties met in Wheeling to adopt a Constitution calling for the formation of the loyal state of West Virginia.

Colonel Robert McCook and his "Bloody Dutch" had spent five months of scouting, skirmishing, and fighting at Rich Mountain, Carnifex Ferry, Summerville, and Gauley River Bridge. Now they were ordered west to help break the long Kentucky line. In Kentucky General William T. Sherman had been replaced by General Don Carlos Buell, and the Army of the Cumberland had been renamed the Army of the Ohio.

Colonel McCook was given command of the Third Brigade, made up of the Ninth Ohio, Second Minnesota, Thirty-fifth Ohio, and Eighteenth U.S. Infantry. The brigade was assigned to the First Division, commanded by Brigadier General George H. Thomas. A forty-six-year-old Virginian who had remained loyal to the Union, Thomas had his headquarters at Lebanon in central Kentucky.

On New Year's Day 1862, while both Union and Confederate armies were snug in their winter quarters, General Thomas started south through rain and sleet toward Confederate Brigadier General Felix K. Zollicoffer's camp at Mill Springs on the Cumberland River in southeastern Kentucky. Marching in the lead was Colonel McCook with two regiments, the Ninth Ohio and Second Minnesota.

On January 18, after slogging through ankle-deep mud, they reached Logan's Crossroads, ten miles from the Rebel camp. With most of his division still struggling to catch up, Thomas set up camp with four regiments, two of McCook's and two of Colonel Manson Mahlon's, to await the rest of his division. Then he would strike Zollicoffer.

Zollicoffer struck first. Aware of Thomas's skeletal force, the Confederate general made an all-night march with eight regiments and attacked amid rain and mist at dawn on January 19. Thomas, outnumbered two to one, held his position for half an hour until his ammunition was getting low and he was fending off flank attacks. Seizing the moment, Thomas ordered McCook to counterattack.

Charging the Confederate hilltop position amid heavy mist and smoke, McCook discovered that while he was moving his men up the hill, the

Rebels were moving down. Meeting in the middle at a rail fence, the enemies were shooting and slashing each other through the slats.

To break the impasse, McCook ordered a bayonet charge. Gathering the Germans of the Ninth Ohio behind a stable, he told them to empty their guns and fix bayonets. Then he drew his sword.

"Charge, my bully Dutchmen!" he shouted.

Screaming their piercing "Hurrah" battle cries, the Germans swept around the corner of the stable with their bayonets glistening in the mist and tore into the "Tiger Rifles" of the Fifteenth Mississippi. The Confederate line cracked in great confusion, with the Rebels fleeing wildly over the top of the hill.

According to the official report of Colonel Speed Fry of the Fourth Kentucky, they flew "like chaff before the wind!"

Three bullets hit McCook's horse, a fourth tore through his overcoat, and a fifth struck him in the lower leg. Unhorsed, he continued to pursue the enemy on foot, stopping only when he limped into Zollicoffer's deserted tent. There the regimental surgeon found him and dressed his wound. Standing beside McCook was the Ninth Ohio flag, a blue silk banner sewn by the German women of Cincinnati. Shot full of holes, it soon flew victoriously over the captured camp.

McCook's bayonet charge at the Battle of Mill Springs

Zollicoffer was killed in the fight. His troops, not able to be rallied, fell back to the Cumberland River and crossed during the night. Left behind were twelve cannon, 150 wagons, more than 1,000 horses and mules, and a large stock of commissary stores. Confederate losses were 125 killed, 309 wounded, and 99 captured or missing. Union casualties were 40 killed, 207 wounded, and 15 captured or missing. The Confederates retreated through the Cumberland Gap, and the eastern end of the long Kentucky line collapsed.

The victorious Battle of Mill Springs was celebrated with the firing of cannon in hundreds of army camps across the North, lifting the morale of soldiers and citizens alike. This time the Confederates were destroyed as a fighting force instead of being allowed to slip away with their arms to fight again.

A grateful North responded with an outpouring of praise. President Lincoln recommended Colonel McCook for promotion to brigadier general. The Ohio General Assembly passed a resolution commending their native son. In the snowbound mountains of western Virginia, where he was in winter quarters, Lieutenant Colonel Rutherford B. Hayes wrote his wife Lucy:

> *I am delighted with the Kentucky victory, and particularly that my friend McCook and his regiment take the honors. We were good friends before the war, but much more intimately so since we came into service. . . . McCook was not seriously but gloriously wounded.*

Bob McCook was granted a furlough to return to Ohio for treatment of his leg. His brother, Colonel George McCook, who was training troops near Steubenville, assessed the wound and wrote a reassuring letter to their father in Washington:

> *Robert is painfully, but not dangerously, wounded. Don't start west.*

Captain Daniel McCook, busier than ever, was in Washington often these days, seeing old friends on Capitol Hill, making new friends among newspapermen, and dropping in at the White House to inform the president about support for the war in the west.

Lincoln, an astute politician, was keenly aware that he was a minority president. Due to the split in the Democrat Party between Northerners and Southerners, Lincoln had been elected with only 40 percent of the vote. In order to maintain the support of the people for the war, he needed to know the pulse of the western Democrats. The obliging Daniel McCook was only too glad to take it for him.

And now, across the White House lawn in the War Department, another good friend of McCook was freshly ensconced in another high place. Edwin Stanton was the new secretary of war.

Stanton was heavier now. At forty-seven years of age, his dark mottled skin was lined, and he had an immense black beard with a wide silver streak running down the middle. But the brown eyes behind the steel-rimmed spectacles were still cunning. He was still irascible and rude. He still loved intrigue, and he was still adept at playing double roles and maneuvering within the labyrinthian world of politics.

Nine months earlier, when President Lincoln was inaugurated, Stanton expected to be named to his cabinet. It would have been a fitting reward for his having played a double role in the dying days of the Buchanan administration. By working with the Republicans in Congress to force Democrat Buchanan to hold onto Fort Sumter, Stanton had helped preserve the Union for Lincoln.

But Lincoln did not return the favor. To those who knew the two men well, it was not surprising. Stanton had been downright rude to Lincoln in 1855 when both attorneys were retained in a patent suit involving the McCormick Reaper Company. It was an important case with millions of dollars at stake. Sizing up the gawky Lincoln in his sweat-stained coat, Stanton had refused to serve with him.

"If that giraffe appeared in the case I would throw up my brief and leave," he said haughtily.

So Stanton sat on the sidelines, caustic and critical, for the first nine months of war. He sneered at Lincoln's "painful imbecility" after the Union disaster at Bull Run.

He sniffed at Lincoln's unpolished persona, calling him the "original gorilla," the "Illinois ape," and a "low cunning clown." He seethed at Lincoln's inability to get General McClellan to attack Richmond with his one-hundred-thousand-man Army of the Potomac, and he scoffed at

Secretary of War Edwin Stanton

Lincoln's attempts to be commander-in-chief, rushing back and forth between the White House and the War Department armed with maps, reports, and battle tactics.

To make matters worse, the War Department itself was plagued with graft and corruption. It was obvious to Stanton that a strong hand was needed at the helm of the ship of state. If the Union was to be saved, he would have to do it. So again, Stanton played a double role.

On December 1, when Secretary of War Simon Cameron issued his report to Congress, he advocated the freeing and arming of slaves. Cameron, like General Frémont, was sabotaging Lincoln's attempts to keep the border states in the Union and, like Frémont, he was removed. On January 15 the new secretary of war was Edwin Stanton who, as chief

*Council of war at the White House in 1861
with President Lincoln seated at left*

legal advisor to Simon Cameron, had been the real author of the very words that got Cameron fired.

Major Donn Piatt, an Ohioan who was one of Stanton's oldest friends, was astounded at his appointment.

"Yes," crowed Stanton, "I am going to be secretary of war to Old Abe."

"What will you do?" asked Piatt, aware of his contempt for Lincoln.

"Do?" snorted Stanton. "I will make Abe Lincoln president of the United States!"

The new secretary of war came into office like a whirlwind. Financially honest, he cleaned up graft and waste. Frenetically energetic, he replaced confusion with order. Fiercely competitive, he transferred his will-to-win-at-any-cost from the courtroom to the war office.

The Union victory at Mill Springs, coming four days after he took office, was a good omen. Stanton issued a congratulatory message to the victors, including his former law student Bob McCook.

McCook's cold cornfield victory in the west contrasted starkly with McClellan's warm dinner parties in the east. This prompted Stanton to write on January 24 to his friend Charles Dana, managing editor of the *New York Tribune*:

> *While men are striving nobly in the West, the champagne and oysters on the Potomac must be stopped.*

Two weeks later, more good news came out of the west. The middle of the long Kentucky line began to collapse. On February 6 Brigadier General Ulysses S. Grant captured Fort Henry on the Tennessee River and announced that in two days he would take and destroy Fort Donelson on the Cumberland. With Grant was Stanton's namesake, and Daniel McCook's seventh son, Captain Edwin Stanton McCook.

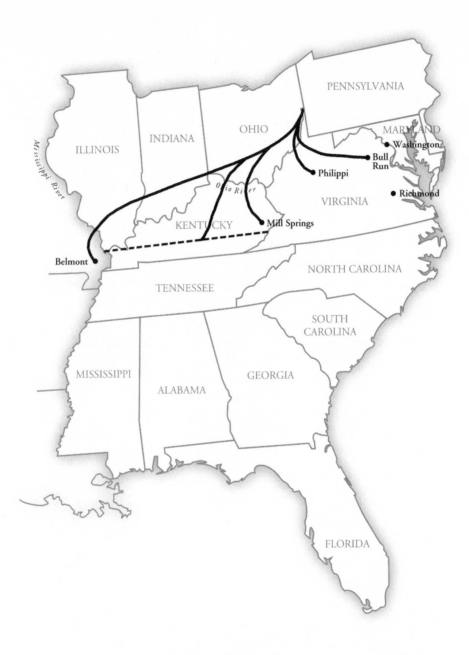

Territory trod by the Fighting McCooks
in their quest to save the Union

Chapter 8

CAPTAIN EDWIN STANTON McCOOK
at Forts Henry and Donelson

It was long before dawn on Valentine's Day, February 14, 1862. A drizzling rain began to fall, and the temperature dropped to twelve degrees. Rain turned into sleet and then into snow that piled up three inches deep.

Captain Edwin Stanton McCook and the hundred or so men in his company, forbidden to light fires that would reveal their position, huddled together on the frozen ground in front of Fort Donelson. Those without overcoats or blankets ran in circles to keep warm.

Edwin McCook, a former steamboat pilot, was gamely trying to live up to the growing fame of the Fighting McCooks, but it was not easy. Although he had the six-foot-one-inch frame and great strength of his grandfather, the Whiskey Boy, Edwin bruised easily. After starting the war with great dash, twenty-four-year-old Edwin was losing all enthusiasm for the struggle.

Daniel and Martha's seventh son was born in Carrollton on March 26, 1837, and named for his father's good friend who was suspected of helping him elude impeachment. But, unlike the brilliant Stanton, Edwin Stanton McCook was not destined for the law. A lackadaisical student, he preferred boats to books, so his politically well-connected father secured an appointment for him to the United States Naval Academy.

Seventeen-year-old Edwin was not destined for the military either. In his first year at Annapolis he incurred 78 demerits for a variety of offenses including skylarking at drill, inattention at battery exercises, using tobacco, and keeping oysters in his room. Failing his examinations, he had to repeat the entire year. The second was worse than the first. Having accumulated 156 demerits, he gave up the ship and resigned.

Heading west, Edwin was hired as a riverboat pilot on the *Polar Star*. The 309-ton side-wheeler plied the Illinois and Mississippi rivers between Peoria and St. Louis. Touted as a good packet, it claimed to have gentlemanly officers, clean beds, and a "number one table."

The rivers were the great highways of the west. Colorful avenues of commerce, they connected Pittsburgh to Cincinnati and Louisville and St. Louis and New Orleans and hundreds of hamlets in between. Churning the waters of the broad rivers were thousands of white steamboats, puffing black smoke from their stacks, spilling yellow cataracts in their wakes, and sounding their shrill whistles as they rounded the riverbends.

Adventurers, soldiers, missionaries, peddlers, hard-eyed gamblers, and immigrant families crowded into their long gilded saloons. Men gathered around a tall cast-iron stove in the bow, chewing tobacco and spitting into cuspidors. Women gossiped around another great stove at the stern, and boisterous, laughing children ran between. For well-to-do travelers there were ample staterooms and delicious meals, ham and cornbread and bacon and buckwheat cakes, served on fine china and tablecloths of snowy white linen.

Ruler of this rootless empire was the riverboat pilot. His crew consisted of five or six roustabouts, drifters of questionable moral character, for whom it was whiskey the first thing in the morning and the last thing at night. Edwin loved the life.

When the Civil War started, Edwin's father tried to get him an officer's commission in the regular U.S. Army. On June 1, six weeks after Daniel

McCook shouldered a musket in the White House to protect Lincoln, the War Department received a memorandum:

> *Edwin S. McCook is excellently well recommended for a Lieutenancy in the Regular Army, and I hope it can, without injustice to others, be given to him.*
>
> *A. Lincoln*
President of the United States

But the U.S. Army, in spite of Lincoln's advocacy, demurred. So Daniel McCook turned to another good friend, Congressman John A. Logan of Illinois, who had been a passenger in McCook's carriage to Bull Run. After the battle, Logan enlisted in the three-year volunteer army and was commissioned colonel of the Thirty-first Illinois Volunteer Infantry Regiment.

On August 19 Colonel Logan announced that Company I would be commanded by Captain E. S. McCook of the famous Fighting McCooks.

The Thirty-first Illinois was assigned to the First Brigade, District of Southeast Missouri, Western Department. The brigade was commanded by another good friend of Daniel McCook, Brigadier General John A. McClernand. A former Illinois congressman, he also had been a passenger in McCook's carriage to Bull Run. Both Logan and McClernand had joined McCook in dodging bullets to carry wounded men to safety at Blackburn's Ford.

The First Brigade was ordered to Cairo, a southern Illinois town of mud and mischief at the confluence of the Ohio and Mississippi rivers. Commanding at Cairo was Brigadier General Ulysses Simpson Grant. A thirty-nine-year-old West Point graduate, Grant had resigned his commission in 1854 amid accusations of heavy drinking. The Civil War gave him a second chance.

Grant was a small man, standing five-feet-seven-inches in height. He was a silent man, uttering only a few terse words. He was a somber man, gazing on life gravely. But Grant was a fighting man, and quick to do so.

On November 6, 1861, Edwin McCook was with Grant when he took a force of three thousand men on steamboats down the Mississippi River to make a demonstration, or show of force, against a small Confederate camp at Belmont, Missouri. Grant had expected to wait for the support

Brigadier General Ulysses S. Grant

of General Eleazer Paine and his Third Brigade, marching from Paducah, Kentucky. With Paine was Edwin's cousin, Chaplain Henry McCook. But when Grant heard a rumor that the Rebels were reinforcing Belmont, he quickly turned the demonstration into a full-scale attack without waiting for Paine.

Disembarking from the boats, Grant's men cut their way through dense woods to surprise the Confederate camp. After a short fight, the Rebels fled. Grant did not pursue.

Heady with their first victory, Edwin McCook and his jubilant comrades began celebrating wildly. Some opened bottles of captured liquor. Others pulled down the Rebel flag and raised Old Glory. The band struck up the "Star Spangled Banner." Everyone gathered around the flagpole to sing. General McClernand mounted a cannon and called for three cheers for the Union. Drunken men danced around the camp, rampaging through tents, gathering up trophies, and reveling boisterously.

Grant, unable to get control of his unruly troops, angrily ordered the camp set on fire. The blaze made them a good target for 140 Confederate cannon mounted on high bluffs across the Mississippi River at Columbus, Kentucky. Rebel artillery began lobbing shells into the Union revelers while Rebel reinforcements, under the command of General Benjamin Cheatham, rowed across the river and rallied those Rebels who had retreated.

Surprising Grant, they quickly had him surrounded. Some of his officers advised surrendering. But Grant was a man of few words, and "surrender" was not one of them.

"Well, we cut our way in and we can cut our way out," he said shortly.

Captain Edwin McCook gallantly led his regiment through enemy lines, carrying the Thirty-first Illinois flag, with Colonel Logan's words ringing in his ears.

"Die with it in your hands!" Logan challenged.

Edwin made it to the river and leaped aboard a steamer. But behind him stretched a long trail of blood. Union losses were 120 killed and 383 wounded, with many of the dead and wounded left behind. Confederate losses were 105 killed and 494 wounded.

Major General Henry Wager Halleck, having just replaced Frémont at St. Louis, was aghast at the defeat and the heavy loss of life. Both were unnecessary. He could not find an order from Frémont to Grant for the attack. Halleck, a forty-six-year-old author of military texts who had taught at West Point, planned to replace Grant.

But Grant, acting first, requested permission to strike again. He and Flag Officer Andrew Hull Foote, commander of U.S. naval forces in the west, were confident they could capture Forts Henry and Donelson. The two Tennessee forts, twelve miles apart, guarded the Tennessee and Cumberland rivers leading to the heartland of the South. Halleck grudgingly gave his approval.

There were two Fighting McCooks with Grant's force leaving Cairo aboard steamboats on February 2 in a raging snow and sleet storm. Edwin had been joined by his eldest brother, Dr. Latimer McCook, a surgeon with the Thirty-first Illinois.

The first target was Fort Henry. Grant's two divisions of seventeen thousand men were to disembark and strike the fort from the land while

Foote's seven gunboats shelled it from the river. The joint attack was set for 11:00 a.m. on February 6.

Flag Officer Foote, in position at the appointed time, waited vainly for an hour and a half for Grant's troops to appear. Finally, Foote went ahead without them. Due to heavy rains, the low-lying fort was partially flooded, and only half of its guns were working. After two hours of shelling by the Union gunboats, a white flag was raised.

It had been a crisp naval victory. Union losses were eleven men killed and thirty-one wounded. Confederate losses were five men killed, eleven wounded, and five missing.

Captain Edwin McCook and the rest of the infantry, struggling through water-logged land, reached the fort about an hour after its surrender, where Grant telegraphed Halleck:

> *Fort Henry is ours. I shall take and destroy Fort Donelson on the 8th.*

Delayed by bad weather, but elated at the ease with which Fort Henry fell, Edwin McCook and his men set out for Fort Donelson on February 12 with high hopes. Even the weather was optimistic. It was so balmy on the twelve-mile march that many of the sweating Union soldiers threw their heavy blankets and overcoats by the side of the road.

Their cockiness evaporated, however, on reaching Fort Donelson. A heavily barricaded stockade on steep bluffs above the Cumberland River, the fort was protected by more than two miles of earthworks, seventeen heavy guns, forty-eight field guns, and some twenty-one thousand Confederate troops commanded by three generals: John B. Floyd, Gideon J. Pillow, and Simon Bolivar Buckner. Grant, outnumbered, sent for reinforcements and ordered the fort encircled.

That night the weather changed drastically. First rain, then sleet, then snow fell as the temperature dropped to twelve degrees and McCook's men, who had thrown their coats and blankets away, suffered without campfires. Valentine's Day dawned gray and dreary. During the night reinforcements had arrived. Grant, now commanding three divisions of twenty-seven thousand men, drew his noose tightly around the fort and let Foote hammer it with his gunboats.

About 3:00 p.m. the navy began shelling. But the six-boat Union fleet, trying to maneuver in the swift current of the narrow Cumberland River, came too close to Fort Donelson's batteries. Foote's flagship took a shot through the pilothouse. The steering of a second boat was damaged. Both vessels drifted helplessly downstream, turning around and around like logs, while the rest of the fleet followed, reduced to floating hulks with shattered smokestacks and smashed decks.

It was a bitter defeat for the navy. The battle ended at 4:30 p.m. with fifty-four sailors killed or wounded. Foote, injured in his arm and ankle, would be forced to take the fleet back to Cairo for repairs.

Grant had expected Fort Donelson to fall quickly. It did not. So he settled in for a siege.

Again, the night was bitterly cold. Edwin McCook's men, again without tents or fires, tramped in the snow to keep warm. Within the fort they could hear sounds of unusual activity, and in the morning they discovered what it meant. Shortly after dawn the entire Rebel garrison burst out of the fort, yelling like tigers. Planning to escape, they descended on McClernand's First Division, which held the right of the Union line, including the Nashville Road.

Word was sent to Grant's headquarters, but he was not there. Having galloped off before dawn to consult with Foote on his flagship five miles downstream, Grant did not anticipate a breakout nor leave anyone in overall command.

McClernand's division, outnumbered three to one, held its position for five hours. Dense smoke enveloped the land like a low-lying fog. The bright flames of the guns tinted everything a lurid red that matched the blood that stained the snow. Finally, out of ammunition, the division withdrew to the rear, leaving the Nashville Road open.

The three Confederate generals, seeing the Union retreat, thought that Grant's entire force was beaten. No longer needing to escape, they ordered their troops back into the fort and telegraphed Confederate Army headquarters in Nashville that Fort Donelson had been held.

The deserted battlefield was an eerie no-man's land when Grant finally rode up on his horse in early afternoon. His face was flushed. His jaw was set. His words were few.

"Gentlemen," he said, "the position on the right must be retaken."

Then Grant went off to send a message to Foote:

> *If all the gunboats that can will immediately make their appearance . . . it may secure us a victory. Otherwise all may be defeated. . . . I must order a charge, to save appearances.*

Brigadier General Charles F. Smith

Brigadier General Charles F. Smith, commanding the Second Division on the Union left, made the charge. The fifty-five-year-old general, who had been commandant of cadets when Grant was at West Point, gave his soldiers a battlefield lesson. They were to feint with a small brigade, charge with a large brigade, rely on the bayonet, and hold their fire until they were within the enemy's works.

The white-haired general mounted his horse, rode to the front and center of the line, and started toward the battlements.

They were under fire instantly. His men kept following him, although some thought that the abatis of sharpened and tangled trees were too thick for a rabbit to get through. Occasionally Smith turned in his saddle to check his lines, but mostly he looked straight toward the enemy, erect as if on review. His scared soldiers, seeing the general's white mustache over his shoulder, kept going. Behind them was a trail of dead and wounded. Reaching the abatis, Smith placed his cap on the point of his sword and held it aloft.

"No flinching now, my lads. Here, this is the way. Come on!" he challenged.

He picked a path through the sharp maze as his men followed his cap, still held aloft. The Rebels in the rifle pits, seeing the bayonets, climbed out and fled. Smith, leaping on the battlement, grabbed a cannon and turned it on the retreating enemy. In less than an hour he had taken possession of their earthworks without firing a shot.

It was nearly midnight when the three Confederate generals at Fort Donelson faced some disagreeable facts. Smith, having gained a commanding position, was certain to attack at dawn. Twelve additional Union transports, carrying reinforcements, had landed. Grant once again had his noose tightly around the fort.

Generals Floyd and Pillow slipped away on boats with some of their men, leaving Buckner to deal with Grant. At 4:00 a.m. on February 16 the notes of a bugle and a white flag alerted Smith's pickets. Buckner's message asked for an armistice of six hours to negotiate for terms of capitulation.

Smith took the note to Grant with the suggestion that he settle for nothing less than unconditional surrender. Grant, agreeing, wrote his reply.

> *No terms except an unconditional and immediate surrender can be accepted. I propose to move immediately upon your works.*

Buckner gave up Fort Donelson with 18,000 troops. Grant marched in with regimental flags flying and brass bands playing. Union casualties were 510 killed, 2,151 wounded, and 224 missing. Confederate losses were about 2,000. It was the first major Union victory of the Civil War.

The North was ecstatic. "Unconditional Surrender Grant" was a national hero. His terms and the phrase "I propose to move immediately upon your works" were quoted admiringly by everyone, including the secretary of war.

⤴

Stanton, since taking office a month earlier, had become increasingly frustrated by General McClellan's refusal to move on Richmond's works.

McClellan, brought from western Virginia to Washington to build a new three-year volunteer army after the Union defeat at Bull Run, had done some things well. He had used his engineering skills to design a thirty-seven-mile ring of forts and batteries around Washington to protect the Capitol, and he had used his organization skills to train a splendid new one-hundred-thousand-man Army of the Potomac.

But as a warrior he was wanting. Constantly overestimating enemy numbers, McClellan hesitated to attack Richmond, as he had hesitated to attack Rich Mountain in western Virginia. Instead, he waged a pompous white-gloved "gentleman's war," putting French princes on his staff, staging endless dress parades with his splendid army, and driving the president and the secretary of war to despair.

"He's got the slows," declared Lincoln.

But while the president shook his head, the secretary of war shook his fist. Stanton performed in the War Department as he had in the courtroom, despotic and spectacular. In times of crisis, when he flew into a frenzy and paced the room like a caged lion, his histrionics were viewed with amusement by Lincoln.

The president, who seemed to have an inexhaustible fund of humorous stories for every occasion, said Stanton reminded him of an old preacher in the west who jumped up and down so frequently during his sermons that his parishioners threatened to put rocks in his pockets to hold him down.

Smith's bayonet charge at the Battle of Fort Donelson

"We may be obliged to serve Stanton the same way," drawled Lincoln, "but I guess we'll let him jump awhile first."

The president, elated by the great victory at Fort Donelson, promoted Grant and Smith to major general. Logan was promoted to brigadier general. Edwin McCook was promoted to lieutenant colonel. However, having displayed enough dash for a while, Edwin requested to be invalided home to recover from a bruised kidney incurred when he fell off his horse.

Although both Edwin and his brother Dr. Latimer McCook were wounded at Fort Donelson, their injuries were not serious. Nevertheless, their names appeared on the front page of the *New York Times*. Their father never hesitated to promote the exploits, large or small, of the Fighting McCooks.

⌢

The fall of Forts Henry and Donelson broke the long Kentucky line and opened the door to the rich middle South. Kentucky fell. Most of

Tennessee fell. The Confederate Army of Kentucky, under the command of General Albert Sidney Johnston, fell all the way south to Corinth, Mississippi.

The North went wild. Recruiting offices were closed. People were sure that the end of the war was in sight. A jubilant Stanton ordered the two main forces in the west, the Army of the Ohio and the Army of the Tennessee, to pursue the Confederates to Corinth and destroy them.

Although Grant was now a national hero, he was still in Halleck's disfavor due to rumors that he was drunk on Foote's flagship while his men were fighting at Fort Donelson. So Halleck, seizing on a minor infraction as a good excuse to shelve him, gave the command of the Army of the Tennessee to Smith.

General Smith led the forty-thousand-man Army of the Tennessee down to Pittsburg Landing, twenty miles from Corinth. However, Smith injured his leg while boarding a boat, and it became so badly infected that he had to relinquish command. Grant, restored to command of the Army of the Tennessee, came down to Pittsburg Landing to await the arrival of Buell's thirty-seven-thousand-man Army of the Ohio. Together, they would attack Johnston's forty-four-thousand-man Army of Kentucky at Corinth.

As Buell's Army of the Ohio marched south, it occupied Nashville, Tennessee, the first capital of a Confederate state to fall. Brigadier General Alexander McCook, commanding the Second Division, was given control of the city while Buell's five divisions gathered there.

When General George Thomas's First Division arrived, it was Alex's first opportunity to congratulate his brother Bob on his great victory at the Battle of Mill Springs and his promotion to brigadier general. The two brothers, now both generals, had a grand reunion.

Buell's army left Nashville in mid-March to join Grant, Alex McCook's Second Division in the lead. Midway in their three-week march, as they headed southwest through Tennessee, Alex dashed off a hurried note to Kate Phillips in Dayton, Ohio.

March 24, 1862

As we move southward . . . I will continue to write you often and keep you well posted in regard to our movements. Be of good cheer, Kate, and tell me how you feel—your happiness,

your ills, joys and all. If I have added to your happiness, I am
happy at the thought. . . . Now Kate I bid you a good night. It
is past twelve, and an early start in the morning leaves me but
a few hours to sleep, which I hope may be passed dreaming of
my darling so far away from me. Good-bye. May God ever bless
and protect you—from your devoted and truly affectionate—
                                              A. McD. McCook

(Postscript) I send you a piece of the 9th Ohio Flag that was
shot all to pieces at Mill Spring. I stole it from Bob and also
told him to whom I was going to send it.

On April 5, as McCook's Division was still twenty-two miles from
Grant's army at Pittsburg Landing, a confident General Grant was
telegraphing a worried General Halleck in St. Louis:

I have scarcely the faintest idea of an attack.

The Confederates attacked the next morning. Struck at dawn, Grant
was almost destroyed by dusk. Leading the Rebel charge was General
William Hardee. Rushing to the rescue was General Alexander McCook.
The two old friends would fight for the first time at the Battle of Shiloh.

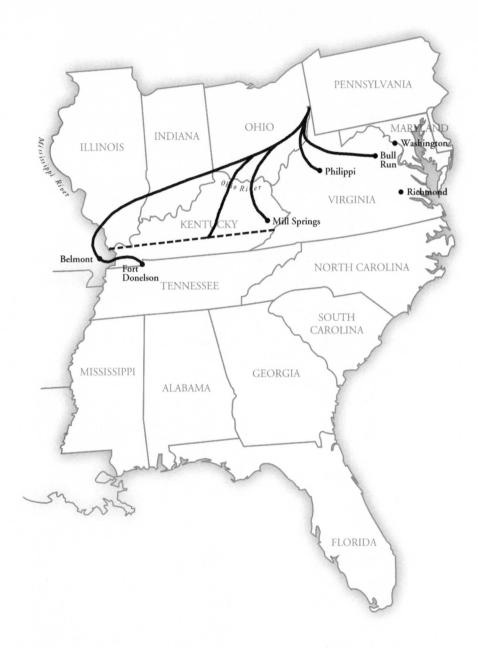

Territory trod by the Fighting McCooks
in their quest to save the Union

Chapter 9

BRIGADIER GENERAL ALEXANDER McCOOK
at the Battle of Shiloh

It was a scene from hell, enacted to the music of Verdi's opera *Il Trovatore* being played by the Sixteenth U.S. Infantry band, as General Alexander McCook arrived at dawn on April 7 at the battlefield of Shiloh.

Alex had reached the Tennessee River at dusk the previous evening after issuing his division two days' rations and forty rounds of cartridges and marching them, at the double-quick, for twenty-two miles after receiving word of Grant's attack. Alex spent the night in a driving rain commandeering steamboats to ferry his men across the river to the battlefield. At 5:30 a.m. he stepped ashore to a horrendous sight.

Some seven thousand to ten thousand of Grant's soldiers had fled from battle on the previous day, and thousands of them, panic-stricken, were hiding under the riverbank, trying to discourage McCook's troops from going ashore. Rations, forage, and ammunition were trampled into the mire by the surging crowd.

Wagon trains were huddled together in sheltered places. Ambulances with their bleeding loads were trying to get to the boats. Sutlers and women camp followers were adding their shrill views to the babel of sound.

"For God's sake, don't go out there or you will all be killed," one straggler cried, describing in grim detail how his regiment had been cut to pieces.

Scarcely hiding his disdain for Grant's ill-disciplined troops, Alex ordered his men up a steep slope to heavily timbered high ground. While they gulped down a hasty breakfast of crackers and hot coffee, he rode among them, telling them that he expected them to fight hard in this, their first major battle. When he reached the men of the First Ohio, whom he had trained in Dayton, he stopped.

"I will blow my brains out if any men of my old regiment run today!" Alex shouted, revolver in hand.

They did him proud. Advancing in battle formation, they came face to face with the enemy standing in close order, shoulder to shoulder, three hundred yards away.

"Ready." The command ran along the line and the click of muskets was the response.

"Aim." All stood awaiting the shock.

"Fire." Amid a deafening crash, the flame from their muskets leaped almost halfway across the field.

The sound scarcely had reached its full volume when it was answered by another. The roar of battle then swelled over all while underneath they could hear the *spitz, spitz, spitz* of the hurtling bullets. The damp air darkened with missiles as the battle line swept back and forth like an undulating thread.

There was no battle plan. Grant and Buell had only agreed to recover Grant's camps. The twenty-five thousand troops of the three divisions of the Army of the Ohio that had arrived, commanded by Generals McCook, Nelson, and Crittenden, took the left and center of the battlefield. Some fifteen thousand of Grant's surviving troops of the Army of the Tennessee took the right.

Union forces steadily pushed the Confederates back in a battle that raged in the rain for eight hours on a broad front one and a half miles wide. The commanding Confederate general, Albert Sidney Johnston,

*Enemy lines three hundred yards apart
at the Battle of Shiloh*

who had been killed during the first day of battle, was replaced by General Pierre Beauregard.

About 2:00 p.m. Beauregard, the hero of Fort Sumter and Bull Run, launched a massive counterattack with three divisions.

McCook's Second Division, in the center, took the blow. Heavy artillery fire spewed from Rebel batteries hidden in a wood of water oaks. Alex ordered a charge to capture the guns. When the Thirty-second Indiana advanced too quickly and was in danger of being flanked, he had to send one of his staff officers through the fire with an order for the regiment to fall back.

The officers went in turn on such missions. This time it was the turn of his younger brother, Captain Dan McCook Jr., who was serving as adjutant general.

"Captain McCook," Alex commanded, "you will go to Colonel Willich and order him to fall back on Rousseau's brigade."

Then, fearing it might be the last time he would see his brother alive, Alex added quietly, "Good-bye, Dan."

Captain Dan McCook made it through the fire. The regiment was saved. The counterattack was repelled. The division pushed the Rebels back. Grant's camps near the Shiloh Meetinghouse, a one-room Methodist church, were recovered. By 4:00 p.m. the Rebels were in full retreat. General Hardee's troops were the last to quit the field.

The Battle of Shiloh, rescued from the jaws of defeat, was a Union victory.

It was a moment of triumph for young General Alexander McCook and his Second Division. With McCook at the head of the column, the men were marching as smartly as if on parade as they approached General Grant, expecting some words of praise.

It was not to be. Grant merely said that, since his troops were exhausted, McCook should pursue the fleeing enemy.

"No," said McCook.

His reasons were many. His men had not slept in thirty-six hours. They had force-marched twenty-two miles the previous day, then spent the night being ferried across the Tennessee River. They had fought a long and hard battle in a driving rain to recover Grant's camps. They had suffered 911 casualties, and it was only because of their superb discipline that they still looked fresh.

McCook, who never wanted to lose a man unnecessarily, refused to order them to face death one more time just to rescue Grant's tattered reputation. The two generals faced each other on the blood-soaked battlefield. Grant was furious. McCook was firm. But in making his decision, he also made another enemy. Grant was not a forgiving man, and he had a long memory.

Criticized by Lincoln for not pursuing the enemy, Grant put the blame on McCook. In fact, the Battle of Shiloh generated much bad blood between the Army of the Ohio and the Army of the Tennessee. It would last throughout the war.

Buell and his generals, certain that they had saved Grant from annihilation, did not mention in their official reports the assistance of his fifteen thousand surviving troops. And Grant, maintaining that he would have won the battle on the second day without them, minimized their role.

However, one of Grant's division commanders gave credit where it was due. General William T. Sherman, after having been removed from command of the Army of the Cumberland the preceding fall, was reinstated in the Army of the Tennessee. It was his camps that were overrun on the first day of the Battle of Shiloh. In his official report, Sherman wrote:

> *I concede that McCook's splendid division from Kentucky drove back the enemy along the Corinth Road, which was the great center of the field of battle, and where Beauregard commanded in person, supported by Bragg's, Polk's and Breckinridge's divisions.*

Grant received much of the blame for the first day's disaster. McCook received much of the praise for the second day's victory, and he was nominated by Lincoln for promotion to major general.

Heady with success, Alex and his brother Dan, in the frank and often reckless manner of the McCooks, made no secret of their contempt for Grant's performance at Shiloh. Not anticipating an attack, Grant had neglected Halleck's warning to entrench his men, and they were easily overrun.

McCook's division fighting the enemy along the Corinth Road

Grant's headquarters were nine miles away on the other side of the Tennessee River. He had not reached the battlefield until shortly before noon.

The casualties at Shiloh were the greatest of any battle in American history. The carnage shocked and sickened the nation. Union losses were 13,047 killed, wounded, and captured. Rebel losses were 10,699. A huge 2,500-patient field hospital was set up under a sea of white tents, and many Northern physicians, including Drs. George and John McCook, rushed south to treat the wounded.

The wrathful secretary of war ordered General Halleck to come down from St. Louis and personally lead a mammoth armada of 120,000 men, the combined armies of the Ohio, Tennessee, and Mississippi, to march on Corinth and crush the Confederates.

There were nine Fighting McCooks with Halleck as he started south on April 29. In addition to Dr. George and Dr. John, there were five sons of Daniel and one son of Dr. John. And, of course, there was the familiar commanding figure of Daniel McCook. Four weeks earlier he had been promoted to major and commissioned as a paymaster with the Army of the Ohio.

Halleck, haunted by the terrible cost of life at Shiloh, advanced at a snail's pace of less than a mile a day. He arrived on May 30, after a four-week march, to find Corinth abandoned. The outnumbered Confederates, saving their strength for another day, had disappeared into the swamps and bayous of Mississippi.

With no one to fight, Lincoln and Stanton could not agree on what to do next. Lincoln wanted to liberate East Tennessee. Stanton wanted to open up the Mississippi River. So they decided to do both. The giant Union force was disbanded. The Army of the Mississippi returned to Missouri. The Army of the Tennessee went west to Memphis. The Army of the Ohio went east to Chattanooga.

But, divided in the Deep South, the slow-moving Union armies became easy targets for sabotage. Galloping out of nowhere came three Confederate cavalry generals, John Hunt Morgan, Nathan Bedford Forrest, and Joseph Wheeler. They led thousands of Rebel troopers tearing at will through Kentucky and Tennessee, nipping at the heels of the Federals and raising hell. Southern boys had grown up in the saddle, and their horsemanship was superb. They rode circles around Union armies,

Confederate cavalry on the prowl

tearing up railroad tracks, pulling down telegraph lines, burning bridges, plundering wagon trains, and capturing millions of dollars in supplies.

The thirty-seven-thousand-man Army of the Ohio, hundreds of miles from its main supply base in Louisville, was forced to forage for food. It needed a minimum of fifty tons daily to feed men and animals. To Southern farmers it seemed that the entire Northern army had been turned loose on the land to "appropriate" cattle and corn for its mess kettles.

In retaliation, the farmers declared guerrilla war. Squads of bushwhackers shadowed the Army of the Ohio to murder marauding soldiers.

Many Southerners were descendants of those Scotch-Irish immigrants who had trekked southwest through the Shenandoah Valley into Georgia and Alabama. Like their Northern counterparts in the Ohio Valley, they knew how to wage a war of terror.

Stanton was convinced by now that the South would never surrender and the North would never win by fighting a white-gloved "gentleman's war." Word came from the War Department to take off the gloves. Northern generals were told to wage a war of total conquest, a war of annihilation to lay waste to the land, a war to destroy the civilization of the South.

Brigadier General Robert McCook, Stanton's former law student, agreed. McCook's Third Brigade was on its 217-mile journey to Chattanooga amid one-hundred-degree heat, swarms of mosquitoes, and squads of guerrillas. During a Fourth of July celebration, when some of his fellow officers in General Thomas's division urged that their "Southern brothers" be treated kindly, Bob McCook jumped to his feet in anger.

"The secessionists are our brothers no more," he said brusquely. "They are enemies; ours and the nation's. If they will not submit peacefully, they must be exterminated. My men and I are ready to do just that, even if it means the South is to be laid waste."

General Thomas, a Southerner who had remained loyal to the North, quickly defused the oratorical jousting.

"If the boys can't keep within bounds," he said, "they must omit celebrating the Fourth of July hereafter."

Bob McCook's angry outburst was aggravated by illness. His leg wound, never having had a chance to heal properly, had reopened. Now he came down with dysentery, the debilitating malady that had struck nearly half of the men and officers during the rainy Corinth campaign. There was no cure except bed rest, but McCook refused to go north to a hospital. Keeping his promise to stay with his Ninth Ohio, he had his camp cot placed in a covered spring wagon improvised as an ambulance, and he turned over the command of his brigade to Colonel Ferdinand Van Derveer of the Thirty-fifth Ohio.

Moving through northern Alabama, they reached Athens on August 3. The village was nervous at their appearance, as three months earlier it had been brutally pillaged by Colonel John B. Turchin's brigade searching for bushwhackers. This time there were no similar atrocities, but many of the slaves who had not fled previously were emboldened by the presence of Northern troops and took this opportunity to escape.

Bound for Decherd, Tennessee, McCook's brigade broke camp at 3:00 a.m. on August 5, taking advantage of the predawn coolness so that it could halt by noon and rest during the hot afternoon hours. The column's order of march was the Ninth Ohio, the Thirty-fifth Ohio, and the Second Minnesota. The Eighteenth U.S. Infantry, attached to the brigade, marched a half day in advance. Colonel Van Derveer led the column, and McCook's covered wagon was in the center for safety's sake.

In the general's entourage were his two headquarters wagons and seven of his First Ohio Cavalry escort, with a few members of the Ninth Ohio band following on foot. In the wagon with McCook was his aide, Captain Hunter Brooke, and at the reins was the general's free black manservant from Cincinnati, John Vincent. Riding horseback beside them for company were Major H. V. Boynton of the Thirty-fifth Ohio and Jacob Aug, Esquire, of Cincinnati, the sutler of the Ninth Ohio.

The road from Athens to Decherd turned abruptly to the right at a little place called Hazel Green. However, Colonel Van Derveer missed his turning point and marched the entire Ninth Ohio, with all its baggage trains, beyond it. When McCook arrived and saw Van Derveer's mistake, he halted the column and sent an orderly forward to tell the colonel to turn back. Then, with narrow roads and his wagons blocking the intersection, Bob turned to his aide, Captain Brooke.

"Let's move out of the way with our wagons and give Van Derveer a chance to come back and take the right road," he said.

This placed McCook in the front of the line of march, but he expected Van Derveer to overtake them easily. So the general's entourage went forward slowly, looking for a camping ground with a good water supply, and halting frequently at farmhouses to make inquiries. There was no idea of danger. The Eighteenth U.S. Infantry had passed over the same road some three hours previously without trouble, and no bushwhackers had been seen north of the Tennessee River for more than two weeks.

Coming to a crossroads, McCook questioned a farmer about water while Major Boynton went to look in one direction and several members of the First Ohio Cavalry searched in another. Captain Brooke was standing outside the wagon talking with the rest of the group when scattered shots were heard and the corporal in charge of the cavalry escort came back at a full gallop, yelling that he had stumbled on a nest of ninety mounted guerrillas.

"The Rebels have fired upon me!" he shouted.

McCook, with only four of his cavalry with him and the enemy fast approaching, yelled to his aide.

"Get in quick, Brooke, we've got to get out of here."

John Vincent wheeled the horses around quickly, almost overturning the wagon in the narrow country lane. Brooke leaped in, and McCook told Vincent to "drive like hell" to meet the main body of his command. They took off at a full gallop, careening down the road with the wagon top torn by low overhanging trees and bullets whizzing all around. After running at full speed for three-quarters of a mile, they saw no friends in front but an abundance of enemies behind.

"Where the hell is Van Derveer?" McCook demanded, looking first to the front and then to the rear where the guerrillas were closing fast.

"Stop! Stop!" they yelled, while bullets and buckshot rattled around the wagon and the Rebel yell split the air.

McCook, seeing that they were trapped and hopelessly outnumbered, said bitterly, "They've got us. We might as well surrender."

Clad only in a hat, shirt, and underwear, he rose from his cot and shouted, "Don't shoot. The horses are running. We will stop them as soon as possible."

The general ordered Vincent to get control of the horses, now almost ungovernable. The terrified driver finally managed to run them into a bank of clay and brush, bringing the wagon to a jolting halt. The general and the captain raised their hands over their heads. But the bushwhackers, most of whom were without uniforms or military identification, kept shooting.

Frank Gurley, the leader of the band, came to within ten yards of the wagon and, disregarding the rules of war, fired his large navy revolver three times in rapid succession.

Two shots tore through Captain Brooke's coat, and the third struck General McCook in the left side of his abdomen. Immediately the wagon was surrounded by a noisy and swearing mob of some thirty men, one of whom aimed his gun at the general.

"You need not shoot," Bob McCook said tersely, holding his hand to his side. "I am already fatally wounded."

The three were taken prisoner. Captain Brooke told the bushwackers they had shot a sick man and asked that he and John Vincent be allowed to carry him to a log cabin by the side of the road. When they got inside, McCook, hardly able to speak, turned to his manservant.

"John," he said, "you are a free Negro from the North, and it will go hard with you here among these people, so you had better make your escape."

Obeying reluctantly, John Vincent climbed out a back window and fled through a cornfield. Captain Brooke was bathing McCook's wound with cold water when the guerrillas came in. Frank Gurley ordered Brooke to be taken away as their prisoner in spite of his entreaties to be left with his dying general.

The guerrillas galloped off, leaving McCook in the cabin bleeding profusely.

Soon the soldiers of the Ninth Ohio, having arrived at the intersection and hearing shots in the distance, came down the road looking for trouble. They found the general's wagon overturned and riddled with bullets.

"What has become of Colonel McCook?" they asked, still calling him the name by which they had followed him into battle.

They found him in the cabin where the guerrillas had left him to die. Furious that he was shot defenseless, not in the midst of battle or leading his men in a charge as he would have wished, they showed their anger by going out and searching for the bushwhackers. They destroyed five plantations before they could be brought under control.

One of the Ninth Ohio wrote home of the consequences when some of the guerrillas were found:

> *The murderers suffered severely. Some of the assassins were taken and hung on the spot. Many more were taken and summarily dealt with, for the soldiers scoured the country for miles on each side of the road and the torch applied to every house that happened to be in the way.*

Bob McCook lingered for twenty-four hours. The physicians of his brigade tried to ease his pain with opiates and stimulants, but he died a slow and painful death. Recovering from a convulsion, he turned to his aide-de-camp, Captain Andrew S. Burt.

"Andy," he murmured, "the problem of life soon will be solved forever."

Private Martin Betz asked if he had a message for his brother, General Alexander McCook.

"Tell him and the rest I lived as a man and die attempting to do my duty," and then he added, "My good boy, may your life be longer and to a better purpose than mine."

He sent for Colonel Van Derveer to draw up his will, leaving his two favorite horses to his closest brothers, Alex and Dan. The rest of his property he left to his mother. Then Bob McCook's troops filed past to bid him farewell, the magnetic man who always got them the best of everything and who refused to leave them when he was ill. What they felt for him was little short of adoration.

McCook was conscious to the last, although frequently unable to speak from the pain he was suffering. Whenever able, he uttered words of advice, gratitude, and consolation to those around him. His last moments found him as firm and calm in the face of death as he was in life, clutching the hands of Betz, the brigade wagon-master, as he went into a final convulsion.

"I am done with life," he groaned. "Yes, this ends it all. You and I part now, but the loss of ten thousand such lives as yours or mine would be nothing, if their sacrifice would but save such a government as ours."

Brigadier General Robert Latimer McCook died at the age of thirty-four at noon on August 6. The next day General Thomas ordered all of the members of his division to wear a badge of mourning for thirty days out of respect for his memory. Throughout the North there was revulsion and outrage at the manner of his death, and the wrath of the press burst forth. *Harper's Weekly* observed:

> *This wanton murder of General Robert McCook has roused the West to a pitch of unforgivable fury.*

Both *Harper's Weekly* and *Frank Leslie's Illustrated* ran full-page artist's sketches of the shooting. The *New York Times* said in a bitter editorial:

> *The rebel assassination of Gen. McCook is one of the most melancholy and disastrous events of the war. There is not a single circumstance to redeem it from classification among the most wanton and savage butcheries that ever occurred in a civilized country.*

The general's body was taken by train to Louisville. It was placed aboard a mail steamer for the trip up the Ohio River, accompanied by a special committee of the Cincinnati City Council, the Hamilton County Bar Association, and the Cincinnati Chamber of Commerce. The boat arrived at the Cincinnati public landing about noon on Sunday, August 9, where the flags throughout the city were flying at half-mast. His coffin was taken to the rotunda of the Hamilton County Court House, where he had fought for the rights of the Germans of Cincinnati. It lay in state until the next afternoon with a constant stream of people passing by the bier to pay their last respects.

Late on Monday afternoon the funeral rites were held. The general's parents, Daniel and Martha McCook, and other members of their family took their places at the foot of the bier.

The members of the city council, headed by the mayor and the judge of the police court, stood at one side with the members of the Bar Committee on the other. The services began with the choir singing an old German hymn, "The Song of the Grave" or "Slumber Lightly." Then Dr. Charles McIlvaine, Episcopal bishop of Ohio and a former West Point

The murder of Brigadier General Robert McCook as printed in Frank Leslie's Illustrated Newspaper, August 30, 1862

chaplain, conducted the burial service. This was followed by an oration in German by the chaplain of the Ninth Ohio, the Rev. Joseph Fuschuber.

Six white horses slowly drew the hearse from the courthouse. Following was a band playing "General Robert L. McCook's Funeral March," composed by F. W. Rauch and dedicated to "Gallant Bob" McCook. The funeral cortege was the greatest ever known in Cincinnati, consisting of some two thousand mourners, military and civic, and over one hundred carriages and buggies. Many of the larger carriages were draped in black, while hundreds of crepe-draped flags waved over the hearse as it passed. As the bells tolled 6:30 p.m. the procession reached Spring Grove Cemetery, where the hero of Mill Springs was buried in the center of the soldiers' lot.

On August 10 at his camp in western Virginia, Lieutenant Colonel Rutherford B. Hayes wrote to his wife Lucy:

> *The sad news that McCook was murdered was in all evening dispatches, casting a deep shadow over all.*

And he noted in his diary:

> *Sad news. The dispatch tells us that General Bob McCook was murdered by guerrillas while riding in front of his brigade in Tennessee. He always said he did not expect to survive the war. He was brave, honest, rough—an "uncut diamond"—a good friend of mine. We have slept together through many stormy nights. I messed with him in his quarters at Mount Sewell. Would that he could have died in battle. Gallant spirit. Hail and farewell.*

Territory trod by the Fighting McCooks
in their quest to save the Union

Chapter 10

LIEUTENANT JOHN McCOOK
and McCook's Avengers

Martha McCook's heart, so often broken, was buffeted anew. On August 12, 1862, the day after General Robert McCook's funeral, her youngest son, seventeen-year-old John, asked if he still had her permission to join the army. She had given it to him, reluctantly, several weeks before Bob was killed.

Now, in spite of her almost unbearable sorrow, Martha McCook found the spartan strength to do what she had taught her sons to do. She honored her word. In so doing, she had given all of her nine sons to the nation.

John was large for his age, standing an awkward six feet tall with the broad shoulders and lanky frame of a country boy. His freckled face was naïve. His frank eyes were bright blue, and his fingers were blunt and battered from his having played catcher on his baseball team before the days of mitts.

John James McCook, the youngest of Daniel and Martha's twelve children, was born in Carrollton on May 25, 1845. He was named for his midshipman brother who had died at sea three years earlier.

During childhood John's best friend was his brother Charlie. As the two youngest boys in the family, they were inseparable. When war broke out, they were rooming together at Milnor Hall, the preparatory school for Kenyon College.

Charlie ran away to enlist, only to die in his father's arms after the Battle of Bull Run. John wanted to volunteer. However, his mother, reminding him that he was only sixteen, made him promise that he would not join the army without her permission.

Reluctantly, John entered Kenyon College in the fall of 1861 after passing examinations in English grammar, ancient and modern geography, classical antiquities, arithmetic, algebra, and Greek and Latin grammar, including two books of Caesar's *Commentaries*, six books of Virgil's *Aeneid*, and four *Orations* of Cicero against Catiline.

There were thirty-three boys in his freshman class. Tuition was thirty-two dollars per year. Room rent was twelve dollars. Students had to deposit one dollar to cover damage to the buildings. Parents got a strict warning:

> *A profuse allowance of money almost invariably works injury to the character and scholarship of the student; and <u>the privilege of purchasing articles on credit is especially dangerous</u>.*

John tried to apply himself, but it was hard to keep his mind on Greek and Latin and Herodotus and Homer. Ancient warfare lost out to current warfare with his brothers and cousins fighting for the Union in the mountains of western Virginia, the hills of Kentucky, and the mud of Tennessee.

By the summer of 1862 he had turned seventeen. All his friends were volunteering. The Army of the Ohio was in the Deep South marching on Chattanooga. The war might be over soon, and John would be the only Fighting McCook not to have the honor of fighting for his country. His mother found it hard to refuse him.

John joined the new Fifty-second Ohio Volunteer Infantry Regiment, commanded by his brother, Colonel Dan McCook. After Dan fought at the Battle of Shiloh, as a captain on Alex's staff, he returned to Ohio to be commissioned a colonel and recruit a new regiment. It was badly needed. After a year of war, not a single regiment in the Army of the Ohio had more than half of its officers and men on duty. Some regiments had only one-third due to furloughs, straggling, desertion, disease, and death.

Much of the Northern enthusiasm for the war had vanished. It was hard to get volunteers. Ohio had to resort to giving prisoners in the Ohio Penitentiary their freedom if they would enlist. One company in the Army of the Ohio contained twenty ex-convicts.

Only boys on the brink of manhood, like John McCook and his friends in the new Fifty-second Ohio Volunteer Infantry Regiment, were eager to fight. The Fifty-second Ohio was a particularly young regiment. Their average age was nineteen. After General Robert McCook's death, they called themselves "McCook's Avengers."

Avenging came quickly after John's brother Alex discovered Confederate plans to invade the North.

Some two hundred miles south, the Army of the Ohio was approaching Chattanooga when Major General Alexander McCook's Second Division cavalry, skirmishing with the enemy, captured a letter revealing the Rebel strategy.

General Braxton Bragg, commanding the Confederate Army of the Mississippi, planned to pull stealthily out of Chattanooga before the Army of the Ohio reached it. Bragg, a forty-five-year-old hero of the Mexican War, would swiftly recapture Nashville and then head to Kentucky to join Major General E. Kirby Smith, marching from Knoxville with his Army of Kentucky. Together they would cross the Ohio River to carry out Bragg's boast:

> *My army has promised to make me military governor of Ohio in ninety days.*

The Confederates hoped that an invasion of Ohio by Bragg, in conjunction with an invasion of Pennsylvania by Lee, would prove to England and France the strength of the Confederacy and its right to be recognized as a nation.

When Alex McCook alerted his commander, General Don Carlos Buell, about the captured letter, Buell ordered McCook to prevent Bragg from reaching Nashville until the scattered Army of the Ohio got there to

General Braxton Bragg

protect it. McCook, with ten thousand men, entered Tennessee's Sequatchie Valley from the west on August 28 as Bragg, with thirty thousand men, entered it from the south.

Outnumbered three to one, McCook split his forces, sending four thousand men and four batteries on a forced march north to Tracy City Gap, which guarded the road to Nashville. With his remaining force, six thousand men, two batteries, and his cavalry, McCook attacked Bragg's flank on the march. Hoping to convince Bragg that he faced Buell's main army, McCook deployed his men on a mile-wide front and added four dummy cannon to each of his batteries.

Bragg, taking the bait, halted and formed for battle. Heavy skirmishing continued until dark, when McCook slipped away and made an all-night march to Tracy City, leaving his cavalry behind to keep campfires going. At dawn Bragg found only smoldering fires. When he reached Tracy City he found McCook in command of the gap. Denied access to Nashville, Bragg headed straight to Kentucky to join forces with Kirby Smith.

Smith, meanwhile, had slipped through the Cumberland Gap with twelve thousand men to whip sixty-five hundred new Indiana recruits at the Battle of Richmond, Kentucky, on August 30. It was one of the most complete defeats of the Civil War. Union losses were over 75 percent, with more than one thousand killed or wounded, and some forty-three hundred captured or missing.

The North panicked. With its veteran armies in the Deep South, it was forced to pour more raw recruits into Kentucky. This included Lieutenant John McCook and the other 981 untrained boys of the Fifty-second Ohio, who had been in camp only four days. Hurriedly issued uniforms and guns that they did not know how to use, they boarded boats to cross the Ohio River and rescue the survivors of the Battle of Richmond, covering their retreat to Louisville.

Colonel Dan McCook, training his boys on the march, taught them their first lesson in warfare: how to serve as rear guard. Citing Napoleon's retreat from Moscow in 1812, Dan showed them it was a post of honor. They had to prevent stragglers from being captured by enemy cavalry that pursued them closely, nipping at their heels.

The weather was oppressively hot. A summer drought had dried up most of the streams. And, like all new recruits, the boys of the Fifty-second Ohio suffered from a wide variety of illnesses including measles, mumps, and dysentery, jokingly called the "Kentucky quickstep." But no matter how tired and thirsty and footsore they were, their spirits never failed to rise when their band struck up a lively march, the color bearer unfolded Old Glory, and someone started the song they all loved.

"Rally 'round the flag, boys . . . ," they sang as they trudged the dusty roads of Kentucky, finally limping into Louisville, headquarters of the Army of the Ohio, on September 6.

Colonel Dan McCook was given command of the new 36th Brigade. It contained his 52nd Ohio and three Illinois regiments—the 85th, 86th, and 125th—and Battery I, 2nd Illinois Light Artillery. Finally able to train his men, the colonel was a demanding drillmaster, as one lad revealed in a letter home:

> *Drill in morning from 5 to 6 o'clock. We then eat breakfast and then go out and drill from 9 to 11 o'clock. We then come in and eat our dinner and then go out at 3 o'clock and drill about an hour or so or a little more. We then come in and go out again on Dress Parade which lasts about 3/4 of an hour. We then come in and have Roll Call and Prayers and then go to bed and sleep til morning. Us boys is learning drill pretty fast.*

And they mastered their guns:

> *We have got Bully good rifles, the Enfield, they shoot and kill 900 yards. I have got so I can handle mine like an old solgier. Woe to the Sesesh that come in the range of old True Love.*

First Lieutenant John McCook, serving as his brother Dan's aide-de-camp, learned what that title meant. He was to assist in camp, on the march, and in battle. He was to reconnoiter the enemy. He was to carry messages, both verbal and written, to commanding generals and regimental officers. He was to ride fast, shoot straight, and not get caught.

Also arriving in Louisville, to visit their sons, were Daniel and Martha McCook. Major McCook, as paymaster with the Army of the Ohio, traveled regularly between Louisville, Columbus, Indianapolis, and Cincinnati. And he brought news about the "Squirrel Hunters."

After his Confederate victory at Richmond, Kirby Smith had captured the state capital of Frankfort and sent advance units toward the Ohio River. Cincinnati, sitting undefended on the northern bank, urgently telegraphed midwestern governors for help. In response, more than sixteen thousand volunteers, including farmers, students, teachers, ministers, lawyers, doctors, and clerks, came by foot and horse and boat and train. Many of the volunteers had squirrel tails on their caps. The Rebels, stopped by the broad

Ohio River as well as the thousands of "Squirrel Hunters" lined up on the opposite bank, did not cross. Cincinnati was safe.

But Louisville feared it would be the next target. Bragg was approaching with his thirty-thousand-man Army of the Mississippi. On his heels was Buell with his thirty-seven-thousand-man Army of the Ohio.

Louisville, milling with thousands of new recruits, threw up barricades and waited nervously to see who would reach them first. It was not Bragg. He had expected thousands of Kentuckians to hail him as their liberator and rush to swell his ranks. But Kentucky did not rally to his cause. Most men were content to stay out of the bloody fight. So, considering Louisville too well-defended for his forces, Bragg turned aside and headed toward Frankfort to join Smith, leaving Louisville to Buell.

On September 25, looking like beggars, the Army of the Ohio straggled into Louisville. It was a sad end to a splendid start. These were the same spit-and-polish troops who had left Kentucky seven months earlier to whip the Rebels at Corinth. Now they were back in tatters after having pursued their elusive enemy in a huge circle through the South.

The Army of the Ohio had marched almost a thousand miles, often covering twenty-five miles a day. Their shoes were in shreds. Many walked barefoot. They were threadbare, lean, and hardened veterans who headed for taverns to get a square meal, partake freely of the "Pride of Kentucky," and grouch. They were angry. They felt that Buell had been outgeneraled by Bragg. Worse, Buell had declined to fight when Bragg stopped several times en route and offered battle.

In Washington the secretary of war was even angrier. Buell had abandoned nearly all the Rebel territory gained since the fall of Fort Donelson. The blood shed at Shiloh had been in vain. After eight months in office, Stanton was being driven almost insane by the failures of his generals.

In the east, there had been one defeat after another. McClellan, after much prodding, finally had started south to Richmond in March with his one-hundred-thousand-man Army of the Potomac. Advancing via the Yorktown Peninsula, he got to within five miles of the Confederate capital and then hesitated. Fearing that the enemy outnumbered him two to one, he did not attack.

Lee, with his smaller seventy-two-thousand-man Army of Northern Virginia, had no such qualms. Counterattacking time after time, Lee outmaneuvered McClellan in a series of savage and bloody battles, forcing him to retreat more than twenty miles.

On July 1 McClellan's four-month-long campaign to capture Richmond was abandoned. The furious secretary of war ordered him to return to Washington and transferred most of his troops to the sixty-three-thousand-man Army of Virginia, commanded by Major General John Pope. Meanwhile, Lee started his drive north into Pennsylvania, in conjunction with Bragg's drive into Ohio.

Lee struck Pope before he could be reinforced with McClellan's troops, defeating him on August 30 at the second Battle of Bull Run. Pope, like McClellan, returned to Washington in humiliation. Lee continued marching triumphantly north.

President Lincoln was desperate. Lee had to be stopped. Over Stanton's strong objections, Lincoln restored McClellan to command and sent him in pursuit of Lee.

McClellan caught up with Lee near Sharpsburg, Maryland. On September 17 they fought at Antietam Creek in the bloodiest one-day battle of the Civil War. Lee, with fifty thousand men to McClellan's one hundred thousand, was defeated, but due to McClellan's habitual caution, Lee was able to slip away to fight again another day.

Stanton ranted and raved and resolved to remove McClellan from command, permanently this time. In the west, Buell was due for the same treatment. However, when Buell managed to reorganize and reinforce his army in three days, refitting it with new uniforms, new shoes, and new recruits, and was ready to pursue Bragg, Stanton gave him a grudging stay of execution.

On October 1, in what seemed like a minor miracle, the enlarged sixty-one-thousand-man Army of the Ohio marched out of Louisville with bands playing and banners flying. Five Fighting McCooks—Alex, Dan, and John, and their cousins Ed and Anson—were with it.

First Lieutenant John McCook and McCook's Avengers marched in the advance. During three weeks in Louisville, Colonel Dan McCook had trained his mob of schoolboys into a well-disciplined fighting force.

Major Daniel McCook, watching them go, was shouldering his new Henry Repeating Rifle #1116. The gun, one of the latest on the market, was a popular lever-action carbine that carried fifteen rounds and had a fire rate of ten shots per minute. Rebels called it "that Yankee rifle that can be loaded on Sunday and fired all week."

The Army of the Ohio was looking for Braxton Bragg. Major Daniel McCook was looking for Frank Gurley, the guerrilla who had killed his son Robert.

Major Daniel McCook with his Henry rifle

*Territory trod by the Fighting McCooks
in their quest to save the Union*

Chapter 11

MAJOR GENERAL ALEXANDER MCCOOK
at the Battle of Perryville

Clumsy as an octopus on dry land, the sixty-one-thousand-man Army of the Ohio crawled slowly across central Kentucky groping for General Braxton Bragg.

General Buell's three corps marched, miles apart, on three somewhat parallel roads. The First Corps, commanded by Major General Alexander McD. McCook, was the left wing. The Second Corps, commanded by Major General Thomas L. Crittenden, was the right. The Third Corps, commanded by Major General Charles C. Gilbert, was the center.

Dust rose in whirlwinds as men and horses plodded over the parched earth. Despite the fact that it was early October, the army was marching in July heat. Streams were dry. Water in canteens emptied rapidly. Nothing was available to refill them. Due to the three-day leave in Louisville, which for many soldiers had been a whiskey binge, scores fell ill by the roadside.

The new recruits balked at the difficulty of the march. Making up nearly one-third of the army, they lugged heavy knapsacks filled with extra boots, blankets, ponchos, frying pans, soup kettles, and coffeepots. The veterans laughed at their naïveté. It was not long until, hot and tired and complaining of blistered feet, the new boys trimmed themselves down, throwing their extra things by the roadside to be snatched up by farmers and sutlers.

Many of the veterans, angry that they had not received their back pay in Louisville, complained that the next campaign had begun before they were paid for the last. Some units in the Army of the Ohio were eight months overdue.

"Paymaster, paymaster," furious members of one regiment began shouting. The chant was picked up by others through the line of march until it approached a mutiny.

Eventually order was restored, but the morale of officers and men was low. Some officers had received promotions in Louisville. Others were jealous. And so, as the army rumbled along at the rate of ten miles per day, there was a lot of grumbling. Much of it was due to the commanding general.

Major General Don Carlos Buell was a forty-four-year-old West Pointer with a stern face and stiff spine. Although he had excellent theoretical knowledge about the science of war, he was a cold and aloof man who had spent most of his army career as a bureaucrat in the adjutant general's office.

Disdainful of volunteers, Buell had no sympathy for their plight. One day, catching sight of a straggler, he tried to drive him back into the ranks by striking at him with his sword. The general's horse shied, throwing Buell on a pile of metal by the side of the road and cutting his thigh so badly that he was unable to remount and had to ride in an ambulance. When the story made the rounds, it did little to improve the morale of his three-corps army.

Buell rode with the center corps, commanded by General Gilbert. A former member of Buell's staff, he had been promoted to acting major general in Louisville.

Never having commanded troops in the field, West Pointer Gilbert was equally intolerant of volunteers. When he discovered an exhausted regiment taking a rest during an all-night march, he demanded that the men get up and form ranks to salute him properly. The colonel of the regiment

Major General Don Carlos Buell

responded that he "would not hold dress parade at midnight for any damn fool living." The men responded by bayoneting the rear end of Gilbert's horse, roaring with laughter as the general took off down the road in a cloud of dust.

Meanwhile, at all hours of the day and night, Buell sent messengers galloping off with orders for the First and Second corps. Aware that he was on borrowed time with the secretary of war, Buell insisted on directing every move of his three-corps army, keeping it as tightly reined as a troika. But he changed his orders so frequently that his wing commanders were often in the dark.

A frustrated Alex McCook, commanding the left wing, sent a wry message on October 5 to Crittenden, commanding the right:

> *Please keep me advised of your movements, so that I can cooperate. I am in blissful ignorance.*

After a week on the march, the soldiers were suffering terribly from the drought. They had been almost entirely without fresh water for nearly thirty-six hours. Some filled their canteens out of hog puddles and held their noses while they drank. Others fell from sunstroke with their empty canteens flung beside them. The desperate army was searching for water as much as it was searching for the enemy, and the men were willing to die for it.

Finally, on the afternoon of October 7, Union scouts told the soldiers what they wanted to hear. There was water ahead at the village of Perryville, and the Rebels were there, too.

General Buell ordered his tent set up in a little valley four miles west of town, got out his maps, and studied the terrain. Perryville sat astride the Chaplin River amid the gently rolling hills and valleys of bluegrass Kentucky.

After deciding on his battle plans for the next morning, Buell sent couriers galloping off in the dark to find Generals McCook and Crittenden. Their orders were to march at 3:00 a.m., form their battle lines, and report to him in person. The attack was set for 10:00 a.m.

At midnight Buell received a report that there were pools of water in Doctor's Creek, two and a half miles ahead. But the Confederates held Peters Hill, which overlooked the creek. Knowing that men and horses would need water before going into battle, Buell ordered Colonel Dan McCook to seize the creek.

At 3:00 a.m. Dan McCook led his novice Thirty-sixth Brigade in attacking the hill, driving two veteran Arkansas regiments off and repelling a counterattack. By dawn he had a firm hold on Peters Hill. It was a fine position, the center of the proposed field of battle. About 6:30 a.m. his division commander rode up. Brigadier General Philip H. Sheridan complimented Colonel McCook on the handsome job of taking the hill, ordered the rest of his division up, and set up his headquarters in a house on the rear slope.

Soon their corps commander arrived. General Gilbert surveyed the scene and told Sheridan not to advance further. General Buell did not want to bring on an engagement until all three corps were in position. Then Gilbert rode off to report to Buell.

In spite of Gilbert's order, Sheridan decided to dislodge a Rebel nest in nearby woods, and it turned into a full-fledged fight. Gilbert, hearing musketry and cannonading, galloped back and angrily ordered Sheridan to limit himself to defense unless there was a general advance.

It was almost 9:00 a.m. The battle hour was set for 10:00 a.m., and the First and Second corps had not yet arrived.

Alex McCook had not been reached by courier until 2:30 a.m., and by the time he had his First Corps up, breakfasted and marching, it was 5:00 a.m. As he approached Perryville on the Mackville Road, he heard Sheridan's cannonading.

"There will be fun before night!" Alex predicted to Colonel William H. Lytle, one of his brigade commanders.

Arriving on the battlefield shortly after 9:00 a.m., Alex surveyed his assigned position on the left flank. It was a broad and high plateau called Chaplin Heights. On his left, below steep bluffs, ran the Chaplin River. In his front the ground sloped down to a broad valley stretching to the village of Perryville. On his right, he saw Gilbert's troops on Peters Hill.

A deep wooded ravine ran between McCook's corps and Gilbert's corps. Doctor's Creek meandered through it, creating a three-hundred-yard gap between the two corps.

The area was deserted. Terrified villagers and farmers had fled at the approach of the two armies, driving off in heavily loaded wagons with household goods thrown in at random and children perched on top.

After setting his battle lines and commandeering an abandoned farmhouse for his headquarters, Alex McCook told one of his division commanders, Brigadier General Lovell H. Rousseau, to hold the position while McCook rode back to report to Buell, two and a half miles in the rear.

There he found the lame and shirt-sleeved Buell in his tent, angry that McCook was late and Crittenden still had not arrived. McCook's explanation—that the courier was late in reaching him—failed to appease the perfectionist commanding general. Furious that his meticulously laid plans had been disrupted, Buell announced that the attack was postponed until the next morning.

Alex McCook, given a written order not to fight that day, put it in his pocket as he walked out of Buell's tent with Colonel James B. Fry, the general's chief of staff.

"Who is down in Perryville?" Alex asked.

"Hardee," answered Fry, "with two divisions."

It was the rear of Bragg's army. Buell planned to defeat the outnumbered Hardee handily in the morning and then pursue the rest of Bragg's force.

Anticipating another win over Hardee, it was a high-spirited Alex McCook who refused a drink as he mounted his horse to go back to his thirsty troops.

"I am going down to drink at the river!" he called out cavalierly as he galloped off.

Shortly after McCook left, Buell sat down to his midday meal, with Gilbert as his guest. Hearing cannonading, the general got up from the table and limped out of his tent to listen.

"There is a great waste of powder over there," Buell said sternly. He sent an order to the front. It was short and clear:

Stop that useless waste of powder.

It was Colonel Dan McCook's batteries that Buell had heard. Dan McCook, having inched his brigade out to a commanding position on a forested spur of Peters Hill, saw Rebel infantry and artillery move toward the wooded ravine, carrying Doctor's Creek, that ran between the two corps.

General Rousseau was sending his men, regiment by regiment, down the Mackville Road to the creek to get water. Stacking their guns, the Union soldiers filled their canteens near a little white house belonging to Squire Henry Bottom. When the enemy appeared, Rousseau's men grabbed their guns and ran for cover. Dan McCook began shelling and was successfully repelling the Rebels when Buell heard the big guns.

Sheridan, getting Buell's message, was aware that it was the second time he had been reprimanded that day. New to high command, Sheridan had been given his general's star a week earlier in Louisville. Now, to avoid fur-

Major General William J. Hardee

ther trouble, he ordered Dan McCook to stop firing and pull back half a mile to his original position on Peters Hill.

Dan McCook was incredulous. From his forward position he was covering the three-hundred-yard gap between the two corps. A withdrawal would leave both corps open to flank attacks. Protesting the order, he galloped back to Sheridan and brought him to the front.

Showing him the position, Dan asked that the order be suspended. Sheridan admitted that the position was strong, said that he would like to remain, but insisted on the withdrawal. McCook, refusing to give up, begged him to exercise his rights as a division commander and delay execution of the order until Gilbert could be brought to the field.

Sheridan hesitated. It was a tense moment between the West Pointer and the volunteer. Both were hot-tempered fighters. Phil Sheridan, short and stocky, and Dan McCook, tall and razor-thin, eyed each other in silence. Then the moment was gone. Sheridan put his hand on McCook's shoulder.

"Colonel McCook," he said, "your facts are right, your conclusions are sound, and we probably should hold this position, but I am a regular and orders must be obeyed."

Dan McCook sullenly withdrew. But scarcely had his brigade returned to Peters Hill when he saw red and white rockets rise above Chaplin Heights. The twofold message from Alex's corps said "the enemy is advancing" and "send reinforcements."

The surprise attack came about 2:00 p.m. as Alex, after returning from Buell's headquarters, was positioning his troops.

Hardee, not waiting to be struck on the morrow, was following the written advice he had given Bragg:

> *There is one rule in our profession which should never be forgotten; it is to throw the masses of your troops on the fractions of the enemy.*

Colonel
Dan McCook

Brigadier General
Philip H. Sheridan

Hardee had been reinforced. Now, with three divisions of 18,000 men, he unleashed them on McCook's 12,500 men who were still moving into position.

One Confederate division commanded by Major General Benjamin Cheatham, their advance hidden by the steep Chaplin River bluffs, came over the rise in perfect battle formation, firing their guns and screaming their blood-curdling Rebel yells.

Alex McCook ordered his artillery to reply, in spite of Buell's "do not fight" order in his pocket.

"If General Buell supposes that Alex McCook is coming in sight of the enemy without fighting him," he muttered, "he is much mistaken in his man!"

He had less than two-thirds of his corps with him. His crack Second Division, which had been trained by him and fought under him at Shiloh, had been sent north by Buell under the command of Brigadier General Joshua W. Sill to make a feint attack against Smith at Frankfort. One of McCook's two remaining divisions, commanded by General Rousseau, had seven thousand battle-tested troops. But the other, led by Brigadier General James S. Jackson, was filled with fifty-five hundred raw recruits who had been in the army less than a month and had never fired guns in battle.

It was General Jackson's recruits, holding the high ground on the left flank, who took the first blow. When the Confederates charged, the recruits ran down the hill and fired one volley. But before they could reload, the Rebels poured hot fire into their ranks.

Jackson, knowing that green troops either break and run or die in place, was trying to rally them when he was shot from his horse and killed. His panicked men ran back up the hill, pursued by the Confederates who were finally stopped by Union artillery commanded by Brigadier General William R. Terrill. McCook's left flank held.

Hardee, like a prizefighter, had advised Bragg:

Strike with your whole strength first to the right and then to the left.

Now, following his own advice, Hardee sent a second division, commanded by Major General Simon Bolivar Buckner, sweeping in broad columns across the valley to hit McCook's center. The veteran Union troops in General Rousseau's Third Division, attacked again and again, knew how to back up a little and regroup. The center held. McCook, recognizing Hardee's plan, anticipated that his right flank at the wooded ravine would get the next blow.

It was about 2:30 p.m. McCook's outnumbered men had been fighting alone for half an hour. There was no response to the signal rockets, even though signal stations existed between Buell's headquarters and his three corps.

Urgently, Alex sent an aide-de-camp, Lieutenant Lewis M. Hosea, to Sheridan on Peters Hill, asking him to see that McCook's right flank was not turned. Sheridan responded by shelling the wooded ravine until he saw an enemy division forming across the valley on his own front. Withdrawing his batteries and men to hidden safety behind the crest of Peters Hill, Sheridan sent a message to Gilbert that he could not hold his position unless he was reinforced.

Dan McCook watched the Rebel division on Sheridan's front start moving, but it did not march toward Peters Hill. Instead, it went diagonally across Sheridan's front toward the wooded ravine.

As if on parade, the Rebel division commanded by Brigadier General James P. Anderson marched across the broad valley. Their long lines of burnished bayonets gleamed brightly in the sun. Passing within seven hundred feet of Peters Hill, they were so close that Dan could see daylight through their ranks.

"Let me go to Alex's help," he begged Sheridan, pointing out that by making a left wheel with his brigade he could hit the Rebels in their flank and rear.

"The orders are not to bring on an engagement," Sheridan repeated.

Then Dan asked to be allowed to shell them with his artillery. But Sheridan said that it would reveal their hidden position. So Sheridan's guns remained silent. The Confederates assumed that Peters Hill had been abandoned. Dan McCook was forced to watch helplessly all afternoon as every third man in his brother Alex's corps was either killed or wounded.

When the Confederates reached the ravine, their brass band announced their arrival by breaking into a triumphant tune that filled the woods with music. The Rebels cheered as they crossed Doctor's Creek and swarmed around Squire Bottom's house. Eighteen Confederate cannon rumbled up and began raking Alex McCook's right flank. A barn filled with hay caught fire, and a heavy wind billowed the dense smoke over the hillside. The Rebels wheeled and struck the end of McCook's line. It crumbled.

"God help our poor boys now," murmured one of Sheridan's hidden men on Peters Hill.

It was 3:00 p.m. Alex McCook had been fighting for an hour. His left and center were holding. But his right was giving way. His ammunition was giving out, and he had not been reinforced. In desperation he ordered his staff engineer, Captain Horace N. Fisher, to ride like hell, find the nearest commander, and get help.

"Minutes are terribly important," shouted McCook.

Taking the quickest route to Gilbert's corps, Captain Fisher rode between the lines that now were about one hundred yards apart. He repeated McCook's message to his orderly, telling him to deliver it to the nearest general in case Fisher was hit. Then the captain took off on his thoroughbred mare, Betty, who had taken a cup at Lexington. He counted on her remarkable speed to get them through, hoping that the enemy would misjudge her stride and their bullets would pass behind her. Just before reaching the zone of fire, he leaned low over her neck and dug in his spurs. There was a hail of bullets. One brought down his orderly's horse. Another carried away Fisher's blanket roll from the back of his saddle. A third dented the scabbard of his sword. Ahead was a lane with two rail fences. The mare took the first and then, with a superb effort, cleared the second as the admiring Rebels gave the gallant horse and its rider a sportsmanlike cheer.

Fisher reached the Springfield Turnpike and halted in front of Brigadier General Albin Francisco Schoepf, marching at the head of his division. General Schoepf agreed to help but said that since General Gilbert was riding at the rear of the column, army regulations required that Fisher make the request of him. Fisher galloped back to Gilbert.

"General McCook's entire command is engaged!" Fisher cried. "His reserves are all in line, and the safety of his corps is compromised."

Gilbert, after his midday meal with Buell, was on his way back to his corps. Having received Sheridan's message about the enemy division, he wanted to assess the situation before committing troops to McCook.

"I'll think about it," Gilbert said and rode on.

Fisher, in an angry outburst, vowed to report Gilbert's eccentric behavior to General Buell. Galloping on to Buell's headquarters, Fisher arrived at 3:50 p.m. and dashed into the general's tent. But instead of the alarm that he hoped to raise, Buell received the news coolly, commenting merely that he was "astonished" at the report.

His headquarters was in a valley with forty-foot-high hills on either side. The wind was blowing toward the battlefield and not a sound, except Dan McCook's artillery, had reached him. Buell limped out of his tent, held his ear toward the battlefield, listened for a few moments, and then turned sharply to Fisher.

"Captain," he said, "you must be mistaken. I cannot hear any sound of musketry. There cannot be any serious engagement."

Bodies of the dead and wounded were strewn across the battlefield as Alex McCook galloped from flank to flank, frantically trying to save his corps. The right was hemorrhaging badly as the enemy advanced up the Mackville Road toward his headquarters. The center, after holding its ground until all the cartridge boxes of living and wounded and dead were empty, fixed bayonets and fell back. The left was battered and bloodied,

Starkweather's brigade holding position at the Battle of Perryville

but Colonel John C. Starkweather was holding with his brigade and twelve cannon. His powder-begrimed artillerymen kept working their guns.

McCook, not hearing from Fisher, sent Captain Hoblitzell to General Schoepf, and Major Bates to General Buell.

Chaplin Heights, after two hours of fighting, was pandemonium. Loose artillery horses were running wild. Wounded men were crying for help. Colonel William Lytle on the right flank had been wounded and captured. Colonel George Webster in the center was killed as he led his green troops. General William Terrill on the left flank fell among his guns, his breast torn away by a shell.

Terrill, a West Pointer and close personal friend of Alex, was a Virginian who had remained loyal to the Union. He had commanded a battery at Shiloh with great distinction, saving many of McCook's men.

A mile away, most of the twenty-one thousand troops in Gilbert's corps were idle. One division filed into the woods, formed in line, and lay down. They could hear the sounds of battle distinctly, were almost in view of it, and wondered why they were not ordered to help. Several officers in Schoepf's division, overhearing Fisher's desperate plea, came to see the battle for themselves and could not believe their eyes.

"We are just back over there a short distance with our arms stacked," cried one. "Why in hell don't they order us in?"

McCook's headquarters was captured. His corps, pushed back a mile, was on the verge of a complete rout. He was frantically rallying them to make a last stand when help finally came. It was a single brigade out of the seventeen or eighteen that were available.

Colonel Michael Gooding's brigade of fifteen hundred men marched up and tore into the fight savagely, as if avenging the wrongs of their commanders who had not sent them earlier. They forced the Confederates back down the Mackville Road and retook McCook's headquarters.

It was about 5:00 p.m. when one of Buell's aides, Major J. M. Wright, arrived on the scene. As the battle came within his sight, he was dumbfounded. He found that one of the fiercest struggles in the western theatre of war had been raging almost within his sight all afternoon. As a military man he thought it was the finest spectacle he had ever seen. And he bore a message for McCook from Buell.

"Hold your ground!" was the order from the commanding general.

It was dusk when Hardee, astride his horse at Squire Bottom's house, sent his last troops up the hill on McCook's right flank. They were the two Arkansas regiments that Dan McCook had driven off Peters Hill earlier that morning. Advancing up the Mackville Road, the Rebels fell on Colonel Gooding's flanks.

Sheridan, after an assault on his own front had been repelled, finally turned his guns on them. But it was too late. They were too far up the hill, and his shells could not reach them.

Forcing Gooding back, the Rebels retook McCook's headquarters. Gooding, having lost more than one-third of his men, was shot from his horse and captured.

It was nearly dark when Union Brigadier General James Blair Steedman galloped up. Although his brigade had been only one-half mile away all afternoon, he had not been ordered to fight until Major Bates convinced Buell that McCook needed help. By now, however, darkness had fallen. The two armies, only yards apart, could not tell friend from foe. They were forced to stop about 6:00 p.m.

By the bright light of the nearly full moon the field of battle was littered with the shadowy figures of the dead and wounded. The men lay quietly, but the dying horses gave out a piteous moan of almost human suffering. Cannon, muskets, wagon wheels, and caissons were thick upon the ground. In the distance, in all directions, lanterns bobbed as injured men were brought in from the fields. Small groups of soldiers carried handkerchiefs tied to sticks, as flags of truce, while they searched between the lines for fallen comrades.

Dominican nuns from Springfield came to carry shattered bodies back to their convent, which was turned into a hospital where surgeons worked through the night amputating arms and legs. By the light of pine torches the white coifs of the nuns moved like silent ghosts across the bloody fields.

General Terrill died a slow death from his chest wound. The previous night he had sat around a campfire with General Jackson and Colonel Webster, discussing their chances of being shot in battle. All three had agreed that, considering the theory of probabilities, the odds were slight that any one of them would be hit. Now all three were dead.

On Peters Hill, Colonel Dan McCook bivouacked his brigade for the night. There was no supper, as Buell had ordered the supply wagons kept far in the rear. The night was frosty. The men wrapped themselves in their blankets and slept on their arms. Nearby, a Union band softly played "Home, Sweet Home" while, like an echo, a mile and a half away in Perryville, a Confederate band picked up the tune.

Back in his headquarters tent, Buell was entertaining Gilbert and Sheridan at supper. Still not aware that a major battle had been fought that day, Buell was discussing his plans to attack at dawn. Although Gilbert and Sheridan told him that there had been quite a bit of action on McCook's front that afternoon, Buell still thought that it was only a minor encounter. Finally about 9:00 p.m., when Rousseau reported, Buell learned the truth.

McCook's corps had been pushed back a mile. Almost a third of his men were killed, wounded, or missing. General Jackson, General Terrill, and Colonel Webster were dead.

Buell listened in stunned silence. Furious that McCook had fought against orders and ruined his carefully laid plans for battle the next day, Buell sent a message for him to report immediately.

McCook arrived about midnight to a cold reception. He asked for two brigades to protect his men during the night. When his request was denied, he asked for one brigade.

"You shall not have another man!" Buell snapped.

There were angry words between the two generals. When provoked, McCook could swear like a pirate. Storming out, he rode back to his shattered corps and, dropping exhausted from the saddle, slept on the ground beside his horse. Meanwhile, Buell and his staff worked feverishly through the night revising battle plans.

At midnight Union pickets reported hearing the rumble of wagons and artillery, indicating that the Confederates were moving their lines. About 4:30 a.m., when the first fingers of light touched the dark, Union officers searched the countryside through their field glasses.

The enemy was gone.

The entire Rebel army had slipped away during the night after Bragg, who had reached the field in time to fight, studied Alex McCook's captured papers. Discovering that more than thirty thousand of Buell's troops were only a mile or two away, Bragg was baffled as to why they had not been thrown into battle. Badly outnumbered, Bragg departed hastily, leaving behind his dead and severely wounded.

The hills and valleys were strewn with the dead and dying of both armies. Some men lay torn to pieces. Some were in the last agony of dying. Friend and foe lay together. Nearly all the faces were quiet and peaceful as though death had come instantly and without pain. On McCook's right flank, near Squire Bottom's house, there were a hundred men lying stiff and cold. On the left flank the Rebel advance was marked by trails of blood a half-mile long. Over five hundred of the Rebel dead appeared to have been killed instantly by bullets or artillery fire. Some heads were missing. Some had upper and lower limbs torn off. Others lay with their chests and stomachs open. The Union sanitary corps moved among the hundreds of Rebel wounded left on the battlefield. During the long night they lay, suffering from the cold and the lack of food and water. Workers gathered up those less wounded and took them to hospitals. The hopeless cases were left to die where they were, writhing in their last agonies.

At 8:00 a.m. Buell was still in his tent, sending messages to his commanders, asking them if they had attacked yet. His note to Crittenden demanded:

Have you commenced the attack? What delays your attack?

The commanding general did not know that the great battle for Kentucky was over.

Blame and recrimination were everywhere. The War Department was shocked to learn that most of the Army of the Ohio sat out the battle and that McCook fought with 12,500 men, half of them new recruits, against a veteran army of 18,000. Meanwhile some 30,000 Union soldiers and eighty pieces of artillery nearby did not fire a shot. Union losses were 845 killed, 2,851 wounded, and 515 missing. Confederate losses were 510 killed, 2,635 wounded, and 251 missing.

And while Buell was never closer than two and a half miles away, Bragg rode the battlefield with five of his generals—William Hardee, Leonidas Polk, Benjamin Cheatham, James Anderson, and Simon Bolivar Buckner. Bragg's official report stated:

For the time engaged it was the severest and most desperately contested engagement within my knowledge.

When Alex's brother, Colonel Dan McCook, wrote his official report, he was blunt. He had not hesitated to proclaim loudly during the battle, and he did not hesitate to proclaim loudly afterward, that the Rebel wheeling movement would not have been possible if he had not been ordered to fall back:

> *The enemy's batteries had begun to play upon General Rousseau's division upon our left when we were ordered to fall back at least half a mile . . . leaving General Rousseau without support on the right, exposing his flank. The enemy was not disturbed any longer by the batteries of our division. . . .*

One of the greatest opportunities of the war had been lost. The universal conviction of the officers and men of the Army of the Ohio was that they could have destroyed Bragg's army if they had been allowed to fight. They denounced Gilbert without stint for failing to come to McCook's aid. And Gilbert, for his part, was discovered not to be a general after all. Never nominated by the president nor confirmed by the Senate, he was really only a captain in the regular U.S. Army. The livid secretary of war sent him elsewhere and ordered a hearing to determine the blame for the botched battle.

By now Stanton's mind was set. He was sure that he, with all the great resources of the North, could win the Civil War. But he needed two things, total control of the war and a commanding general who would unquestioningly follow his orders and fight. It was not McDowell. It was not McClellan. It was not Halleck. It was not Pope. And it certainly was not Buell.

Buell's official report on the Battle of Perryville attempted to put the blame on Alex McCook, stating that he had failed to report the fighting until 4:00 p.m.:

> *I was not apprised early enough of the condition of affairs on my left. . . . I ascribe it to the too great confidence of the general commanding the left corps (Major-General McCook) which made him believe that he could manage the difficulty without the aid or control of his commander.*

Reporters had their own theories. Some wondered whether McCook, who could direct a division well, was mature enough to command a full corps in battle. William Furay, of the *New York Times*, wrote that McCook was

> *a brave man, cool under fire, but he lacks the eagle eye to behold, and the quick mind to plan. He is not a man of decision; he is not a man of energy. Brave, gallant and spirited, his virtues are all of the heart. Slow and undecided, his faults are all of the head.*

Alex McCook did not lay the blame on anyone else. He credited General Rousseau and his other commanders for their great courage. He praised his gallant corps for its steadfast fighting. And for himself, he had a frank admission:

> *I was badly whipped.*

However, he claimed for his corps the honor of leading the pursuit of Bragg. Racing through Union Army camps was a report of the angry exchange of words in Buell's tent at midnight after the Battle of Perryville.

Buell had threatened to court-martial McCook for bringing on the battle, and Alex had a sharp retort, "I'll send you to hell in a minute if you do!"

*Territory trod by the Fighting McCooks
in their quest to save the Union*

Chapter 12

MAJOR GENERAL ALEXANDER McCOOK
at the Battle of Stones River

"We move tomorrow, gentlemen!" announced Major General William Starke Rosecrans, slamming his empty brandy mug on the table.

It was Christmas night 1862 in Nashville, Tennessee. Two and a half months had passed since the Battle of Perryville. The Army of the Ohio had been reorganized and renamed, again, the Army of the Cumberland. The cold and cautious General Buell had been replaced by the fiery and feisty General Rosecrans.

But the quarry was the same. The crafty General Braxton Bragg who, with his renamed Army of Tennessee, was in winter quarters thirty miles south at Murfreesboro.

On the evening of December 25 Rosecrans was holding a council of war at his headquarters in a commandeered Nashville mansion with his three wing commanders: Major Generals George Thomas, Alexander McCook, and Thomas Crittenden. Rosecrans sat balanced on the edge of his chair in whispered conversation with Thomas while McCook and Crittenden stood at the fireplace smoking cigars and sipping hot brandy toddies.

Alex McCook, with his elbow on the mantel and his florid face aglow in the light from a stack of cedar sticks burning brightly on the hearth, was singing the praises of his gallant corps when Rosecrans suddenly silenced the room with one stroke.

"We move tomorrow, gentlemen! Strike hard and fast! Give them no rest! Fight them! Fight them! Fight them, I say!" he cried exuberantly.

Rosecrans was a charismatic man, extremely popular with his troops. They called him "Old Rosey" and threw their hats in the air when he appeared on his charger, nattily attired in black breeches with a blue coat and snow-white vest.

Well-read, Rosecrans was a brilliant conversationalist who often sat up until 4:00 a.m. arguing philosophy, literature, religion, and politics. Multifaceted, he could dictate three letters simultaneously while talking with a visitor and smoking a cigar. However, his hot temperament rendered the forty-three-year-old general charming and irritable by turns.

Imperious and argumentative, Rosecrans was bound to clash with Edwin Stanton, the imperious and argumentative secretary of war.

They first clashed in the spring of 1862, shortly after Stanton took office. Rosecrans, fresh from driving Lee out of western Virginia, had overstepped his authority by trying to improve the Shenandoah Valley campaign plans of Lincoln and Stanton. Rosecrans considered both men as amateurs at war.

Stanton, for all his bluster on the surface, was highly sensitive inside. Feeling that he had been treated like nothing more than Lincoln's clerk, Stanton never forgot nor forgave Rosecrans.

Lincoln, for all his affability on the surface, was highly secure inside. Recognizing that Rosecrans was a skillful strategist, Lincoln had ignored the slight. Six months later, after the Battle of Perryville, the president gave him command of the Army of the Cumberland.

Stanton was vehemently opposed. But the president, as commander-in-chief, had the last word. Lincoln also said that Rosecrans's three corps commanders would be Generals Thomas, McCook, and Crittenden.

Major General William Starke Rosecrans

"Well," Stanton muttered angrily to his good friend Major Donn Piatt after returning from the White House to the War Department, "you have your choice of idiots; now look out for the frightful disasters."

During that fall of 1862 there was no shortage of frightful disasters.

First was a political disaster. Lincoln had announced that he would sign an Emancipation Proclamation on January 1, 1863, freeing all slaves in seceded states. Democrats were strongly opposed. They would support a war for the Union but not a war to free the slaves. Campaigning against the controversial measure, the Democrats won overwhelmingly in the 1862 congressional elections, sweeping Ohio, Pennsylvania, Indiana, Illinois, and New York, and carrying New Jersey. It was a severe rebuke to Lincoln.

The next disaster was a military one. Major General Ambrose E. Burnside, who had replaced McClellan as commander of the Army of the Potomac, again took it south to capture Richmond. On December 13 Burnside was whipped by Lee at the Battle of Fredericksburg, one of the worst defeats in the history of the U.S. Army. Union casualties totaled some 12,600. The Confederates lost 5,300.

The North rebelled against the slaughter. Convinced that the South could never be conquered, and strengthened by their fall election wins, Peace Democrats demanded that the war be negotiated to an end. If that meant independence for the Confederacy, so be it.

Lincoln needed a victory badly.

Rosecrans had planned to keep his army in winter quarters at Nashville until spring. But as Christmas approached, his soldiers recognized the stockpiling of supplies that signaled they would soon march against their old foe Braxton Bragg, thirty miles south at Murfreesboro.

The Confederates were enjoying a festive holiday season. December in Tennessee was beautiful, with warm and sunny days for military reviews and clear starlit nights for parties. Confederate President Jefferson Davis came out from Richmond to inspect the troops and attend festivities preceding the wedding of the dashing cavalry commander John Hunt Morgan to Mattie Ready, a Murfreesboro belle. The most lavish wedding of the year in the South, it started a spate of parties in plantation mansions that culminated in a formal Christmas Eve ball.

Hardee's headquarters at Eagleville, fifteen miles west, was a gay scene of reviews and tournaments, horse races, banquets, and balls. Recently promoted to lieutenant general, the highest rank in the Confederate Army, Hardee received Christmas gifts from his many admirers. John Hunt Morgan gave him a fine thoroughbred horse.

Even Union officers sent Hardee gifts. Old army friends with Rosecrans in Nashville sent Hardee greetings, under flags of truce, accompanied by a bottle of his favorite liquor. Volunteers in both armies found these gallantries hard to swallow. However, among West Pointers it was the highest form of chivalry to send Hardee brandy today and bullets tomorrow.

The bullets were packed on Christmas night when Rosecrans told Thomas, McCook, and Crittenden that they would march at dawn. McCook, commanding the right wing, was to attack Hardee at Eagleville. Crittenden, commanding the left wing, would strike Bragg at Murfreesboro. Thomas, commanding the center, was positioned to come to the aid of either.

As the generals left his headquarters, Rosecrans stood at the door shaking hands warmly.

"Spread out your skirmishers far and wide! Keep pushing ahead! They will not stand it!" he encouraged them.

Later that night Rosecrans was visited by Stanton's close friend Major Donn Piatt, who had been sent out to Nashville to serve as judge advocate at the Buell Hearings investigating the Battle of Perryville. In spite of the fact that Alex McCook had been exonerated by a military tribunal for any blame in the battle, Piatt still tried to persuade Rosecrans to remove him as a corps commander.

Alex's headstrong past was catching up with him. Major Piatt had been chief of staff to General Schenck at the Battle of Bull Run when Alex, leading a revolt of the colonels, turned his back on the political general and left Schenck and Piatt standing in the rain.

Piatt, insisting that he liked Alex McCook personally, said he feared the young general was not capable of handling a full corps in battle. Rosecrans, well aware of the political and military infighting in Washington, assured Piatt smoothly that McCook had his full confidence to command the right wing.

At 6:00 a.m. McCook's sixteen-thousand-man corps, accompanied by nine batteries of artillery, started marching south in a torrential rainstorm. His three division commanders were Brigadier Generals Jefferson C. Davis, Richard W. Johnson, and Philip H. Sheridan. Behind them rolled three hundred white-topped mule-drawn wagons with supplies and ammunition.

Two miles beyond McCook's picket line he met Hardee's cavalry. Heavy skirmishing lasted all day as McCook fought his way south and Hardee, cool and skillful, fell back fighting.

Late that night Rosecrans rode to McCook's camp. The two generals sat on the floor of a wagon drawn up in a cedar grove and, by the flickering light of a candle stuck into the socket of a bayonet, they pored over a map and agreed on McCook's advance the next day.

"Good night, General," Alex called out confidently as Rosecrans remounted his horse. "With the blessings of God, General, I will whip my friend, Hardee, tomorrow."

It rained all night. At murky daylight McCook advanced cautiously in a dense fog, fighting with his unseen enemy, who kept slipping away all day into the mist. When night came, the rain stopped and the temperature dropped.

The next day was bright and cold, and there was a fine coating of ice on the land. It was Sunday, a day on which Rosecrans did not like to march or fight. A devout Catholic, he had Father Patrick Treacy of the Fifty-fifth Indiana say Mass every morning at his headquarters. While the army rested, McCook sent out scouts, who reported that Hardee was heading east to join Bragg at Murfreesboro.

McCook pursued the next morning, skirmishing with Hardee's rear guard, until he reached a cedar forest on the banks of Stones River, three miles north of Murfreesboro. The armies of Rosecrans and Bragg were there, drawn up for battle.

McCook fought his way into position on the right of the Union line. The ground was extremely rough, interfaced with huge limestone boulders and dense cedar thickets. He placed the divisions of Sheridan and Davis along a ridge at the edge of the cedars. In his front, beyond a fallow cotton field, the Confederates lay hidden in more thickets.

About noon, when McCook was positioning Johnson's division in the rear as his reserve, he got bad news. His entire three-hundred-wagon supply train had been destroyed.

Confederate Brigadier General Joseph Wheeler with two thousand cavalrymen had encircled Rosecrans's army, discovered McCook's wagons, and obliterated them. Wheeler captured some seven hundred men, nearly a million dollars in ammunition and food, plus over one thousand mules and horses. He torched the rest. It was a scene of total devastation. Burning wagons stretched for miles over ground littered with empty valises and trunks and broken guns. In forty-eight hours of hard riding, Wheeler had shown what strong cavalry could do.

"Give me more cavalry," Rosecrans had pleaded with the War Department for two months, to no avail. Bragg's cavalry outnumbered his, four to one.

About 2:00 p.m. McCook got more bad news. A farmer reported that Hardee's troops extended far beyond the right end of McCook's line. After sending the farmer to Rosecrans with the message, McCook moved two brigades from his reserve division to the right flank, ordering them to hook back in a crochet to protect against a flank attack. Commanding the brigades were two of McCook's best and most experienced brigadier generals, August Willich and Edward N. Kirk, veterans of Shiloh.

About 4:00 p.m. McCook sent his aide, Captain Horace Fisher, to Rosecrans to report that his corps was in position but that the right of his line rested directly in front of Hardee's center. Rosecrans, preoccupied with his battle plans for the next morning, told Fisher that he could not spare any troops to reinforce McCook. He added that he was not disturbed to hear that the Rebels were in heavy force opposite McCook.

"Tell General McCook," said Rosecrans, "to prepare for battle tomorrow morning. While he holds Hardee, the left under Crittenden will swing around and take Murfreesboro. Let Hardee attack if he wants to. It will suit us exactly."

Rosecrans, who earlier had been anxious and uncharacteristically silent after the loss of McCook's wagon train, now warmed his hands over a fire and murmured, "It is looking better."

But later, on reflection, Rosecrans resorted to the ancient stratagem of false campfires. He ordered enough campfires for a full division of infantry to be built in the empty cedar thickets beyond the right end of McCook's line. Rosecrans gambled that Bragg would swallow the bait, think that the Union Army was shifting to the right, and shift his forces accordingly.

About 6:30 p.m. Rosecrans's chief of staff, Colonel Julius Garesche, sent McCook his written battle orders:

> *Take a strong position; if the enemy attack you, fall back slowly, refusing your right, contesting the ground inch by inch. If the enemy do not attack you, you will attack them, not vigorously, but warmly. The time of attack by you to be designated by the General commanding.*

That evening, just before tattoo, one of the Union bands struck up "Yankee Doodle." A Confederate band responded with "Dixie." Other bands joined in, and soon the damp night air was filled with the competing tunes of "Hail Columbia" from the North and "Bonnie Blue Flag" from the South. The battle of the bands continued until one played "Home Sweet Home." Others picked it up, and thousands of soldiers in both armies raised their voices together in the old refrain. Then they cut cedar boughs for beds, wrapped themselves in their blankets, and dropped off to sleep before waking up in the morning to cut each other's throats.

After tattoo McCook rode to Rosecrans's headquarters to report, expressing concern about the strong concentration of the enemy opposite him. Rosecrans assured him that it fit his battle plan exactly. Crittenden's 7:00 a.m. attack from the left would be on the weak end of the Confederate line. As it gave way, Thomas would assault the center. McCook simply had to hold firm on the right.

"You know the ground, you have fought over it, you know its difficulties," Rosecrans said. "Can you hold your present position?"

"Yes, I think I can," McCook replied.

Later the two men would argue over whether Rosecrans asked McCook if he could hold his position for "three hours." Rosecrans said he did. McCook said he did not.

It was about midnight when Alex arrived back at his headquarters in the cedar forest. Dismounting, he stretched out on a pile of hay in an angle of a worm fence. A north wind shrieked through the cedars, and the night turned bitterly cold.

Rosecrans and Bragg, each trying to deceive the other, had ordered no campfires. So their men huddled shivering on the ground while McCook's aide shouted commands to nonexistent troops and his pickets fed the false campfires that extended nearly a mile beyond his lines. In response Bragg shifted his army.

Union pickets, hearing the slashing of guns and jingling of canteens as the Confederates moved during the night, were worried. About 2:00 a.m. they woke Generals Davis and Sheridan. They in turn woke McCook, who repeated Rosecrans's assurance that all would be well.

"His attack upon their right in the morning will be so vigorous that they will be compelled to withdraw their forces to support that portion of their line," McCook said. "I am only to hold my line and wait for orders from headquarters."

A little later McCook was awakened again. This time it was Rosecrans's chief of cavalry, Major General David S. Stanley, who had been ordered by Rosecrans to take his cavalry north to protect incoming wagon trains. Stanley warned McCook about the shifting Rebels and later told his aides that the young general was in his usual high spirits.

"McCook seemed utterly indifferent and laughed, joked, and rolled around his hay bed with the good nature and love of fun of a big boy on his first picnic," Stanley related.

But beneath McCook's show of bravado was a professional soldier who prided himself on making no mistakes. He sent another message to Rosecrans at 3:00 a.m. that the Confederates were continuing to shift to the right.

Sheridan, in spite of McCook's assurances, had his division up at 4:00 a.m. Davis awakened his men soon after. By 5:00 a.m. the brigades of Willich and Kirk were hooked in their crochet behind split-rail fences and limestone boulders.

The cold gray dawn filtered through the cedars about 6:00 a.m. All was still. The enemy had stopped moving. The rain also had stopped. The five hundred yards of open ground between the two armies was shrouded in eerie fog.

Alex McCook was shaving in the cedar forest shortly before 6:30 a.m. when he heard the stutter of heavy musketry coming from his lines.

"That is contrary to orders!" McCook shouted, throwing down his razor.

An aide ran up to tell him that it was the Confederates, not the Federals, who were firing. Enemy battle flags were sailing like ships through the fog.

"Who is opposing me today?" McCook demanded.

"Major General Cheatham," the aide replied, recognizing the flags.

Confederate General Benjamin Cheatham was a hard fighter and a hard drinker, sometimes riding into battle so inebriated he could barely sit his horse. But, drunk or sober, he was a formidable foe. It had been he who struck first at Perryville.

"Is it possible that I have to meet Cheatham again?" McCook muttered as, with shaving lather on his face, he galloped off to the Battle of Stones River.

He found not only Cheatham's flags but the colors of much of the Confederate Army, including the familiar blue banner of Hardee, with cannons crossed on a full moon. After five days of falling back, Hardee filled the canteens of his shivering men with whiskey and gave his former assistant a lesson both brilliant and brutal.

Moving noiselessly out of the mist, their gray uniforms melding with the gray dawn, some ten thousand Rebels advanced in double lines of perfect order that stretched to the right and left as far as the eye could see. Holding their fire until they were on top of the Union line, they smashed into it screaming the Rebel yell and spitting orange-red musketry.

Overrunning the empty campsites, Hardee's men wheeled and fell with double force on the end brigades of Kirk and Willich. In a few minutes almost 700 of Willich's men were captured and 463 killed or wounded. General Willich was captured. General Kirk was mortally wounded. The right end of the Union line collapsed.

Hardee started to roll up the line, and McCook, outnumbered three to one, was in the thick of the battle trying to stop him. McCook was rallying his men behind fences and boulders when a courier galloped up, shouting that Confederate cavalry was in their rear.

First at a trot and then at a gallop, two thousand cavalrymen under General John Wharton had swept around McCook's right flank. Smashing through the false campsites and finding no Union cavalry to stop them, they would soon have McCook surrounded and cut off from the rest of the army. McCook sent the courier to Rosecrans for help.

Rosecrans, three miles away on the other side of the cedar forest, had heard the fighting almost from the start. Confident that McCook could

McCook's right flank hit by Hardee

hold his position, Rosecrans sent Crittenden's corps across Stones River at 7:00 a.m. as planned. Suddenly a sound erupted from McCook's corps like the distant rumble of heavily loaded wagons. Rosecrans recognized it as the full roar of battle. He was listening intently when fleeing figures emerged from the forest. On their heels came McCook's courier.

"The right wing is broken!" he shouted. "Rebel cavalry is charging the rear!"

"Tell General McCook," replied Rosecrans, "to contest every inch of ground. If he holds them, we will swing into Murfreesboro with our left, and cut them off."

To reassure his staff and himself, Rosecrans murmured, "It is working right."

But the distant rumble grew louder. Wounded soldiers straggled from the forest. Soon a second aide from McCook galloped up, asking for reinforcements.

"So soon?" Rosecrans blurted.

It was not yet 8:00 a.m. Rosecrans stalked the soggy ground, silently pacing up and down, listening to the distant rumble. The trickle of figures from the cedar forest became a panic-stricken mob of teamsters and servants running for their lives. Then the rumble swelled to an earthquaking roar.

Rosecrans's florid face turned pale. He realized that he and Bragg had the identical plan: to make a massive wheeling attack with their left while pivoting on their right. But Bragg did it first. He had broken McCook's wing and was forcing it back on the main body.

Rosecrans, sending an order to Crittenden to abort his attack, improvised a defense line along the Nashville Turnpike. It was his only escape route.

The roar of battle was like a runaway locomotive. Bullets spattered against boulders, hit trees, and whizzed around Rosecrans as he whirled into action, galloping from corps to corps, an unlit cigar clamped between his teeth, while his staff at his heels tried to keep up.

Within the cedar forest McCook was contesting the ground, as ordered, inch by inch. After the initial surprise, his resistance was gallant and obstinate. The *New York Times* correspondent wrote that McCook was

> *brave to a fault and self-possessed. He narrowly escaped death many times. His horse was killed under him and he was severely hurt.*

Actually McCook, fighting with Davis's division, had two horses shot from under him. Then, when Davis fell back on the main body of the army, McCook went to help Sheridan.

The last of McCook's three divisions to be hit by Hardee's avalanche, Sheridan's battled valiantly against overwhelming odds. They repelled four attacks before, out of ammunition, Sheridan was ordered by McCook to fall back with bayonets fixed. His men made their way single file, Indian style, through the cedar forest, using each tree as a shield. Sheridan reached open ground about 10:30 a.m., having lost one-third of his men. Three brigade commanders and sixty-nine junior officers were dead. But Sheridan's resistance had won time for Rosecrans to marshal his forces on a sliver of ground between the Nashville Turnpike and Stones River.

Suddenly from the cedars came a curious sound. A combination of men shouting in a high-pitched whine and the Rebel yell, it sounded like steam escaping from a kettle.

Cannonballs were everywhere. One struck Colonel Garesche, Rosecrans's chief of staff, and severed his head. Blood and brains spewed all over Rosecrans's overcoat as Garesche's headless body rode on eerily before toppling to the ground.

Hardee had succeeded brilliantly. It was his finest hour. He had closed up McCook's corps like a jackknife. He held a large part of the forest battleground, strewn with prisoners, cannons, guns, ammunition trains, and the dead and wounded of both armies. Now he planned to destroy the rest of Rosecrans's beleaguered army with one piercing thrust.

The Confederates emerged from the cedars and lined up in battle array. Across some four hundred yards of open ground, the Federals dug in their heels and waited. Hardee ordered a charge.

Newspaper reporters, watching from some high ground, were spellbound. They thought it was splendid. It was magnificent. It was a tournament with flags flying and bands playing and regiments marching four lines deep as if on parade. It was why men went to war. They knew that this was what they had come to see, and that they might see it only once in their lives. The Confederate lines were perfect as the men moved steadily across the plain.

Union artillery, massed on high ground behind the infantry, held its fire. Then, at a signal, the earth trembled as fifty cannon, double-shotted

Union cannon stopping a Confederate charge

with canister, belched smoke and flame into the oncoming gray lines. Men dropped, but the lines keep coming. More shells fell. More men dropped. It was men against machines, flesh against iron.

At long last the iron won. The thinned gray lines faltered, broke, and fell back across the body-strewn field into the forest. There was a lull. Then Hardee tried again with fresh troops. Again he was repulsed. Then Bragg tried. He, too, was repulsed. The battlefield was silent as the Federals watched the woods.

About 4:00 p.m. another gray line emerged to make one last effort to crack the blue line. Although it came nearer to success, again Union artillery drove it back. When Hardee asked for more men and Bragg replied that he had none to send, Hardee refused to order another assault. Both the Confederates and the sun disappeared into the cedars shortly before 5:00 p.m.

Rosecrans's army, after ten hours of desperate fighting, held onto its thin slice of ground. It was low on ammunition. It was out of food. It was New Year's Eve. Under the bright light of a full moon, a man in gray called out to a man in blue crouched behind a rail fence digging a trench.

"Hello, Yank. How do you like *that* for a New Year's gift?"

Rosecrans called a council of war. When his generals arrived at his log cabin headquarters, they found the commanding general seated on a campstool in front of the fireplace. The only light came from the fire and a pale candle stuck in the socket of a bayonet. Rosecrans offered his seat to General Wood who hobbled in on crutches, but Wood declined, saying he would stand. The mud-covered generals were solemn as their commander asked them for their thoughts.

Alex McCook, never at a loss for words, said shortly, "I would like Bragg to repay me for my two horses lost today."

He was downcast. His corps, which did the bulk of the fighting, had lost more than 5,000 men: 676 were killed, including two generals; 2,821 were wounded; and 2,110 were captured or missing. McCook advised withdrawing to Nashville. General Stanley concurred. His cavalrymen were outnumbered four to one by Rebel troopers. But Thomas and Crittenden, whose corps were still in fighting shape, opposed falling back. Rosecrans agreed.

"Gentlemen," he announced, "we fight or die right here."

Morning came, and the Union Army braced itself for battle. There was none. Scouts reported that Bragg's army was as badly crippled as theirs. So Rosecrans held. Some of his men had only a few ears of corn to eat. Some had a little coffee and hardtack. Some cut meat from dead horses and boiled it. When night fell it rained again. The weather was raw and miserable.

At dawn on January 2, 1863, Rosecrans and his army were still in position in front of Murfreesboro.

Bragg made another attack in the afternoon, but again Union artillery drove him back. That night, with only 20,000 men fit to fight, Bragg examined McCook's papers, captured when his wagon train was burned. They indicated that Rosecrans commanded 70,000 men, and Bragg assumed that by now they all were at Murfreesboro, or soon would be.

The next day Bragg held a council of war. His corps commanders agreed to withdraw. After dark the Confederate Army retreated south in a drenching rain. Hardee led the way, leaving behind nearly 2,000 badly wounded.

Sunday morning, January 4, dawned bright and quiet. Rosecrans, after attending Mass at his headquarters, learned that Murfreesboro had been evacuated. Since Bragg quit the field, the victory went to Rosecrans.

The Union Army spent the Sabbath burying its 1,730 dead, a ritual that one man described in his diary:

> *What terrible sights we behold! We found men with their heads torn off, some with their bowels torn from them, some with their faces half gone, some with both legs torn off. One boy was lying with his hands clasped above his head, as though his last words were a prayer.*

The Battle of Stones River had the highest casualty rate of the Civil War, with both sides losing about one-third of their men. Union losses—killed, wounded, and missing—were 13,249. Confederate losses—killed, wounded, and missing—were 10,266.

Many soldiers, after a year and a half of war, were inured to death. During battle they were so engrossed with their own struggles that when they saw one or another go down, they thought, *There goes poor so and so. Well, it will be my turn next.* The dangers did not concern them until afterward when they went out with details to bury the dead.

On January 5 Rosecrans marched triumphantly into Murfreesboro, banners waving and bands playing, to telegraph President Lincoln:

> *God has crowned our arms with victory! The enemy are badly beaten, and in full retreat.*

Although it was a dubious victory, it helped bolster the Emancipation Proclamation, which had been signed on January 1. Lincoln wired back:

> *God bless you, and all with you. Please tender to all, and accept for yourself, the nation's gratitude for your and their skill, endurance and dauntless courage.*

Now the battle of the official reports began. Although Rosecrans was accorded the victory, he had failed to destroy Bragg's army. A scapegoat was needed. It was Alex McCook.

Rosecrans's first official report, written on the battlefield on January 3, cited McCook for having a faulty position, stating that McCook faced southeast instead of due south, causing his corps to be *partially surprised, thrown into confusion and driven back.*

McCook fought back. His official report, written five days later, defended himself by stating that he formed his lines exactly as ordered by Rosecrans:

> *At one o'clock A.M. on the thirtieth I received an order from General Rosecrans . . . that the left of my line should rest on the right of General Negley's division and my right was to be thrown forward until it became parallel, or nearly so, with Stone River. . . .*
>
> *I have been thus particular on account of the Commanding General's dispatch to the General-in-Chief, and also from erroneous reports sent to the public by newspaper correspondents.*

Scathing articles appeared in the press about the fighting ability of McCook's corps. Reporters also criticized McCook personally. This was his second disaster. The *New York Times* correspondent wrote:

> *At present the sentiment of the entire army is hostile to . . . McCook. . . . I imagine it will not be many days before there will be a change in the leadership. . . .*

But there was no change. One of Lincoln's strongest traits was loyalty to his generals. Not only did Lincoln retain McCook, but he sent his eldest son, Robert Todd Lincoln, on vacation from his studies at Harvard, out to Dayton, Ohio, several weeks later when Alex was married to Kate Phillips. It was one of the most lavish war weddings in the North. On January 29 the *Dayton Daily Empire* reported,

> *The city is electrified today by the arrival of a number of distinguished guests . . . for the marriage of Major-General A. D. McCook to a beautiful, amiable, and accomplished young lady of this city.*

It was high noon when a radiant Kate Phillips came down the stairway of her home on the arm of her father, Jonathan Dickinson Phillips, Esquire.

The marriage was celebrated in the parlor by the Reverend Thomas E. Thomas, pastor of the First Presbyterian Church.

The *Empire* reported on the affair:

> . . . *the most brilliant wedding that, within our knowledge, ever transpired here. Among the visitors were Governor Tod and staff, General Wright and staff, Governor Morton (Ind.) and staff, ex-Governor Dennison. . . . Mr. Bob Lincoln (son of the President), Judge McCook and wife . . . and other members of the groom's family and guests.*

After the reception the bride and groom, accompanied by their wedding party, took a train south to Cincinnati for a large reception in their honor. The January 30 edition of the *Cincinnati Times* reported:

> *A very brilliant party took place . . . last evening. Today the bridal party took passage on the steamer General Buell for Louisville. The General will return immediately to his post and will, no doubt, fight the harder as he now has two Unions to defend.*

In Louisville the wedding party stayed at the Galt House Hotel, where formal pictures were taken. Then Kate returned to Dayton and Alex returned to Murfreesboro. There he found that Rosecrans's slain chief of staff had been replaced by Brigadier General James A. Garfield.

Garfield, sent out from Washington by Stanton, urged Rosecrans to remove both McCook and Crittenden from command and replace them with Buell and McDowell. Garfield argued at length but in vain.

"I hate to injure two such good fellows," Rosecrans replied.

Quick to lose his temper and quick to cool off, Rosecrans often would fling his arm impulsively around the shoulder of a person whom he had just castigated. Now, weighing the defeats of Buell and McDowell against the faults of McCook and Crittenden, Rosecrans decided to keep the generals with whom he was pushing Bragg south.

At Murfreesboro, Rosecrans rested and rebuilt his Army of the Cumberland. At Tullahoma, twenty miles south, Bragg rested and rebuilt

Alex and Kate on their wedding trip in Louisville

his Army of Tennessee. Like two bloodied lions, they licked their wounds and growled at each other.

Meanwhile, spring came to Tennessee. So did many Northerners whose sons were in Rosecrans's army. Homes of Murfreesboro residents, who had fled with Bragg's army, were occupied by visitors. Rosecrans and his staff lived in a large townhouse with a beautiful garden, while his three corps surrounded and protected the town.

McCook's Twentieth Corps was camped on a plantation two and a half miles south of Murfreesboro. For his men Alex scheduled ballgames, boxing and wrestling matches, dances, and religious services. And for their visiting families he staged parades and reviews.

Kate McCook, arriving in March, discovered that Alex's plantation mansion headquarters was a lively place overflowing with hospitality. The general and his staff were a very jolly set, and there was a good deal of fun with athletic games, singing of songs in chorus, and a continuous flow of official and unofficial callers. During the day Alex and Kate rode horseback and reviewed troops. In the evening they entertained at dinner parties.

General Garfield was a frequent guest. In spite of his reservations about McCook's fighting abilities, Garfield admired his fine singing voice. Writing to his wife Lucretia, Garfield enclosed a stanza of a song that Alex had sung

> *finely. It is very beautiful. His wife copied it for me.*

As Kate's visit neared its end, Alex sat down to write his new mother-in-law.

> *Headqtrs: 20th Army Corps*
> *Murfreesboro, Tenn. April 1, 1863*
>
> *My dear Mama Phillips,*
>
> *As I have a little time, before going to ride, I write you to let you know how happy and comfortable my precious Kate is.*
>
> *Old Mr. A. McD. McCook makes no mistakes, and never did he enjoy such a complete success as his marriage to Kate, your much cherished daughter. She is everything that a wife should be and I am, I assure you, much more happy than I ever dreamed I could be.*
>
> *Her visit to me, my dear Mama, will ever be remembered both by her and myself as one of the very brightest spots in the springtime of our existence.*
>
> *Your affectionate and devoted son,*
>
> *A. McD. McCook*

After Kate departed, Clement Vallandigham arrived. He was the boyhood friend of Alex's brother, Colonel George McCook, who had argued successfully for Vallandigham's right to take his seat in Congress in 1858.

Vallandigham was now the leader of the Peace Democrats who wanted to negotiate peace with the South. Since this was certain to result in independence for the Confederacy, Republicans considered them traitors and called them Copperheads, after the poisonous snake.

While campaigning for governor of Ohio that spring, Vallandigham had been arrested for making antiwar speeches. Tried and convicted of disloyalty, he was sentenced to prison. But Lincoln, loath to make him into a martyr, commuted the sentence to exile in the South. Vallandigham was taken to Murfreesboro where Rosecrans had him escorted to the Confederate lines under a flag of truce and handed over to the pickets.

Stanton was not happy about Lincoln's leniency toward traitors, nor his choice of generals, nor his strategies for winning the war. But Stanton knew that his powers as secretary of war were limited. He could push the president only so far. Lincoln's "no" was a firm "no."

The secretary of war, after a year in office, was a driven man. Barely tolerating the lesser minds around him, he worked feverishly day and night in his third-floor office at the War Department. Standing behind a high desk, he bullied and threatened and courted and cajoled everyone from generals and admirals to cabinet members and congressmen, turning on them savagely and whiplashing them with his sarcastic tongue if they failed him.

Stanton spared no one, least of all himself, in his messianic mission to save the Union.

Desperate for battlefield victories, Stanton had decided to put his commanding generals in competition with each other. On March 1 he sent identical letters to each one, offering the position of a vacant major generalcy in the regular U.S. Army to the first general who achieved an important and decisive victory.

All of the generals silently pocketed their letters, except one. Rosecrans took his as an insult and fired back an outraged reply, saying that as an officer and citizen he was

> *degraded at such an auctioneering of honors. Have we a general who would fight for his own personal benefit when he would not for honor and for his country?*

Your Obt Servt
A. Lincoln

President Lincoln in 1863

Rosecrans had only contempt for the author of such an offer. As the simmering hostility between the two men boiled over, Rosecrans criticized the secretary of war openly to reporters, predicting that Stanton would have to go. But the general underestimated his foe.

From this time forward, Rosecrans discovered that all his requests—from cavalry to revolving rifles—were treated coldly by the War Department. The Army of the Cumberland, so ignored that it began calling itself the "stepchild army," nevertheless was badgered to give battle.

Angrily, Rosecrans called a conference of his corps and division commanders. After being bloodied at Stones River, they refused to fight Bragg again until they were strong enough to whip him. All agreed that they would ignore Stanton's order and remain in Murfreesboro until they were prepared to launch a successful attack.

"Stanton is a natural-born fool!" exploded Alex McCook in disgust.

The unfortunate and impolitic remark was likely to reach the secretary of war within the hour. Rosecrans's chief of staff, General Garfield, was a good friend of Stanton. Behind Rosecrans's back, Garfield was telegraphing Stanton that, regardless of Rosecrans's protestations, the Army of the Cumberland was ready to march.

Rosecrans, deciding to have nothing more to do with Stanton, went directly to Lincoln. The president, informed that sixteen of Rosecrans's generals advised against a premature advance, countermanded Stanton's order.

The incensed secretary of war became obsessed. He would get rid of Rosecrans. He would get total control of the war. It was just a matter of time.

Meanwhile, he turned his vast energies toward the one general who obeyed his orders promptly and unquestioningly: Ulysses S. Grant. For months he had been trying to capture Vicksburg, the key to control of the Mississippi River.

With Grant was Daniel McCook's eldest son, Dr. Latimer McCook.

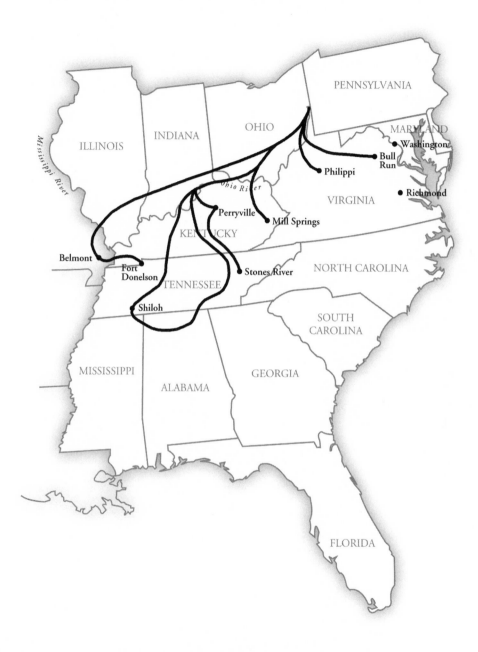

*Territory trod by the Fighting McCooks
in their quest to save the Union*

Chapter 13

DR. LATIMER McCOOK
at Vicksburg

Vicksburg crouched like a snarling white tiger atop the two-hundred-foot clay bluffs overlooking the mighty Mississippi River. Fiercely protecting some 250 miles of river still in Confederate hands, Vicksburg's 172 heavy cannon were bared, like iron fangs, to devour any Union gunboat within range.

Secretary of War Edwin Stanton desperately wanted Vicksburg. It would give the North control of the Mississippi and cut the Confederacy in half. No longer could food and arms from Texas, Arkansas, and Louisiana come east to resupply Rebel armies.

Grant had been given the Army of the Tennessee to do the job. Accompanying the army was a tall and lanky physician with a finely chiseled face and curly chestnut beard. Accompanying the physician were two dogs always by his side.

Forty-three-year-old Dr. Latimer Abraham McCook was Daniel and Martha's first child. Born on April 26, 1820, above the former Black Horse Tavern in Canonsburgh, Pennsylvania, he was named for his maternal grandfather, Abraham Latimer, a prosperous merchant. In 1824, when Daniel McCook moved his family to Ohio, four-year-old Latimer shared the wagon with his two-year-old brother George and the little brass cannon.

Not as hot-tempered nor as high-spirited as his younger brothers, Latimer was the quiet and sensitive one, as gentle as the legendary Johnny Appleseed who trod the fields and forests of eastern Ohio sowing apple seeds. There were Johnny Appleseed orchards scattered from the Ohio River to the Great Lakes. Two were near the McCook home in Carrollton.

Studying medicine came naturally to Latimer. His mother, besides bearing and raising twelve children, served as a midwife for the people of Carrollton. His Uncle John was an old-fashioned country doctor, and his Uncle George was a renowned surgeon.

Latimer apprenticed with his Uncle George in New Lisbon, working beside his cousin, George Latimer McCook, the surgeon's elder son. In 1844, when Dr. George was appointed professor of surgery at Willoughby Medical College in Chagrin, Ohio, the two cousins entered as students. Their costs were three dollars for matriculation, fifty-five dollars for lecture tickets, and fifty-five dollars for room and board for forty weeks.

Graduating from Willoughby in 1845, Latimer married Eliza McLain, the seventeen-year-old daughter of a New Lisbon drover. They settled in the village of Sullivan, Ohio, where he established his practice and she gave birth to a son, Alexander, who died in infancy. Then, in the fall of 1847, the young couple joined the McCook family in southern Illinois, where Daniel McCook was building Martha Furnace, his iron-making venture.

While Daniel was going west, his elder brother was going east. After one of Dr. George's innovative eye surgeries was written up in the British medical journal *The Lancet*, he was offered the chair of surgery at Washington University in Baltimore. After teaching there for two years, Dr. George returned to the Ohio Valley in 1849. Finding New Lisbon in decline, he moved his family to Pittsburgh, where he established a large practice and became chief surgeon for the Pennsylvania Railroad.

Unfortunately, the success that always surrounded Dr. George seemed to elude his brother Daniel. When Martha Furnace failed, Daniel McCook hit bottom. He also hit the bottle, and his close-knit family began to unravel. Martha and the children remained in Illinois while Daniel went east to Washington. Also leaving Illinois, but heading west, was Daniel's daughter-in-law Eliza. The mysterious disappearance of Latimer's young wife was never explained by the tight-lipped McCooks. Eventually, everyone just referred to Dr. Latimer as a widower.

After four years, when Daniel took the pledge to stop drinking, Martha and the younger children joined him in Washington. But Latimer remained in Illinois, practicing medicine in Pekin. He lived alone at the Tazewell House, until his brother Edwin joined him after resigning from the U.S. Naval Academy.

The two brothers were close. When Edwin joined Colonel John Logan's Thirty-first Illinois, Latimer also volunteered to serve the regiment as a contract surgeon.

There had been 115 surgeons in the U.S. Army Medical Department when Fort Sumter fell. Twenty-four went South. With each Union volunteer regiment needing a surgeon and an assistant surgeon, Northern physicians rushed to fill the vacuum. Surgeons, commissioned as majors, were paid $165 a month. Assistant surgeons, serving as first lieutenants or captains, earned $130.

Latimer, for his own reasons, was not a "Fighting" McCook. Declining to take the medical exam that would make him an officer, he served as a civilian contract surgeon, receiving $100 a month.

During the Civil War, twice as many soldiers died from diseases—pneumonia, dysentery, typhoid fever, and malaria—as were killed in combat. Dysentery, striking almost three-fourths of the men, was treated with epsom salts in the morning and opium in the evening. Malaria, suffered by about half of the men, was relieved by quinine six times a day and opium when the pain became unbearable.

During battle doctors worked near the front lines, usually in a commandeered farmhouse. Bullets caused almost 95 percent of wounds, with about 5 percent coming from artillery fire and only a fraction from bayonets. Often minié bullets splintered the bones so badly that there was no choice but to amputate. Protesting soldiers had to be held down on kitchen tables and chloroformed so that surgeons could saw off their arms and legs. The amputated limbs were thrown out a window where farm hogs often finished them off.

During battle the gore was bad enough. After battle it was worse. Physicians found the dead, wounded, and dying from both sides lying where they fell. There were men with their heads torn off, some with their faces half gone, some with both legs missing. Some, still alive, had their entrails torn out and piled on the ground beside them. Some had both eyes shot out. Others had their jaws torn off, hanging by a strip of skin with their tongues lolling out of their mouths, still trying to talk.

Many of the western soldiers in the Union Army were grandsons and great-grandsons of the tough Scotch-Irish immigrants who had trudged

Charles Dana

over the Allegheny Mountains to settle in the Ohio River Valley. Most of the western soldiers, in trying to save the nation, bore their wounds as stoically as their forefathers had borne their hardships in trying to settle it.

During the Civil War, as during the Whiskey Rebellion, liquor played a leading role. Plentiful in hospital supplies, it often posed problems. After the Battle of Shiloh, Major General John Logan heard that his soldiers were obtaining large quantities of whiskey. Investigating, he discovered that Dr. Latimer McCook's signature had been forged on orders directing the dispensary to release it for "medicinal purposes." The culprits were never discovered.

Liquor also played a role in the rocky career of Dr. Latimer's commanding general, Ulysses S. Grant. Grant had been removed from command after the Battle of Fort Donelson, in part because Halleck heard rumors of heavy drinking. Grant was removed from command after the Battle of Shiloh, in part because Halleck again heard rumors of heavy drinking.

Grant was going to resign, but Sherman talked him out of it. Citing his own removal from command of the Army of the Cumberland in the fall of 1861 and his subsequent reinstatement in the Army of the Tennessee, Sherman advised him to stick it out. Grant did, and their friendship was cemented.

Halleck's continued animosity toward Grant, the "Unconditional Surrender" hero of Fort Donelson, perplexed Lincoln and Stanton. They needed to know more about the controversial general whom they had never met. So Stanton sent Charles Dana west.

Dana was the former managing editor of the *New York Tribune*, responsible for the phrase "Forward to Richmond" that had helped precipitate the disastrous Battle of Bull Run. After the equally disastrous Battle of Shiloh, Horace Greeley, publisher of the *Tribune*, turned against the war. He also turned against Dana, who was fired in April 1862. Stanton hired him in May, and in June he sent Dana west.

Ostensibly Dana was to audit unsettled claims against quartermasters. Actually he was to assess Grant and report back to Stanton by secret telegraphic code. Arriving at Grant's headquarters on July 4, Dana found a commonplace man whom he described as "modest," "honest," and "disinterested." Grant was dominated by his chief of staff, Lieutenant Colonel John A. Rawlins, who ran the headquarters with an iron hand and kept Grant sober.

Unlike Rosecrans, Grant was not brilliant. Unlike McClellan, he was not arrogant. Unlike both, he was not hard to handle. Grant's assessment of himself was found in his own words:

> *For a soldier his duties are plain. He is to obey the orders of all those placed over him and whip the enemy wherever he meets him.*

Stanton had his man.

Grant was restored to command of the Army of the Tennessee. Halleck was ordered back to Washington to serve as general-in-chief of the army and military advisor to Lincoln. It would suit his bureaucratic talents and get him off Grant's back in the west.

Dana's report also secured the support of Lincoln. In the future, whenever people complained about Grant's heavy drinking or heavy casualties, the president had a ready answer.

"I can't spare this man," Lincoln would say. "He fights."

Stanton ordered the telegraph lines kept open late at night at the War Department so he could hold private "conversations" with Grant at his headquarters in Memphis, Tennessee. Foremost on Stanton's mind was capturing Vicksburg and opening up the Mississippi River.

By the fall of 1862 most of the river was in Union hands. On April 7 General John Pope, commanding the Army of the Mississippi, had captured Island #10 and opened up the northern portion of the river. On April 25 Rear Admiral David G. Farragut, commanding the West Gulf Blockading Squadron, had captured New Orleans and opened up the southern portion. Only Vicksburg and Port Hudson, 240 river miles south, were still held by the Rebels. If Vicksburg fell, Port Hudson would not be far behind.

After spending the fall gathering supplies, Grant launched a two-pronged attack against Vicksburg in mid-December. He, with forty thousand men, marched south from Memphis to strike from the land while Sherman, with twenty-three thousand men, boarded transports to strike from the river.

However, on December 20, while the campaign was under way, Confederate cavalry, under Generals Nathan Bedford Forrest and Earl Van Dorn, destroyed Grant's telegraph communications and his supply depot at Holly Springs, Mississippi. Grant, calling off his attack on

Vicksburg, returned to Memphis. Sherman, not notified of Grant's retreat, carried out his part of the campaign on December 29 and was defeated with heavy loss of life.

During that winter Grant tried again and again. Moving his army to the west bank of the Mississippi, he made a series of assaults on Vicksburg by land and water. All ended in failure. Finally, Grant decided that if he could not capture the town, he would move the river.

He ordered Major General James P. McPherson's Seventeenth Corps to dig a canal from the Mississippi to Lake Providence, a small Louisiana lake some fifty miles west. Part of the Mississippi would be diverted into the lake and then sent south on a meandering 470-mile course through swamps and bayous until it rejoined the main channel far below Vicksburg. The Confederate bastion would be bypassed.

Grant's men digging a canal to divert the Mississippi River

The Mississippi refused to move. Its strong current widened canals. Water flooded the countryside. Snakes and wildcats attacked soldiers who were dredging tons of mud from swamps and sawing off trees eight feet under water to clear channels for gunboats. Dr. Latimer McCook and the other physicians in Grant's army could not save the hundreds of men who were dying from cholera, smallpox, pneumonia, typhoid, and dysentery. Furthermore, there was no dry land in which to bury them.

By spring Vicksburg was still a Southern stronghold, and the Army of the Tennessee was mired in the mud. Grant was depressed. The press reported him drinking heavily again. Some members of the president's cabinet were calling for his removal. Lincoln's support for Grant was wavering.

Then Charles Dana reappeared. On March 23, 1863, he called on Rear Admiral David Porter at his Mississippi Squadron headquarters in Memphis. Two weeks later Dana arrived at Grant's headquarters on a Mississippi riverboat. Explaining his mission, Dana stayed at Grant's side until it was completed.

Presently a new plan was announced for capturing Vicksburg.

The Army of the Tennessee would march down the west bank of the Mississippi while Admiral Porter's gunboats and transports slipped past Vicksburg's batteries on a moonless night. Thirty miles south of the city, the navy would ferry the army across the river to the east bank. Grant would attack Vicksburg from the south.

It was a most unmilitary maneuver. Grant's West Point–trained corps commanders, Sherman and McPherson, were opposed. But Charles Dana was enthusiastic. He rode horseback down the west bank of the river to show how easily it could be done. And, as his clinching argument, he said that Admiral Porter was willing to try it.

So on the moonless night of April 16, Porter's fleet slipped down the river. Confederate batteries, discovering their presence, fired 525 rounds of ammunition and scored sixty-eight hits. Five of the seven transports and all eight gunboats got through.

By the end of April Grant's army had been ferried back across the river to the high and dry east bank. Then, after routing smaller Rebel forces at Port Gibson, Raymond, Jackson, and Champion Hill, Grant galloped swiftly toward Vicksburg with Dana by his side, struggling to keep up.

As Grant's sixty-thousand-man Army of the Tennessee approached, Confederate Lieutenant General John C. Pemberton withdrew his thirty thousand men behind the Vicksburg fortifications. Mammoth earthworks surrounded the town. Massive forts guarded the roads. Batteries on steep bluffs were buttressed by tangled masses of felled timber.

Grant assaulted the citadel in a frontal attack on May 19. It failed. He tried again on May 22. Again and again men were sent forward over blood-soaked ground. Again and again they were repulsed. Union casualties climbed to 3,119 while the Rebels, behind their battlements, lost fewer than 500.

Grant had expected Vicksburg to fall quickly. It did not. So he settled in for a siege.

Twelve miles of trenches, like a noose, were dug around the city. Union soldiers started firing from 50 to 100 rounds of ammunition every day. An around-the-clock artillery and gunboat barrage began with 220 cannon dispatching as many as 2,800 missiles every twenty-four hours. Inside the city, thirty thousand Rebel troops dug in their heels while some three thousand starving civilians burrowed in caves and began eating their horses and mules and dogs and cats.

May passed into June. As the siege slogged on, Grant's chief of staff, Colonel Rawlins, began to worry. Rawlins knew that Grant, when not fighting, was bored. When bored, he drank. Although Grant had promised Rawlins that he would not touch liquor again during the war, Rawlins found a case of wine outside Grant's tent on June 5. He heard that the general had been imbibing with one of the surgeons.

The next day Grant left from Chickasaw Bayou on a steamboat with Charles Dana to make an inspection tour of the Yazoo River.

A newspaperman, Sylvanus Cadwallader of the *Chicago Times*, was aboard and saw Grant stagger out of the barroom on the boat. When the captain refused to try to get the tipsy general to bed, Cadwallader took the job on himself. After getting Grant into his stateroom, the reporter locked the door, began throwing bottles of whiskey out the window into the river, got Grant into his bunk, and fanned him to sleep.

The next morning at breakfast Grant was sober. An hour later Cadwallader was shocked to find that he was as intoxicated as the night before. Again the reporter got the bottles away. However, when they returned to Chickasaw Bayou that evening, Grant slipped over to a sutler's boat and was enjoying himself at a party when the reporter found him. Again self-appointed, Cadwallader got the tipsy general on shore and mounted on a borrowed horse named Kangaroo for the five-mile ride back to Grant's headquarters.

Grant, an expert horseman, dug in his spurs. Kangaroo reared on his hind legs and they tore off at a full gallop. The road meandered through the army camps, but the general went straight, leaving behind him a trail of toppled tents, scattered campfires, and shouted curses. When Kangaroo finally slowed down, Cadwallader seized the reins, stopped the horse, and got Grant to lie down on the ground. While the general slept, Cadwallader delivered word to Colonel Rawlins to send an ambulance. Arriving about midnight at his headquarters, Grant climbed out of the ambulance, straightened his vest, calmly said, "Good night" to the glaring Rawlins, and went to bed.

There was plenty of camp gossip about the wild excursion up the Yazoo River, but Lincoln never heard about it from Charles Dana. Although Dana corresponded by secret telegraphic code with Stanton every day, Lincoln was told only that Grant needed reinforcements.

Although Rosecrans did not get the cavalry or supplies that he needed to attack Bragg, Grant received everything he wanted to help him capture Vicksburg. By the third week in June there were some eighty-five thousand Union troops ringing the besieged town.

The soldiers waited expectantly for the explosion that would herald their triumphant entry into the barricaded place. Grant had ordered a trench dug under the largest fort in the Confederate defenses. It was to be packed with twelve hundred pounds of powder and ignited. When the fort blew up, volunteers could charge through the breech, and the rest of Grant's army would follow.

On June 25 everything was ready. The trench was ready. Volunteers from General John Logan's brigade, the Forty-fifth Illinois, Thirty-first Illinois, and Twenty-third Indiana, were ready. Union artillery, which had been pounding Vicksburg for thirty days and nights, fell silent. All eyes were fixed on the massive A-shaped fort. At 3:00 p.m. Grant nodded.

Earthquakes rocked the ground. Mountains of yellow dirt flew into the air. Fires sprang from burning powder. Confederate soldiers were tossed about like rag dolls. Some were buried under falling clods of earth. Others

Union soldiers charging the Vicksburg defenses

fell into Union lines. A crater, thirty-five feet in diameter, was glimpsed through the whirling smoke and dust.

With a cheer Logan's men jumped in and ran to the far side. But, climbing out, they came face to face with Confederate cannon belching grape and canister.

Falling back into the crater, torn and mangled, the Union soldiers were trapped. Lighted grenades and shells were tossed down on their cringing bodies, so tightly packed that one explosion could kill and wound a dozen men. For almost twenty-four blood-filled hours they held the position called the "slaughter pen."

"My God," Logan cried in horror. "They are killing my bravest men in that hole!"

Another brave man, carrying a medical bag, jumped in to bandage their wounds. A month earlier, Dr. Latimer McCook had looked on help-lessly as thousands of Union soldiers, dead and wounded from the failed assaults of May 19 and 22, lay unburied and untended for six days between enemy lines in the broiling Mississippi sun. Corpses swelled to twice their size, some bursting open and spewing a nauseous stench. Wounded men cried desperately for help.

During battle Grant did not see dead men, nor did he hear the pleas of the injured. Feeling that it would indicate weakness on his part, Grant refused to ask for a truce to bury his dead and rescue his wounded.

Confederate General Pemberton, a Pennsylvanian who was fighting for the South, finally sent a message to Grant under a flag of truce:

> *For God's sake remove your dead and care for your wounded or*
> *I will.*

When Grant still did nothing, Pemberton ordered a cease-fire so those Union soldiers still alive could be pulled to safety.

On July 3, 1863, after forty-seven days of siege, Pemberton asked for terms of surrender. Grant, as at Fort Donelson, said that he would accept nothing less than unconditional surrender.

Then, several hours later, in a strange and uncharacteristic move that was opposed by all his corps and division commanders, Grant countermanded himself and paroled Pemberton's entire army. Over thirty thousand Rebel officers and men were set free after promising not to fight again unless they had been exchanged for Northern prisoners.

A week later, when Port Hudson fell, its eight thousand prisoners were also ordered to be paroled. A total of thirty-eight thousand Confederate soldiers were freed in the west.

The paroles were unenforceable and the orders were surprising, especially in view of Lincoln's ire over those Union generals, including Grant, who did not pursue and capture Rebel armies but let them slip away to fight again another day.

⌣

Charles Dana's mission was over. Never having left Grant's side, and having been in constant touch with Stanton by telegraph, Dana returned to Washington to await his next assignment.

Meanwhile, in the east, the Army of the Potomac had been fighting two more battles with Robert E. Lee.

Union Major General Joseph Hooker had been appointed by Lincoln, without consulting Stanton, to replace the defeated Burnside after the Battle of Fredericksburg. In April Hooker took the Army of the Potomac on what western soldiers dryly called "its annual excursion to Richmond."

On May 1 Hooker's 130,000 met Lee's 60,000 at Chancellorsville. After three days of heavy fighting, it was another Union defeat. Northern casualties were 17,000. Confederate losses were 12,800.

"My God, my God," cried Lincoln in despair. "What will the country say? What *will* the country say?"

Meanwhile, Lee was invading the North again. Marching up through the Shenandoah Valley into Pennsylvania, Lee's advance units almost reached the state capital of Harrisburg. Lincoln, hurriedly replacing Hooker with Major General George G. Meade, sent him after Lee. Meade was the fifth commander of the Army of the Potomac in a year.

On July 1 Meade's 85,000 caught up with Lee's 65,000 near the village of Gettysburg. The fighting raged savagely for three days in the greatest battle ever fought on the North American continent. On the third day, in a desperate attempt to break the impasse, Lee ordered Brigadier General George E. Pickett's division to charge the center of the Union line. Some 13,000 Confederates marched in perfect parade formation across an open field and up the slope of Cemetery Ridge into Union cannon. It was mass slaughter. Finally, Lee quit the field, having suffered more than 25,000 casualties.

The victory went to Meade. But, to Lincoln's disgust, he did not pursue. Lee slipped away to fight again another day.

Nevertheless, July 4, 1863, was a glorious day in the North. Cannon boomed continually to celebrate three major Union victories. Grant had defeated Pemberton at Vicksburg, Meade had defeated Lee at Gettysburg, and Rosecrans had defeated Bragg at Tullahoma.

Rosecrans, finally attacking, had followed the West Point wisdom of not moving until completely ready and then moving with great speed. Advancing on June 25, Rosecrans skillfully outmaneuvered Bragg at Tullahoma and sent him reeling back across the Tennessee River into Chattanooga. The masterly campaign, waged in seventeen consecutive days of rain and mud, was the least bloody major Union victory of the war.

Union losses were 83 killed, 473 wounded, and 13 missing. Confederate casualties were not reported by Bragg. The Union Army, however, captured 1,634 Rebel officers and men.

On July 4 General Alexander McCook was in his usual high spirits. His corps had fought well against Hardee at Liberty Gap. His old rival was in full retreat. Alex, always an expansive host, held a festive Independence Day dinner party at his headquarters in Winchester. Two brass bands entertained Rosecrans and all his corps and division commanders.

But Rosecrans's victory attracted little attention from either the War Department or the Northern press, overshadowed as it was by the great Union victories at Vicksburg and Gettysburg. Stung, the testy Rosecrans telegraphed Stanton:

> *I beg in behalf of this army that the War Department may not overlook so great an event because it is not written in letters of blood.*

Rosecrans's tart tongue did nothing to alleviate his private war with Stanton. When Rosecrans sent emissaries to Washington to plead for more cavalry, they got a rude reply.

"He shall not have another damned man," growled the secretary of war.

Rosecrans, fighting Bragg in front and Stanton in the rear, nevertheless was ordered to act quickly and get to Chattanooga. But Bragg acted first. He sent Brigadier General John Hunt Morgan with twenty-five hundred cavalrymen into Kentucky to destroy the railroads and bridges in Rosecrans's rear, cutting off his supplies from the main Union Army depot in Louisville.

Then, after successfully completing his assignment, Morgan took off on a long-cherished mission. On July 8, despite Bragg's orders forbidding it, Morgan ferried twenty-five hundred troopers and their horses across the Ohio River in captured steamboats to raise hell in Indiana and Ohio.

Morgan's Raiders swept through southern Indiana like locusts. They cut telegraph lines. They burned military supplies. They seized mills and factories and sold them back to their owners in return for not putting them to the torch. They repeated this over and over until the name "Morgan's Raiders" paralyzed entire communities.

Brigadier General John Hunt Morgan

Heading east into Ohio, they covered ninety miles in thirty-five hours. Crossing the Whitewater River on July 13, they burned bridges behind them to slow down more than four thousand pursuing Union troops under the commands of Brigadier Generals Edward H. Hobson and James M. Shakelford. Meanwhile a fleet of steamboats chugged up the Ohio River carrying thousands of Union cavalrymen under Brigadier General Henry Moses Judah, commanding the Third Division of the Army of the Ohio.

By General Judah's side was Major Daniel McCook. Ever since his son Robert's death at the hand of guerrilla Frank Gurley a year earlier, McCook had been looking for Gurley.

Daniel and Martha McCook were living at Mrs. Hannah Garrison's boarding house in Cincinnati. Whenever a new batch of Confederate prisoners arrived in town en route to Northern prison camps, McCook went down to the railway station with his Henry rifle. There was no doubt in anyone's mind what he planned to do when he found the guerrilla leader.

Now, hearing that Gurley was riding with Morgan, Daniel slipped away without telling Martha, and joined General Judah's staff as a volunteer.

In the spirit of the ancient Scottish clan chieftains, Daniel McCook's eyes sparkled at the thought of avenging his son's death. With relish he told General Judah that, regardless of the orders he received or how much restraint was placed on him, he was determined to kill Frank Gurley at the first opportunity. McCook vowed to do so even if Gurley were taken prisoner.

Disembarking from the steamboats at Portsmouth, Ohio, on July 16, Judah's troopers mounted their horses and headed east after Morgan. Daniel McCook was with the lead party as they dashed through the rolling hills of southern Ohio.

Union gunboats *Moose* and *Allegheny Belle* kept on Morgan's right flank up the Ohio River. They were carrying two regiments from West Virginia under the command of Bob McCook's close friend, Colonel Rutherford B. Hayes. More troops and militias joined the chase until an estimated fifty thousand men and boys pursued Morgan at one time or another.

For most, it was pure fun and merriment, the liveliest and jolliest campaign of the war. Bands were playing. Men were singing. Women were frying chicken and baking pies to feed the pursuers. Everyone was collecting trophies of the chase, spurs and swords and guns, as proof of one of the happiest events in their lives. It was such a good time as men rarely see.

Finally Morgan was brought to bay in a narrow valley in southeast Ohio filled with ancient Indian burial mounds. With only nineteen hundred men remaining with him, Morgan knew that his last chance to escape and recross the Ohio River was the ford at nearby Buffington Island. He was moving his men across the river in a heavy fog about 4:00 a.m. on July 19 when he heard musketry in the distance.

It was General Henry Judah, with Major Daniel McCook by his side. They and their force of cavalrymen had been riding all night in the rain. Placing his artillery on a bluff above the valley, General Judah ordered an advance detachment of troopers down the slope to make a probe into the thick fog.

McCook was advised not to go. But, giving a mock salute, he spurred his sorrel charger and dashed out of sight into the fog. He and the advance scouts almost rode into the Confederate skirmish line before either side saw the other. In a barrage of rifle fire, thirty Union soldiers were captured, two were killed, and twelve were wounded.

One, shot in the abdomen, fell from his horse still clutching his rifle. It was Daniel McCook.

In the ensuing Battle of Buffington Island, Morgan was caught in the crossfire between gunboats and cavalry. Outnumbered, with his ammunition almost gone and his river crossing aborted, he escaped northward with fewer than one thousand troopers through a narrow gap in the valley. But some eight hundred of his men were captured and marched to the gunboats that would take them down the river to Cincinnati.

Also carried aboard was the mortally wounded Daniel McCook. Long aware of the dangers from his frequent displays of rashness, he had predicted that, like his sons Charles and Robert, he would die from a Rebel bullet. On the evening of July 21, 1863, his premonition came true. It was one month after his sixty-fifth birthday and two years to the night that he had nursed the dying Charlie.

The sun was setting over the great Ohio River as it wound its way west, carrying the ambitious man who had traveled it so often in his quest for success, the impatient man who had cut so many corners and stepped on so many toes, the loving man who would move heaven and earth for his sons, the charming man who had so many friends in high places, and the feisty man who on its broad bosom lost his last fight.

Major Daniel McCook had been extremely well-liked in Cincinnati, and when his body arrived, an editorial appeared in the *Daily Commercial*:

> *This community, nay, the whole State and Country, will be shocked by the intelligence of the death of Major Daniel McCook, the well known father of so many distinguished soldiers in the loyal service. . . . The record made by the McCooks is, and always will be, a part of the history of the country. . . . Let all homage by rendered to the memory of a model patriot!*

Funeral services were conducted on July 25 at Mrs. Garrison's boarding-house with the burial at Spring Grove Cemetery. The casket was escorted by an army band and military unit, followed by the carriages of General Burnside, Episcopal Bishop Charles McIlvaine, Mayor Harris, members of the city council, and the general public. Even though it was raining hard, the procession was the largest the city had seen since General Robert McCook's funeral a year earlier. Graveside rites were performed by Bishop McIlvaine, and then Daniel McCook was laid to rest with his son Robert.

Meanwhile, John Hunt Morgan had continued fleeing into northeast-ern Ohio. He and his pursuers fought the most northern engagement of the Civil War in Carroll County, near Daniel McCook's former home in Carrollton. Morgan escaped but was finally brought to bay in Columbiana County near the McCook family farm, three miles from New Lisbon, where even the little brass cannon came out to do battle.

Morgan was cornered with about four hundred men, ending an eighteen-day rampage during which he destroyed thirty-four bridges, miles of rail lines, and more than five hundred thousand dollars in property. Taken to Cincinnati, Morgan was tried as a horse thief and imprisoned in the Ohio State Penitentiary.

Then it was discovered that Frank Gurley had not been with him after all.

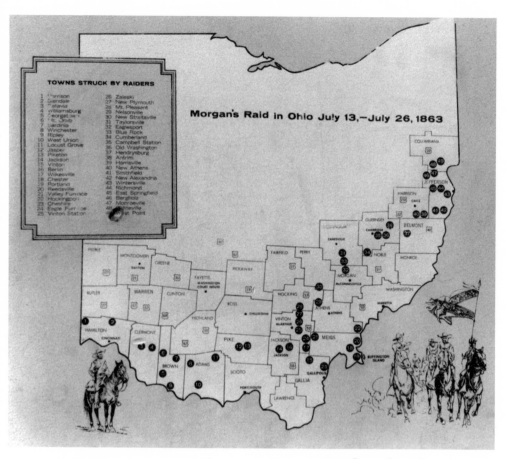

TOWNS STRUCK BY RAIDERS

1 Harrison
2 Glendale
3 Batavia
4 Williamsburg
5 Georgetown
6 Mt. Orab
7 Sardinia
8 Winchester
9 Ripley
10 West Union
11 Locust Grove
12 Jasper
13 Piketon
14 Jackson
15 Vinton
16 Berlin
17 Wilkesville
18 Chester
19 Portland
20 Reedsville
21 Valley Furnace
22 Hockingport
23 Cheshire
24 Eagle Furnace
25 Vinton Station

26 Zaleski
27 New Plymouth
28 Mt. Pleasant
29 Nelsonville
30 New Straitsville
31 Taylorsville
32 Eaglesport
33 Blue Rock
34 Cumberland
35 Campbell Station
36 Old Washington
37 Hendrysburg
38 Antrim
39 Harrisville
40 New Athens
41 Smithfield
42 New Alexandria
43 Wintersville
44 Richmond
45 East Springfield
46 Bergholz
47 Monroeville
48 Smithville
49 East Point

Morgan's Raid in Ohio July 13,–July 26, 1863

Morgan's Raiders rampaging route through Ohio

Territory trod by the Fighting McCooks
in their quest to save the Union

Chapter 14

MAJOR GENERAL ALEXANDER McCOOK
at the Battle of Chickamauga

"My God, we are doomed!" cried Alex McCook, rushing into General James Garfield's tent, holding a telegram. "My father was shot today while pursuing John Morgan!"

Alex had warned his father about taking risks. Now that indomitable and domineering man, who considered himself just as young and vigorous as any of his sons, was gone. And so it was with a heavy heart that Alex prepared his corps for the most audacious undertaking of the war in the West.

General Rosecrans was ready to attack Chattanooga.

John Hunt Morgan's earlier handiwork of ripping up the railroads had accomplished its purpose. Rosecrans, hampered in getting supplies, had to delay his pursuit of Bragg until the rails could be repaired. This brought a barrage of telegraphs from the War Department, including one on July 24:

> *The patience of the authorities here has been completely exhausted. . . . It has been said that you are as inactive as was General Buell, and the pressure for your removal has been almost as strong as it has been in his case.*

Union armies in the east and along the Mississippi River moved their supplies by water with ease. But those fighting in the vastness of the middle west had to rely on single lines of railroad running for hundreds of miles through enemy territory. Confederate cavalry was constantly tearing up the tracks and burning bridges.

Without the railroad it would mean keeping some thirty-five hundred supply wagons, each pulled by six mules, on the road continually. Since each mule ate twelve pounds of corn every twenty-four hours, it would require some 40,000 bushels or 125 tons of corn a day. The War Department did not seem to appreciate these logistics.

However, by mid-August the railroad had been repaired and Rosecrans was ready to march. Food and ammunition were flowing south to the fifty-seven-thousand-man Army of the Cumberland. On the evening of August 15 Rosecrans summoned his three corps commanders to his headquarters to reveal his plan for capturing Chattanooga. It was bold. It was brilliant. But it was difficult.

Chattanooga! The vital railroad center was the Gibraltar of the Deep South. Union armies had been lusting after it for two years. It nestled in a valley protected by the six-hundred- to one-thousand-yard-wide Tennessee River and surrounded by a tangled mass of mountains rising to twenty-four hundred feet above sea level. The South was certain that Chattanooga could not be captured.

Rosecrans, however, planned to trap Bragg in his own fortress. While Crittenden shelled the city from across the river and built pontoon bridges in preparation for crossing, it would just be a feint. The real crossings would be made by McCook and Thomas far downstream, hidden by the mountain ranges that lined the winding river. Once across, the two generals would encircle Chattanooga from the south.

Thomas was to capture the village of LaFayette, twenty-five miles south. McCook had the longer route. He was to cross two mountain ranges and seize the Western and Atlanta Railroad, forty-two miles south. It was Bragg's supply line. He would be trapped in Chattanooga.

Nothing so difficult on such tough terrain had been attempted in the war.

On August 29, as the first rays of light hit the wide, silver Tennessee River, McCook's Twentieth Corps started crossing. Thousands of silent soldiers, their gun barrels glistening in the mist, passed over a pontoon bridge at Caperton's Ferry, Alabama, forty miles west of Chattanooga. Behind them, as the water turned blue in the sunlight, came supply wagons with enough food and forage for men and animals for forty-five days plus ammunition for two major battles.

One week later the entire Twentieth Corps, three divisions of fourteen thousand men with cavalry and artillery, had crossed one of the major rivers of the South without being detected.

In the minds of McCook's men, Napoleon's passage of the Alps presented less formidable obstacles than what lay ahead. Led by General Stanley's cavalry, McCook's corps crossed Sand Mountain on narrow bridle paths over which no wheeled vehicle had ever traveled. Without unloading the wagons, four rails were inserted through each set of wheels. Then, to the music of the bugle, twenty-four men on each side lifted the lorries and carried them over seven-hundred-foot heights with much singing, yelling, and hurrahing. The mules scrambled up the steep slopes behind them. It was all one grand frolic for the young men with hard, bronzed muscles.

The march was more like a sporting event than war. The mountains were magnificent. The air was fresh as fall approached. Spirits were high as the long lines snaked through the narrow valleys, their banners waving proudly. They sensed victory as they entered Georgia. With luck "Old Rosey" would capture Atlanta and end the war. They would all be home for Christmas.

Alex sent a buoyant message off to Rosecrans by galloping messenger:

All goes on swimmingly.

Bragg, thinking an attack impossible through the mountains, had made no effort to defend the passes. By September 8 McCook was nearing his goal. However, that was the day when Bragg finally discerned that Crittenden's shelling was a feint and that McCook and Thomas had already crossed the Tennessee River. Mountaineers told Bragg that Thomas was moving toward LaFayette, but no one had any idea of McCook's whereabouts. Bragg, fearing that he soon would be trapped, had no choice but to abandon Chattanooga.

Two days later Rosecrans rode triumphantly into the vaunted citadel. Within three weeks he had crossed the mighty Tennessee and forced Bragg from Chattanooga without losing a single man. It was hailed in the Northern press as "brilliant." Rosecrans was called the greatest strategic general of the war.

Stanton telegraphed him not to halt in Chattanooga but to pursue immediately. Rosecrans agreed. It was his chance to destroy Bragg and not let him, like Lee after Gettysburg, slip away to fight again another day.

Confederate deserters told Rosecrans that Bragg's army was fleeing in panic toward Atlanta. Rosecrans sent a message to McCook, forty-two miles south, to cut off their retreat.

McCook, however, was uneasy. From his mountaintop position, he could see large clouds of dust rising over LaFayette, midway between him and Chattanooga. It indicated large forces of men and cavalry. McCook sent Stanley's cavalry to reconnoiter and discovered that Bragg was not in headlong flight after all. He had halted at LaFayette and was lying in wait, like a crouched lion, to devour Rosecrans's separated corps, as each emerged from the mountains.

McCook, knowing that Thomas was heading unsuspectingly into Bragg's trap, sent him a warning:

> *I am not desirous of fighting Bragg's whole army, and in case he is concentrated at LaFayette I am in a false position, for I could not reach you. Where is Crittenden's corps? LaFayette is the strategic position for Bragg. . . . His object will be to oppose his whole force to our fractions as they debouch from the Mountain.*

Thomas alerted Rosecrans, who now realized that Bragg had lured him out of Chattanooga with sham stories told by "deserters." With his three corps scattered some sixty miles from flank to flank, Rosecrans ordered McCook and Crittenden to unite immediately with Thomas "as a matter of life and death."

McCook received his order at midnight on September 13. Leaving Stanley's cavalry behind to harass Bragg and cover his retrograde movement, McCook started on his long and exhausting march back over the mountains and through the valleys to reach Thomas.

Bragg, in his camp at LaFayette, finally had received a report that McCook was in the mountains south of him. He could not believe it.

"Lies!" Bragg cried. "There is not an infantry soldier of the enemy south of us."

When he learned it was true, Bragg knew he would have to guard against an attack in his rear. Unaware that McCook had left the mountains and was marching north through Lookout Valley, Bragg worried about his whereabouts.

So did Rosecrans. Furious that McCook was taking the safer but longer valley route and fearful that Bragg would attack before he arrived, Rosecrans ordered McCook to find a shorter road over the mountains. McCook refused. Certain that a mountaintop march would be spotted by Bragg, McCook halted his corps until the order was rescinded.

Meanwhile, more bad news reached Rosecrans. The War Department belatedly telegraphed him what had been rumored in the east for a week or more. Bragg was being reinforced by troops from all over the Confederacy. Three of Lee's divisions had passed through Atlanta nine days earlier. General Joseph E. Johnston had sent fifteen thousand men from the Mississippi. General James Longstreet's corps had disappeared from Virginia amid reports that trains were leaving Richmond day and night.

Moreover, on September 17, Halleck telegraphed Grant:

> *Major-General Grant:*
> *The rebel government has announced that some 16,000 of the prisoners paroled by you at Vicksburg are released from their paroles and will return to duty. It is also understood that they intend to put in the ranks against Rosecrans, without exchange, all the prisoners paroled by you and General Banks.*

Rosecrans was in a state of nervous collapse. Realizing that he had made the classic military blunder of dividing his forces, he tried to unite them before Bragg could strike. So worried and anxious that he could not sleep or eat, Rosecrans paced and smoked incessantly.

By his side was the newly arrived Charles Dana, the ubiquitous aide to the secretary of war.

"I was sent here for the purpose of finding out what the government could do to aid you," Dana assured Rosecrans.

Rosecrans's staff, however, regarded Dana as an evil omen, a sinister spy who had come to undo their chief. Every evening Dana reported by telegraph to Stanton, using his secret code.

To Rosecrans's relief, Bragg had not struck by the time McCook finally emerged from the mountains on September 17 after an epic march of fifty-seven miles. Rosecrans's three corps were now within supporting distance of each other in a long narrow valley, thirteen miles south of Chattanooga, called McLemore's Cove.

A desolate place of dense forests and thick underbrush, it was scattered with crude cabins and patches of corn, tilled by settlers who barely subsisted. Through the valley ran a meandering stream called Chickamauga, a Cherokee word meaning "river of death." It was where the Indians went to cool their fevers after catching smallpox and other diseases of civilization from white settlers.

It was a poor place to fight. But if Bragg offered battle, Rosecrans could not avoid it without dishonor. He started positioning his three corps along the LaFayette Road, his escape route to Chattanooga.

Great clouds of dust rising from the forest on the other side of the creek warned Rosecrans that Bragg was moving up. By late afternoon of September 18, it was clear that the Confederates were massing opposite the Union left. Rosecrans perceived the battle plan. Bragg would try to turn Rosecrans's left flank, capture the LaFayette Road, force Rosecrans back into the valley, and destroy him at his leisure.

Rosecrans, playing a desperate game of battlefield chess, shifted his army to the left during the night. Thomas, his oldest and most experienced corps commander, was entrusted to hold the left. Crittenden took the center. McCook was to hold the right.

McCook's corps started moving at midnight. The temperature had dropped to near freezing. His troops were no longer the singing, spirited warriors who carried the wagons over the mountains. They were exhausted, hollow-eyed men who had marched continuously for five weeks and now knew that, tired and cold, they would face battle in the morning. Moving solemnly like silent ghosts, they were still moving at dawn as the fighting erupted.

The Battle of Chickamauga was touched off accidentally with both armies groping for position in the dense forest. They simply stumbled into each other. A sudden chorus of throbbing guns reached the startled ears of Rosecrans and Bragg to tell them that the battle had started.

Rosecrans had his headquarters in a little hillside cabin belonging to the widow Eliza Glenn. Since he could not see the fighting in the forest, he paced back and forth, rubbing his hands together nervously while a curious haunting smile of half-pleasure/half-pain writhed behind his beard. Nearby sat his engineer, with a map and compass and pencil, trying to pinpoint the fighting as the young widow by his side ventured guesses from the sounds of firing.

". . . about a mile fornenst John Kelly's house" . . . "nigh out about Reed's Bridge somewhar . . . ," she allowed.

The battle was reported almost hourly by Charles Dana to the secretary of war over wires that the signal corps had strung from the Glenn cabin to Chattanooga. From there the messages were relayed to Washington at 10:30 a.m., 1:00, 2:30, 3:00, 3:20, 4:00, 4:30, 5:20, and 7:30 p.m.

The fighting was fiercest on the left flank. Thomas kept calling for reinforcements, and Rosecrans kept sending divisions from Crittenden and McCook to his aid. Thomas, with most of the army under his command, held firm until late afternoon when the Confederates made a savage attack. Then he was driven back more than a mile.

The exultant Rebel yells were heard above the screaming of shells, the whistling and crackling of bullets, the neighing of frightened horses, the cries of the mangled, the shouts of the defiant, and the moans of the dying. Dead men were piled like cordwood so that fresh troops could charge. And Chickamauga Creek flowed red with blood.

Merciful darkness put an end to the madness.

As the Union Army fortressed itself, the woods echoed with the sounds of trees being felled and artillery being wheeled into position. Rosecrans ordered no campfires as they would reveal Union positions. So his men

Battle of Chickamauga

shivered in the cold and huddled together for warmth as they crouched behind barricades waiting for dawn.

Bragg no longer had Hardee with him. The two men, long antagonistic, had parted company after the Confederate retreat from Tullahoma. But formidable foes had taken Hardee's place. Rosecrans now knew, from prisoners, that some of the best fighters in the Confederacy were at Chickamauga: D. H. Hill, John B. Hood, Simon Bolivar Buckner, John C. Breckinridge, Thomas C. Hindman, and Lee's old "war horse" James Longstreet.

Longstreet had brought most of his twelve-thousand-man corps on a circuitous 925-mile train ride from Virginia. They were veterans of Bull Run, Antietam, Chancellorsville, and Gettysburg. Rosecrans refused to believe that his old West Point roommate was on the field until one of Longstreet's men was captured.

"You Yanks will find fighting tomorrow such as you have not found hitherto!" he warned.

Rosecrans estimated that Rebel reinforcements totaled about twenty-four thousand men. That would give Bragg more than seventy thousand to Rosecrans's fifty-seven thousand, approximately the forces of Napoleon and Wellington at Waterloo. Still, Rosecrans was outwardly optimistic when he wired Washington at 8:00 p.m.:

We have just concluded a terrific day's fighting and have another in prospect for tomorrow. . . . The army is in excellent condition and spirits and, by the blessing of Providence, the defeat of the enemy will be total to-morrow.

In contrast to the telegram, pessimism pervaded every dark corner of the widow Glenn's cabin at 9:00 p.m. when Rosecrans summoned his corps and division commanders to a council of war. Thomas, who had done most of the fighting, dozed in his chair. Whenever Rosecrans asked for his opinion, Thomas's large frame straightened up and he repeated, over and over, the same words.

"I would strengthen the left."

"Where are we going to take it from?" Rosecrans demanded each time. Thomas already had most of the army under his command.

Rosecrans, his eyes heavily rimmed with fatigue, revised his line to cope with the unfavorable odds. Thomas would continue to hold the left. McCook would cover both center and right. Crittenden would pull back in reserve in order to come to the aid of either.

It was 11:45 p.m. by the time Rosecrans's orders were written and read aloud by chief of staff General Garfield.

"You will defend your position with the utmost stubbornness. . . . In case our army should be overwhelmed, it will retire on Rossville and Chattanooga."

Hot coffee was served. Although his generals had been under strain for many days, some without sleep for forty-eight hours, they lingered to savor the drink. Rosecrans, as if to fortify them for the struggle ahead, asked McCook to sing a ballad of courage called the "Hymn of the Hebrew Maid." McCook's rich voice filled the little cabin.

"HER FATHER'S GOD BEFORE HER MOVED,
AN AWFUL GUIDE IN SMOKE AND FLAME. . . ."

Midnight was at hand. Thomas slept in his chair. The dozen or so other generals sipped their coffee and gazed solemnly into the fire on the hearth. They knew that in a few hours they themselves would be awful guides in smoke and flame as they led their men in fighting for the very life of the Army of the Cumberland.

Dawn arrived, cold and eerie, with the frosted and forested battlefield lying under a thick blanket of fog. The rising sun sent millions of silver threads slanting through the trees. Then the threads changed to gold and finally reddened into liquid fire that flooded the narrow valley.

It was the Sabbath, a day on which Rosecrans did not like to fight. After hearing Mass he stepped from the cabin and mounted his horse. It had been another nearly sleepless night, and Rosecrans's nerves were taut to the snapping point.

Starting on an inspection tour, he began changing picket lines and moving divisions. When General Wood seemed to move too slowly, Rosecrans was fuming when Wood finally rode up and saluted.

"Good morning, Wood," said Rosecrans, returning the salute. Then he added sternly, "General, why didn't you move sooner?"

"I moved promptly on receipt of the order," Wood replied good-naturedly. "You know I always do."

Wood's calm civility in the face of disaster was too much for Rosecrans. His nerves exploded in anger and, amid a torrent of profanity, he gave Wood a good dressing-down for his "damnable negligence." Delivered in front of Wood's staff, it was unusual and embarrassing.

Battle of Chickamauga

"Hurry up and relieve General Negley on the line!" snapped Rosecrans as he galloped off.

Riding to a hillside orchard on the southern slope of Missionary Ridge, Rosecrans established a field headquarters. For the first time he would have a partial view of the battlefield. When the fog lifted, he could see across the fields of the Brotherton farm to the woods where the enemy lay.

Starting about 9:30 a.m. the Confederates hit Thomas again and again and again. Three times they attacked, and three times they were repulsed. Thomas, already commanding six divisions, kept sending requests for more.

In contrast, a mile away, all was quiet in the Union center and right. The droning of insects was interrupted only by the distant rumble of battle. McCook's troops huddled behind their barricades, fingered their guns, and peered toward the woods where the enemy was hidden, almost a stone's throw away. The fog lifted and the day warmed. By mid-morning it was so drowsy at Rosecrans's field headquarters that Charles Dana lay down under a tree and went to sleep.

Meanwhile, Thomas kept requesting more troops and Rosecrans kept sending them. At 10:10 a.m. chief of staff Garfield sent a message to McCook:

> *General Thomas is being heavily pressed on the left. The general commanding directs you to make immediate disposition to withdraw the right, so as to spare as much force as possible to re-enforce Thomas.*

Twenty minutes later Rosecrans dictated another order for Garfield to send McCook:

> *The general commanding directs you to send two brigades, General Sheridan's division, at once and with all dispatch to support General Thomas, and send the third brigade as soon as the line can be drawn in sufficiently.*

At that moment a courier, arriving from Thomas with the thirteenth request of the morning for troops, shouted a warning that there was a gap in the line between the divisions of Reynolds and Wood.

"Brannan is out of line, and Reynolds's right is exposed!" he cried.

Rosecrans, aghast, did not take time to check the report. He ordered Wood to close ranks with Reynolds immediately. And, since Garfield was busy writing the message to McCook, Rosecrans dictated Wood's order to an aide, Major Frank S. Bond. Lacking official paper, Bond hurriedly scrawled the order on the margin of a newspaper, put it in an envelope, and marked it "Gallop." It was handed to Crittenden's chief of staff, Lieutenant Colonel Lyne Starling, who took off in a cloud of dust.

It was about 11:00 a.m. when Starling found Wood and his staff under a tree in the rear of his lines. Starling gave the envelope to one of Wood's aides, who opened it, removed the scrap of paper, wrote a receipt on the envelope, gave it back to Starling, and handed the message to Wood:

> *The general commanding directs that you close up on Reynolds as fast as possible, and support him.*

Wood was mystified. He knew that Brannan was hidden in the forest between Reynolds and himself. If he were to close up on Reynolds he would have to pull his troops out of line and march them around the rear of Brannan. It would create a quarter-mile gap in the Union line.

"My God!" exclaimed Wood. "I can't pull out of here. The very moment my troops commence to move, the Rebels will bulge right through."

At this moment McCook rode up. Wood handed him the order and asked what he should do.

"The only thing for you to do is to obey the order," replied Alex. "You do not know what assistance is wanted on the left, and you could be court martialed for not obeying it."

Wood, still stinging from the reprimand Rosecrans had given him earlier, muttered angrily, "I am glad that Catholic son-of-a-bitch put it in writing. I'll ruin him now!"

McCook galloped off, shouting reassuringly, "I will have Sheridan here before you are out."

But on his way to find Sheridan, McCook finally got the 10:30 a.m. message that he was to send Sheridan to Thomas. This left McCook with only one small division of fourteen hundred men, commanded by Davis, to put into Wood's position.

It was 11:10 a.m. Most of McCook's men were moving, having left the barricades of stone and logs they had thrown up during the night. At that moment a bone-chilling sound split the morning air. It was the Rebel yell.

Eight Confederate brigades burst out of the woods and came marching across the fields of the Brotherton farm. Twenty-three thousand Rebels, massed in battle array, came with their hats down, their bayonets at a charge, and their guns firing. It was perfect precision with flags flying and bugles blaring and cavalry galloping and cannonballs whistling through the air. It was a Napoleonic charge. It was warfare at its most triumphant. It was Longstreet.

Rosecrans, seeing them come across the sunlit fields, blanched and blessed himself. Bullets whizzed around the awakened Charles Dana, who, observing Rosecrans preparing himself for death, leaped on his horse and headed pell-mell over the ridge for Chattanooga.

Rosecrans, in removing a division to cover a gap that did not exist, had created one. Longstreet swept through it.

Davis's paltry force of fourteen hundred men, outnumbered more than ten to one, managed to fire several rounds before they were hurled like toy soldiers against Missionary Ridge. Sheridan, rushing to the rescue with two brigades, waged a ferocious fight. But in minutes his dead were lying thick upon the ground. Sheridan and his survivors were swept from the field.

"Charge them once for Old Rosey, boys!" cried Rosecrans as he stood on the hillside, trying to rally his fleeing men.

*The Brotherton farm
where Longstreet charged McCook's line*

"I will send in Laiboldt's brigade," shouted McCook as, sword in one hand and pistol in the other, he went forward with Sheridan's reserve brigade.

It was too late. Longstreet had wheeled and was rolling up the Union line. It was a complete rout. Rosecrans, McCook, Crittenden, Davis, Sheridan, Negley, Van Cleve, the general staff, and newspaper correspondents were borne to the rear by a flood of fleeing troops. They refused to rally.

"We'll talk to you, my son, when we get to the Ohio River," one old soldier shouted.

Rosecrans, his sword drawn, was last seen leading a charge. Afterward it was rumored that he was dead or captured.

No one knew what had happened to Thomas. Rumors said that he, too, had been routed and that the entire army was retreating to Chattanooga. The back road to Chattanooga was a confused mass of limping men, ambulances, mules running loose, squads of cavalry, baggage wagons, and abandoned artillery. It was the dregs of a broken army.

Word came, finally, that Rosecrans had not been killed or captured but had gone to Chattanooga to rally what remained of the Army of the Cumberland. Alex McCook followed Rosecrans's midnight orders:

> In case our army should be overwhelmed, it will retire on Rossville and Chattanooga.

McCook arrived in Chattanooga shortly after 4:00 p.m. to find that Dana had arrived first to send a frantic telegraph to Stanton:

> My report to-day is of deplorable importance. Chickamauga is as fatal a name in our history as Bull Run.

Dana had thought, as they all thought, that the entire army had been driven from the field. But Rosecrans learned by telegraph from Garfield, who had gone to investigate, that Thomas still held his position. Unaware of the rout, he was fighting with seven divisions, two-thirds of the army, on a high piece of ground called Horseshoe Ridge.

McCook and Crittenden asked permission to return to the field, but Rosecrans ordered them to wait until he had more news from Thomas. By 8:00 p.m. things were encouraging enough for Dana to wire Stanton:

> *I am happy to report that my dispatch of 4 p.m. today proves to have given too dark a view of our disaster.*

And he suggested a scapegoat:

> *The disaster might perhaps have been avoided but for the blunder of McCook in marching back from his previous advanced position. That blunder cost us four days of precious time.*

By midnight McCook and Crittenden had collected their scattered corps and joined Thomas at Rossville, where he had fallen back on a new defense line. By daylight, Thomas decided that the new Union position was too weak to defend and advised pulling back into Chattanooga. With Rosecrans's army leaving the field, the victory went to Bragg.

Chickamauga was the bloodiest battle in the western theatre of war. Union losses were 1,656 killed, 9,749 wounded, and 4,774 captured or missing. Confederate losses were greater: 2,389 killed, 13,412 wounded, and 2,003 captured or missing.

Rosecrans, in his official report, offered his explanation for the disaster. It, too, was McCook:

> *The battle of the 20th was fought with all the troops we had, and but for the extension and delay in closing in our right, we should probably have driven the enemy.*

Stanton was with Lincoln's secretary, John Hay, in the War Department when he received Rosecrans's reasons for the defeat.

"I know the reasons well enough," Stanton snorted. "Rosecrans ran away from his fighting men and did not stop for thirteen miles."

Moments later the secretary of war finished his thoughts.

"No, they need not shuffle it off on McCook. He is not much of a soldier. I never was in favor of him for a major general. But he is not accountable for this business. He and Crittenden both made pretty good time away from the fight to Chattanooga, but Rosecrans beat them both."

Northern newspapers glowed with praise for Thomas, the "Rock of Chickamauga," who held his position. They glowered with disdain for

Rosecrans, McCook, and Crittenden, who had fled from the field. Stanton planned to remove all three. But he bided his time until after the fall elections to fire Rosecrans, a popular general whom many Republicans had been touting for the presidency.

Dana continued to lay the groundwork for the removal of Crittenden and

> *that dangerous blunderhead McCook, who always imperils everything.*

In his dispatch of September 27, Dana reported that he had it on good evidence that many of the division generals would not serve under McCook and Crittenden if they retained their commands:

> *This feeling is universal among them, including men like Major Generals Palmer and Sheridan and Brigadier Generals Wood, Johnson and Hazen. The feeling in the case of McCook is deepened by the recollection of his faults at Perryville and Murfreesboro, and of the great waste of life which they caused. . . . In my judgment the removal of Crittenden and McCook is imperatively required. . . .*

Dana's dispatch was shown at once to Lincoln. Daniel McCook was no longer around to drop in at the White House and have a little chat with Lincoln to rescue his son's tattered reputation. McCook and Crittenden were relieved of their commands and ordered to report for a court of inquiry. Their corps were dissolved and consolidated into a new Fourth Corps under the command of Major General Gordon Granger.

Alex McCook, while trying to appear unscathed, took it very hard. The supremely self-confident young general, who prided himself on making no mistakes, now had made a fatal one. But he maintained for the rest of his life that he had faced death on too many battlefields, and in the presence of too many men, to require any defense of his conduct at Chickamauga.

Those who knew him agreed. While his generalship might be questioned, his courage was not.

Some people felt that Alex McCook had been elevated to high command before he had the maturity to handle a full corps in battle.

Unfortunately, his rollicking good nature and irrepressible witticisms often made him appear boisterous and swaggering. Personal mannerisms obscured his ability to fight hard and, on occasion, out-general older and more experienced commanders.

In disgrace, Alex McCook left Chattanooga. However, before he went, he issued a last message to the men of "his gallant corps" whom he had led in five battles: Shiloh, Perryville, Stones River, Tullahoma, and Chickamauga.

> *Head Quarters 20th Army Corps*
> *Chattanooga, Tenn., October 6th, 1863*
> *Officers and Soldiers of the Twentieth Army corps*
>
> *An order will soon reach you, consolidating your gallant Regiments, Brigades, and Divisions with the 21st Corps. With that order I am relieved from command in this Army and directed to report to Indianapolis, Indiana; there to appear before a Court of Inquiry.*
>
> *After being relieved from Command, I could ask no greater favor of the War Department than a thorough investigation of my conduct during the two memorable days of Chickamauga, for I do not fear the issue. My great regret will be the breaking up of the glorious associations formed after so long service in the Army of the Cumberland, and the bidding farewell to the gallant Officers and Soldiers of this Corps.*
>
> *You will have new Corps and Division commanders. To them, as you have at all times to me, yield obedience. Give them additional evidences of your discipline, zeal and patriotism in our great cause, and never lay down your arms until this unholy rebellion is crushed—the Union permanently restored and a peace secured that will allow you to return to your homes and firesides.*
>
> *You have been slandered and maligned by news scribblers who, unfortunately, in our country mould the public mind. Official reports will do you justice before the world.*
>
> *I return my thanks to every Officer and Soldier of the Corps for his gallantry in action and his hearty cooperation and devotion to duty.*

With this I leave you, and my earnest prayer ever shall be, that God may prosper you as a Corps, and as individuals, and ever give you victory when struggling for your Nation and Glorious Flag.

A. McD. McCook
Major General

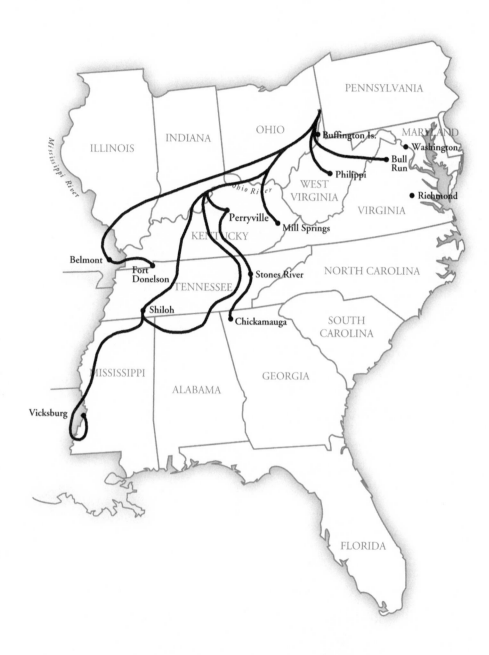

*Territory trod by the Fighting McCooks
in their quest to save the Union*

Chapter 15

COLONEL ANSON McCOOK
at the Battle of Chattanooga

Two days after Alex left Chattanooga in disgrace, his cousin Anson wrote to Alex's older brother, Mexican War veteran Colonel George McCook, who was training troops in Ohio.

Chattanooga
Oct 8th, 63

Dear George:

Long ere you receive this you will have heard from other sources, the last and this time the successful attempt to slaughter Alex.

It is what I have long anticipated and . . . Mr. Dana is the man who has assumed the responsibility.

Colonel Anson McCook, commanding the Second Ohio Volunteer Infantry Regiment, admitted that it was unfortunate that Alex had left the field but pointed out that he returned the same night.

> *The whole thing is a most infamous outrage, and Alex is determined to have the matter thoroughly ventilated. I wish you to see him or write him, cautioning him particularly about making use of unguarded expressions in regard to the possible political bearings of the case, or he is a "goner".*

The "political bearings" were the beliefs of some Democrat generals, like Alex, that they were being made scapegoats by the secretary of war. It was true. Stanton and the Radical Republicans in Congress, accusing the Democrat generals of being soft on the South and not fighting hard enough, were determined to get rid of them.

The Radical Republicans were members of Congress who had formed a powerful Joint House and Senate Committee on the Conduct of the War. Propelled by politics and consumed by hate for the Southern Democrats who had started the war, the Radicals were determined to wage war more aggressively and crush the South so completely that it could never rise again.

Stanton was in their ranks. A former fierce Democrat, he was now a fierce Republican. He had taken up the Radicals' cause as easily as a lawyer takes up a client's case. And, like most converts, Stanton was exceedingly zealous.

Lincoln was not in their ranks. A native Kentuckian and moderate Republican, Lincoln was not driven by hate. Dedicated to winning the war, he was equally dedicated to bringing the South peacefully back into the fold. The Radicals were not happy with Lincoln.

And the Fighting McCooks were not happy with the Radicals.

The McCooks were staunch Democrats who were fighting and dying to save the Union. There was not a family in the nation, North or South, Republican or Democrat, who had given more sons to their side of the fight. They deeply resented any slur on their loyalty, as Anson said in ending his letter to George:

> *I scarcely know what to do. My regiment is torn to pieces and that, in addition to the attempt to disgrace Alex, makes me feel very much like resigning.*

Twenty-eight-year-old Anson was the most modest of the Fighting McCooks. Desiring neither high rank nor glory, Anson just wanted to do his duty and not bring disgrace on his clan. Although he had fought in several major battles in the west, he minimized his military prowess and considered it something of a minor miracle that he had not been shot.

Actually, his only "war wound" came when he was just a boy. It was inflicted by the little brass cannon.

Anson George McCook, the second son of Dr. John and Catherine, was born in New Lisbon on October 10, 1835. At the age of ten, Anson watched his parents drive off in the buggy to see his cousin George leave for the Mexican War. They were scarcely out of sight when Anson and some friends decided to wage their own war. Dragging the little brass cannon from the stable, they loaded it with powder and shot and lit a wick to "touch her off." While it was sizzling, Anson ran in front. At that moment it fired, sending shot into his hand.

Splattered with blood, he was taken to his Uncle George, a stern surgeon unsparing in his denunciation of anything that incurred his displeasure. Dr. George removed the pellets with a few deft strokes of his surgical knife, dressed the painful wound, and sent Anson home to bed. The escapade confirmed Dr. George's opinion that his nephew was a very troublesome boy indeed.

With his father and uncle as doctors, Anson toyed with the idea of studying medicine. But, after watching them operate on kitchen tables without anesthetics, he quickly changed his mind. Instead, he took the advice of Horace Greeley, publisher of the *New York Tribune*, who was famous for his exhortation: "Go west, young man!"

In 1854 eighteen-year-old Anson caught "California Fever." Although the great Gold Rush of '49 was over, newspapers were still full of stories about overnight millionaires. Anson and three friends caught an Ohio River steamboat to Missouri, where they joined a teamster taking two hundred head of cattle across the plains. The vast region known as the "Great American Desert" was dotted with graves of those who did not finish the trip. After a month on the trail, Anson sent his father a letter from Wyoming to assure him that he was still alive and trekking.

June 10, 1854

Dear Father,

I take the opportunity of mailing a letter at Ft. Laramie so that you and the parents and relations of the other boys may not be uneasy at our long silence. I am writing this in camp about 80 miles from the Fort with my paper resting upon a carpet sack, so if you find any bad orthography or syntax do not blame me too hastily.

We are now one third of the way and if we get along as well the balance of the trip I will be well satisfied.

Tonight I ate some jerked Buffalo meat. . . . It is not a very tempting morsel but the novelty of the thing enabled me to get it down. Tomorrow I don a pair of moccasins, and with my pistol and knife will be quite a <u>savage</u> looking animal.

How is Mother's health? Tell her the first spare money I make she shall have for pin money, and I hope to come home someday and furnish her with those things I know she loves.

Ans

After 135 days on the trail, Anson arrived in California with $1.25 in his pocket. For five years he mined for gold but rarely found any. By 1859 he was homesick. Returning to Ohio, he studied law with his cousin George in Steubenville and was admitted to the bar in 1860.

When Fort Sumter fell, Anson was one of the first men in Steubenville to volunteer. He was elected captain of Company H, Second Ohio Volunteer Infantry, and by July they were in camp with General McDowell's Army of Northeastern Virginia.

Before marching to the Battle of Bull Run, Anson wrote his Connecticut cousin, Mary Sheldon. True to her promise, she was being a faithful correspondent with all of her McCook cousins in uniform.

Camp Upton, Va.
July 10, 1861

Dear Cousin,

Your very welcome letter was received some time ago and would have been answered ere now except that I plead guilty to con-

The Butler home in Hartford, Connecticut, where Mary Sheldon wrote her McCook cousins during the Civil War

stitutional laziness and my disease is much aggravated by the mercury standing at 95° in the shade.

I have nothing to write that can possibly interest or amuse you. You, through the medium of the press, are much better informed as to the movements of the army than those who are actually engaged as actors. I know of nothing that is transpiring until I receive the N.Y. papers, which are eagerly sought for as the prevailing impression is that their reporters are ubiquitous and know everything.

The only reliable information I can give you is that . . . a very lively fight is anticipated. Our two regiments will be in the advance and the probability is that some of us will never come back.

Possibly your correspondent (as the papers say) may be unlucky to be of that number, in which case the army will lose an efficient officer and society will have to mourn the loss of one of its brightest ornaments.

But seriously, Coz, from present appearances we will have a brisk offense, and should anything happen, remember your western country cousin and pray for the repose of his soul.

Yours as ever,
A. G. McCook

After the Battle of Bull Run Anson helped bury his cousin Charlie. Then he went back to Steubenville to recruit a three-year company. Within forty-eight hours he had enough men for a battalion and went to Columbus to report to Governor Dennison. The governor, pleased with his promptness, offered to promote him to major. Anson, dumbfounded, did not reply.

"Well, what do you say?" the governor demanded.

"You might spoil a fairly good captain," Anson finally allowed, "and make a doubtful major."

"I will risk it," Dennison declared.

And so Major Anson McCook, third in command of the Second Ohio, diligently began studying *Hardee's Tactics* and outfitting himself. Officers paid for their own uniforms, horses, and body servants. Those servants, who cooked and did the laundry, were usually runaway slaves who received wages, clothes, and small tents to pitch near their officers.

By September Anson was in central Kentucky, finely mounted on a spirited little black Morgan horse given to him by his father. Writing to his cousin Mary, Anson reported that his first fight was much overblown by the press.

> *Camp near Louisville*
> *Dec. 1st, 1861*

> Dear Coz:

> *Our fight at Middle Creek was grossly exaggerated. It was a sharp and very creditable little affair, in which the . . . enemy stood their ground for an hour and twenty minutes, with courage and determination.*

> *My personal exploits and adventures were neither numerous or brilliant. I was riding my little black horse . . . and presented a fair mark, which they fully appreciating, indulged in twice. . . . I jumped off my horse, seized a musket and followed by two or three companies started up the almost perpendicular mountainside after them.*

> *I managed with my usual bad luck to get near the color bearer . . . and the "secesh" showed their malignity by firing at him, placing me again in hot water. I however went ahead and shot four times, once I think with fatal effect. So ended the fight.*

Excuse wordy and bad orthography for it is cold, and my early education was neglected.

Your cousin
A. G. McCook

His next letter, two months later, ached for action.

February 4, 1862

Dear Coz:

Camp life is very monotonous, the same dull routine, and unless a man has a newspaper correspondent's vivid and brilliant imagination, it is destitute of items.

I can form no idea when we will move. We are expecting the order every day and probably while you are reading this the armies may be in deadly conflict.

I intend in the impending fight to do my duty, and hope I will not disgrace my name. . . . I would rather, much rather die, unprepared as I know I am, than to bring disgrace on a name heretofore undishonored.

Yours,
A. G. McCook

Action finally came when the long Kentucky line collapsed and the Army of the Ohio pursued the Confederates to Nashville, Tennessee.

Camp Andrew Jackson near Nashville
March 7, 1862

Dear Coz:

Since I last wrote I have been (to us a Westernism that may perhaps shock your Yankee ears polite) knocking around at a frightful rate. . . . Now here we are in possession of the pride of the South West as they style it . . . where nearly the whole population is arrayed against us.

I always was skeptical about a re-construction of the Union, but I am now satisfied that unless a wonderful change takes place, that we will always be two people.

> *The enemy has evacuated Columbus and are falling back to Georgia and Alabama, where in my opinion will be fought the battle that will decide the matter.*

The battle was fought at Shiloh. Anson's regiment was not there, and the battle did not decide the matter.

Four months later, after the death of his cousin Bob at the hands of guerrillas, Anson's letter to Mary was bitter:

> *Aug 7, '62*
>
> Dear Cousin:
>
> *It is a terrible mortality and makes me curse the day when this unholy, causeless and ungodly rebellion reared its devilish head. Oh, how I hate them, and feel more than ever it incumbent upon me to remain in the army until the final crushing out of the infamous thing.*
>
> *Had he fallen at the head of his Brigade amid the roar of battle, I could have resigned him without a sigh.*
>
> *Alex is very much depressed. . . . Poor Bob, after going through two or three severe fights with comparative safety, winning his "Star" by gallantry and ability . . . is shot like a dog in an ambulance.*
>
> *Unfitted as I know I am to die, I am ready and willing to cheerfully peril my life against the devils, and if I must fall I only pray that my death may not be unavenged.*

Anson was in his first major battle, two months later, at Perryville. The Second Ohio, in his cousin Alex's corps, fought stubbornly and held its position most of the day. Anson was promoted to lieutenant colonel for his "coolness and bravery."

The next battle, two and a half months later, was fought under the command of Rosecrans at Stones River. As the Union Army of the Cumberland braced itself for a Confederate charge, Anson checked his company commanders to see if they and their men were all right.

"Oh, we are all right," replied Captain James Murdoch, son of a well-known Shakespearean actor, quoting Sir John Falstaff, "'Honor pricks me on. Yea, but how if honor pricks me off, when I come on. How then?'"

The wry lines from Shakespeare's *Henry IV* were interrupted by the Rebel charge. The Second Ohio had been ordered to defend one of the Union batteries at all costs, using bayonets if necessary. As the Confederate line came closer, the colonel of the Second Ohio turned to Anson.

"McCook, if anything happens to me today," said Colonel John Kell, "I want you to promise to send me home in charge of Will and Old Sol." Will was his son and Old Sol his body servant.

"Did you hear me?" Kell demanded, when Anson did not reply.

"Certainly I heard you," said Anson. "But, Colonel, this regiment is like the Democratic Party, where none resign and few die, and I don't know but my chances to be killed are as close as yours. However, as you have asked me, I promise to do it."

Minutes later a bullet pierced Kell's chest, killing him instantly. Anson, taking command of the regiment, ordered his men to fire when the enemy came within two hundred yards. After a fierce fight, which used up all the bullets on both sides, Anson led his men in a bayonet charge.

Fighting hand-to-hand, the Second Ohio pushed the Rebels back into the cedars and surrounded them. When a white flag was raised in surrender, Anson sent in two companies of skirmishers who captured twenty men of the Thirtieth Arkansas. Their battle flag, a white cross on a blue field, was one of only two Rebel flags taken that day.

Ten days later, Anson enclosed two skeins of thread from the captured flag when he wrote his cousin Mary:

January 10, 1863

Dear Mary,

Poor Kell's death will I presume make me a Col. If so, I will be the youngest one I know of in the service, and I fear poorly qualified to fill the places of those who are gone. I can do my duty however let what come.

Yours,

Ans

Excuse the hastily written letter. I have no time for a better one.

Confederate flag being captured at the Battle of Stones River

Soon Anson was wearing a colonel's eagles, but it did not stifle his self-effacing sense of humor. Writing to Mary from Murfreesboro, he said that the only things breaking the monotony were burying dead horses, speculating about the fall elections, and witnessing military executions.

April 5, 1863

Dear Mary,

As far as I am individually concerned, I am afraid I would have committed suicide had I not been <u>fortunately</u> attacked with something that at one time gave promise of blooming into full grown typhoid fever.

I am now recovering under the reviving influence of a genial sun and a judicious application (internal) of whiskey.

No present indication of a move or fight, although "Rosey" has a happy faculty of keeping his own counsel and may be contemplating it without anyone knowing it.

Yours ~
Ans

By early June, although the War Department had not given Rosecrans the cavalry that he requested, Anson felt a Union attack was imminent.

> *Murfreesboro*
> *June 6th, 1863*
>
> *Dear Mary,*
>
> *I am perfectly well satisfied that Rosecrans intends moving upon the enemy, and notwithstanding my great confidence in this army, I fear the result. The rebel army in our front is as large, perhaps larger than our own, composed of gallant and desperate men, ably led.*
>
> *I have lost all my chivalry and do not want to again fight them unless the advantage is so decidedly in our favor that the prospect of victory is almost certain.*

The stepchild status of the Army of the Cumberland, caused by the animosity between Rosecrans and Stanton, infuriated Anson.

> *But for the imbecility or cowardice of our government and the apathy of our people, we could meet them at every point with superior forces.*
>
> *I am getting heartily sick and tired of this dreadful war. It drags its slow length along fearfully and it seems to me that the people at home with but few exceptions have lost their interest in it. In comparison to the enthusiasm and determination manifested by the South, we make but a sorry show, and I fear the worst.*
>
> *Yours as ever,*
> *Ans*

After Rosecrans successfully maneuvered Bragg out of Tullahoma and back into Chattanooga, McCook requested leave. Since the Army of the Cumberland could not advance until the railroads were repaired, Anson took advantage of the lull to go to Hartford to see his youngest brother, Little Johnny, graduate from Trinity College as valedictorian of his class.

But while Anson was up north, the Army of the Cumberland suffered its crushing defeat at Chickamauga. Hurrying back to his regiment, Anson arrived in Chattanooga to find Rosecrans barricaded in the town while Bragg bombarded him from the surrounding mountains. Confederate artillery commanded the roads and the Tennessee River by which Rosecrans would be resupplied.

Bragg's plan for recapturing Chattanooga was to starve Rosecrans out, forcing him to recross the river and retreat north. Rosecrans's plan for holding onto Chattanooga was to open up a new supply route and then, strengthened in the "Gibraltar of the South," maneuver Bragg from his mountaintop positions and force him to retreat farther south.

So optimistic was Rosecrans that he telegraphed Lincoln with a political proposal on October 3:

> *If we maintain the position in such strength that the enemy are obliged to abandon their position . . . would it not be well to offer a general amnesty to all officers and soldiers in the rebellion? It would give us moral strength and weaken them very much.*

Lincoln's reply arrived the next day:

> *I intend doing something like what you suggest whenever the case shall appear ripe enough. . . .*

To Stanton, who oversaw all telegraphs in the War Department, such a plan of amnesty was anathema. He and the Radicals had no intention of allowing it. For the moment, however, they said little. Arguing with Lincoln was like "throwing water on a duck's back," declared Salmon B. Chase, the secretary of the treasury.

Meanwhile, by mid-October, Bragg's starvation of Chattanooga was succeeding. Rosecrans's Army of the Cumberland was on half-rations. Horses were eating the bark off trees. Carcasses of thousands of mules lay north of the Tennessee River where they had been slain by Confederate cavalry while trying to haul supplies to the besieged city.

While Rosecrans was working on a plan to open a new supply route, Charles Dana was flooding Washington with false reports that the general had lost his nerve and was planning to abandon Chattanooga. Dana's daily dispatches were deciphered at the War Department and shown to Lincoln:

> *The soldiers have lost their attachment for him since he failed*
> *them in battle. . . . I have never seen a public man possessing*
> *talent with less administrative power. . . . I consider this army*
> *to be very unsafe in his hands . . . seems difficult to believe him*
> *of sound mind . . . If the army is finally obliged to retreat, the*
> *probability is that it will fall back like a rabble. . . .*

General Garfield, Rosecrans's chief of staff, also was writing secretly to his friends in Lincoln's cabinet urging the general's removal. The president had supported Rosecrans throughout the war, aware that he was the only Union general who had been able to outmaneuver Lee. But finally Lincoln was persuaded by Dana and Garfield that the defeat at Chickamauga had made Rosecrans wobbly.

"Like a duck hit on the head," Lincoln said sadly.

Dana also telegraphed Stanton that Rosecrans, in writing his official report of the Battle of Chickamauga, planned to lay the blame for his defeat on the secretary of war. Rosecrans was to cite Stanton's failure to reinforce him or tell him that Bragg was being reinforced until it was too late.

Rosecrans had powerful friends in the North who were touting him for the presidency. He also had powerful friends in the press. Horace Greeley, publisher of the *New York Tribune*, made no secret of the fact that he thought Stanton should be removed and replaced by Rosecrans.

Stanton, as he always did in times of crisis, flew into a frenzy and paced the room like a caged lion.

"The tycoon of the War Department is on the war path," Lincoln's secretary John Hay reported. "His hands are red and smoking with the scalping of Rosey."

It was done with a few deft strokes. First, the three western armies, the Cumberland, Ohio, and Tennessee, were reorganized into the Military Division of the Mississippi, under the command of Grant, the victor of Vicksburg.

Then Stanton, taking the document to Grant himself, rushed west on a private train. The engineer was ordered to throw the throttle wide open. As the train careened around mountain curves and dishes came crashing to the floor, there was fear that the swaying cars might leave the rails. But Stanton, in high dudgeon, ordered the breakneck speed to continue until they came to a screeching halt in Indianapolis. In the station was Grant's train, which had just arrived from the Mississippi River. Stanton climbed aboard.

"How do you do, General Grant?" Stanton said effusively, extending his hand to Grant's doctor. "I recognize you from your pictures."

There was an awkward moment before Stanton was introduced to a stubby, round-shouldered man with a slightly seedy look in a rumpled uniform. Recovering his poise, Stanton handed Grant two orders signed by Lincoln. One retained Rosecrans in command of the Army of the Cumberland. The other replaced him with Thomas. Grant was told to make the decision.

Stanton was well aware of the enmity between Grant and Rosecrans. Rosecrans was bitter that Grant outranked him. Grant was jealous of Rosecrans's victories and good press. Although Grant had been telegraphed by Halleck on September 13 to send troops to help Rosecrans, it was a full two weeks before Grant complied. By then the Battle of Chickamauga had been fought and lost.

"This is to be expected," Rosecrans said when he got the telegram on October 19 relieving him of command. He slipped out of Chattanooga the next morning.

Grant arrived in Chattanooga on October 23 and put into motion Rosecrans's plan to break the siege. General Joseph Hooker had arrived from Virginia with fifteen thousand men from the Army of the Potomac. General William T. Sherman was on his way from Memphis with seventeen thousand men from the Army of the Tennessee.

So it was with optimism that Anson wrote his cousin the next day:

October 24, 1863

Dear Mary,

I wish you were here this morning to enjoy the finest view in America in peaceful times, but doubly so now. My tent is on the highest peak around Chattanooga with the exception of Lookout Mt., now occupied by the rebels. Away below me is the valley in which the town is situated, dotted all over with the tents of our men, while beyond, at the foot of Missionary Ridge . . . are the tents and cannons of the enemy. Lookout Mt. looms

up on my right, studded with rebel batteries, while . . . at my
feet the Tennessee, bank full, rolls along in sullen grandeur.

One month later, with some sixty thousand men from three armies, Grant began the drive to oust Bragg from his mountain entrenchments surrounding the town. On November 23, Thomas captured the Confederate anchor position on Orchard Knob. The next morning, in a thick fog, Hooker assaulted Lookout Mountain, the nearly perpendicular pile of rock that rose to twenty-four hundred feet above sea level.

Anson watched as Hooker's troops started up Lookout Mountain under fire. He followed their progress by the sounds of gunfire echoing down the mountain and saw occasionally, when the fog lifted, flashes of light from the advancing blue line. By noon the Stars and Stripes were fluttering from a plateau halfway up the mountain.

By 4:00 p.m. Hooker's troops were almost out of ammunition. The Second Ohio, with the rest of Brigadier General William P. Carlin's brigade, was ordered up to reinforce. Anson led his regiment in scrambling up the steep wooded slopes, over rocks and fallen trees and through ravines and

Union foot soldiers charge the heights at the Battle of Chattanooga

gullies. It was dark by the time they reached the plateau and waged a sharp fight by the light of a full hunter's moon.

"Hello, Yank, how many rounds have you?" yelled a voice with a Southern drawl.

"Only sixty, Johnnie!" shouted someone with a Northern twang.

As soon as the Yank started talking, a bullet whistled over his head.

"There, damn you," drawled the Rebel. "Take that and you'll have sixty-one!"

Anson felt it was rather a grim joke. But, judging from the laughter, it was appreciated on both sides. The enemies continued to spar until 11:00 p.m. when the mountain became unusually quiet. About 3:00 a.m. McCook's skirmishers crawled cautiously toward the Confederate trenches and found them deserted. So the Second Ohio lit fires, boiled coffee, and counted its casualties. Four men had been killed and three wounded.

By dawn the Stars and Stripes were flying briskly from the top of Lookout Mountain, while down in the valley thousands of Union troops sent up loud huzzahs, and even the undemonstrative General Thomas threw his hat in the air. Anson buried his dead on the mountain and descended to join the assault on the last Rebel bastion: Missionary Ridge.

Stretching for six miles, Missionary Ridge was considered impregnable. Its five-hundred-foot height was strewn with boulders and fringed with trees. The Confederates had three strong lines of defense: rifle pits at the base of the mountain, trenches halfway up the steep slopes, and, on the top, some fifty cannon placed every hundred yards.

Grant ordered Sherman, commanding the Army of the Tennessee, to make the main attack on the left. Thomas, in command of the Army of the Cumberland, was to wait and play a supporting role.

The ill will between the Army of the Tennessee and the Army of the Cumberland, begun after the Battle of Shiloh, still existed. Grant said he expected little from the Army of the Cumberland, telling Sherman that the men had been demoralized by their defeat at the Battle of Chickamauga.

"I fear they cannot be got out of their trenches to assume the offensive," said Grant.

Sherman attacked on the left in the morning. By mid-afternoon he was stopped. He faced rugged terrain and a heavy concentration of enemy troops under the command of Hardee, who had returned from the Mississippi to join Bragg.

Grant, hoping to draw Hardee away from Sherman, ordered Thomas to assault the center of the mountain and capture the first line of rifle pits. The Army of the Cumberland, jubilant that it would have a chance to avenge its defeat at Chickamauga, dressed ranks enthusiastically.

Six cannon signaled the assault shortly before 4:00 p.m. Then hundreds of shrill bugles sent some twenty-three thousand men forward, three lines deep on a two-mile front, marching shoulder-to-shoulder in quick time with their rifles at a right shoulder shift. This time it was Union bands that were playing and Union flags that were flying and Union gun barrels that were gleaming in the sun as the soldiers marched across the plain with the precision of a dress parade.

Bright flames flashed from the top of Missionary Ridge, smoke curled into the sky, and thunder shook the earth as Confederate cannon opened up. Union batteries replied with a deafening roar. The soldiers in the long blue lines increased their pace to double-quick.

Reaching the rifle pits, they found them empty. The Rebels had fled and were scrambling up the steep slopes to the top of the mountain. There, in great confusion, they attempted to re-form their ranks.

The Army of the Cumberland had no orders to go up the mountain. But the rifle pits were a death trap. Enemy musketry and canister rained down on them from the top. Their only hope was to take the whole mountain. The men of the First Ohio, whom Alex McCook had trained in Dayton, clamored for permission to mount the ridge.

"Boys," shouted an officer as he galloped by, "if you want to go, why go!"

And so up they went. The First Ohio, with the rest of Brigadier General William B. Hazen's brigade following, charged up Missionary Ridge. First it was companies, then regiments, then brigades that haphazardly clawed their way up the side of the mountain. The day was bright and clear, and the whole scene was in full view as General Grant watched in surprise through his field glass.

"Thomas, who ordered those men up the ridge?" Grant demanded.

"I don't know," replied Thomas. "I did not."

Grant then turned to General Granger, who commanded the men from McCook's and Crittenden's corps. "Did you order them up, Granger?"

"No," said Granger, "they started up without orders. When those fellows get started all hell can't stop them."

Grant, chomping on his cigar, muttered that someone would suffer if it did not turn out well.

"Chickamauga! Chickamauga!" The men of the Army of the Cumberland shouted in revenge as they charged wildly up the boulder-strewn, almost perpendicular side of Missionary Ridge like a herd of stampeded cattle.

It was a soldier's assault. The officers had little control over it. Sixty regimental flags raced each other to the top, and when flag bearers fell, others picked up the banners and carried them forward. In some places it was too steep to stand, and so they crawled up on their hands and knees, clutching at branches and boulders.

Meanwhile there burst forth from the brow of the ridge a tornado of fire, smoke, and thunder as Confederate artillery raked the sides of the ridge in a murderous cross fire. When the batteries could not depress enough to shoot the upcoming hoards, the Confederates threw lighted shells and huge boulders down on them. But nothing stopped the furious charge.

Drunk with excitement, the Union regiments raced each other to the top . . . First Ohio . . . Twenty-third Kentucky . . . Sixty-eighth Indiana . . . Thirty-fifth Illinois . . . Ninth Kentucky . . . Eighth Kansas . . . Eighty-ninth Illinois . . . Forty-first Ohio . . . Second Minnesota . . . Sixth Indiana . . . Fifth Kentucky . . . Sixth Ohio . . . Sixth Kentucky . . . Ninety-third Ohio . . . Twenty-fifth Illinois . . . Thirty-second Indiana . . . and on and on.

The First Ohio surged over the top and charged with fixed bayonets to capture six cannon as Hazen's brigade claimed to have won the race. Many made the claim. No one knew for certain. It was simply a magnificent victory for the foot soldiers of four divisions—Wood, Baird, Sheridan, and Johnson—of the Army of the Cumberland.

Their charge ended the Battle of Chattanooga in an hour.

The Confederate line swiftly collapsed with Rebels flying down the other side of the ridge in wild disarray, tossing away knapsacks and muskets, while their raging officers tried to halt the panic-stricken men. It was the first time in the Civil War that an entire Confederate Army had fled in panic.

"Here is your commander!" shouted Bragg, trying in vain to halt their headlong flight. Finally, nearly surrounded, he had to abandon the field.

Colonel Anson McCook, on the extreme right of the Union line, reached the crest to seize a commanding knob and find the Thirty-eighth Alabama running straight into his guns. He captured the lieutenant colonel, 2 majors, 25 line officers, 282 men, and their battle flag. The officers, in surrendering, handed over their swords silently, except for one young lieutenant.

"It is a shame, a shame," he lamented, "to have lost the position."

He tried to remove his sword belt, in spite of great pain from a badly shattered hand, until Anson took pity on him.

"Oh, lieutenant," said one of the least vengeful of the Fighting McCooks, "I don't want your sword."

*Territory trod by the Fighting McCooks
in their quest to save the Union*

Chapter 16

COLONEL DANIEL MCCOOK JR.
at the Battle of Kennesaw Mountain

Shortly after midnight on November 26, 1863, Colonel Dan McCook Jr. awakened his brigade to lead them in pursuit of General Braxton Bragg.

Eight hours earlier, the foot soldiers of the Army of the Cumberland had captured Missionary Ridge, and the Confederates had fled in wild disarray. Dan McCook was given the honor of leading the chase. He grabbed it eagerly.

He had been itching for action for over a year. Recognized early in the war as a superb warrior, Dan had been shelved, doing dull garrison duty or stuck in a reserve corps, ever since the Battle of Perryville.

An intense man with a hot temper, he was twenty-nine years old, six feet tall, and razor thin. An intellectual man with steel-gray eyes, he could flare them quickly with eagerness or anger. An impetuous man with a strong strain of poetry running through his veins, he had raised his glass in a spirited toast upon leaving for war:

"Here's for a general's star or a soldier's grave!"

The sixth son of Daniel and Martha was born in Carrollton on July 22, 1834. A frail youth with chronic respiratory problems that were aggravated by the humidity of the Ohio Valley, Dan was sent to the dry South for his college education. At LaGrange College in Leighton, Alabama, his health improved, and he became active in the Literary and Debating Society, wrote for the college newspaper, and played field sports. Graduating in 1857, Dan returned north to study law with his brother George in Steubenville, Ohio, living with George and Margaret at their Hillside estate.

A year later, after passing the bar, Dan headed west to the Kansas Territory. Gold had been discovered in the Rocky Mountains, and men stampeded west shouting "Pikes Peak or bust." Reaching Leavenworth in the fall of 1858, he joined a law firm whose dingy office on the second floor of a flimsy cottonwood building, on the corner of Main and Delaware streets, had a sign on the rickety stairs that said:

THE LAW SHOP OF
SHERMAN, EWING AND McCOOK

Attorneys Tom and Hugh Ewing were members of a prominent Ohio family. Their father was a U.S. senator. Their sister Ellen had married Sherman.

William Tecumseh Sherman, called "Cump," was a West Pointer who had become discouraged at the lack of promotion in the army for Northerners. Resigning his commission, he joined the Ewings. Although not a lawyer, Sherman was admitted to the Kansas Territory Bar on the basis of "general intelligence." He handled real estate transactions for the firm.

Sherman was a bundle of nervous energy. Tall and wiry, with sharp blue eyes and dark reddish hair that stood straight up on his high-domed forehead, he was constantly in motion. Talking and laughing and chomping on his ever-present cigar, he was able to hold the floor for more than an hour on any subject. He had a firm opinion on everything.

Dan McCook, the junior member of the firm, handled probate and lower court cases. Eloquent on his feet, he excelled in courtroom jousting where words were sword and rapier. In May his success was reported in the press:

His speech in a murder case a short time ago is spoken of as one of the best that has ever been made in the territory.

But by the summer of 1859 the "gold mania" had become a "humbug mania." Almost everyone was bankrupt, and most of the fifty thousand to sixty thousand people who had flocked to the Kansas Territory were leaving. That included Sherman, who moved his wife and children to Louisiana, where he took a job as superintendent of a military academy.

Dan McCook remained in Leavenworth to become involved in the politics of "bleeding Kansas." The territory had been torn by violence between free-staters and slave-staters ever since Senator Stephen Douglas pushed the 1854 Kansas-Nebraska Act through Congress. Leaving the question of slavery up to the citizens, it was called "popular sovereignty."

Dan, writing to his father, warned him that Douglas should deal carefully with the issue of slavery in Kansas as it would affect his try for the presidency in 1860.

Leavenworth City
August 20, 1859

My Dear Father,

    I am going to write you a political letter, knowing that to a certain extent you have the ear of Judge Douglas and in my humble judgment the position he takes upon the admission of Kansas . . . will have a great deal to do with his nomination at Charleston, and his subsequent race before the people.

Dan felt that Douglas, bound by his policy of popular sovereignty, would be compelled to support the admission of Kansas as a free state. This would alienate him from those Southern Democrats whose backing he would need.

He should be slow in taking any position, and he should be fully advised by some reliable men here, as to the popular pulse in the territory. . . . Give my love to all at home. . . .

your dear
Dan. McCook

In the fall of 1859 Dan was elected probate judge of Leavenworth County, becoming the second "Judge McCook" in the clan. He also fell in love. A letter from law partner Tom Ewing to his sister Ellen Ewing Sherman asked:

> *Did you ever see Julia Tebbs of Platte County? McCook is committed in that quest beyond hope of redemption.*

Julia Tebbs was a beautiful seventeen-year-old Southern belle from a fine old Leesburg, Virginia, family. Her father, Algernon Sidney Tebbs, had moved west to purchase a plantation and practice law. Dan and Julia were married in her parents' parlor on December 5, 1860.

Two weeks later South Carolina seceded. After three more Southern states left the Union, Dan recruited a volunteer company called the Shields Guards. Elected captain, he became the second person in the country to make a private tender of troops to Washington.

> *Leavenworth City, February 20, 1861*
>
> Hon. Joseph Holt,
> Secretary of War,
>
> Sir:—*I have the honor to tender to you and the government the service of the volunteer militia company, consisting of sixty rank and file, infantry, which I at present command. We are willing to serve in any capacity and any way, and against any powers which the public need may require, or the constituted authorities order. Hoping that you will at least give us an equal chance, I remain, with sentiments of highest respect,*
>
> > *Your obedient servant,*
> > *Daniel McCook*
> > *Captain Leavenworth State Guard*

However, by March Dan was angry. His offer had not been accepted by the War Department. Worse yet, the newly inaugurated Lincoln was following a course of "masterly inactivity." Having expected stronger action from Lincoln, Dan vented his frustrations in a letter to his politically astute brother George in Steubenville.

March 10, 1861

My dear Brother,

Tell me with your superior political wisdom, where are we drifting. Can secession of all the southern states be avoided? And will not that be followed by immediate or at least ultimate war? Everything seems dark to me. We are borne upon a relentless overwhelming tide to anarchy in my humble judgment. But when our rulers and would be statesmen are at a loss for conjectures, it cannot be expected that I should anticipate evils unheard of, and unrecorded, with any degree of accuracy.

As the "war clouds lower" my old army fever returns; but like the Huns as they hovered upon the Danube, menacing both Constantinople and Rome, I am hesitating against which Empire to turn my "weighty sword". The "tangled woof of wrong" enwarps both causes.

While my education has been so cosmopolitan (at least in an American sense) and my prejudices are so ill defined that I know not whether to support the Administration or oppose "coercion".

My wife says when I dream of the army that she did not marry an army officer but a lawyer and says if I go into it she will look upon it as a breach of one of the implied conditions of the contract. She says moreover that she discarded a captain in it for me and this she considers should settle the question conclusively against the army and in favor of the law.

Your brother,
Danl McCook

The fall of Fort Sumter settled the question. Dan and his law partners, after hasty consultation, sent a telegram to Washington:

We are yours to command—

Sherman, Ewing and McCook.

Dan was serving as captain of the First Kansas Voluntary Infantry Regiment when his old pulmonary problems returned. Hospitalized in

Kansas City with pneumonia, he was listed in critical condition. His parents were telegraphed that it might be fatal.

Pneumonia did not kill Dan, but it forced him to resign from field command. He took a staff position as assistant adjutant general with his brother Alex, who was in central Kentucky, commanding the Second Division of the Army of the Cumberland.

After fighting at Shiloh, where he helped recover his former law partner Sherman's camps, Dan insisted he was strong enough for a field command. Returning to Ohio, he began to recruit the Fifty-second Ohio Volunteer Infantry Regiment.

Riding horseback throughout the eastern part of the state, Dan made impassioned speeches on tree stumps and at crossroads and in drowsy villages. To his old friends, who had not seen him since he moved to Kansas, Dan was no longer a buoyant poetry-quoting law student. He was a warrior wielding words like a weapon as he urged farm boys to do their duty for their country.

Commissioned a colonel on July 15, 1862, Dan also became a father that month when his wife Julia presented him with a son. The baby, born at Hillside, was nicknamed "the pocket colonel." But he was christened Robert after his Uncle Bob, the famous hero of Mill Springs.

A month later, when Bob was killed by guerrillas, Dan's grief took the form of rage. In Louisville, where he was given command of the Thirty-sixth Brigade, Eleventh Division, Army of the Ohio, Dan trained his recruits so hard and so relentlessly that one of them wrote home angrily:

> *The Gen. commanding our brigade is McCook, who is held in utter contempt by all who know him, so much so that the boys say that if ever they get into battle, he is the first man who will fall by their own hand.*

But Dan produced a brigade that was so well-trained and disciplined that General Buell chose him to capture Peters Hill at Perryville. McCook's raw recruits took the hill handily from Hardee's Arkansas veterans and, instead of shooting him as threatened, his men cheered him for their victory.

After the Battle of Perryville, Colonel Dan McCook was cited for "great gallantry" in General Sheridan's official report. But Dan remained furious about his restricted role in the battle. Appearing before the Buell Hearings in Nashville, he repeated in sworn testimony what he had written in his official report—that he had been ordered to pull his brigade back to Peters Hill and, in spite of repeated requests, was not permitted to go to the aid of Alex's corps. Sheridan did not testify.

Alex McCook, in his own testimony, observed of Sheridan, a fellow West Pointer:

> *It is the duty of a general to relieve a brother general, whatever his orders may be.*

Boiling-mad and sharp-tongued Dan McCook refused to stop talking to newspaper reporters about the battle and taking them out on the battlefield to see where he had been ordered to pull back. Abruptly, on December 10, 1862, his brigade was removed from Sheridan's Eleventh Division and assigned to the Fourth Division doing dull garrison duty in Nashville.

It was a disciplined and disappointed Dan McCook who watched with envy as Rosecrans left Nashville two weeks later to attack Bragg at Murfreesboro. Dan could hear the cannon, thirty miles away, during the Battle of Stones River. On New Year's Day Rosecrans, bloodied but unbeaten, was holding on to a thin sliver of ground and calling for reinforcements. Some three hundred Union wagons, loaded with food and ammunition, left Nashville only to be destroyed by Confederate cavalry Generals Joseph Wheeler and John A. Wharton.

Dan McCook tried next. He left Nashville at 11:00 a.m. on January 2 with an ammunition and hospital train of ninety-five wagons protected by cavalry and infantry from four regiments, including his Fifty-second Ohio. Seven miles south of town he was attacked by Wheeler with some three thousand cavalrymen and three pieces of artillery. Sixty Confederate troopers reached the wagons and surrounded McCook, who held them off with his pistols until he was rescued by his own cavalry. Fighting his way through the ambush, McCook finally drove Wheeler off. Forty of Wheeler's men had been killed, wounded, or captured. Two of McCook's men were wounded.

The Union wagon train moved on, and as it neared Murfreesboro, it was hailed by a friendly civilian on horseback. Dan McCook, suspecting that he was a Confederate scout, called out to him.

"I know you're a Union man by your looks, and I want to tell you a secret. Do you see these troops? They're some of Rosey's Mississippi veterans. There are twenty-five thousand coming, and we're going to give old Bragg hell. Good-bye, mind you don't say a word to anyone."

"Oh, no," replied the civilian.

Relating the story to Rosecrans when he arrived at 3:00 a.m. the next morning, McCook said with a wide grin, "I reckon he's been at Bragg's headquarters more than three hours by this time."

That night Bragg withdrew to Tullahoma. Dan McCook returned to garrison duty in Nashville.

During the spring of 1863, while Rosecrans rebuilt his army, Dan spent his time educating the field officers of his brigade. Using his many military volumes, he taught them about the great campaigns of Saxe, Turrenne, Napoleon, and Wellington. As solicitous as his own father, Dan McCook carefully watched over "my boys," as he called them.

And they reciprocated. On the Fourth of July his field officers presented him with a handsome gift. It was a pair of Smith and Wesson .32-caliber six-shot revolvers, ivory-gripped and engraved:

Col. D. McCook from the officers of his brigade—
July 4th, 1863.

But pleasure turned to pain that night when he received a telegram. "The pocket colonel," his one-year-old son Robert, had died after a brief illness. Just three weeks later another devastating wire arrived. His father had been killed at Buffington Island while pursuing John Hunt Morgan.

Again, Dan's grief took the form of towering rage. Sometimes he took it out on delinquent members of his own brigade. However, he saved the worst for Frank Gurley, the guerrilla who had killed Bob.

In late August, as Rosecrans advanced his army to capture Chattanooga, Dan McCook's brigade was assigned to the Second Division, Reserve Corps, commanded by Major General Gordon Granger. On September 6 McCook's brigade was marching through southern Tennessee when they passed Gurley's farm. Dan sent fifty mounted men from his Fifty-second Ohio, McCook's Avengers, to ravage it.

"Make it an utter desolation," he ordered.

They burned down the house where Gurley was born and torched twenty-four other buildings on the farm for good measure. Everything was leveled except two slave shanties. And, as a parting gesture, they deadened the fruit trees and fired the fences.

Two weeks later the Battle of Chickamauga was fought. It was Colonel Dan McCook, stationed three and a half miles away in Granger's Reserve Corps, who fired the first and last shots.

On September 18, as Union and Confederate armies jockeyed for position in the forest, McCook was ordered to march to the support of Union cavalry holding Reed's Bridge over Chickamauga Creek. Approaching the bridge at dusk, Dan ran into the rear of an enemy brigade that had managed to cross the stream. During a brief skirmish McCook's troops took twenty-two prisoners, including a major whose fine horse was presented to Dan. It was called "McCook's Chickamauga pacer."

Bivouacking that night in the woods, Dan allowed no campfires as he planned to capture the entire brigade at dawn. At 2:00 a.m. he sent one regiment to burn the bridge so that the enemy could not escape. At 3:00 a.m. he was joined by Colonel John Mitchell and his brigade. At 6:00 a.m., as they were preparing to attack, a messenger arrived with an order from Rosecrans:

Withdraw McCook and Mitchell if not already too late.

Always furious when not allowed to fight, Dan galloped off to find General Thomas, commanding the left of the Union line. Telling him about the isolated brigade, Dan asked Thomas to overturn Rosecrans's order so that he could capture it. Thomas, declining to change the commanding general's order, sent his own troops to do the job. Colonel John T. Croxton found the Confederate brigade all right, along with five or six others.

"Which brigade do you want us to catch?" Croxton inquired dryly in a message to Thomas.

Almost two-thirds of the Rebel army had crossed Chickamauga Creek during the night. Unknowingly, Dan had bivouacked in the dense forest surrounded by three enemy divisions. One was in his front, another in his rear, and a third on his left flank. And so the Battle of Chickamauga began.

Dan, returning reluctantly to Granger's Reserve Corps three and a half miles away, paced impatiently as the outnumbered Army of the Cumberland fought for its life.

On the second day of battle his brother Alex, along with Rosecrans and Crittenden and one-third of the army, was routed. Dan demanded to be allowed to take his brigade to aid Thomas, still holding out on Horseshoe Ridge. Denying his request, Granger sent him an order to remain in his position and protect Thomas's escape route to Chattanooga, fighting to the last man.

"Tell General Granger," Dan replied, "when my brigade retreats he can report Dan McCook among the killed."

Later that afternoon, McCook finally was allowed to move up and fight on Thomas's left flank at Horseshoe Ridge. That night, when Thomas retired from the field and fell back on Rossville, Dan's brigade was the last to leave. At 10:00 p.m. he ordered two final six-cannon charges near the spot where, forty hours earlier, he had touched off the battle.

Cited for "gallant and meritorious conduct at the Battle of Chickamauga," Dan was recommended for promotion to brigadier general. With his star finally in sight, the frustrations of the past year disappeared. His color improved and his spirits, too, as his cousin Anson noted in a letter from Chattanooga to George in Steubenville on November 15:

> *I saw Dan the other day. He is as irrepressible as formerly, and looks better than I have seen him for some time.*

Dan's revived spirits were also due to the fact that his old law partner had arrived. After Rosecrans was removed from command, Grant took over in Chattanooga. Joining him was Sherman with his seventeen-thousand-man Army of the Tennessee.

Sherman had been altered by the vicissitudes of war. Now forty-four years old, his red hair was tinged with gray, his lean face was furrowed with wrinkles, and his eyes were as cold and hard as steel. A black felt slouch hat sat carelessly on his head, and his old blue coat had weathered to a dingy bottle green.

Dan McCook, transferred to Sherman's command, now would get all the fighting he wanted. Given the honor of the pursuit of Bragg after the

Major General William Tecumseh Sherman

foot soldiers of the Army of the Cumberland took Missionary Ridge, McCook followed Bragg twenty-five miles south to the mountain fortress of Rocky Face Ridge in northern Georgia. Then Grant, considering the Rebel position impregnable, ordered the Union armies of the west into winter quarters.

On returning to Chattanooga, Dan received another tragic telegram. It was from his brother George. Margaret, the great love of George's life who had given birth to her seventh child in the summer of 1862, had died suddenly after complications from another pregnancy.

During her girlhood, when she made the European grand tour with her parents, Margaret had written home comparing the Rhine River to the Ohio River:

> *To be sure the scenery on the Rhine is very beautiful . . . its vine covered terraced hills . . . wild and romantic scenery . . . isolated castles whose days of glory have passed away . . . but wait 200 or 300 yrs. hence, until we get some desolate mansions and romantic tales attached thereto on our Ohio. . . .*

It had taken only twenty years. The desolate mansion was Hillside. The romantic tale was of George and Margaret. Now it had ended.

Dan, knowing how devastated his brother must be, requested leave and reached Steubenville just before Christmas. There he found his mother presiding over the household and caring for George's four surviving children. Martha McCook, although sixty years old, was a strong and loving woman who made the holidays at Hillside as warm and welcoming as possible for all the McCook clan who, as usual, gathered there.

In January Dan went to Washington. Despite recommendations of his promotion to brigadier general—from Generals Rosecrans and Thomas, as well as Governors Tod of Ohio and Yates of Illinois—four months had gone by, and there still was no coveted star.

Since his father was no longer around to drop in at the White House and have a little chat with the president, Dan did. He was just as persuasive. On January 28 Lincoln endorsed the request for his promotion.

One month later his brother Alex was exonerated by a court of inquiry at Louisville for his retreat at the Battle of Chickamauga. On February 23 the court declared:

> *The small force at General McCook's disposal was inadequate to defend against greatly superior numbers.*

The court also vindicated Alex of cowardice, which had been inferred in some Northern newspapers.

> *The Court are of the opinion . . . that in leaving the field to go to Chattanooga, General McCook committed a mistake, but his gallant conduct in the engagement forbids the idea that he was influenced by consideration of personal safety. . . . The Court cannot regard this act of General McCook other than an error of judgment.*

Confident that his honor had been redeemed, Alex went to Washington to await assignment to a new command. He was optimistic. Other generals, including Grant and Sherman, had been removed from command and later restored.

Grant, due to his foot soldiers' victory at Chattanooga, was now the North's greatest hero. On March 9, 1864, he was named general-in-chief of all the armies of the United States and promoted to lieutenant general, a rank held previously by George Washington.

Lincoln was convinced that he finally had his winning general. He told Grant that he had never professed to be a military man and that he had dictated strategy only because of the procrastination of his generals. Giving Grant a free hand, Lincoln said that he would no longer interfere in army matters.

"The particulars of your plans I neither know or seek to know," promised Lincoln.

Grant knew, however, that although he was general-in-chief of the armies, he was not general-in-chief of the strategies. Twice, after his victories at Vicksburg and Chattanooga, he had wanted to attack Mobile, Alabama. But Stanton, after assuring Grant that he was always glad to hear his ideas, promptly ignored them.

The master of the double role was now firmly in control. Major Donn Piatt, one of the few persons to glimpse Stanton's private life, saw him drunk with the lust of great power. He reveled in it. Having outwitted his rivals and vanquished his enemies, he ravenously quaffed his frothing cup of revenge as he prepared to destroy the South. So began the grand campaign to end the Civil War.

Grant was ordered to make the main advance against Lee in the east. Leading a mammoth, well-equipped army against the ragged troops of Lee, Grant was expected to be in Richmond within a week.

Simultaneous and secondary roles would be played by Generals Franz Sigel in the Shenandoah Valley, Benjamin F. Butler up the James River, Nathaniel P. Banks against Mobile, and Sherman against Atlanta.

Sherman's main task was to keep General Joseph E. Johnston, who had replaced Bragg as commander of the Army of Tennessee, too busy to reinforce Lee.

With three western armies to lead—the Cumberland, the Tennessee, and the Ohio—Sherman suggested to Grant that Alex McCook and Thomas Crittenden be restored to command. Both had been exonerated by courts of inquiry. Sherman was told to do nothing, as Grant would have to check with Stanton.

March turned into April. The Union armies, east and west, were poised for the grand campaign. But Dan McCook, in spite of Lincoln's endorsement, had not received his star. And Alex, in spite of his exoneration, had not received a command.

In a desperately blatant move, Dan tried to pour balm on an open wound festering since Shiloh. After the battle he and Alex had made no secret of their disdain for Grant's failure to anticipate an attack or entrench his men and the resultant fleeing and cowering of thousands of his troops. In their frank and outspoken way, Alex and Dan had made a bitter enemy of a man who neither forgot nor forgave.

Unabashedly swallowing his pride, Dan wrote a "mea culpa" version of the Battle of Shiloh and sent it to *Harper's New Monthly Magazine*. It was accepted for the May issue.

THE SECOND DIVISION AT SHILOH
By a Staff Officer

> *The highest romance in military life centres in a succoring army. The sturdy heart of England throbbed responsive to the tread of Bulow's legions . . . the fortunes of consular France rested on Dessaix's eagles . . . the hopes and fears of the loyal North marched with Buell's soldiers, surging to the redfield of Shiloh.*

> *Thousands of soldiers, panic-stricken, were hiding under the bank and, not satisfied with their own infamy, were discouraging our troops newly arrived. How we loathed them!*

But Grant's soldiers, Dan wrote, later redeemed their honor by capturing Vicksburg.

> *I am convinced now that we thought too harshly of them. . . .*

And, finally, they had come to rescue the Army of the Cumberland at Chattanooga.

> *Providence, in His inscrutable ways, permitted these men, thirty months later, to pay the debt of Shiloh with compound interest when, gathering from the plains and savannahs of the Southwest, they marched with eager feet to our relief in beleaguered Chattanooga, and with their brawny shoulders helped bear our banners up the blazing heights of Mission Mountain.*

Summing up his case, Dan reached into his lawyer's lexicon for his final desperate plea:

> *The intellect of Beauregard was no match for the genius of Grant.*

It did not work. He and Alex were still pariahs.

On May 4 the grand campaign began. Grant crossed the Rapidan with the 118,000-man Army of the Potomac to attack Robert E. Lee's 62,000-man Army of Northern Virginia. The next day Sherman started south with 98,000 men in three armies to attack Johnston's 53,000-man Army of Tennessee.

Although the Confederates were still entrenched behind the sheer wall of Rocky Face Ridge, Sherman simply skirted it. By feinting in the center and attacking on the flanks, he forced Johnston to pull out and retreat. Time and time again the strategy worked. Rocky Face Ridge fell on May 12. Dalton fell on the thirteenth. Resaca fell on the fifteenth. Adairsville fell on the seventeenth. Rome fell on the eighteenth. In two weeks Sherman advanced ninety miles.

Reaching the heavily fortified Allatoona Mountains, he swung widely west. Johnston, discovering his movement, also moved west. The two armies slugged it out in five days of hard fighting at Dallas, New Hope Church, and Pickett's Mill. It was a stalemate. Sherman was stopped.

Shifting back to the Allatoona Mountains, Sherman used his long-range artillery. During a week of almost constant rain, he pushed Johnston from one mountain to another until he was barricaded on mighty Kennesaw Mountain. It was the last natural barrier before Atlanta.

Sherman rested his men and studied his maps. In forty-five days of feinting and flanking and fighting, his losses had been light. But in the east it had been a bloodbath.

The grand campaign, starting out with bright hopes, had brought some of the darkest days of the war. Grant's march to Richmond, expected to take a week, had been six weeks of battlefield carnage: he lost almost eighteen thousand men at the Wilderness, another eighteen thousand at Spotsylvania Court House, some twenty-six hundred at North Anna River, and almost thirteen thousand at Cold Harbor. Hospitals in Washington overflowed with thousands of mutilated and dying men.

After losing more than fifty thousand of his army, Grant was no closer to Richmond than McClellan had been in 1862. Northern newspapers, as well as Northern people, castigated him for being destitute of strategy or skill.

"He is a butcher," cried Mary Lincoln, "and is not fit to be at the head of an army."

Grant had expected Richmond to fall quickly. It did not. So on June 20 he settled in for a siege of Lee's supply depot at Petersburg.

Three other secondary campaigns had also failed. Sigel had been thwarted in the Shenandoah, Butler had been defeated at Drewry's Bluff, and Banks had been bloodied on the Red River.

Lincoln was deeply depressed. The war, which cost $2 million a day to wage, was bankrupting the Union. Northern morale was at its lowest. Presidential elections were coming up in four months, and the Radical Republicans, fearful of Lincoln's defeat, were conspiring to get him to withdraw as a candidate. The Democrats, standing on a "peace-at-any-price" platform, had high hopes of winning the White House and negotiating a peace.

If Lincoln were to be reelected, and the fight to save the Union continued, a major victory had to be won soon.

On June 24 Sherman abruptly changed his tactics. He announced that he would feint on the flanks of Kennesaw Mountain and attack the center. Most of his generals considered it little short of madness. But Sherman was adamant. He believed that the enemy's long line on the mountain, although strongly constructed, was thinly held. One sharp thrust would break through. If Kennesaw fell, Atlanta was next. An attack with eight brigades was ordered for June 27 at 8:00 a.m.

Mighty, two-humped Kennesaw rose eight hundred feet above the wooded Georgia plain. Its top bristled with abatis and was crowned with batteries. For months slave labor had fortified the mountain with barricades and trenches protected by twelve feet of spiked logs. The Confederate line was shaped in a wide V, and the key to its defense was the angle where the two wings meet. Dan McCook was selected to charge the angle.

Union trenches below Kennesaw Mountain

Spies reported that it was lightly held because Johnston did not think Sherman would make a frontal attack. But Hardee did. Commanding that segment of the line, he fortified the angle heavily the night of June 25. That was the night that Dan McCook moved his brigade up and bivouacked in the woods below.

On June 26 the rain stopped and at eventide a beautiful sunset seemed to set the woods on fire. Dan's cousin Anson came to his tent for dinner and found Dan's enthusiasm almost boyish in its fervency as he described in detail the plan of attack. Anson, who had assaulted Lookout Mountain and Missionary Ridge, knew what it meant to charge an entrenched position. He was privately apprehensive when the cousins bade each other good night.

The brigade was up at 4:00 a.m. with orders to move at 6:00 a.m., canteens filled with water, forty rounds in cartridge boxes, guns loaded, and bayonets fixed. To veteran soldiers this meant battle. They wore their old clothes and tightened their belts. Officers, who rarely wore their finery on the battlefield, put on torn bars and battered eagles for the assault.

The morning of June 27 was clear and cloudless and already oppressively hot. After a short march, the brigade came to a halt on the crest of a hill in an old peach orchard some six hundred yards from the enemy battlements. Around their ranks sunbeams played. Five regiments of almost eighteen hundred men were deployed in lines of battle, a regiment to each line. The 85th Illinois, acting as skirmishers, were followed by the 125th Illinois, 86th Illinois, 22nd Indiana, and 52nd Ohio. Five pairs of silk flags flew, one for country and one for state. Five regimental commanders sat in the shade of a tree with Dan McCook.

"Officers," he said, "we are going to charge the enemy's works."

He ordered the troops to assault the mountain in silence. They were to rely on their bayonets until they reached the breastworks. Then, as they went over the top with a cheer, they were to fire their guns as a signal for the rest of Sherman's army to follow. Finally, Dan said that he had just learned the mountain had been reinforced and that he would lead the charge.

"Don't be rash, Colonel, don't be rash!" barked a voice from behind a large tree where Generals Thomas and Davis were standing.

"No," Dan said firmly, "I do not send my men where I fear to lead."

Those were the same words that his brother Bob had used in the mountains of western Virginia three years earlier.

Several hundred yards behind him, Sherman climbed up to a platform built on a tall hickory tree. A telegraph key would keep him in touch with his generals as he viewed the assault. Kennesaw's rugged brow stood out clearly, its top bristling with batteries, entrenchments, and abatis, its steep sides strewn with boulders. Sherman watched through his field glass, his wrinkled face working nervously as he paced the platform, chewing on his cigar.

At 8:00 a.m. some two hundred Union heavy guns opened in a furious cannonade along the ten-mile front, pouring shot and shell into the mountain. In reply, Rebel sharpshooter bullets started to crack and whiz. Dan ordered his men to lie flat on the ground. A corporal noted that McCook was standing and might get his head shot off too.

"'Tis an easy matter to fill my place and a very hard matter to fill yours," Dan replied. "Now lie down."

Shortly before 9:00 a.m. the batteries ceased firing. Dan strode to the center of his command. There, in his clear shrill voice, he recited the twenty-eighth stanza of Thomas Macaulay's epic poem "Lays of Ancient Rome," better known as "Horatius at the Bridge."

> *Then out spoke brave Horatius,*
> *The captain of the gate;*
> *To every man upon this earth*
> *Death cometh soon or late.*
> *And how can man die better*
> *Than facing fearful odds*
> *For the ashes of his fathers,*
> *And the temples of his gods?*

Signal guns fired. Bugles blared. Dan, drawing his sword from its scabbard and lifting it high, pointed it toward the deadly angle outlined against the clear blue sky and gave the command.

"Attention battalions, charge bayonets!"

The brigade, as one man, sprang to its feet with a loud cheer. Shoulder to shoulder, the five lines marched at quick time down the long slope toward a marshy vine-tangled creek. Changing their pace to double-quick time, the men jumped across the creek, straightened their lines, and marched in splendid order through a meadow of tall yellow wheat. Rebel batteries opened up from the heights. Grape, canister, shot, and shell rained down on their heads.

The first man fell, his tongue protruding from his mouth. His comrades longed to take him in their arms and minister to his sufferings but could not. Another soldier, white as death, started to flee but returned to the line at two words from his colonel:

"Stop, Joe!"

Reaching a belt of timber, they overran the Confederate skirmish line with bayonets and rifle butts. Winded by the long run, searing heat, and red rasping dust, they halted briefly. Then, at a command, they leaped to their feet and started up through the timber into the open where the ground rose steeply to the crest and where the enemy had a clear range.

Dan led them up through a cross fire of shot and shell. Sheets of flame rained down. Lighted hand grenades plummeted through blue smoke from muskets and white smoke from artillery. Four color-bearers fell. Others caught the flags and carried them up through the roar of the Napoleons. Bodies of fallen men dotted the hill. It was a seething cauldron of hell. Mitchell's brigade on the right was repulsed. Harker's brigade on the left fell back.

McCook's brigade kept climbing. Reaching a sheltered embankment thirty feet from the enemy trenches, they crouched down, out of breath and almost overcome with heat in the broiling Georgia sun.

"Come on, boys, the day is won!" shouted Dan.

He led the sprint to a parapet of spiked logs. Just one breach in the line and the whole army could pour through. They stormed the works with brutal hand-to-hand fighting. The front line pulled the logs back to make an opening. Dan leaped to the parapet with his sword in his right hand and his hat in his left hand as he called back to flag-bearer Private Samuel Canterbury of Company C, Eighty-sixth Illinois.

"Bring up those colors!" Dan shouted.

He was parrying the thrusts of enemy bayonets with his sword and fighting like a man possessed when Private Canterbury pulled on his coattail.

"Colonel Dan," he cried, "for God's sake, get down. They will shoot you."

"Goddamn you," McCook yelled over his shoulder. "Attend to your own business!"

Turning back to the trench, he cried, "Surrender, you damn traitors."

In answer a shot rang out. Fired from a musket a foot away, the flash singed his blue wool blouse as the bullet entered his chest. As McCook fell, Private Canterbury pulled with all his might to keep the colonel from going into the trench.

"Stick to them, boys," Dan ordered as he collapsed on the ground.

"Come on, boys," cried Captain Charles Fellows, "we'll take—." He never finished the sentence. A Confederate volley cut him down. Next Colonel Oscar Harmon rose and ordered, "Forward." He was killed instantly with a bullet through his heart.

Almost one-fourth of McCook's men fell with him at the "Dead Angle," as they called it, in twenty minutes. Dripping wet from blood and sweat, faces blackened with powder and smoke, men vomited from exhaustion and sunstroke. The mangled blue line, torn and bleeding, fell back behind the embankment. The temperature climbed to one hundred degrees in the shade.

The dead were piled high. The living, unable to get back down the mountain, took shelter behind the dead. Bursting shells caught the undergrowth on fire. It crept closer and closer to wounded soldiers of both armies. Then a Confederate colonel stepped out waving a white flag on his sword. He pulled one Rebel soldier to safety. Then he pulled another. The mountain became silent. In an unspoken truce, both sides carried fallen comrades to safety as Hardee watched from the mountaintop.

Dan McCook was lifted tenderly and borne from the field. In the woods they placed him on a stretcher. One of the men carrying him still had his bayonet fixed to his rifle, and Dan was sure that the bayonet would finish him if the bullet did not.

"Soldier, throw that gun down!" he ordered.

Carried past some of his men hugging the ground in the wheat field, he rose on the stretcher and asked, "Boys, what regiment is this?"

Told it was his own Fifty-second Ohio, he gave his last command. "Go on up, boys, you can take the works."

At the field hospital a surgeon dressed his wound. The bullet, shot from the trench below him, had entered Dan's right chest, breaking two ribs. Then the ball split in two. One piece passed through his back, leaving a gaping hole. The other, after striking and breaking his collarbone, remained buried in his body.

"This is to be my last battle, doctor," Dan said.

"Oh, let us hope not," Major M. M. Hooten replied, even though he felt it was true.

Sherman, watching McCook through his field glass, had seen him reach the works and turn around, urging his men on. Sherman was sure he had his breach. But when Dan went down, the day was lost. No one else got so close. Hating to admit failure, Sherman ordered his men to try again at noon. Then, mercifully, he suspended the assault about 2:00 p.m.

Sherman at Kennesaw Mountain and Grant at Cold Harbor tried to duplicate the feat of the foot soldiers at Missionary Ridge. Both failed. Sherman's loss was nearly three thousand killed and wounded. Refusing to admit he had made a mistake, he maintained that the frontal assault was necessary "and for which I assume the entire responsibility." In private he blamed himself for Dan's mortal wound, writing Thomas later that day:

> *I regret beyond measure the loss of . . . Dan McCook.*

When Anson reached the field hospital, he found Dan stretched out on some hay under a little shelter tent, pale and quiet. But when Dan saw his cousin, some of his old fire returned.

"Ans," he said, "in another minute I would have had their works."

That evening he was carried, with two thousand other wounded men, aboard a northbound train and laid on the straw-covered floor of a boxcar. His eldest brother, army surgeon Dr. Latimer McCook, was detached from his Thirty-first Illinois regiment to care for him. The locomotive was painted bright red, and three red lanterns were hung below the headlight to tell Confederate cavalry that it was a hospital train.

As Dan left, he had the satisfaction of knowing that his brigade was still up on Kennesaw Mountain. It refused to surrender what had cost so much to gain. And, in the fighting spirit of its fallen leader, it intended to stay.

It was nearly one thousand miles from Kennesaw Mountain to Steubenville, Ohio. When Dan was removed from the train, station attendants carried the stretcher awkwardly, aggravating the pain of the wound in his back. Without opening his eyes or raising his head, he took command.

"Break step, men, break step," he ordered.

At Hillside they carried him through the front door into the cool center hall where the old Dutch grandfather clock was ticking calmly, then up the wide stairway into a front bedroom where the breeze off the Ohio River ruffled the white curtains and mosquito net over the bed. There he hovered between life and death as his wife and mother tended his wounds. His doctors, Uncle John and Uncle George, could do little except try to keep him comfortable.

His youngest brother John, who had been his aide-de-camp at the Battle of Perryville, was also back at Hillside. After the two brothers protested loudly about the lack of support for Alex's corps at Perryville, they had been separated.

John was assigned to the staff of General Thomas Crittenden. Promoted to captain, John fought at the Battles of Stones River, Tullahoma and Chickamauga. After Alex and Crittenden were relieved of their commands, John served on the staff of General Thomas at the Battle of Chattanooga.

Crittenden, like Alex, was exonerated by a court of inquiry. But Crittenden, unlike Alex, was restored to command. John rejoined him in the east when Crittenden was given command of the First Division, Ninth Corps, Army of the Potomac in Grant's campaign against Lee.

John fought at Spotsylvania, celebrated his nineteenth birthday at the Battle of North Anna River, was wounded in the neck at Shady Grove, and fought at Cold Harbor. When gangrene and blood poisoning developed in his wound, he was invalided home.

By mid-summer John had undergone thirty-seven surgeries on his neck. Finding it hard to sleep, he nursed Dan through the night to relieve his mother and Julia. Told by his doctors that he could not return to active duty, John reviewed Kenyon's sophomore courses in the hope that he could pass the tests and reenter college as a junior in the fall. Studying and nursing Dan were the only things that gave him relief from his pain.

When the large open wound in Dan's back was flushed out with water and probed for the piece of bullet, he tried not to wince. It was not in the blood of the Scots, even in a supreme moment, to make a great demonstration of what was happening within. His family did not encourage him to talk, but Dan wanted to do so, describing the battles in which he fought.

His promotion to brigadier general still had not come from Washington, but other mail came to the famous fighter from grateful countrymen. In answer to one letter, requesting an autograph, he wrote in a firm hand:

He lives best who for himself lives least.

As he neared death he looked forward eagerly to every scrap of news about "his boys" in the Third Brigade, Second Division, Army of the Cumberland. His eyes glowed with pride when he heard of their heroic performance on Kennesaw Mountain after he was shot. Under Dan McCook, they had never turned their backs to the enemy. This was no exception.

Refusing to fall back or to be replaced, they entrenched themselves thirty yards from the enemy's works. Holding their ground for six days and nights with the colors of the Fifty-second Ohio planted in the red soil, they shot one Rebel who tried to grab the flag. No one else dared to try again. On June 28 they hit upon the scheme of digging a tunnel to the Rebel line, charging it with explosives and setting it off at daylight on the Fourth of July. They had burrowed almost to the enemy works when, early on the morning of July 3, a tall lanky Reb who had enough fighting called down that his comrades were all gone.

Johnston had abandoned Kennesaw during the night after discovering that Sherman had returned to his flanking tactics again and had almost reached the Chattahoochee River. Dan McCook's men scrambled to the top of the mountain where, twenty-two miles away, they could see the tall white church spires of Atlanta.

On July 4 Sherman was starting his final drive on Atlanta. Grant still was besieging Petersburg, and Lee was sending a corps to capture Washington.

Slipping away unnoticed by Grant, Lieutenant General Jubal A. Early marched north with some fifteen thousand men through the Shenandoah Valley. He took Harper's Ferry on July 4, crossed the Potomac River into Maryland, and marched into Hagerstown where he collected twenty thousand dollars for not burning the town. At Frederick he upped the ante to two hundred thousand dollars. Then, after defeating six thousand men under General Lew Wallace at the Monocacy River, Early headed for Washington.

Lieutenant General Jubal A. Early

The capital panicked. Since the first week of war, when Daniel McCook stood guard at the White House, the city had feared invasion. During the summer of 1861, under McClellan's direction, the Corps of Engineers had started building a thirty-seven-mile ring of fortifications.

Washington was encircled with over sixty forts and ninety-three batteries containing a total of 837 heavy guns. Every important point, at one-thousand-yard intervals, had a fort. Every approach, not covered by a fort, was swept by a battery of field guns. Rifle pits, with enough room for two ranks of men, connected the entire perimeter. And within these battlements the capital had felt secure, until now.

Now its forts were nearly empty. All able-bodied men, including eighteen thousand experienced artillerists, had been sent to Grant long ago to replace his killed and wounded. Ohio National Guardsmen, partially trained, guarded the northern forts toward which Early was marching.

There were only eighteen hundred infantrymen, an equal number of artillerists, and sixty troopers. The rifle pits were empty.

Military leadership was in disarray. Grant, with Charles Dana again by his side, was more than one hundred miles away at Petersburg. Confusion reigned at the War Department, where they had to wire Grant for permission to do anything. Caution reigned at the White House, where Lincoln had promised he would not interfere with military matters. Orders were issued, suspended, issued anew, and suspended anew.

And the mercurial secretary of war, who usually exploded into a frenzy of action in times of crisis, seemed strangely detached. Although he was always two jumps ahead of everyone else, had a small army of spies, and knew everything that was happening North and South, Stanton gave the impression that he was out of touch.

Early's approach was heralded by terrified people flocking into town. Newspapers printed extra editions. Banks packed up currency and bonds to be shipped down the Potomac River. Confederate sympathizers sent word to Early to hurry, as Washington could be captured easily. Lincoln telegraphed Grant, suggesting that he return. Grant telegraphed Lincoln, declining to come but offering to send the Sixth Corps. The War Department implored every available man to volunteer.

General Alexander McCook, still awaiting orders that had not come, reported for duty on the morning of July 10. He was assigned a small force of one thousand men—invalids, convalescents, and volunteers—at a reserve camp several miles north of the White House.

Assessing the situation, the panic in the capital, and the power vacuum at the War Department, Alex took matters into his own hands, made a hurried inspection of the thinly held forts, and assumed command of the entire northern perimeter.

Getting a report in the late afternoon that Confederate cavalry was skirmishing on the Georgetown Pike, Alex ordered Fort Reno strengthened. Men were to stand by their guns, rifle pits were to be manned, and pickets were to be on the alert all night.

July 11 dawned hot and clear. Signal station officers at Fort Reno in Tennalytown, the highest elevation on the northern perimeter, were watching Early's cavalry column come up Georgetown Pike when they spotted large clouds of dust several miles away on the Seventh Street Pike.

Realizing that the cavalry in their front was a feint and that Early's main force was advancing on Fort Stevens, held by only 209 men, they sent a courier to warn McCook.

Jubal Early, riding at the head of his column, sighted Fort Stevens shortly before noon. Through his field glass he could see it was thinly manned, just as he had been told. It was ripe for picking, like the peach orchards and fields of corn surrounding it.

The usually irascible Early was in high spirits. The greatest prize of the war—the white dome of the Capitol—was only five miles away. The stout, bewhiskered warrior, sitting hunched and stoop-shouldered in his saddle, ordered up a division. But before it could arrive, Early saw a cloud of dust whirling toward the fort from Washington. It was Alex McCook's invalids and convalescents in faded coats of blue.

The lame and the halt came on crutches, arms in slings, heads bandaged, minus an eye or an ear or an arm or a leg that they had given for

Fort Stevens, held by only 209 men, before McCook arrived

the Union. Marching his men at the double-quick and escorted by a small force of cavalry, Alex reached the fort first. He ordered his convalescents and citizen militias into the empty rifle pits. He told his invalids to ram powder into the cannons. He sent Ohio National Guardsmen out in a skirmish line, aided by the timely arrival of some six hundred dismounted troopers. And at 12:30 p.m. he wired the War Department:

> *The enemy is advancing on my front with infantry, cavalry and artillery.*

Alex McCook might have been a pariah, but the former Indian fighter knew how to hold a fort. Outnumbered ten to one, he held his fire until the enemy was within 110 yards of the battlements. Then he opened up with everything he had.

The convalescents in the pits launched a furious barrage, shifting from left to right to give an impression of greater numbers. The Ohio Guardsmen and dismounted cavalrymen on the skirmish line moved forward, firing rapidly with their breech-loading carbines. The batteries, manned by men in bandages, sent out a steady stream of shell and canister from four twenty-four-pounder cannon, six twenty-four-pounder siege guns, two eight-inch howitzers, five thirty-pounder Parrotts, one ten-inch siege gun, and a twenty-four-pounder mortar.

Jubal Early was stopped in his tracks.

Driven back almost a thousand yards, surprised at the ferocity of the attack, and seeing the faded coats of blue, Early thought that Grant's crack Sixth Corps had arrived. Deciding that the fort was too strongly defended to assault, the old warrior withdrew to find another way into Washington, unaware that he had been out-generaled.

President Lincoln, arriving shortly after noon, saw his first fight of the Civil War. He was in excellent spirits, exhilarated by the furious fusillade. But, standing on the rampart in a long yellow linen duster, his plug hat made him a seven-foot-tall target.

"Get down, you damn fool," someone yelled. The president did.

Alex maintained his show of force all afternoon, his thin line augmented by more and more volunteers, young and old, until he had a heteroge-neous collection of citizen militias, messengers, orderlies, male hospital nurses, and some fifteen hundred quartermaster clerks. Fresh ammunition was brought up in a citizen's carriage.

About 3:00 p.m. Grant's best unit, the Sixth Corps, arrived. It was eager to take over.

Alex told them to bivouac in the rear. His ragtag force was doing just fine. The furious commander of the Sixth Corps, Major General Horatio G. Wright, wired the War Department for a clarification of commands. Shortly after midnight a telegram arrived at Fort Stevens:

> *The Sixth Corps, Maj. Gen. H.G. Wright, U.S. Volunteers, commanding, to be held in reserve, and the entire line and troops to be commanded by Maj. Gen. A. McD. McCook, U.S. Volunteers.*

During the night, aided by a full moon, Alex lined his parapets with nearly eight thousand men, including twenty-eight hundred additional convalescents and nine hundred men from the Sixth Corps. At 4:20 a.m. he wired the War Department:

> *Everything is quiet on our front this morning.*

Jubal Early, unable to find another way into Washington, had intended to renew his attack on Fort Stevens at dawn. But when he saw the solid blue line shoulder to shoulder on the parapets, he called it off. Peppering the fort with his sharpshooters, he waited for night to cover his retreat.

During the day visitors streamed out from Washington. The president came again, joined by Mrs. Lincoln and the secretary of war. Also arriving were Secretary of the Navy Gideon Welles, Secretary of State William H. Seward, members of Congress, and streams of citizens who took streetcars to the end of the line and walked the rest of the way, hoping to see a battle.

Charles Dana, hurriedly arriving from Grant's headquarters at Petersburg, assessed the situation and fired off a surly telegram to Grant:

> *Unless you direct positively and explicitly what is to be done, everything will go on in the deplorable and fatal way in which it has gone for the past week. . . .*

In another dispatch, Dana complained that the one-armed general commanding at Fort Reno

if possible, is a bigger fool than McCook.

Jubal Early slipped away during the night. Lincoln wanted the Sixth Corps to pursue him, but it was noon before a telegram arrived from Grant giving permission. By that time Early had escaped across the Potomac River with hundreds of wagons of plunder and $120,000 in greenbacks.

Alex counted his casualties. Fewer than one hundred men were killed and wounded, aside from nearly three hundred casualties incurred by Wright when he sent some of his men out in an attempt to silence Early's sharpshooters.

On July 16 Alex requested a leave of absence to go home as his brother Dan was sinking rapidly. Alex also requested permission to take him a brigadier general's commission. The War Department replied that one already had been sent for "gallant and distinguished service at Kennesaw Mountain."

Dan McCook lingered until 2:00 p.m. on Sunday, July 17, remaining conscious until about noon when he fell into a coma. His family was at his bedside when he took his last breath. As he wished, the funeral ceremonies at Hillside were private.

Then his brothers George and Alex accompanied his body to Cincinnati. The city officials had hoped to have a public ceremony as an expression of their regard for the lionhearted fighter. But mortification, brought on by putrefying gangrene, had commenced before death, and the decomposition of his remains was so rapid that George and Alex decided not to delay his burial. Dan was laid quietly to rest near the graves of his father, his two brothers, and his little son.

Colonel Dan McCook had commanded a brigade for almost two years without the accompanying star of a brigadier general. The recommendation that he be promoted for gallantry in battle had been made by most of his commanding generals, including Sheridan. President Lincoln's endorsement had been made on January 28. The honor, however, was denied until death was near.

But the proud Dan McCook had the last word. When the commission arrived at his bedside on July 16, he wrathfully rejected it and told the officer to take it back.

"The promotion is too late now," Dan said, with the old fighting fire in his steel-gray eyes.

"Return it with my compliments, saying, 'I decline the honor.'"

Sketch of Dan McCook that appeared in Harper's Pictorial History of the Great Rebellion in the United States, May 1866

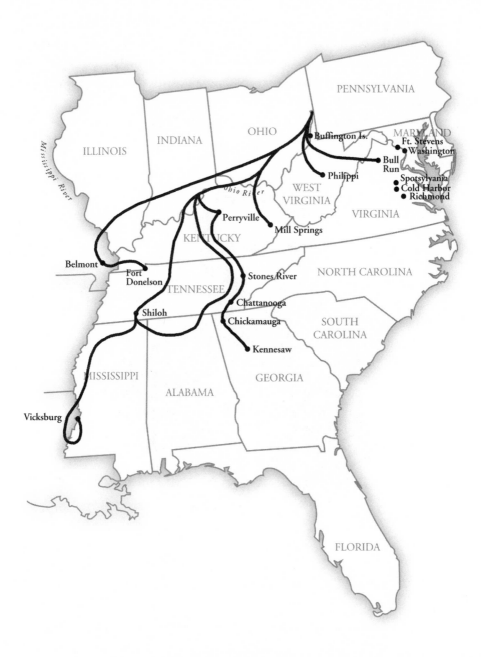

*Territory trod by the Fighting McCooks
in their quest to save the Union*

Chapter 17

BRIGADIER GENERAL EDWARD McCOOK
in the Battle for Atlanta

Splashing across the Chattahoochee River stark naked, except for their hats and cartridge boxes and carbines, Brigadier General Edward McCook's cavalrymen routed a Rebel outpost and drove the enemy through the woods.

It was a scorching day in northern Georgia as Sherman neared Atlanta.

When General McCook's troopers were ordered to dismount, cross the Chattahoochee River, and scout the country, they shed their uniforms and boots before wading across at Cochran's Ford. Surprising the Confederates, they drove them from their rifle pits, capturing an officer, three soldiers, and two boats.

An amused Ed McCook wrote in his official report:

They would have got more, but the rebels had the advantage of running through the bushes with clothes on. It was certainly one of the funniest sights of the war, and a very successful raid for naked men to make.

"Horse Ed," as he was called by the McCook clan, had been in the saddle for three long years of war. Known for leading saber-wielding cavalry charges and riding roughshod over official orders to fight the war his own way, Ed reveled in his reputation as a

dashing officer who never refuses a fight and invariably whips the opponent when the forces are about equal . . .

He was a thirty-one-year-old bachelor with a luxurious jet black mustache and fashionable sideburns. He was a charming rogue who wore a large feather in his hat, drank fine wines, smoked expensive cigars, and kept a French Cajun chef on his staff. He was a renowned ladies' man who had promised to marry at least three belles during the course of the war.

Edward Moody McCook, the eldest of the five sons of Dr. John and Catherine, was born in New Lisbon on June 15, 1833, and grew up to the sounds of men digging the Sandy and Beaver Canal. By the time he was fourteen, the canal still was not finished. But New Lisbon was.

Finding life in the declining town incredibly dull, Ed persuaded his twelve-year-old brother Anson to run away with him. They would get jobs as cabin boys on an Ohio River steamboat and work their way down to New Orleans.

Slipping out of the house early one morning, the boys started walking thirteen miles to the nearest Ohio River landing. Halfway there, tired and hungry, they sat down by the side of the road to rest. Soon they heard a galloping horse and saw a familiar figure.

"Good morning, young gentlemen," said their father calmly as he rode by.

Halting his lathered steed, Dr. John suggested that the erstwhile cabin boys start marching home. The retreat was a quiet one with Ed and Anson shuffling along dispiritedly while their father brought up the rear on his horse. The truants had plenty of time to consider the various punishments they might receive but, to their everlasting gratitude, the only thing they got was a big hot breakfast from their mother.

Adventure came twelve years later when, as a young lawyer, Ed headed for the Kansas Territory. Following the lead of his cousin Dan who had gone west the previous fall, Ed joined the "second stampede" of the Pikes Peak gold rush in the spring of 1859.

Journalists Horace Greeley of the *New York Tribune* and Henry Villard of the *Cincinnati Daily Commercial* had traveled to the Rocky Mountains and reported that a single sluice could yield anywhere from $26 to $494 per day. Over the next few months, on the strength of their reporting, some five hundred prospectors arrived daily in Arapahoe County. Unfortunately, there were not enough workable claims, and soon the "second stampede" was over.

A few men became wealthy. Most lost everything. Some went home. Some drifted farther west. Some were killed by Indians. Some simply disappeared.

Edward McCook, Esquire, remained in the Rocky Mountains to practice law, mine for gold, and fight the Indians who were trying to hold onto the last vestiges of their ancestral land. By 1860 Ed was living in Central City, in the Gul Lake district of Arapahoe County, where he shared a house with four other men.

Their housekeeper, who lived next door, turned out to be the missing wife of his cousin, Dr. Latimer McCook. Eliza McLain McCook's disappearance from Illinois and her reappearance in a small mining town in the Rocky Mountains was never explained by the tight-knit McCooks. Latimer was a widower, they said, and that was that.

Ed, a natural politician like many in his clan, was elected to the Kansas Territorial Legislature in the fall of 1860. But, after traveling some eight hundred miles by oxcart to Lecompton, he discovered that his district was not included when Congress voted Kansas into the Union as a free state on January 29, 1861. Arapahoe County, instead, was assigned to the Colorado Territory. Ed immediately left for Washington to look out for his interests.

Two months later, after the organization of the Colorado Territory, he was on his way back to the Rockies when Fort Sumter fell. Turning around, Ed came back to help defend the capital. He and his brother Henry were on the last train to arrive in Washington before the Rebels tore up the tracks. After registering at Willard's Hotel, they hurried to the White House to join their Uncle Daniel in the Frontier Guards.

During the weeklong siege, Ed also served as a secret agent. With bridges burned and telegraph lines down, he volunteered to ride horseback through Maryland carrying dispatches from General Winfield Scott. On April 23 eight couriers were sent out. Only two reached their destinations and returned. One was Ed McCook.

In recognition of his equestrian boldness and daring, General Scott offered him a second lieutenant's commission in the elite First U.S. Cavalry.

Two days later Ed wrote to his Connecticut cousin Mary Sheldon.

> *Washington City*
> *May 10, 1861*
>
> *My Dear Cousin,*
>
> *I am almost as much surprised as probably you were to find myself in the Army of the United States. I had started for my home in the mountains when the intelligence of that barbarous attack on Sumter reached me, and of course I returned at once and offered my services to my country.*
>
> *It was a great, a very great sacrifice for me to make; all that I possess in the world I left behind me on the mountains, and in that lawless country where the strong arm only protects your rights, absence is utter ruin, but I would rather feel the consciousness of having done my duty than possess all the wealth that lies buried in those lonely mountains.*
>
> *If I meet a soldier's fate, it is well; I know that kind friends will sometimes think of me with pride, and that posterity will do justice to all who have stood by their country in this the hour of her greatest need.*
>
> *When the big wars "that make ambition virtue" are over, when we have fought and triumphed, as we will triumph, then I may return once more to peaceful pursuits, that is if I don't find that peace which the preachers say is only found in the grave.*
>
> *Your affectionate Cousin*
> *Edward.*

His next letter to Mary was from Carlisle Barracks, Pennsylvania, where he awaited the arrival of the First U.S. Cavalry, on its way east from Fort Leavenworth.

Carlisle Barracks
June 3, 1861

My Dear Cousin,

Lieutenants have very few opportunities of distinguishing themselves, at least they do the fighting and others gain the credit for it, but if I have an opportunity I will endeavor to do something that will give me a mention in the returns.

If you do not see my name in the first fight we are fortunate enough to get into, you must have confidence enough in me to suppose either that I am not there, or else that some injustice has been done.

I never did set a very high value on my life, and as I have nothing, or rather no person particularly to live for, I don't intend to be at all careful about exposing it.

Your affectionate cousin,
Edward

A month later he wrote her after visiting his brother Anson at camp in Virginia.

Carlisle Barracks
July 2, 1861

Dear Cousin:

I found Ans there in the advance, looking and living like the brave true soldier that he is, God bless him! I saw three of your regiments there. They are fine looking men. . . .

Their gallantry had got them into some trouble however, as three of their number had been attacked by the bright eyes of some fair secessionists in the neighborhood, yielded to their fascinations, and were captured and carried off away down to Dixie. Heigho! So it has always been with soldiers ever since the beginning of the world; Venus disarmed Mars, Delilah Sampson, and Calypso Ulysses. Your sex has always made fools of ours, even down to the days of your innocent Connecticut men who are fooled into a trap by the soft glances of the sunny eyed southern maids, and who are now no doubt heartily cursing themselves for having forgotten the strict teaching of the land of steady habits.

Write soon, and keep sending those papers if not too much trouble. I have been confined to my bed for several days by an injury received from a vicious horse, and they have afforded me great amusement.

Yours affectionately,
Edward

The "vicious horse" was, in truth, a case of vicious syphilis that landed Ed in the hospital for several weeks.

By the time he was able to sit a horse, the Battle of Bull Run had been fought. Angry that he had missed the battle, he was even angrier to be assigned to recruiting duty, as the North began building its three-year army.

Cincinnati, Aug. 28, '61

Dear Cousin Mary:
I am very lonely here, discontented and unhappy. I know no person, and the thought that I am compelled to remain here recruiting while others die doing the fighting makes me feel dissatisfied with myself and the service.

Though no reputation has yet been won by any of our officers in the field, yet there is certainly none to be gained inspecting recruits.

Your affectionate cousin,
Ed

One month later things were looking better.

Indianapolis, Indiana
September 29, 1861

Dear Cousin Mary:
I have been offered the Lieut. Colonelcy of a volunteer cavalry regiment and of course if the War Department will give me a three year furlough will accept it. I will then have just what I wish for—high rank, and an opportunity for service and distinction.

Ed had heard that his youngest brother, Little Johnny, planned to go to Trinity College in Hartford and live with Mary and her half-sister Eliza.

> *If John goes to Hartford keep him away from the young ladies;*
> *that is a weakness very early developed with the McCook family,*
> *and it will seriously interfere with his studies. Give my love to all.*
> *Yours affectionately,*
> *Ed*

Two months later Ed was on his way to "service and distinction" as major of the Second Indiana Cavalry, Fourth Division, Army of the Ohio.

Cavalrymen were elite. Paid more than infantrymen, they were finely mounted on bays and chestnuts and dappled grays and took care of their horses before they took care of themselves. Bronzed men in short blue jackets with yellow braid, they wore polished boots, spurs of gleaming brass, and wide leather belts that held their six-shot revolvers and glistening sabers. Living by the bugle calls of "Trot," "Gallop," and "Charge," they moved thirty miles a day on the march, sleeping in the open with their heads on their saddles and their horses tethered to their wrists.

In the spring of 1862, after Forts Henry and Donelson had fallen, Buell's Army of the Ohio marched south to join Grant's Army of the Tennessee. Ed, now colonel of his regiment, dashed off a quick note to Mary.

> *Camp Near Columbia, Tenn.*
> *March 29, 1862*
>
> Dear Little Cousin:
> *This is the first time I have had leisure to write, for I am now*
> *Col. of my regiment and working day and night to bring it to*
> *such a state of efficiency as will make me proud of their conduct*
> *at all times. It has taken all the flesh off me, and the other field*
> *officers say that I begin to look like one of the swamp natives of*
> *this bilious region.*
>
> *Yours affectionately*
> *E. M. McCook*

One week later the Battle of Shiloh had been fought.

Camp on the Battlefield
April 13, 1862

Dear Cousin Mary,

I suppose the telegraph has furnished you before this with an account of the terrible battle. . . . When our division arrived here on Sunday evening Grant's forces were whipped and almost driven into the river. The enemy had advanced so close that men were killed in their regiments while forming on the landing. Reinforcements from Crittenden and McCook's Divisions came up during the night, and on Monday morning we attacked. . . .

Alex and Dan McCook were both in the fight. It seems to be the fortune of our family to be represented on every hard fought field. Pray for us, dear cousin. . . .

Yours affectionately,
Ed

The carnage at Shiloh forced Lincoln to call for three hundred thousand more men. States were given quotas and told that if they did not meet them, a draft would be applied. Ed, in his next letter to Mary, wondered whether his brother would be tempted to leave Trinity College and reenlist.

August 17, 1862

Dear Cousin Mary,

I forgot to ask Father how the draft would affect "Little Johnnie". Does he want to go? He has seen enough of the pomp and circumstance of glorious hard bread and fat pork, and gunpowder and wet, tentless nights, and muddy dreary days, not to be tickled any longer into patriotism by the rattle of a drum; but I fear the McCook may be in him strong enough to lead him back to his youthful folly again.

Don't do it my boy! Stay at school and get wisdom, and after while a wife and children; I'm proud of the name and want it perpetuated—leave the rest of us to gather the glory, and be gathered in the harvest of the sword.

Speaking of matrimony reminds me—your Northern girls are not doing the fair thing by us poor fellows who are growing old and ugly and uninteresting in the field. You are marrying home guards, and unwarlike citizens and playing smash with our hopes. . . .

Then Ed quoted from English playwright Richard Sheridan:

"A man who weds today and may be sent the Lord knows where before night, then returns in a twelve month perhaps, like a colossus, with one leg in New York, and the other in 'Chelsea hospital'".

Three sweethearts have I lost already, since the war commenced . . . and if I lose the fourth, the one you promised me, it will drive me to arms—the arms of the first fair southern maiden I can persuade to drink to <u>our</u> Union—how would you all like a fascinating young rebel for cousin, sister-in-law & etc. I hold this over you in <u>terrorism</u>, to keep that promise of yours good, and to prevent the sacrifice of another of my intended to those insatiable Home Guards.

Affectionately yours,
Ed

Three weeks later Ed was given command of the eleven-hundred-man First Brigade of the Cavalry Division in Buell's army. After fighting at the Battle of Perryville, Ed was with Rosecrans at Murfreesboro in the spring of 1863. Twenty miles south, at Tullahoma, was their archenemy, Braxton Bragg.

February 24, 1863

Dear Mary,

The great Army of the Cumberland, heroes of Shiloh & Perryville & Murfreesboro is at last conquered, stuck fast in the mud. . . .

Here the two armies are face to face, growling because they can't get at each other, and quietly waiting until the day dry roads will enable them once more to indulge in the pleasant and pious occupation of cutting each others throats.

He added that he was expecting a promotion to brigadier general.

> *It has not come yet, I suppose, because I scorn to use the usual*
> *political applications for gaining rank. I bide my time, certain*
> *that if life is spared I can win it . . . without degrading myself*
> *by asking political influence.*
>
> *Affectionately yours,*
> *Ed*

As the weather improved, Stanton was prodding Rosecrans to move against Bragg. But Rosecrans reminded Stanton that Bragg's cavalry outnumbered Rosecrans's cavalry two to one. And when Nathan Bedford Forrest and John Hunt Morgan joined Bragg after their raids, the ratio was four to one.

"Give me more cavalry," Rosecrans implored time and time again.

When weeks went by and additional cavalry did not appear, Ed McCook tried a new tack. Writing Stanton on June 3, he asked for permission to raise an all-Negro cavalry brigade:

> *They are almost without exception good riders and accustomed to*
> *the care of animals. Their excellent facilities of imitation and*
> *habits of obedience render them readily susceptible of drill and*
> *discipline. Their simple wants and fine physical development,*
> *produced by hard and continuous labor, fit them well for the*
> *endurance of the hardships incidental to the arduous duties of the*
> *cavalry in this war. Their keen sense of locality and familiarity*
> *with their native regions make them invaluable as scouts and for*
> *flying expeditions into the interior of the enemy's country.*
>
> *What I would wish is your impression as to the propriety or*
> *feasibility of recruiting, from contrabands now being and likely*
> *to be within our lines, select men enough to form a brigade of*
> *cavalry. . . . I would propose to mount the men, if possible, at*
> *the expense of the enemy. In this event arms and uniforms will*
> *be all I should ask of the Government.*
>
> *I have a fine brigade at present, one I would be reluctant to*
> *relinquish, but I submit this project to you, believing that its*

successful accomplishment would be of incalculable service to the country.

Stanton did not act on McCook's suggestion. Although the enlistment of Negroes had been sanctioned by the Emancipation Proclamation and Stanton planned to have one hundred thousand blacks in uniform by mid-summer, none would go to Rosecrans. He would get no more cavalry, black or white.

By now Stanton was increasingly autocratic, reveling in his reputation as the most hated man in Washington, arresting more than thirteen thousand persons during the war on suspicions of being traitors, and using the power of the federal government to crush those he hated and elevate those he liked.

Highly secretive, Stanton did not attend half of Lincoln's cabinet meetings. When he did come, he was late and uncommunicative, openly disdainful of the president's humorous stories. The War Department, containing the telegraph office, was where Stanton presided and where Lincoln usually went to lie on the worn leather couch near the window and wait to learn of battles won or lost.

Lincoln was aware of Stanton's high-handed machinations, but the president needed him. He needed Stanton's superior strengths in the man-killing job, and he needed his tremendous will-to-win-at-any-cost.

In the west, after Ed McCook was turned down in his request for an all-Negro cavalry brigade, he continued to command the Second Brigade, First Division, Cavalry Corps, in Rosecrans's Army of the Cumberland.

After Rosecrans was defeated at Chickamauga and limped back into Chattanooga to lick his wounds, Union wagon trains started south to resupply him. On October 3 a ten-mile-long Union supply train, with eight hundred six-mule-team wagons and a procession of sutler's lorries, snaked its way through Tennessee's Sequatchie Valley, bound for Chattanooga.

Confederate General Joseph Wheeler, roaming the valley with some five thousand to six thousand troopers, discovered the great prize near Anderson's Crossroads. After eight hours of plundering, Wheeler took off with half the wagons, ordering the rest to be burned and the mules to be killed.

Ed McCook, scouting in the valley with two regiments, spotted smoke curling into the sky and belatedly reached the scene of carnage. Galloping past the burning wagons and dead mules, McCook caught up with Wheeler at dusk. Charging the Rebel rear guard in a running fight, Ed recovered most of the stolen wagons and about five hundred mules, stating in his official report:

> *The rebel loss was about 120 killed and wounded and 60 prisoners, among the latter 2 majors and 7 other officers. I know it will gratify you when I tell you that nearly every wound was inflicted with the saber.*

McCook and Brigadier General George Crook, commanding the Second Division, pursued Wheeler and fought him in several battles until, finally, with many of his Rebel troopers killed or captured, Wheeler was forced to retreat south across the Tennessee River.

"Horse Ed," commended by Rosecrans, looked forward to his general's star. Unfortunately, two weeks later, Rosecrans was removed from command.

So Ed unabashedly resorted to the political pressure that previously he had disdained. His cousin Mary was a warm friend of the wife of the secretary of the navy, Gideon Welles, whose ancestors were early settlers of Hartford. Mrs. Welles was close to Mrs. Lincoln.

> *Smithville, Tenn.*
> *Nov. 28, 1863*
>
> Dear Cousin:
>
> *I only have time to write these words and they will be selfish ones.*
>
> *I want you to write to your friend Mrs. Secy Welles (Secy of the Navy) or see her, or see him, and secure his influence and efforts to procure my promotion to the rank of Brigadier General. I think I have been serving long enough as a Colonel. I have always had the command of a brigadier and for the last 5 months of a Major General (this division).*
>
> *I don't know that I can urge any other particular claims, except that I have had more fights than any other man in this department, and never got whipped; however that ain't much of a recommendation probably.*
>
> *You can set Eliza to work too. Tell her I can never marry her*

until I have a star on my shoulder and my buttons set far apart.
The eagle is a beautiful bird certainly and our national emblem
and all that sort of thing, but to add interest and importance
to the wedding ceremony, give me a star.

Your cousin,
Ed. M. McCook

But, after two more months of hard wintertime fighting in the mountains of East Tennessee, there still was no star in sight, and Ed was angry.

Near Marysville, Tenn.
Jan 31, 1864

Dear Cousin Mary:
There was a big cavalry fight on the 27th near Leversville. The
division I commanded engaged the whole of Gen. Martin's
Corps, routed them completely, captured two pieces of artillery,

Cavalry charge

*about 800 small arms, 200 prisoners, 17 commissioned offi-
cers, horses without number, and killed and wounded about
300 of the enemy. None were engaged except my own cavalry
and the enemy had two to our one.*

*I charged them with the saber, and rebels never can stand
the cold steel and the terrible hand to hand fighting that my
men do. Providence again carried me through safely. I exercise
a Major General's command with a Colonel's rank; the only
man in the army that does.*

*I grow intensely disgusted sometimes with these shoddy sol-
diers and tinsel generals, men of neither courage nor capacity,
and then I become home sick as a child, and long oh so much
to see my dear little cousins, Mary and Eliza, and all my dear
friends until the feeling makes me almost sick.*

*It may seem to you comical that big rough soldiers should
feel this way, but you know in some things the bravest are the
tenderest, and the ties of home and kindred twine themselves
stronger around hearts that are exposed day after day to the fire
of the enemy, than those that never beat a pulsation quicker
except at the clink of gold or news from the stock market.*

Included in his disdain were those Northern men who refused to volunteer.

*Tell me really, little cousin, don't you in your heart of hearts despise
these sweet little fellows who can stand behind counters and measure out tape or discount bills, when every man is needed to help
our country in this terrible struggle for existence?*

Affectionately yours,
Ed

A month later Ed took matters into his own hands and applied for a
twenty-day leave of absence:

*The request is not based on a sick wife, important business, or
any of the standard reasons. I simply want to go home <u>very</u> <u>much</u>.*

He also wanted to go to Washington *very much*. After a visit to his parents in Steubenville, he headed for the White House.

After three years of war, Lincoln had aged greatly. Lost battles, high casualties, and sleepless nights had taken their toll. His shoulders sagged, his melancholy eyes were sunken, and his face was more deeply etched.

Unceasingly he had juggled the demands of the war. He had to raise the men and money to wage it, find the generals to fight it, maintain the support of the people to continue it, fend off the demands of the Radical Republicans to run it, and outwit the demands of the Peace Democrats to stop it. At the same time he was trying to cope with the death of his eleven-year-old son Willie and the histrionics of his difficult wife Mary.

President Lincoln in 1864

But Lincoln had not forgotten that Ed, during the first week of war when the capital was threatened and most people fled, had the courage to remain and protect him. On April 23 the president nominated him for brigadier general, and four days later it was confirmed by the Senate. Ed's star, unlike his cousin Dan's, was not held up by a grudge.

One week later Brigadier General Edward McCook commanded the First Cavalry Division, Army of the Cumberland as Sherman began his campaign for Atlanta. Sherman used his four cavalry divisions mainly for reconnaissance, screening flanks and guarding rail supply lines. But Ed McCook chafed under such strictures, feeling that the cavalry, now larger and better equipped, should be more aggressive.

On June 23 he sent a message to the commander of the Cavalry Corps, Brigadier General Washington Lafayette Elliott:

> *I am so tired of taking my share of this fight in little skirmishes and scouting parties that I would risk cheerfully the lives and wind of the few anatomical steeds I have left for the purpose of getting my proportion of the glory, if there is any for the cavalry, of this campaign.*

Ed's "proportion of the glory" finally came in late July after Sherman fought his way to the gates of Atlanta. One of the South's fiercest fighters, Lieutenant General John Bell Hood, had replaced Johnston. Hood was firmly entrenched in Atlanta. Lincoln needed Atlanta.

After failing in two battles on July 20 and 22 to penetrate into the city with his infantry and artillery, Sherman switched to his cavalry. In an effort to strangle Hood within Atlanta, Sherman wired the War Department that he was sending his two best cavalry divisions on a sweeping raid around the city to wreck the Macon and Western Railroad, Hood's main supply line:

> *I send by the right a force of about 3500 cavalry, under General McCook, and round by the left about 5000 cavalry, under General Stoneman, with orders to reach the railroad about Griffin.*

Sherman ordered them to leave at dawn on July 27 and encircle Atlanta, McCook on the west and Stoneman on the east. They were to join forces south of the city near Lovejoy's Station on the night of July 28. Sherman added:

> *The railroad, when reached, must be substantially destroyed for a space of from two to five miles, telegraph wires pulled down as far as possible and hid in water or destroyed.*

But Stoneman, unknown to McCook, had another mission in mind. Privately, he asked Sherman for permission to make a dash down to the infamous prisoner of war camp at Andersonville and free some thirty-three thousand Northern prisoners. Sherman, hoping for success from its very boldness, sanctioned the rescue try but stressed that, first, the railroad must be wrecked.

McCook's troopers, armed with sabers, revolvers, and new Spencer seven-shot repeating carbines, trotted out of their Marietta camps at 4:00 a.m. on July 27 in a torrential rainstorm. After swinging wide to the west to escape detection, they crossed the Chattahoochee River behind enemy lines and dashed rapidly through the pine forests in the rear of Hood's army.

Reaching the town of Palmetto about 6:00 p.m. on July 28, they tore up two and a half miles of Atlanta and West Point Railroad track, downed telegraph lines and destroyed freight cars, set the torch to one thousand bales of cotton, one thousand sacks of corn, three hundred sacks of flour, large quantities of bacon and tobacco, and galloped off, leaving a holocaust of fire lighting the sky behind them.

Tearing through the night like a tornado, they found a five-mile-long Confederate supply wagon train and, without firing a shot, captured 72 officers and 350 men who had been asleep and protested the intrusion profanely.

Before burning five hundred wagons, including those containing the luggage of Hood and Hardee, McCook's cavalrymen confiscated liquor, of which they partook freely, tobacco, and a payroll chest containing thousands of Confederate dollars intended for troops in Atlanta. After trading their tired mounts for fresh horses, the finest they had ever seen, they slaughtered eight hundred mules with their sabers, lest gunfire disclose their location, and headed for Fayetteville.

Reaching the town well before dawn, prisoners in tow, they captured another 130 Confederates, mostly officers, sleeping in homes near the

*"Horse Ed" capturing Confederate
wagon train near Fayetteville*

town square. After destroying mail sacks, boxes of tobacco, and barrels of whiskey, some troopers broke into private homes searching for silver and other valuables. Many citizens, seeing the fires of Palmetto in the distance, had hidden their family treasures. Others displayed Masonic colors in their windows, hoping that Northern officers might be fellow Masons and order their men to spare the houses.

Finished with Fayetteville in two hours, Ed McCook galloped out at 5:00 a.m. headed for Lovejoy's Station, thirty miles south of Atlanta, where he was to meet Stoneman. Marching his 550 prisoners behind him, McCook destroyed wagons and supplies and fought a successful skirmish at Flint River where Confederate pickets attempted to burn a covered bridge to keep him from crossing. He reached his rendezvous point at 7:00 a.m., twelve hours late.

Stoneman was not there. Nor was there any evidence that he had arrived earlier and departed.

While waiting for him, McCook carried out his orders by burning the depot, ripping up two and a half miles of Macon and Western Railroad track, tearing down five miles of telegraph poles and wires, and burning several railroad cars containing thousands of dollars worth of cotton, tobacco, and bacon. By this time he had destroyed a total of 1,160 wagons and 2,000 mules, badly needed by Hood.

It was about 2:00 p.m. when Ed McCook, resting his men, was warned by his scouts that a large cavalry force was approaching from the east. It was Wheeler.

McCook had intended to complete a circle of Atlanta. But now, having wasted precious hours waiting for Stoneman, McCook had to retrace his steps with Wheeler and two brigades of cavalry in hot pursuit. Avoiding Fayetteville, McCook left the main road and wound through fields and wooded byroads, heading back toward the Chattahoochee River.

Dusk descended, and the cavalrymen, weary from little or no sleep, dozed in their saddles on their exhausted horses. Behind them several hundred mules, pulling captured wagons, halted in their tracks and slept. When shouted curses failed to awaken the beasts, troopers poked them with sabers until they came to life with uncouth noises fore and aft and, tails in the air, stampeded down the road, scattering wagons and baggage through the woods.

On his nighttime odyssey Ed McCook captured another fifty wagons, which he smashed rather than burn so that they would not betray his position. But, burdened with several hundred prisoners plus a large pack train and artillery pieces, McCook was slowed. And Wheeler was gaining on him.

After passing over a high wooden bridge at Line Creek, McCook ordered his rear guard, the Fourth Kentucky, under the command of Colonel Granville West, to hold the span until dawn and then burn it. However, Wheeler arrived in the early morning hours and West, forced to torch the bridge, was surrounded and out of ammunition by dawn.

"Surrender, you damn Yankees!" yelled a Confederate.

"Go to hell!" Colonel West shouted in reply.

With about seventy of his cavalrymen, West crashed through the enemy lines and escaped, catching up with McCook as he reached the town of Newnan.

"The Yankees! The Yankees!" townspeople shouted in terror.

Six hundred Confederate soldiers, halted in two trains at the railroad depot due to the wrecked rails at Palmetto, jumped out to defend the town. Families fled with their household treasures thrown hurriedly into carriages and carts. Negro servants were hustled away, cattle and sheep were driven on the run, and seven Confederate Army hospitals were emptied of their physicians, nurses, and convalescents. Only the bedridden were in the wards.

McCook, however, skirted the town and was heading for the Chattahoochee when he was brought to bay at Brown's Mill. Wheeler, reinforced by the infantrymen from the stalled trains, had him surrounded and outnumbered. McCook tried unsuccessfully to break through to the river, managing during the attempt to capture a Texas brigade with its commander and all his men and horses.

As darkness descended once more, McCook called a council to consider a Confederate demand that they surrender. His commanders asked to be allowed to cut their way out with their brigades. He agreed.

"Save yourselves and your commands," he said.

While Ed McCook held off the enemy, Colonels John Croxton and William Torrey fought their way out with their brigades and scattered. Then McCook led twelve hundred cavalrymen in a charge by column through the Confederate lines, leaving his prisoners behind. Keeping one jump ahead of the Rebels, he and his men made their way through woods and swamps until they reached the Chattahoochee, crossed on commandeered boats, and limped into Marietta.

Sherman, who had feared McCook was captured, sent a relieved dispatch to Nashville on August 3:

General McCook is safe. He is in with 1,200 of his command.

Stoneman, it turned out, never had any intention of rendezvousing with McCook. Instead, he headed straight for Andersonville to release the prisoners. Discovered near Macon, Stoneman was captured with part of his command.

McCook lost some five hundred officers and men, killed, wounded, or missing, in the misadventure. Furious at Stoneman's failure to meet him, Ed was defiantly defensive in his official report:

I regard the raid as a brilliant success, and had the forces of General Stoneman been able to unite with mine near McDonough, as I understood was contemplated by the general

commanding the military division, I think we might have suc-
cessfully carried our arms wherever desired, and accomplished
more magnificent results than any raid in the history of the war.

    I conclude my report by expressing gratitude to the kind
Providence which enabled me, through the gallantry of my
brave men and faithful officers, to extricate my command from
the perils which surrounded it, and to bring them back, not
only in safety, but crowned with success.

    I am, general, very respectfully, your obedient servant,

E. M. McCook

Brigadier-General, Commanding Division

Sherman, reinforced in his belief that the best use of cavalry was for reconnaissance and flank-guarding, did not agree with McCook's term "success" when he reported to Washington:

General McCook is entitled to much credit for thus saving his
command, which was endangered by the failure of General
Stoneman to reach Lovejoy's. But on the whole the cavalry raid
is not deemed a success, for the real purpose was to break the
enemy's communications, which though done was on so limited
a scale that I knew the damage would soon be repaired.

Meanwhile, in the east there had been another disaster. Grant, still besieging Petersburg, had resorted to the same tactic that he used at Vicksburg. A 511-foot tunnel was dug under Confederate lines and filled with gunpowder. At dawn on July 30 it was exploded, creating a crater 170 feet long, 60 feet wide, and 30 feet deep. As at Vicksburg, Union soldiers jumped into the hole and, as at Vicksburg, they were slaughtered. Grant suffered four thousand casualties and the bitter denunciations of the North.

The days of August were some of the darkest of the Civil War. Despair and humiliation engulfed the North. Lincoln's defeat at the polls seemed inevitable. His closest friends felt he was unequal to the task. He himself expected to lose. Editorials in Northern Democrat newspapers demanded:

STOP THE WAR!

That was exactly what the Confederates wanted. They counted on Northerners, sick of the slaughter, defeating Lincoln at the polls and suing for peace. If the South could hold onto Richmond and Atlanta, independence might be just around the corner.

But on August 30, Hood made a disconcerting discovery. Sherman, unnoticed, had pulled most of his infantry out of their entrenchments north of Atlanta and circled them south of the city to do the job that his cavalry had failed to do. Hood's last railroad was cut. He faced strangulation. Hardee came out to fight. Sherman mauled him at Jonesboro. Hood was forced to evacuate Atlanta. Sherman marched in and telegraphed the War Department on September 3:

So Atlanta is ours, and fairly won.

Sherman's victory, added to that of Admiral David Farragut in taking Mobile Bay on August 5 and General Philip Sheridan in defeating Early in the Shenandoah Valley on October 19, assured Lincoln's victory at the polls on November 8, 1864.

Lincoln, running on the Union Party ticket, a combination of Republicans and War Democrats, received 55 percent of the popular vote and carried every loyal state except Kentucky, Delaware, and New Jersey.

Now Lincoln had the luxury of concentrating on his plans for a peaceful restoration of the nation. It was a goal he had dreamed of all during the war.

Four months earlier, the Radical Republicans in Congress had tried to circumvent him by passing the Wade-Davis bill, giving Congress the power of reconstruction. Lincoln vetoed the bill by simply pocketing it. Then he took his case to the people by issuing a proclamation that said the subject was too complicated, including the issue of black suffrage, to be solved by a single plan of restoration.

The enraged Radicals issued a rebuttal, called the Wade-Davis Manifesto, which appeared in the *New York Tribune*. A savage attack on Lincoln, it accused him of usurping the power of Congress. But when Sherman won Atlanta and Lincoln won reelection, the Radicals were forced to bide their time.

One week after the election, Sherman started on his 256-mile march across Georgia to the sea. Stanton had his doubts about the march. It had not been part of his grand campaign. But he finally agreed when Sherman insisted:

I can make this march and make Georgia howl.

There was only one McCook on Sherman's march, and he was not even a Fighting McCook. Dr. Latimer had tended wounded and dying men in more than thirty fights and battles. He had been injured twice himself, at Fort Donelson and Vicksburg, and had served for three years without taking a single day of leave.

Sherman's force of more than sixty-one thousand cut a fifty-mile wide swath through Georgia, burning and looting. Designed to break the South's will to continue fighting, Sherman destroyed over $100 million in property and left a wasteland of blackened chimneys in his wake. Thirty-two days later he arrived at Savannah to find Hardee in command with a skeletal force of nine thousand.

Refusing to surrender, Hardee evacuated the city and headed for Charleston. Sherman marched in on December 21 to send a telegraph to Lincoln:

I beg to present you, as a Christmas gift, the city of Savannah.

A Union fleet was waiting in the harbor with clothing and supplies. Dr. Latimer McCook boarded the steamer *Harvest Moon* where he met a naval officer who knew his cousin, Naval Lieutenant Roderick McCook. Latimer sent a message to Roderick that he hoped to see him in Charleston as Sherman continued his march up the coast.

Roderick had been waging war for three and a half years on the high seas. He was truly a Fighting McCook.

Territory trod by the Fighting McCooks
in their quest to save the Union

Chapter 18

NAVAL LIEUTENANT RODERICK MCCOOK
Fights the Civil War at Sea

Two days after Sherman took Savannah, Naval Lieutenant Roderick McCook wrote to his wife from his ironclad ship U.S.S. *Canonicus,* one of the Monitor-like vessels that were derisively dubbed "iron coffins."

On Board the Canonicus
December 23, 1864

My dearest Lizzie,
Tomorrow the battle takes place and I can now tell you that the ironclads will take a very prominent part in it. It may be that this is my last letter to you. I hope otherwise, but if it should be, remember that I loved you to the death. . . .

Roderick Sheldon McCook was the executive officer of the U.S.S. *Canonicus,* one of seven ironclad ships in the North Atlantic Blockading Squadron commanded by Rear Admiral David Porter. The sixty-vessel armada, the largest in the history of the U.S. Navy, was poised to attack Fort Fisher at Wilmington, North Carolina. The massive fort protected the last major seaport in Confederate hands.

Handsome and dashing "Shed" McCook, as his family and friends called him, was a zealous twenty-five-year-old naval officer who throughout the Civil War had been impatient for action, thirsty for glory, and anxious to "hold up my end of the line."

The fourth son of Dr. John and Catherine McCook was born in New Lisbon on March 10, 1839, and named for his maternal grandfather, Roderick Sheldon of Hartford, Connecticut. He inherited his New England ancestors' love of the sea. On September 21, 1854, fifteen-year-old Shed was appointed by Ohio Congressman Wilson Shannon as acting midshipman in the United States Naval Academy at Annapolis.

Shed, in his first adventure away from home, discovered the joys of whiskey and tobacco and Southern belles. The results were disastrous. At the end of his second year he fought with another midshipman, was cited for insubordination, and was forced to resign in June 1856. Six months later, after cooling down, he wrote a chastened letter to the formidable superintendent of the Naval Academy, Captain Louis M. Goldsborough.

> *Steubenville, Dec. 14th / 56*
>
> *Capt. Goldsborough*
>
> > *Sir . . . when I entered the Academy I was young and inexperienced. I knew nothing of the world, or of the hardship of maintaining myself when cast upon it alone. I went there determined to do my duty, and at first I succeeded pretty well, as the records of the Academy will show. For the first few months I stood well in my class, and my conduct was good.*
> >
> > *Gradually, through the influence of seeming friends, my attention became attracted from my studies to foolish amusements . . . and as a natural consequence my conduct became worse until it ended in my dismissal from the Academy.*
> >
> > *Others have gone back after being dismissed. Give me but*

the same chance, and I know that I can and will behave myself
as well as the best.

Hoping that you will grant my request, I remain Sir
Yours Respectfully,
R. S. McCook

Five days later, through the influence of Shed's Uncle Daniel who had good friends in high places in Washington, Captain Goldsborough received a letter from James C. Dobbin, secretary of the navy.

Dec 19 / 56

Commander Goldsborough
Dear Sir:

Well, my dear Captain, you and I know that first rate boys are
sometimes at the beginning irregular and can't stand the bit—
but will have free reins. Then they are checked and become the
best. I have confidence in your judgment and generosity.

Yours truly,
J. C. Dobbin

Roderick McCook, given another chance, graduated on June 9, 1859, standing seventh in seamanship and eighth in naval tactics in his class of twenty midshipmen. He was ordered to the steam frigate U.S.S. *San Jacinto*, whose commander, Captain William Armstrong, reported that McCook was "a most promising young officer."

The *San Jacinto*, flagship of the African Squadron, operated on the west coast of Africa to stem the slave trade. Although Congress in 1807 had prohibited importation of slaves and imposed a heavy fine on slave traders, the law was generally ignored.

In the summer of 1860 the *San Jacinto* chased and captured the slave brig *Storm King* off the mouth of the Congo River. There were 719 slaves aboard. On boarding the captured ship, McCook met an unbearable stench. During the pursuit the naked slaves, both male and female, had been packed below deck so densely that the confinement and foul air killed twenty of them. The worst cases were brought on deck where several women gave birth to children. The others, covered with dirt and vermin and open sores from beatings, were washed with a combination of saltwater and gunpowder. The navy had discovered that this was a good disinfectant.

Midshipman McCook, given the honor of commanding the captured ship, set the slaves free in Liberia and sailed the *Storm King* to Norfolk, Virginia, where he took the crew to Richmond for trial. It was October 1860. Presidential elections were less than a month away, and Richmond was seething with anger about the possibility of a "black Republican" becoming president.

Southerners, drilling and arming themselves, expressed open contempt for McCook's uniform and declared that one of theirs could lick ten Yankees. Shed, seeing their militancy, sent his brother Anson a copy of *Hardee's Tactics* to study.

Home in Steubenville for Christmas, Shed asked his family incredulously, "When will they wake up in Washington?"

Four months later Fort Sumter fell. U.S. Army General-in-Chief Winfield Scott, forecasting a bloodbath if the North invaded the South, advocated strangling the Confederacy economically by blockading Southern ports and seizing the Mississippi River. Scott, the seventy-five-year-old hero of the Mexican War, estimated that it would take three years to bring the South to terms.

The Northern press, demanding a quick victory, derided Scott's strategy and dubbed it the "Anaconda Plan" for the South American snake that slowly strangled its prey. Scott was lampooned for being old and out of touch. But on April 19 President Lincoln, seeing the value of the naval blockade, ordered it for the 3,550 miles of coastline from Virginia to Texas.

It was a large task for a small fleet. When war began, more than half of the navy's ninety vessels were ancient and useless. Of the forty-two ships in commission, twenty-seven were sailing the seven seas. Secretary of the Navy Gideon Welles had to charter a makeshift fleet, everything from merchant ships to private yachts to ferryboats, to impose the blockade.

It would not be easy. Many of the South's swift blockade-runners were commanded by skilled former Annapolis graduates. One-fourth of the thirteen hundred officers of the U.S. Navy had resigned to fight for the Confederacy.

Midshipman McCook was ordered to the U.S.S. *Minnesota*, a forty-seven-gun steam frigate blockading the Charleston harbor. She was the flagship of the Atlantic Blockading Squadron under the command of Commodore Silas H. Stringham. In Hampton Roads on May 19, one week after the blockade began, the *Minnesota* captured the prize-master Confederate privateer *Argo*, bound for Europe with tobacco worth $150,000. McCook, given the honor of commanding the captured vessel, took her to New York.

A few days later, back at sea, he found time to write at night to a young lady in Ohio. Elizabeth Sutherland, the daughter of Judge and Mrs. John K. Sutherland of Steubenville, had promised to correspond when Shed went off to war.

> *Flag Ship "Minnesota"*
> *At Sea May 26th, '61*
>
> Dear Friend Lizzie,
>
> *We are now broad off "Dixie Land", the lights on the coast of South Carolina are plainly visible, looming up like false devils, tempting unwary ships to their destruction; they can't fool anyone in this ship with their false lights. . . .*
>
> *We have just caught, after an hour's chase, a poor miserable schooner loaded with corn from some fort in N.C. bound to Florida. I suppose we will send her north for a change of climate and I will send this letter in her. . . .*
>
> *I am beginning to find my time hang heavy on my hands; blockading is dull business but very hard work. I find myself frequently wishing I was in Pine Street. . . . Indeed I am afraid I have left my heart in some of those houses. . . . If you find it won't you please keep it until further orders? Write soon and often to your friend.*
>
> *R. S. McCook*

Early in June, when the *Minnesota* captured the privateer *Savannah*, McCook was given command of the prize and took her to New York, where she was impounded and her crew imprisoned. Upon Shed's return to blockade duty, he received a letter of congratulations from his Connecticut cousin, Mary Sheldon, to which he replied.

Flag Ship Minnesota
Hampton Roads
June 25, '61

My dear Cousin,

I am much obliged to you for your congratulations on bringing
home the Privateer; I am undoubtedly proud of having done so.
I am the first officer who ever hoisted an American flag over
that of the secessionists on the sea. I hope I may live to perform
the same holy duty a thousand times.

But he was jealous.

I am afraid all the glory will be carried away by the army, and
so anxious am I to see some active service that I <u>did</u> think of
resigning and entering the army in some capacity. You know my
education at Annapolis has fitted me to command on land as
well as on the sea.

And he was zealous.

The Yankee boys will give the chivalry as fierce a fight as they
desire, and probably after a battle or two they will not look
down upon us with such supreme contempt. I want to see the
"peculiar institution" effectually and forever wiped out; let the
South suffer everything we can inflict upon them; they have
provoked the war and must abide by the consequences.

Your affectionate cousin
Shed

Late in August McCook got the active service he craved. The *Minnesota*
led a fleet of fourteen ships from Hampton Roads to Cape Hatteras to
make the first joint navy-army attack of the war on Forts Hatteras and
Clark. Naval gunfire bombarded the forts while troops under the command of Major General Benjamin Butler stormed the bastions.

The successful attack on August 29 came off without a single Union
casualty, as Shed wrote Lizzie.

September 7

Dear Lizzie,

The papers have doubtless informed you of our complete success at Hatteras. . . . On Wednesday we commenced the attack on their smaller battery and after four or five hours firing, completely silenced it. Most of their shots were delivered at us but went over the ship. Nobody was hurt.

The troops we had landed, about 250 in number, took possession of it that evening. The next day we opened on the larger fort, and fired from 7:00 a.m. til a little after noon when they hoisted the white flag.

We have now 650 prisoners aboard. We are bound for New York where we expect to be tomorrow morning.

Shed

In New York McCook was promoted to naval lieutenant and assigned as executive officer of the steamer U.S.S. *Stars and Stripes*. She was ordered to the North Atlantic Blockading Squadron, patrolling the storm-tossed Virginia and North Carolina coasts. It was the navy's most difficult station.

Commanding the squadron, from his flagship U.S.S. *Philadelphia*, was Flag Officer Louis M. Goldsborough, the former superintendent of the Naval Academy who had given Shed another chance to prove that he was a "first-rate boy."

Throughout the fall of 1861 the *Stars and Stripes* prowled the waters of Hatteras Inlet. Shed considered it dull work in a desolate place. He was envious when the South Atlantic Blockading Squadron, commanded by Flag Officer Samuel Francis Du Pont, captured Port Royal, South Carolina. His next letter to Mary revealed his angst.

U.S.S. Stars & Stripes
Hatteras Inlet Nov 28, 61

My dear Cousin,

You cannot imagine how disappointed I am at not being present at Port Royal. My only consolation is that we will probably soon have a chance down here. If the reinforcements promised

us come down, you may expect to hear of a fierce battle, and as
a natural consequence, of a gallant McCook.

In Mary's last letter she had inquired about Shed's "Judge Love." He and Lizzie had managed to see each other during his trips to New York. Now they were betrothed, and Mary asked him to give Lizzie her love.

My "Judge Love" is, so far as I know, "all right". I feel tolerably
secure in that quarter. She is a perfect little gem. I will be most
happy to transmit your love, although I tell you candidly she
does not care a fig for anybody's love save mine, at least she says
so and of course I believe her.

Your affectionate cousin,
Shed

Shed's longed-for action finally came on January 11, 1862, when the *Stars and Stripes* joined a fleet of one hundred ships slipping out of Fort Monroe, near Hampton Roads, bound for Roanoke Island. The North Atlantic Blockading Squadron needed the island as a year-round port. The attack was another joint navy-army operation.

On February 7 the ships lined up in three columns, one headed by *Stars and Stripes*. Approaching the shore, she opened fire with a twenty-pounder Parrot gun and two twelve-pounders. Throughout the afternoon the gunships continued their bombardment, and by midnight ten thousand soldiers under the command of General Butler had landed. By 5:00 p.m. the next day they had captured Roanoke Island with three thousand prisoners and forty pieces of artillery, as Shed related to Lizzie.

February 9

My dearest Lizzie,
The fight is ended and we have complete possession of the
Island. Our victory is a glorious one. . . .

Your own Shed

Anxious for another fierce battle and a chance to be a gallant McCook, Shed got it on March 11. *Stars and Stripes* joined twelve warships and transports, carrying twelve thousand Union troops under the command of Brigadier General Ambrose Everett Burnside, for a combined navy-army attack on Newbern, North Carolina.

Lieutenant Roderick McCook, commanding a naval battery of six howitzers, went ashore at sunrise on March 13 and became the first Northern naval officer to capture a Southern army regiment. Four days later he recounted the feat to Lizzie from Goldsborough's flagship.

> *U.S. Philadelphia*
> *Newbern City, March 15th*
>
> Dear Lizzie,
>
> *We have had a big fight and have thrashed the rebels well. . . .*
> *General Burnside himself told me to take a position in front of*
> *the enemies battery of 11 guns, several of them rifled. He said I*
> *<u>must</u> hold it and I did. . . . We fought well and held our ground*
> *under the fire of these guns and a number of rifle men behind the*
> *breastwork. I had three or four men killed and ten wounded.*
>
> *. . . I am nearly worn out; my feet are covered with blisters. The*
> *mud was up to our knees and raining all the while. . . . We have*
> *the whole city; all their field guns and quite a number of prizes.*
>
> *Will you forgive me for writing no more at this time? I have*
> *worked in the rain all day at dragging down my battery. Please*
> *tell Father and Mother that "My end of the line is all right".*
>
> > *With as much love as ever I remain your devoted*
> > *Shed*

Two weeks later Goldsborough, referring to Shed as "one of his boys," gave him another "glorious chance," as Shed wrote Lizzie.

> *U.S.S. Philadelphia*
> *March 28*
>
> Dearest Lizzie,
>
> *I expect to start for Beaufort tomorrow or next day. It will be a*
> *rather "skeery trip". I intend to go by water and will have to*
> *pass pretty close to Fort Macon. Our troops are down there now,*
> *but have nothing by which they can carry men and guns across*

> *Cose Sound. I am going to take a stern wheel boat down to them. If I succeed it will be a big thing for me, if I happen to be knocked out of the water it will not be so big.*
>
> Your own Shed

He succeeded. It was a big thing, and when the captain of the *Stars and Stripes* became ill, Shed was promoted to acting commander of the ship.

> Stars and Stripes
> Elizabeth City, April 25
>
> *Dearest Lizzie,*
>
> *I now command the Stars and Stripes. It is a large vessel for one so young (23 years and little over a month) but I do not either fear or hesitate about assuming it. I know I can do well, and while I look to a higher power for assistance, I will use my own abilities to the best advantage.*
>
> *When I think nine or ten months ago I was a Midshipman and that now I have command of the finest gunboat in these waters, I certainly have cause to thank our Almighty Father who has so favored me.*
>
> Your own Shed

But blockade duty on the navy's most difficult station meant battling shifting winds and strong currents off Cape Hatteras and the treacherous North Carolina coast, while keeping up a head of steam to pursue swift blockade runners, often on a moment's notice from Goldsborough.

> U.S. Flag Ship "Minnesota"
> June 9, 1862
>
> *Sir:*
>
> *I want you to be off at the earliest possible moment for Wilmington, N.C. I have just received dispatches of a large number of vessels, with immensely valuable cargoes, intending to run the blockade. Go and catch them and make your future.*
>
> In haste,
> L. M. Goldsborough

Shed rose to the challenge. However, by August he was increasingly worried about the safety of his storm-battered ship, particularly with the hurricane season approaching, as he wrote his cousin Mary.

> *U.S. Steamer Stars and Stripes*
> *Off Wilmington, N.C. Aug 26th*
>
> *My dear Cousin,*
>
> *I am so tired of this miserable blockade. . . . I do not see how we can possibly live through the heavy Sept. gales that will soon be upon us. To tell the truth I think if we are kept here we will go to the bottom, and so I have written to the Admiral.*
>
> *You ask me when I intend to get married. I have been considering that question for a long while, and have at length concluded to marry just as soon as I can get long enough leave of absence to do so. I did intend to wait until the war was over, but we are making such miserable headway that I fear we will be finished before the war. Besides, I have been engaged more than a year and that is about long enough to keep any young lady waiting.*
>
> *Your affectionate cousin*
> *Shed*

The next month, when the *Stars and Stripes* was ordered to the Philadelphia Navy Yard for repairs, Lieutenant Roderick McCook received a ten-day leave. On September 23, 1862, he and Elizabeth Ashmead Sutherland were married in Steubenville.

Assigned shore leave until January 1863, Shed was then named executive officer of the U.S.S. *Bienville* and assigned to the Western Gulf Blockading Squadron in the Gulf of Mexico, commanded by Rear Admiral David G. Farragut. Farragut had been the executive officer on the U.S.S. *Delaware* when Shed's cousin, Midshipman John McCook, had died at sea in 1842. Now Admiral Farragut was the Union's greatest naval hero for his capture of New Orleans.

But blockading Southern ports, in order to keep Confederate cotton from reaching English mills, was deadly dull. After almost a year of longing for another glorious chance and post of honor in battle, Shed finally got it.

Rear Admiral David Glasgow Farragut

On December 3, 1863, he was named executive officer of the U.S.S. *Canonicus*, one of nineteen new ironclads built at the Boston Navy Yard.

Ironclad ships, already in use in European navies, had made their first appearance in American waters in the early months of 1862. The Confederates put armor on the old U.S.S. *Merrimac*, renamed her C.S.S. *Virginia*, and showed what an ironclad could do. On March 8 at Hampton Roads she sunk or disabled three of the Union's proudest ships: U.S.S. *Cumberland*, U.S.S. *Congress*, and U.S.S. *Minnesota*.

Hearing this news, Secretary of War Stanton went into a rage, glaring at Secretary of the Navy Gideon Welles as though he were to blame. Fearful that the Confederate ironclad would come up the Potomac River and attack Washington, Stanton flew into a frenzy, rushing frantically about the War Department, scolding and raving and waving his arms like a wild man.

Welles tried to calm Stanton down by disclosing that the Union also had a new ironclad ship, called the U.S.S. *Monitor*. She had just arrived at Hampton Roads and had orders to attack the *Merrimac* the next day. But when Stanton learned that the *Monitor* was a much smaller ship, with only two guns to the *Merrimac*'s ten, he gave Welles an indescribable "look of incredulity and contempt," as the secretary of the navy noted in his diary.

Haughtily ignoring Welles, Stanton ordered Naval Commander John A. Dahlgren to sink sixty rock-filled canal boats in the Potomac River to keep the *Merrimac* from reaching Washington. Welles, protesting this infringement on his authority, argued that the scheme would not work. And, in spite of Stanton's insistence that he have control over all land and sea forces, Lincoln upheld the navy's autonomy. It was just one more instance of Lincoln's putting "rocks in Stanton's pockets to hold him down."

The next day the little *Monitor* came out to fight and gave as good as she got. After a slugging match of six hours, it was a draw. Armor-plated ships had arrived in American waters. The U.S. Navy, catching "iron fever," began building the strange craft that looked like "a cheese box on a raft." Unfortunately, as seamen said, it had all the sailing skills of a stone.

U.S.S. *Canonicus* was launched on August 1, 1863, and completed that fall to the tune of $621,215.63. Similar in design to the *Monitor*, she was a flat-bottomed vessel propelled by steam and covered with eight layers of iron plate. With her deck flush with the water, she had only two projections: a

U.S.S. Canonicus

small armored cupola for the pilot and a revolving turret amidships for two eleven-inch Dahlgren guns. Larger than the *Monitor*, the *Canonicus* weighed 1,034 tons, was 225 feet long, had a maximum speed of seven knots, and carried a crew of eighty-five.

Her guns had such perfect range that they never failed to put a shell just where they wanted it. But, like all the ironclads, she was unseaworthy and would have to be towed to her battle station. After her trial run in March 1864, she was assigned to the James River Division of the North Atlantic Blockading Squadron.

By mid-1864 the Union Navy, numbering more than six hundred vessels, had closed all but one of the South's major ports. Only Wilmington, North Carolina, remained open to Confederate blockade runners.

In October Rear Admiral David D. Porter, the hero of Vicksburg, assumed command of the North Atlantic Blockading Squadron. By December he had assembled a fleet of nearly sixty warships, including the *Canonicus*, for a joint navy-army assault of the massive fortress protecting the port of Wilmington.

Fort Fisher was an L-shaped bastion, over a mile in length on its seaward side, built with sand walls twenty-five feet thick and thirty feet high. Long sloping banks on every front gave its forty-seven guns a clear field of fire. It was a monstrous fort to attack. The South, needing the port of Wilmington desperately, was prepared to hold Fort Fisher at all costs.

On December 13 Admiral Porter's armada sailed from Hampton Roads, the *Canonicus* and six other ironclads towed by steamers, and rendezvoused off Fort Fisher with transports carrying sixty-five hundred troops under the command of General Butler. However, on December 18 a strong breeze from the southeast made the water too rough to attempt a landing. The next day a heavy gale swept in from the southwest. Porter, fearing that he could not make it to a safe port without scattering all his ships, was forced to ride out the storm at sea.

For the heavy and awkward ironclads it was not a pleasant experience. The *Monitor* had gone down in heavy seas off Cape Hatteras in December 1862 with sixteen men aboard. The U.S.S. *Weehawken* had sunk off Charleston in December 1863, taking thirty-one seamen down with her.

Shed's letter to Lizzie reflected his uneasiness about the ironclads in rough seas.

Canonicus
Off New Inlet N.C.
Dec 20, 1864

My own dear wife,

For the first time since our marriage I am writing to you from my old Blockading Station. In my last letter to you I told you that the weather looked far from promising. It turned out to be as bad as one could wish. We arrived at the rendezvous on the evening of Sunday and never in my life did I feel so anxious for the weather. I cannot remember seeing the sky look more threatening than it did all through that night.

We anchored in sight of the land and are there now. No chance of attacking today, and I begin to feel the bad effects of this constant strain upon my mind. I cannot help being very anxious about the vessel. Any man who has been to sea in a gale can understand my feelings. It would be the greatest relief to go into battle, and remain there, rather than feel this constant anxiety about the weather and vessel.

I will never again go to sea in a monitor. I have suffered more in mind and body since this affair commenced than I will suffer again if I can help it. No glory, no promotion can ever pay for it. I have always been willing to take my share of the danger, but I now think I have seen my full allowance in an ironclad.

Goodbye now, darling. I will finish when I get a chance to
send the letter. May God bless you always, dear, darling wife—
Your own Shed

The next day he continued:

Yesterday was a day I shall remember through life. It was one
of the most terrible and awful in every respect that I ever expect
to see. I never saw the sea higher and all the day it formed in
torrents over us, breaking with green seas over our turret,
awning and all. We could do nothing and to add to our trou-
bles the ship commenced to drag her anchor. The next thing was
to get an anchor down to keep us from going to sea. The sea was
breaking so heavily over us that it seemed impossible to get a
man out to let our spare one go. One man tried and was
washed back three times to the turret; at length an officer and
man tried it, and succeeded. It was at the risk of their lives but
it was done.

Our next trouble was to stop the water coming in through
our house pipes, out of which the chain runs. The ship was
doing badly at best, and every drop of water added to her heavy
motion. At last I went out with a man and stopped it up, and
was nearly washed overboard for my pains. Just about this time
our wheel chains broke and there we were completely at the
mercy of the sea.

Thank God it is now all over and we are safe. What we will
have tomorrow I do not know; but I feel that one more such
gale as yesterdays will send us to the bottom. The fleet is scat-
tered all around; the weather very cold, and no one has an idea
when the attack will come off.

It came off at dawn on December 24. The *Canonicus* lumbered toward
Fort Fisher and cannonaded for five hours. Having expended eighty-five
shells, she withdrew and anchored in eight fathoms of water. It was
Christmas Eve. At dawn he wrote again.

Christmas Day—morning

My darling Lizzie,

> *I have only time to say a word. Yesterday we went into them and of all the terrible, awful tremendous fighting I ever saw, this fight beat. We drove them from their guns, dismounted them, hammered their forts unmercifully and burnt them out. We will probably go at them in an hour or so and I hope will give the people a Christmas gift in the shape of Fort Fisher.*

> *A Merry Christmas to you, though it seems strange to think of you having a merry time while I am fighting. Our vessel was the nearest in of the whole fleet all through the fight. We have done as well as could be done.*

> *Do not worry. I will come out all right. The Captain is going on board the flag ship and will take these letters.*

> *Good bye dearest.*
>
> *Your own Shed*

At 9:00 a.m. the *Canonicus* again steamed for the fort. In a four-hour duel she fired forty-nine shells and nine shrapnels. She dismounted two of the fort's guns and took four hits herself, one on the side armor and three on the smokestack.

Naval bombardment of Fort Fisher with the ironclads in advance

In the bowels of the ship, the sailors had no idea what was happening in the battle above. Their ears pounded with the hissing of the steam machinery that turned the turret and ran the ventilators and pumps. Their eyes stung from the boiling hot and foul air. Their nerves jumped with the muffled roar of the guns and the sounds of shots bouncing off the armor. All around them was chaos. Runners were carrying orders from the captain's pilothouse to the gunnery officer in the turret. Soot-covered stokers were shoveling coal into the boilers in the engine room. Every minute threatened to take the chugging and clanging monster to the bottom.

Fort Fisher, despite the two-day bombardment, failed to fall. Its thick sand walls had absorbed most of the shells. General Butler, after getting several thousand of his troops ashore, decided that he did not have suffi-cient force to storm the fort. Withdrawing his men, he told Admiral Porter that he was taking them back to Hampton Roads.

An exhausted Shed wrote his wife.

Canonicus, Dec 26th '64

My own dear Lizzie,

I cannot write much now. I only want you to know I am safe. I am used up completely.

After going through enough to kill an ordinary man, up to the 24th, I was up at 4 o'clock on that morning and fought all day. Was up half the night and out at daylight on Christmas; fought all day Christmas and at night we anchored; had to get up the anchor again and run out further and anchor. At nine o'clock turned in very tired, and at half past ten was called on account of bad weather, and told to get one of our anchors on deck as the sea was smashing it against our side. I worked in the rain and water until 3 o'clock in the morning and at last had to let go the anchor. At 4 I turned in and was called at half past 7 to get up anchor as we were to go to Beaufort for coal and ammunition.

My clothes are all wet, torn, powder stained—ruined. I have only one suit (my best) fit to wear. Where the money will come from to get more I do not know. I have suffered more anxiety of mind and bodily labor than a man ought to see in a life time. I pray God I may not be called upon to go out in her again.

Good night now love. I must sleep while I can.

Your own Shed

But he did go out in her again. Two and a half weeks later another navy-army attack was made on Fort Fisher. Admiral Porter was eager to have another try. This time General Butler was replaced by Brigadier General Alfred Howe Terry, and the troops were increased to eight thousand.

On the night of January 12 Admiral Porter's armada again gathered off Fort Fisher. Four days later Shed wrote his wife triumphantly.

Off New Inlet
Jan 16th

Dearest Lizzie,

We have gained a grand victory, thank God. From the 13 till late last night we have been hard at work fighting like devils. All day fighting; all night taking in powder and shell, and now Fort Fisher is ours, and the port of Wilmington is <u>closed</u>. . . .

Our vessel is covered with glory as well as scars. We kept the lead, and went in to within 700 yards of the fort. We were struck about forty times: our boat all cut to pieces and every-thing generally smashed up.

According to Shed, the navy lost some two hundred men and the army about seven hundred.

There is a feeling of sadness through the fleet at the loss of so many gallant officers; still we rejoice for the victory. . . .

A loving kiss from your loving
Shed

Admiral Porter was unstinting in his praise of the officers and crews of the ironclads:

Riding out heavy gales on an open coast, without murmuring or complaining of the want of comfort, which must have been very serious. They have shown a degree of fortitude and perseverance seldom witnessed.

Charleston was the next port of call for Shed and his ship. On January 19 they were ordered to report to Admiral John Dahlgren, commanding the South Atlantic Blockading Squadron. The *Canonicus* was to replace a sister ironclad, the U.S.S. *Patapsco*, which had been struck by a torpedo off Charleston on January 15. It sank in less than a minute, taking sixty-two men down with her.

Charleston was where the war began. On the night of February 17 General Pierre G. T. Beauregard, the South's "Hero of Fort Sumter," ordered General Hardee to evacuate the city. Admiral Dahlgren shelled Charleston from sea. General Sherman, having marched up the coast from Savannah, shelled it from land.

At daylight the *Canonicus* steamed toward the city and fired two shots. There was no answer. Hardee had abandoned Charleston during the night after blowing up the ammunition depot. The explosion set fire to the city and, as the flames raged, McCook accompanied Admiral Dahlgren ashore. In the morning he returned to the *Canonicus* to write his last letter of the war to his wife.

Feb. 19th

My own darling,

Will you think it funny if I say that I slept in Charleston last night? It is true enough; before you receive this, the papers will inform you of our having charge of the city.

Later that morning the Union Navy captured the *Deer*, a Confederate blockade-runner. Admiral Dahlgren gave Shed the honor of taking the prize to Boston. He was not sorry to leave the *Canonicus*.

Now he would have the spray in his face again and the wind in his sails again and the throb of the ship under his feet again as it sliced through the sea.

Shed was a changed man. He was no longer anxious for action, anxious for glory, or anxious to "hold up my end of the line." He was a man who, after almost four years of war at sea, confessed to his wife:

> *I am anxious for smooth waters.*
>
> *Your affectionate husband*
> *Shed*

*Territory trod and sailed by the Fighting McCooks
in their quest to save the Union*

Chapter 19

"HORSE ED"
Sweeps through the South

Buglers sounded "Boots and Saddles," and Brigadier General Edward McCook's 4,069 troopers trotted out of their camps, two by two, at 5:30 a.m. on the fine morning of March 22, 1865, with guidon flags flying. "Horse Ed" was leading his First Division on the largest Union cavalry raid of the Civil War.

One month earlier, his brother Shed had seen the fall of Charleston, where the Civil War began. The Confederacy was tottering. Sherman was fighting his way up the Eastern Seaboard to join Grant at Petersburg. Lee was on his last legs.

The end of the war, finally and at long last, was in sight.

But the president of the Confederacy, Jefferson Davis, refused to admit defeat. So Secretary of War Edwin Stanton sanctioned a massive cavalry raid through the Deep South. His plan was to destroy the factories that made the weapons that allowed the South to continue to fight for a cause that was lost.

"Horse Ed" received his orders while he was on leave in Peoria, Illinois, living in royal style and courting a beautiful eighteen-year-old heiress.

Mary Thompson, whose late parents had left her a fortune from iron manufacturing and distilling, was lonely in her twenty-two-room mansion with fourteen black marble fireplaces and a ballroom. Understandably, she did not want her dashing sabreur to go back to war. Succumbing to her charms, Ed went off to enjoy a merry holiday with her in Chicago before rejoining his division, as his brother Anson related to their Connecticut cousin Mary Sheldon.

> *March 8th, '65*
>
> *Dear Mary,*
>
> *Ed, failing to resist either the charm of Miss T's companion-ship and society or, what is more probable, her importunities, went with her to Chicago, and from there goes to Cincinnati and the front.*
>
> *Yours as ever,*
> *Ans*

Betrothed by the time he left Chicago, Ed arrived at Chickasaw Bluff, Mississippi, just in time to lead the First Division, Cavalry Corps, Army of the Mississippi as it started south under the command of Major General James Harrison Wilson.

Wilson and McCook, unfortunately, were not members of a mutual admiration society. Wilson, a West Pointer who went strictly by the book, disliked McCook's cavalier tendency to toss the text aside and improvise on the march. And McCook was ready to blame Wilson's self-righteous rigidity if the raid failed, as he confided to his cousin Mary.

> *March 10, 1865*
>
> *Dear Mary,*
>
> *The experiment is a dangerous one, but I think will be success-ful—at any rate, if it is not, the fault will not be that of the men or subordinate commanders. General Wilson starts with*

Major General James Harrison Wilson

the finest appointed cavalry force in the world, and ought to accomplish almost anything.

A thousand kisses and blessings for you all!

Your Cousin Ed

Wilson's three divisions, commanded by Brigadier Generals Edward McCook, Eli Long, and Emory Upton, comprised 13,480 lean and hard men, most of whom had been in the saddle for four years.

Union cavalry had come into its own.

The troopers were well-mounted. In addition to their sabers, they were equipped with Spencer carbines, deadly seven-shot repeating rifles. Each man carried five days' rations for himself, twenty-four pounds of grain for his horse, one hundred rounds of ammunition, and an extra pair of horseshoes.

Rolling behind the cavalry were 58 lorries loaded with 30 canvas pontoon boats and enough lumber for the construction of a four-hundred-foot bridge, plus 250 quartermaster wagons stocked with a sixty-day supply of rations for the troops and forage for the animals. If the campaign lasted longer, they would live off the land.

There should be little opposition from the three famous Confederate cavalrymen who had ridden circles around Union armies in the west for most of the war. John Hunt Morgan, after escaping from the Ohio Penitentiary, had been killed in battle on September 4, 1864. "Fightin' Joe" Wheeler had gone to the Carolinas to try to stop Sherman. Only Nathan Bedford Forrest, with eleven thousand men in widely scattered forces, was in the west.

Forrest, who once killed a man with a pen knife, had vowed to fight to the bitter end. He fought in fifty battles during the Civil War, inflicting sixteen thousand Union casualties and capturing or destroying 67 artillery pieces, 38 vessels, 40 blockhouses, 36 railroad bridges, 300 wagons, and 200 miles of railroad track. The cost to the North was some $15 million.

Wilson hoped to get deep into Alabama before Forrest discovered he was there.

Wilson's Raiders, moving swiftly, rode unchallenged for six days through the swamps and forests of northern Alabama. After wrecking iron works and rolling mills and blast furnaces that produced from ten to twenty tons of iron daily, they headed for the shipbuilding city of Selma.

Forrest, finally discovering their presence, tried to unite his scattered forces to protect the city. But Ed McCook and one of his brigades, swiftly covering fifteen miles in two hours, captured and destroyed a bridge over the Cahaba River, preventing two of Forrest's divisions from reaching him.

With only a small portion of his forces, Forrest was badly outnumbered and whipped at Montevallo. Offering battle again at Ebenezer Church, he was wounded in a saber duel and fell back into Selma. Wilson stormed the city on April 2 with his unmounted dragoons and captured it, obliterating the armament industry and taking twenty-seven hundred prisoners. Forrest escaped, but as a warrior he was finished.

Unhampered now, Wilson headed east toward Montgomery. It was the capital of Alabama. It was also the "Cradle of the Confederacy," the birthplace of the Confederate States of America.

Ed McCook, having missed the fight at Selma due to destroying the bridge over the Cahaba, was given the honor of the advance to Montgomery. McCook had only his Second Brigade, under the command of Colonel Oscar H. LaGrange, with him. The First Brigade, under the command of Brigadier General John T. Croxton, had been sent to tear up the town of Tuscaloosa and had not been heard from since.

As McCook's troopers approached Montgomery, the mayor and a delegation of citizens, carrying a white flag, rode out to surrender at 7:00 a.m. It was April 12, the fourth anniversary of the attack on Fort Sumter. An hour later McCook sent a message to Wilson:

I occupied the city this morning at 8 o'clock without opposition.

Ordering the Stars and Stripes raised over the Alabama statehouse, Ed McCook decreed that all homes and public buildings were not to be harmed. Then, when Wilson arrived, the entire corps made a victorious entry into the city.

Wilson and McCook, their bright brass buttons and brilliant epaulets shining, rode at the head of the column with sabers drawn. Behind them the troopers trotted four abreast. The triumphant parade lasted nearly all day with guidons flying, sabers and spurs jingling, bands playing patriotic airs, and bugles sounding the call.

Southerners watched silently from their windows.

McCook, commanding the city, supervised the destruction of all military property, including several locomotives, five steamboats, five artillery pieces, and the armory in which twenty thousand rounds of ammunition were stored. Then Wilson's Raiders headed east into Georgia, destroying everything of military value in their paths.

McCook took Fort Tyler on the Chattahoochee River with its 265-man garrison. At West Point he wrecked nineteen locomotives, five hundred stands of small arms, and two hundred railway cars. But he still had only one-half of his division with him. The other half, Croxton's "Lost Brigade," had not reappeared.

Meanwhile Wilson, with his Second and Third divisions, captured Columbus with over one thousand Confederate officers and men. They destroyed the ironclad ram *Jackson*, the arsenal, navy yard, four cotton mills, a foundry, three paper mills, fifteen locomotives, two hundred railway cars, one hundred thousand bales of cotton, one hundred thousand rounds of artillery ammunition, and the factory that produced most of the South's swords.

At Macon, Georgia, McCook's "Lost Brigade" finally reappeared. They had been missing for almost a month. Croxton and his men, after destroying much of Tuscaloosa, Alabama, searched fruitlessly for McCook. Finally, learning that Wilson's Raiders had headed east, Croxton followed, fighting and destroying as he went, and finally tracked them down.

Wilson's Raiders, due to downed telegraph wires in the South, had no idea what was happening in the North. They only knew that they had little opposition in Georgia as most Confederate units had gone to the Carolinas to try to stop Sherman.

Whirling like a hurricane, Sherman had pursued Hardee up the coast. In South Carolina, Union soldiers wreaked vengeance on the state that had started the war, putting a torch to everything in sight. In North Carolina, a Confederate Army of thirty-five thousand under General Joseph E. Johnston offered battle to Sherman's eighty-thousand-man army near Bentonville.

During three days of fighting, Hardee's sixteen-year-old son Willie, who had ridden on Alex McCook's shoulders at West Point, was mortally wounded while charging with Wheeler's cavalry. It was his first day of battle, and it was his father's last day of battle. Bentonville was the Confederates' final attempt to check Sherman.

Leaving his army in North Carolina, Sherman went up to Virginia to join Grant, who for nine months and with another forty-two thousand casualties had been besieging Petersburg. On March 28 Grant and Sherman met with Lincoln aboard the steamer *River Queen* anchored on the James River. The president had come south to make known his wishes about the terms of surrender.

"With malice toward none, with charity for all" were the words Lincoln had used in his second inaugural address on March 4.

He had always held that, since secession was illegal under the Constitution, the Southern states had never left the Union. Now he planned to embrace them warmly as prodigal sons.

Like President Washington after the Whiskey Rebellion, President Lincoln wanted no reprisals, no hangings, and no harsh military rule that

President Lincoln in the spring of 1865

would fester into another war. However, he was well aware that the Radical Republicans in Congress and in his cabinet were violently opposed to him. Some Radicals believed that those who were soft on the South were traitors. All the Radicals felt that Lincoln was giving away the fruits of victory.

"Did Grant surrender to Lee?" Stanton demanded.

On Palm Sunday, April 9, the president arrived back in Washington. There he learned that Lee had surrendered that morning at Appomattox Court House. Lincoln was assured that the terms were in the spirit of his wishes for leniency. Lee's troops were to be paroled and permitted to go home, with officers keeping their sidearms and their horses for spring plowing.

Five days later, on Good Friday morning, there was a cabinet meeting at the White House. It was April 14, the fourth anniversary of the surrender of Fort Sumter.

Stanton had worked late the previous night on his Reconstruction plan. It was to be a military rule that would erase state boundaries and treat the South as a conquered province, with no political or economic rights for its vanquished people.

Lincoln turned it down, saying he would not tolerate hate and vindictiveness. Since Congress had adjourned until December, he would have seven months to bring the South peacefully back into the Union without their interference.

"No bloody work," he insisted. And he meant it.

Everyone had always underestimated Lincoln. Considering him nothing more than a backwoods bumpkin, smooth city lawyers were surprised to find themselves outsmarted. Considering him unlettered because he had less than one year of schooling, college graduates were astounded to hear him quoting Shakespeare and the Bible. Considering him uncouth for telling raunchy stories, "proper" people were awed by the poetic beauty of his Gettysburg Address. He was a contradiction: soft as a feather, hard as a rock.

President and Mrs. Lincoln had invited Stanton and Grant, with their wives, to join them at Ford's Theater that evening. Grant's presence had already been announced in the morning and afternoon editions of the *National Republican.* But after the cabinet meeting, both Stanton and Grant declined, citing other engagements.

That night, while watching the play *Our American Cousin*, Lincoln was assassinated. As the president lay dying in a little house across the street from the theater, Stanton gathered the reins of government into his hands. According to one of his friends, Stanton "continued through the night, acting as president, secretary of war, secretary of state, commander-in-chief, comforter and dictator."

When Lincoln died, so did his dream of reuniting all thirty-five states peacefully. Three days after Lincoln's death, Sherman accepted the surrender of Johnston in North Carolina. Sherman's terms were generous, as he

FORD'S THEATRE. — Lieut. Gen. Grant, President Lincoln and lady, and other distinguished personages, are to visit this theatre this evening, on the occasion of Laura Keene's farewell benefit; and in honor to the distinguished military hero, a patriotic song and chorus has been written expressly for the occasion by Mr. H. B. Phillip, with music by Mr. William Withers, jr., which will be sung by the entire company. In addition to the attractive entertainment announced in the bills of the day.

Notice in the National Republican, April 14, 1865

understood Lincoln's intent on the *River Queen*, guaranteeing Southerners their economic and political rights.

But when the surrender document reached Washington, Stanton flew into a frenzy. A cabinet meeting was called. Sherman's terms went far beyond what Stanton and the Radicals would permit. Denouncing the document vehemently, Stanton turned his almost incoherent wrath on Sherman and released to the press a scathing implication that the general was guilty of treason.

Grant was told to go to North Carolina, relieve Sherman of his command, and either renegotiate the terms or restart the war. Grant, for once not following Stanton's orders, convinced his old comrade-in-arms to make the terms of surrender the same ones that Lee had accepted at Appomattox. Sherman did. Johnston signed the revised document on April 26, and Sherman wired Wilson in Georgia:

I regard the war as over.

That day John Wilkes Booth, the actor who had shot Lincoln, was trailed by Stanton's men to a tobacco shed in Virginia. Booth was brought in dead, and eight alleged conspirators were quickly rounded up. Their trial, by a military tribunal, was to start on May 10.

At dawn that day in the woods of southern Georgia, Ed McCook's troopers of the First Wisconsin helped capture the fleeing president of the Confederacy, Jefferson Davis. Although Lincoln had been willing to allow Davis to escape the country like a troublesome mule, Stanton put a one-hundred-thousand-dollar bounty on his head, and McCook's regiment shared in the reward.

Ed McCook did not witness the capture. That day he arrived in Tallahassee with five hundred troopers to accept the surrender of Florida. It was the last Confederate state east of the Mississippi to capitulate.

McCook paroled 7,200 Rebel troops and took possession of 40 pieces of artillery, 700 pounds of musket balls, 25,000 small arms, 450 sabers, 1,618 bayonets, 121,000 rounds of ammunition, 170,000 pounds of bacon, 70,000 bushels of corn, 300 barrels of salt, 150 barrels of sugar, 100 barrels of syrup, and 1,200 head of cattle.

Four years earlier, a McCook had fired a cannon to start the Civil War and now a McCook fired a cannon to end it.

Ordering the Stars and Stripes raised over the Florida State House, Ed McCook told his artillery to fire one salvo for each of the thirty-five states in the indivisible Union.

Alabama . . . New York . . . Georgia . . . Ohio . . . South Carolina . . . Pennsylvania . . . Texas . . . Wisconsin . . . Tennessee . . . California . . . Missouri . . . Michigan . . . Arkansas . . . Oregon . . . Florida . . . Maine . . . Kansas . . . Minnesota . . . Kentucky . . . Iowa . . . Mississippi . . . Illinois . . . Virginia . . . New Hampshire . . . Indiana . . . North Carolina . . . Vermont . . . Louisiana . . . West Virginia . . . Connecticut . . . New Jersey . . . Delaware . . . Maryland . . . Massachusetts . . . Rhode Island.

Lincoln would have approved. But Stanton would not. Neither would Wilson. But then he never did approve much about McCook. When Wilson recommended a promotion to major general for all his cavalry commanders, he could not resist a parting thrust at the Scotch-Irishman who liked to ignore orders and fight the war his own way. Wilson wrote:

> *With the exception of McCook, I think the officers I have just mentioned are the best cavalry officers I ever saw.*

"Horse Ed" was unscathed. The hard-drinking, hard-fighting, saber-wielding, woman-loving rascal with a smile on his face and a cigar in his mouth would go home, put his sword in the attic, marry his heiress, and fulfill a prediction he had made to his cousin Mary on May 10, 1861.

> *When the big wars "that make ambition virtue" are over, when we have fought & triumphed, as we will triumph, then I may return once more to peaceful pursuits. . . .*

Not the least of those pursuits was the one his grandfather had sought seventy-one years earlier:

> *"A' thought A' was a-comin' til a land of liberty!"*

The Whiskey Boy found that it was, indeed, a land of liberty—*under the law.* His sons and grandsons fought to save it. That fight restored liberty to those people from whom, ages earlier on a distant continent, it had been snatched.

*Territory trod and sailed by the Fighting McCooks
in their quest to save the Union*

Epilogue

The victorious Union armies of the West marched up Pennsylvania Avenue in a grand review on May 24, four days after General Edward McCook ordered the Stars and Stripes raised over Tallahassee.

Some seventy-five thousand westerners in their faded and tattered uniforms swung along in the loose-limbed strides with which they had traversed the vastness of the West. They were led by General William Tecumseh Sherman and escorted by torn and tattered battle flags from Fort Donelson, Shiloh, Perryville, Stones River, Vicksburg, Chickamauga, Chattanooga, Kennesaw, and Atlanta.

The parade stretched for fifteen miles. Regiments marched twelve abreast, gleaming bayonets fixed, as thousands of people lined the avenue to cheer wildly, throw flowers, and cry. Newsmen noted that the westerners were taller and more raw-boned than the easterners who had marched the previous day.

That was true. The quartermaster general had discovered early in the war that western men required larger uniforms. They were also less formal than the easterners. Lumbering behind each brigade were wagons filled with wartime pets—a menagerie of raccoons, dogs, goats, chickens, roosters, eagles, and pigs.

Ohio dominated the day. She had sent more men than any other western state to save the Union—some 320,000 volunteers in 234 regiments of infantry, 29 companies of cavalry, and 27 batteries of artillery.

She also sent 227 Ohio-born men who rose to the rank of general, including Ulysses S. Grant, William T. Sherman, Philip H. Sheridan, Irvin McDowell, Don Carlos Buell, William S. Rosecrans, William H. Lytle, James A. Garfield, Rutherford B. Hayes, George A. Custer, James B. McPherson, David S. Stanley, Ormsby M. Mitchel, Robert C. Schenck, and six Fighting McCooks.

Another prominent Ohioan, watching the parade from the reviewing stands in front of the White House, was the controversial secretary of war. Edwin McMasters Stanton, having transferred his tremendous will-to-win-at-any-cost from the courtroom to the battlefield, took a large share of credit for the victory. But his autocratic ways of waging war and dictating peace had earned him the enmity of many men.

One of them was the national hero leading the grand review. When General Sherman joined President Andrew Johnson and his cabinet in the reviewing stands, Sherman glared scornfully at Stanton and refused to shake the hand of the "two-faced scoundrel" who had accused him of being a traitor to his country.

Missing from the cabinet was Secretary of State William H. Seward. He was still recovering from multiple knife wounds inflicted during a brutal assassination attempt on his life the same night that Lincoln was murdered. Both men had advocated a lenient and peaceful reconciliation with the South.

The only McCook marching in the grand review was not even in the Union Army. The tall solitary figure of Dr. Latimer McCook, accompanied by his two dogs, limped up Pennsylvania Avenue with the aid of a cane. He had been wounded for the third time at Pocotaligo Bridge during Sherman's advance up the coast. Dr. McCook and the Thirty-first Illinois had marched a total of 4,076 miles during the war, arriving in Washington just in time for the grand review.

Many did not march. More than 1 million men were casualties of the Civil War. The North listed 364,511 men killed and 288,881 wounded. The South estimated that 260,000 men had been killed and 194,000 wounded.

Sitting in the bleachers along Pennsylvania Avenue was the McCook doctor who, according to Ohio Valley lore, had fired the first shots of the Civil War at the Ohio River steamboat with the little brass cannon.

— DR. JOHN —

He also had foreseen the terrible bloodbath. Ten days after Fort Sumter fell, Dr. John McCook made a dire prediction in a letter to Connecticut cousin Mary Sheldon:

> *This useless fratricidal war may have in store for our family a cup of bitter sorrow.*

Reviewing stand in front of the White House

After the grand review, Dr. John visited his son, Colonel Anson McCook, commanding a brigade in the Shenandoah Valley. Dr. John, a Democrat who had stumped for Lincoln in 1864, proposed making a speech to the troops. Anson objected, saying that he did not believe in political speeches at army camps. When Dr. John persisted, Anson countered that he was in command.

"Well," his father replied calmly, "occasionally you find boys who are too large for their clothes."

That evening after dark a procession of flickering lights moved through the camp. Over two thousand soldiers, candles stuck into the shanks of their bayonets, marched to brigade headquarters, gave three cheers for Dr. McCook, and demanded a speech. The good doctor mounted a horse block, spoke eloquently for nearly an hour, then stepped down and turned to his son.

"I told you I would make it and I did," he said.

"Yes," Anson laughed heartily, conceding defeat, "you are in command!"

The next fall Dr. John, again visiting Anson, was overcome by severe dysentery. Army surgeons put him in the hospital, but he failed to improve. Diagnosing his own case, the fifty-nine-year-old physician told Anson that he would not recover and pointed to a corner of the room.

"I saw Mother there last night," Dr. John said, "beckoning me to come."

His wife Catherine had died seven months earlier, wasted and wan after many years of suffering from epilepsy. He was very lonely without her. It had been an old-fashioned love match that never withered.

"How did Mother look?" asked Anson.

"As young and beautiful as the night she was married," said his father. The next day, October 11, 1865, he slipped away to join her.

— LATIMER —

After the grand review, Dr. Latimer McCook went to Steubenville, Ohio, and the welcoming warmth of Hillside, his brother George's home. There, Martha McCook nursed her eldest son. Latimer, after mending broken men on thirty-eight battlefields, had broken down himself. His nerves shattered, he was as helpless as a child.

In 1868 he returned to Pekin, Illinois, where his last year was as solitary as was much of his life. His wife Eliza never reappeared. His bills were paid by his mother, his brothers, his sisters, and his uncle, Dr. George. Passing away on August 23, 1869, at forty-nine years of age was the most gentle of the Fighting McCooks.

— Dr. George —

Still financially astute, Dr. George went into business after the war with two of his favorite nephews, George and Anson. Speculating in real estate, they bought sixty-five hundred acres of West Virginia land and developed it into a successful coal mining venture.

After retiring from his medical practice, Dr. George left Pittsburgh and moved back to New Lisbon. But the former candidate for Congress in 1836 did not live long enough to enjoy the victory when his son-in-law, Jonathan H. Wallace, defeated William McKinley for the U.S. House of Representatives in 1882. Dr. George died on June 23, 1873. Buried near his father, the Whiskey Boy, in the New Lisbon cemetery by the Sandy and Beaver Canal, was the oldest of the Fighting McCooks.

The surgeon's son, Dr. George Latimer McCook, also served the Union during the Civil War. Volunteering without military rank or compensation, he took a corps of physicians to Virginia during McClellan's Peninsula campaign in 1862 and contracted a fever from which he never recovered. Unable to resume his practice, he died in 1874, the most unknown of the Fighting McCooks.

— Edwin —

Edwin Stanton McCook was breveted a major general in the volunteer army on October 9, 1867. The brevet rank was an honorary one, created by the Articles of War in 1776, permitting the president to reward outstanding army officers. Edwin's star was due largely to the efforts of Daniel McCook's good friend, General John Logan, who reminded Secretary of War Edwin Stanton of the many sacrifices of the Fighting McCooks.

Edwin was appointed secretary of the Dakota Territory in 1873 and moved to Yankton with his wife Lorain and son Charles. Involved in a controversy over the Dakota Southern Railroad with local banker Peter P. Wintermute, Edwin got into an argument with him in the billiard parlor of the St. Charles Hotel. When the diminutive 135-pound Wintermute challenged him to a fight, the six-foot-one-inch, 207-pound McCook merely laughed.

The banker shouted, "If I can't whip you, I'll shoot you!"

In response, Edwin punched him in the jaw, knocked him against the bar, threw him into a mirror, and rubbed his face in the contents of a spittoon. When Wintermute swore he would get even, McCook laughed again and went to wash his hands. But when he returned, the banker shot him four times with a borrowed pistol.

One bullet hit Edwin in his chest, passed below the collarbone and came out under the shoulder blade, severing a vital artery. Although mortally wounded, he still possessed the legendary physical strength of his grandfather, the Whiskey Boy. Knocking over chairs and a nearby stove, McCook picked up Wintermute, kicked out a window, and was about to throw him into the street when spectators intervened.

Wintermute was arrested, and McCook was taken to his hotel room. Three doctors could not stop the excessive bleeding, which soaked the bedding and could be heard dripping to the floor. Aware that he was dying, Edwin called his wife and son to his bedside, told Charles to "be a good boy and mind your mother" and died on September 12, 1873. Conscious to the end, he maintained that he really did not mind dying half as much as being taken unaware. He still was trying gamely to live up to the fame of the Fighting McCooks.

— GEORGE —

After his wife Margaret's death in 1863, George volunteered for active duty and was placed in command of the Union prisoner of war camp at Fort Delaware, on Delaware Bay. After the war, he returned to Steubenville to resume his law and business activities and to host family and friends at Hillside. Occasionally that included his former law partner, Edwin Stanton.

Stanton was still the secretary of war, and he was still irascible, cunning, and manipulative. He clashed repeatedly with President Andrew Johnson over Reconstruction of the South. Although the Radical Republicans had thought that Johnson was one of them, he turned out to be as moderate as Lincoln.

When Stanton continued to be hell-bent on revenge, Johnson fired him on February 21, 1868. The secretary of war, flying into a frenzy, locked himself in his office and refused to leave.

The Radicals in the House of Representatives moved to impeach Johnson on grounds that he had violated the Tenure of Office Act. It was a law that they had passed (subsequently declared unconstitutional), preventing the president from dismissing members of his cabinet without Senate approval.

Andrew Johnson, the first president of the United States to be impeached, was acquitted by one vote in the Senate trial on May 26.

Stanton, having failed in his effort to get rid of Johnson, finally vacated his office after holding out for three months. But he left the War Department wrecked in health and ruined in fortune. Having used up all the money he had made as a successful attorney, Stanton was a poor man. Even Riggs National Bank turned down his application for a loan. Having made countless enemies while in office, Stanton had few friends.

Ulysses S. Grant was not one of them.

Grant's election as president in 1868 was inevitable, due to his great popularity as the victor of the war. Stanton expected Grant to appoint him to the Supreme Court, a seat he avidly coveted. But Grant, having been handled roughly by Stanton in the past and now having the upper hand, ignored him. Stanton was cut.

"His name and fortune he owed at critical moments to me," Stanton fumed.

That was true. But it was also true that, while Stanton publicly built Grant up, he privately tore him down. Stanton never hesitated to express his contempt for Grant while admitting, "The man will fight."

According to Major Donn Piatt, Stanton's close friend, the enmity stemmed from their first meeting in the railroad car in Indianapolis in the fall of 1863.

After Stanton gave Grant the honor of the command of three western armies, the two men proceeded to Louisville. There they held talks and agreed to meet again in the evening. When Grant failed to appear, Stanton frantically sent his aides searching for him. They finally found the general, long after midnight, drunk in a bar. Stanton, already suffering from a cold, savagely tore into him and came down with an acute asthma attack that plagued him throughout the war and ultimately caused his death.

Nevertheless, the die had been cast, and the fortunes of the two men were entwined.

According to Donn Piatt in his book *Memories of the Men Who Saved the Union*:

> *The true story of the late war has not been told. It probably never will be told.*

Late in the fall of 1869, when Stanton was at death's door, the Radical Republicans in Congress went in a body to the White House and demanded that Grant appoint the former secretary of war to the Supreme Court. Reluctantly, it was done.

But before the fifty-four-year-old Stanton could take his seat, he took his last painful breath early on Christmas Day, still firmly convinced that he, with his overwhelming will-to-win-at-any-cost, had saved the Union.

Two years later another major figure in the war, and another old friend of George McCook, died. Clement Vallandigham, the former leader of the Copperheads, was serving as a defense attorney in a murder trial in Lebanon, Ohio. While rehearsing in his room at the Golden Lamb Inn to show a jury how a man could shoot himself in the head, Vallandigham accidentally killed himself. George McCook, as a last favor, was a pall-bearer for his boyhood friend.

"Gentleman George," as he was known in Ohio, never remarried, although there were several attractive ladies in Steubenville who would have liked to console the wealthy Colonel McCook. Sociable as ever, he still loved playing cards, smoking cigars, eating good food, drinking good wine, reading the classics, going to the theater, and participating in politics.

In 1871 George was the Democratic nominee for governor of Ohio. But several weeks before the election he had a stroke, was forced to quit campaigning, and lost the election. Eventually he recovered enough to resume his law practice, look after his business interests, and travel in Europe where, like other wealthy Americans, he sent his children to school.

On Christmas Day 1877, while in New York City with his family enjoying dinner at his cousin Anson's home, George complained of dizziness and suffered another stroke. Dying on December 28 at the age of fifty-six, he was buried in Steubenville's Union Cemetery with Margaret, the great love of his life, for whom he gave up a general's star and the honor of leading troops into battle like the best of the Fighting McCooks.

— MARTHA —

While raising George's motherless four children at Hillside, Martha McCook ruled the household with a hand that was loving but firm. One day, when the youngest child punched holes in the new kitchen floor with an ice pick, George gave the boy a spanking that Martha thought was too severe.

"He is my son, Mother," said George, "and I can punish him as I see fit."

That evening when George came home from the office, the dining room was dark and the table was bare. When he inquired about dinner, his mother had a prompt answer.

"You can punish your son, and I can punish mine," she replied. "There will be no dinner tonight."

The servants could hear Colonel McCook laughing to himself as he walked down the hill to get his dinner in town. His spunky mother still outmatched him.

Martha Latimer McCook outlived all but two of her sons, Alex and John, and when the time came for her to go she was ready, drifting away gently at the age of seventy-eight on November 10, 1879. She had designed a memorial for her family—a small Greek temple with two urns and twelve columns—to be built in Spring Grove Cemetery in Cincinnati. There, reunited with her husband Daniel, was lain the indomitable mother of eight of the Fighting McCooks.

McCook Monument in Spring Grove Cemetery, Cincinnati, Ohio

— RODERICK —

After the war, Shed was promoted to naval lieutenant commander and assigned to the Naval Academy at Annapolis, where he commanded the midshipmen's practice ship, U.S.S. *Macedonian*. After a three-year tour of duty, he went to sea as executive officer of U.S.S. *Kearsarge*, U.S.S. *Albany*, and U.S.S. *Congress*. In 1873 he was promoted to commander of U.S.S. *Kansas*.

But in 1876, when he was commanding U.S.S. *Yantic* in China, he suffered a nervous breakdown. It was a result, his doctors believed, of the intense heat and ear-splitting concussions in the bowels of the ironclad *Canonicus* during the Civil War.

In 1885 Shed retired from the navy and the life at sea, which he loved. The next year, while living in New Jersey with his wife Lizzie and son, Shed was thrown from his carriage. Suffering a brain injury, he died three days after his forty-seventh birthday. Commander George Belknap, former commanding officer of the ironclad *Canonicus*, wrote Lizzie in 1888 regarding her eligibility for a widow's pension. He said that Roderick

> *was a splendid executive; he never suggested any doubts of success nor ever wanted to hold back when the enemy was to be approached. His lionine courage and vigorous effort in battle inspired all those about him and could not be surpassed. He fully proved himself a worthy representative of the "Fighting McCooks".*

— ALEXANDER —

Immediately after the Civil War, Alex reverted to his former U.S. Army rank as captain of infantry, expecting to be promoted when the army was reorganized in 1866. But, with Grant as general-in-chief, Alex was passed over.

The next year, however, when Grant was elected president and Sherman succeeded him as general-in-chief, Alex was promoted to lieutenant colonel and assigned to Austin, Texas, attached to the Twenty-sixth Infantry.

In 1875 he was promoted to colonel and assigned as Sherman's chief of staff in Washington. When Alex's brother Bob's good friend, Rutherford B. Hayes, was elected president the next year, the McCooks were frequent guests at the White House. The lovely Kate McCook was a warm friend of First Lady Lucy Webb Hayes.

In 1880 Alex was given command of the Sixth Infantry at Fort Douglas, Utah. A year later Kate became ill. She, who had never been afraid to join Alex at his army camps during the Civil War, did not respond to treatment and died at the age of forty-four in Salt Lake City, leaving a devastated husband with three daughters to raise.

Three years later Sherman received a letter from Alex announcing that he planned to marry Miss Annie Colt of Milwaukee. Sherman, retired from the army, still had firm opinions on everything and did not hesitate to express them.

> *St. Louis, Mo.*
> *August 23, 1884*
>
> *Dear McCook,*
>
> *I got back this morning after an absence of 5 weeks in Minnesota to attend a meeting of the Grand Army of the Republic and of the Army of the Tennessee. I calculated this as my show for 1884, to the hundred if not thousand of army reunions all over the land—but you now come with a wedding which upsets all calculations. I confess when I read your letter of the 14th of August, announcing your engagement to Miss Colt I was dumbfounded. I devoted all of August to army meetings and have pleaded that as an excuse for refusing hundreds of others, but I must be at your wedding, therefore count me in.*
>
> *I have written to Miss Colt a letter—an honest one, I hope, "characteristic" at all events—one you will be sure to see. And though I could not suppress my surprise, and a tribute to that extraordinary beautiful and angelic woman who shared with you some of your best years, I endeavored to write in kindness and respect. Our days on earth are numbered, and when death intervenes there is no good reason why man should be alone— therefore I hope that the woman you have chosen to succeed your Kate may be all your fancy paints her.*
>
> *I am back to my old condition of 1861—without aide or clerk—do my own writing and copying. The Tax collector and I*

*will likely compromise to divide my pay, and allow me to worry
through the year without debt. This is the best I can expect.*

in always yr frd. W.T. Sherman

His letter to Miss Colt was, indeed, characteristic.

August 23, 1884

My Dear Lady,

*I am just back from a long absence in Minnesota and find in
the letters awaiting my return one from my good friend and
former aide-de-camp General Alex McD. McCook a letter of
August 14 that you have consented to share with him in the
holy relation of wife the remainder of his period of life.*

*I knew McCook's first wife Kate Phillips well, and a more
loveable creature never existed on Earth. Too good for this
world and called early to another and I hope a better one.
McCook is the soul of kindness—hearty, jovial and cheery at
all times and I cannot blame him for wishing another close
companion to share his life; yet I am jealous of you for taking
his Kate's place.*

*From his description I infer you have all the graces and
accomplishments of womanhood and that you will make his
home what he always wants it to be—a hospitable and generous place for his children and his host of friends.*

*I can only at this time send you the assurances of my best
wishes for a long life of contribution and usefulness—that
whatever contributes to McCook's happiness and success will
ever be precious to me.*

Hoping to see you in person at the time of your marriage.

I am affectingly yours, W.T. Sherman

Colonel Alexander McDowell McCook and Miss Annie Colt were married on October 8, the twenty-second anniversary of the Battle of Perryville. Alex remained forever proud of his corps' gallant fight on that memorable day.

Some years later, Civil War journalist Henry Villard wrote about the Battle of Perryville in his memoirs. Citing General Don Carlos Buell's claim that Alex McCook did not notify him of the Rebel attack until 4:00 p.m., Villard revealed an important discovery:

> *In closing my description of the battle, I deem it my duty to state that, while I was writing it in the spring of 1896—nearly thirty-four years after the event—the curious fact was discovered that General Buell was informed, by signal message, as early as 2 P.M. of the rebel attack in force upon General McCook's division. The discovery rests on the evidence of the signal-officer who received the message.*

In another memoir of the Civil War, General Grant, dying of throat cancer, still blamed McCook for not pursuing the enemy at the Battle of Shiloh. Grant, after leaving the White House, had made bad investments and eventually found himself almost penniless. To make money, he began writing his memoirs. In the February 1885 issue of *Century Magazine* he wrote:

> *I saw troops coming up in beautiful order, as if going on a parade or review. It was McCook's division. The column halted and General McCook rode up. He suggested that his division be sent no further inasmuch as the men were worn out from marching and fighting. It was not the rank and file or the junior officers who asked to be excused but the division commander.*

A storm of criticism broke out in the press, reminding Grant that McCook's division had marched twenty-two miles to rescue him, spent a sleepless night crossing the Tennessee River in the rain, and then fought and whipped the enemy. Their "beautiful order" was due to McCook's training and discipline. Grant apologized in a footnote when his article was reprinted later in the book, *Battles and Leaders of the Civil War*:

I did General McCook injustice in my article in "The Century" although not to the extent one would suppose from the public press.

Alex headed the Infantry and Cavalry School at Fort Leavenworth, Kansas, from 1886 until 1890 when he was nominated by President Benjamin Harrison for brigadier general. This would promote him over several officers ahead of him in rank, but his cause was advocated by many of his old army colleagues who wrote to the president in support of him.

One letter was from General Lew Wallace, now world-famous as the author of the popular novel *Ben-Hur*:

There can be, I think, no question of his merit from whatever standpoint it may be viewed; besides which, judging others by myself, his selection would be received by every veteran as a personal compliment.

. . . As a rule, I am a stickler for seniority, but this is one of the cases in which it ought to be set aside; for, privately, McCook would have been ranking colonel at the end of the Rebellion but for the causeless prejudice of General Grant. You could not please the old soldiers better than by giving him his due now that the opportunity is at hand.

Alex received his second star in 1894 when President Grover Cleveland appointed him major general. Two years later President Cleveland gave him the great honor of representing the United States at the coronation of Czar Nicholas II of Russia.

Then Alex retired to Dayton, still the life of the party and a fine raconteur who could keep everyone amused and laughing. He loved to sing, in his deep rich voice, the battle hymn, "Hold the Fort for I Am Coming." It was reminiscent of his gallant defense of Washington in 1864 when he held Fort Stevens with a small band of invalids.

Suffering a stroke at the age of seventy-two, Alex passed away on June 12, 1903, still the most colorful of the Fighting McCooks.

*Major General Alexander McCook
representing the United States at the
coronation of Czar Nicholas II of Russia*

— EDWARD —

When he married Mary Thompson on June 21, 1865, Ed had everything he could desire. She was beautiful, brilliant, and wealthy. And, as a major general, he had two of those celestial items he had mentioned several years earlier in a letter to his cousin Mary:

> *To add interest and importance to the wedding ceremony, give me a star.*

The marriage was a lavish affair performed by the Episcopal bishop of Illinois. The next year President Andrew Johnson appointed Major General Edward Moody McCook as minister to the Sandwich Islands.

During his tenure in Honolulu, Ed negotiated a commercial treaty between the Islands and the United States. And when the McCooks' first child arrived, Mary had some dirt shipped from the United States and placed under each foot of her bed so that Edward McPherson McCook could be born on American soil.

On April 15, 1867, President Johnson appointed McCook to a four-year term as governor of the Territory of Colorado. And so Ed returned to his beloved Rocky Mountains.

In Denver he was energetic and progressive, overseeing the development of the Colorado mines, organizing a school system, encouraging the building of railroads, and developing an irrigation system for agriculture. His wife was an advocate of women's suffrage, and he supported her interest, recommending the extension of voting rights to women and inviting suffragettes Elizabeth Cady Stanton and Susan B. Anthony to campaign in Colorado.

But McCook's administration came under financial scandal when it was discovered that "Horse Ed," riding roughshod as usual, had overcharged the U.S. government for cattle sent to the Ute Indians, depositing a "commission" of $22,335.19 in his personal bank account. In 1873 Colorado citizens petitioned President Grant not to give McCook another term.

At first Grant acquiesced. Then he changed his mind. Grant, whose administration was scarred by corruption, was honest himself but able to be manipulated by clever men. After Ed convinced him that the new governor of Colorado was involved in an illegal land grab, Grant submitted McCook's name to the U.S. Senate for a second term.

During the height of the struggle, Ed's wife died in Washington at the age of twenty-seven after a long bout with tuberculosis. Mary McCook was described by the publisher of the *Daily Central City Register* as a

> *beautiful, brilliant, and fascinating woman, highly educated, a welcome guest in the first circles of society by reason of her splendid attainments and rare conversational powers. In her death General McCook lost the great potential influence which had sustained and advanced his political aspirations. When the grave closed over her remains, McCook began to sink far below the position to which her beauty and wiser judgment had elevated him.*

Ed McCook's second term was worse than the first. As he took up his old habits of wine, women, and song, his moral conduct caused public scandal. Outraged Senate Republicans told Grant that they would block Colorado's statehood bill unless McCook was removed from office, and so he was ousted for the second time.

Remaining in Denver, Ed remarried in 1884, taking as his bride twenty-three-year-old Mary McKenna. His financial interests—including extensive real estate holdings, mining ventures in Arizona and New Mexico, and investments in European telephone companies—made him the wealthiest man in Colorado. But the depression of 1884 and panic of 1893 combined to deplete his fortune.

Promised a position in Manila by Judge William Howard Taft, Ed was en route to the Philippines in 1900 when he became ill in San Francisco. Penniless, he was supported in his final years by his brothers until he died of Bright's disease in 1909 at the age of seventy-six. Buried with most of Dr. John's family in Steubenville's Union Cemetery was saber-wielding "Horse Ed," the most reckless of the Fighting McCooks.

— JOHN —

After the war, Daniel's youngest son returned to Kenyon College, was elected to Phi Beta Kappa, and received his bachelor of arts degree in 1866. Entering Harvard Law School, he graduated in 1869 and joined the prestigious New York law firm of Alexander and Green, with whom his brother George had long-established ties.

John traveled for the firm, visiting Europe in 1874 and 1875. On one of his visits, he was presented to Queen Victoria by the U.S. minister to Great Britain, former General Robert C. Schenck. He was the political general whom John's brother Alex had left standing in the rain after the first Battle of Bull Run.

On February 17, 1876, John McCook and Janetta Alexander, daughter of Henry M. Alexander, were married in New York City. It was a large society wedding, with carriages of guests stretching for blocks down Fifth Avenue. To them was born a son, who died in infancy, and five daughters.

John McCook sat on boards of directors with some of the nation's wealthiest men, including August Belmont, John Jacob Astor, and J. Pierpont Morgan. One New York newspaper described him in words of which his ambitious father, Daniel McCook, would have been proud:

> *It has long been a common saying in Wall Street that if any great financial deal is under way, Colonel McCook is the first man to know it. He is sought by everyone for information and advice. He is not a mere mouthpiece of capital and capitalists. He has risen above that. He is one of them.*

Although the press called him "colonel," due to his recommendation for that rank because of his "gallant and meritorious services" during the Civil War, the War Department had not approved the promotion. John was still a captain.

Other awards he received, however, included honorary master of arts degrees from Kenyon College and Princeton University, and honorary doctor of laws degrees from Lafayette College and the University of Kansas. He was a director of Princeton and a trustee of Kenyon, where he and his mother donated the largest bell in the church tower in memory of his brother Charles, who had died at Bull Run.

In 1896 John and his family accompanied his brother Alex and his family to Moscow to represent the United States at the coronation of Czar Nicholas II of Russia. And in 1897 John received tentative overtures from

President-elect William McKinley for the position of attorney general. He was endorsed by the *New York Express* in glowing terms:

> *Mr. McCook would be a positive factor in any Cabinet. He is a character of courage and firmness, as his conduct on the battlefield early illustrated. His appearance is striking. He stands at about an even six feet, and is of powerful and energetic frame. Broad of shoulder, square of jaw, clean cut of face, with a pair of frank eyes . . . his presence is the embodiment of physical and tempermental strength.*

But when McKinley offered him the post of secretary of the interior, instead of the attorney generalship, John turned it down to remain in New York and practice law. In 1911 he suffered a heart attack and died with his wife and daughters by his bedside. Laid to rest in Princeton Cemetery was the former seventeen-year-old freckle-faced boy who had been the youngest of the Fighting McCooks.

— HENRY —

After resigning as chaplain of the Forty-first Illinois in protest against escaped slaves being sold back to their masters, the Reverend Henry McCook, D.D., returned to his church in Clinton, Illinois. In 1863 he accepted a call from the Biddle Market Mission in St. Louis to attend to the suffering poor. During two cholera epidemics, he ministered to those struck by the dread disease.

In 1878 Henry became pastor of Philadelphia's Seventh Presbyterian Church, where he earned a reputation as a fine preacher. A prolific author, he wrote numerous books on nature, history, and religion. And in 1897 he penned a historical novel, *The Latimers: A Tale of the Western Insurrection of 1794*, based on family recollections about his grandfather's role in the Whiskey Rebellion.

His boyhood friend Mark Hanna was now the "boss" of the Republican Party. Hanna had helped elect President William McKinley in 1896 by persuading businessmen to contribute heavily to his campaign. Shortly after the turn of the century, Henry and Mark were involved in another fight.

The Hannas, who had left New Lisbon after the failure of the Sandy and Beaver Canal, moved to Cleveland where they made a fortune in the iron and coal business. In 1902 a strike was called by the 140,000-member United Mine Workers to protest low wages and unsafe working conditions. Henry McCook, on behalf of the miners, and Mark Hanna, on behalf of the owners, worked together to settle the dispute.

On Thanksgiving Day, 1902, Henry retired to his country home and continued to write until he died of heart failure in 1911 at the age of seventy-four, still the most stubbornly principled of the Fighting McCooks.

— Anson —

Breveted a brigadier general in the volunteer army for his four years of service, Anson went home to join his cousin George and uncle Dr. George in a successful coal mining venture in West Virginia. Then in 1873 Anson moved to New York City to become manager and part owner of the *Daily Register Law Journal.*

Active in the Republican Party, Anson was surprised to find himself a candidate for Congress three weeks before the election. He campaigned among longshoremen in his Lower Manhattan district, got the support of Civil War veterans of both parties, and was the only Republican elected to Congress from New York City in 1876.

Occupying the White House was Rutherford B. Hayes, and serving with Anson during his three terms in the House of Representatives were the former vice president of the Confederacy Alexander Stephens, former Confederate General Joseph E. Johnston, and former Union General William S. Rosecrans.

In 1883 Anson became the secretary of the Senate, and in the spring of 1886 the fifty-year-old bachelor fell in love. The object of his affections was Hettie McCook, the twenty-seven-year-old daughter of his cousin George. Anson's love letters were typically modest:

> *You perhaps know by this time that I have not the faculty of either saying or writing pretty things, for some parts of my education were sadly neglected; but Hester, I love you and that should and I believe will support many deficiencies.*

The McCook clan, convinced that Anson would never find anyone good enough for him, was delighted at the match. Three children were born to them in Washington before Anson returned to New York and his paper, renamed the *New York Law Journal*. In 1894 he became the city chamberlain, responsible for the finances of New York City.

The McCooks' dinner table invariably hosted a lively assortment of guests—generals, admirals, senators, congressmen, and diplomats—as well as relatives and cronies from all over the country. But it was with Civil War veterans whom Anson was most comfortable. Having fought the war with a great deal of civility, he counted some of his former opponents among his warmest friends.

In 1917, at the age of eighty-two, he passed away after a short illness. By his bedside were his wife and two surviving children, for whom he had written his memoirs seven years earlier.

October 10th, 1910

Dear Katherine and George;

I do not think that my life has been an especially eventful one but there certainly has been a good deal of variety in it, and as I am seventy-five years old today, I know of no better way to celebrate it than by writing these recollections or reminiscences, especially as I hope that some day they may not be without interest to you.

It was a typical understatement from the most self-effacing of the Fighting McCooks.

— LITTLE JOHNNY —

After graduating from Trinity College in Hartford in 1863 as valedictorian of his class, Little Johnny entered Columbia College of Physicians and Surgeons in New York to study medicine. But after a month he decided, once and for all, that he was meant for the ministry. Graduating from Berkeley Divinity School in 1866, he became rector of St. John's Episcopal Church in East Hartford, a mission parish for poor tobacco farmers.

John and Eliza Butler, the "quiet little mouse" half-sister of his cousin Mary Sheldon, were married that summer. Seven children were born to them in the comfortable Butler home on Main Street in Hartford. They were raised by numerous servants—cook, housemaid, governess, and Swiss-French nurse—as well as by Mary Sheldon, who ran the household as faithfully as she had corresponded with her McCook cousins during the Civil War.

With money plentiful, there were leisurely trips to Europe and summers spent at their Long Island Sound estate. But disaster struck in 1883 when it was discovered that Eliza's inheritance had been mismanaged by her financial guardian.

The family fortunes having suffered a serious reversal, John McCook joined the Trinity College faculty to teach Latin. Since he was also fluent in French and German, proficient in Italian and Spanish, and had a working knowledge of six other languages including Greek and Hebrew, he was appointed head of the department of modern languages in 1888.

The former Beau Brummel became a spartan man of frugal habits who rode a bicycle to work and devoted his life to the poor and criminal. He investigated the causes of drunkenness, vagabondage, and crime. He was president of the board of directors of the Connecticut Reformatory. He was chairman of the Hartford Board of Education. And for a short time he served as president of Trinity College.

He retired from teaching in 1923. The next year the graduating class had his likeness carved over the Seabury Hall doorway through which he had walked on his way to class. A month shy of his eighty-fourth birthday, he died in 1927 of angina pectoris, leaving behind these apt words:

I am aware that the best material for history is found in the plain stories of individual lives.

It was a fitting testament from the last of the Fighting McCooks.

On Fame's Eternal Camping Ground

The lapse of years has obscured the individual achievements which make up a record astonishing and glorious, if not absolutely unprecedented under any flag; but the appellation of "the Fighting McCooks" is still almost as familiar as his own name to any American boy.

The mists of time have enveloped those fields of valor and sacrifice, but the thought of such a race of patriots will always touch the heart and stir the blood of every one who is fit to be an American citizen.

The New York Tribune
June 13, 1903

Today

Proud descendants of the Fighting McCooks live in every corner of this great nation that they fought so valiantly to save.

These things also remain. . . .

Daniel McCook's house in Carrollton, Ohio, where he and Martha raised their nine sons and three daughters sits on the town square. A marble bust of Martha graces the mantle in the parlor. The house is owned by the Ohio Historical Society and managed by the Carroll County Historical Society. It is open to the public on weekends from Memorial Day through the second week of October and again during the Christmas holidays.

In Lisbon (formerly New Lisbon) the home of Dr. John McCook no longer exists. The home of Dr. George McCook is a private residence, as is the home of his son, Dr. George Latimer McCook. It sits by the side of the old Sandy and Beaver Canal.

The remains of Lock 24 of the Sandy and Beaver Canal, whose dry bed winds through Columbiana County, is in Elk Run Township near the site of the McCook family farm.

Stone steps lead up to where Hillside once stood in Steubenville. The hospitable mansion above the Ohio River was destroyed by fire many years ago. But the view is the same as loved by George and Margaret.

A stone tablet with the words "Martha B.F." (Blast Furnace) sits by the side of a country road in Hardin County, Illinois. It was the cornerstone of Daniel McCook's great dream of an iron manufacturing empire.

The Butler-McCook Homestead at 394 Main Street in Hartford, Connecticut, where Mary Sheldon wrote her McCook cousins and where

John and Eliza McCook raised their seven children, is owned by the Antiquarian and Landmarks Society. Listed in the *National Register of Historic Places*, it is open to the public throughout the year.

The likeness of the Reverend John McCook is carved over doorway 40-49 of Seabury Hall at Trinity College, Hartford, Connecticut. McCook Hall, a college classroom building, contains the McCook Auditorium.

A memorial bust of General Robert L. McCook stands in Washington Park, opposite the Music Hall, in Cincinnati, Ohio. It faces the former parade ground where he first commanded his all-German Ninth Ohio Volunteer Infantry Regiment. Surviving members of his regiment erected the monument in 1878.

At Perryville, Kentucky, Squire Henry P. Bottom's little white house still sits beside Doctor's Creek where General William Hardee broke through General Alexander McCook's right flank during the Battle of Perryville on October 8, 1862.

Bullets are still embedded in the trees at Kennesaw Mountain in Georgia where Colonel Dan McCook led his gallant charge. Thirty-five years later, his surviving "boys" bought sixty acres of the battlefield and erected a monument where their colonel fell.

World War II photographs show the U.S.S. *McCook*, the destroyer named in honor of Commodore Roderick Sheldon McCook, fighting at Normandy on D-Day, June 6, 1944. The *McCook* remained on duty for fifty-four hours, bombarding the shore as assault troops hit the beaches under its protective fire.

McCook Field in Dayton, Ohio, was established in 1917 as the U.S. Army Signal Corps engineering center and experimental airfield. Jimmy Doolittle and other pioneer test pilots helped make it the "Cradle of Aviation." It is now a recreation field.

The little chapel at Walter Reed Medical Center in Washington, D.C., near the site of old Fort Stevens where Alex McCook stopped Jubal Early, honors the Fighting McCooks. Their descendants contributed the altar, stained-glass windows, and furnishings in memory of those "Who Served Their Country in the War for the Preservation of the Union."

The Ohio Historical Society in Columbus owns the large oil painting of Daniel McCook and his sons, entitled *The Tribe of Dan*, by Charles T. Webber. They also own other memorabilia—including Major Daniel

McCook's Henry rifle, number 1116, which he was holding when shot at Buffington Island, and Colonel Dan McCook's sword with which he led the charge up Kennesaw Mountain.

Historical markers on many battlefields—Mill Springs, Shiloh, Perryville, Stones River, Buffington Island, Lookout Mountain, Chickamauga, Chattanooga, and Kennesaw Mountain—tell of the exploits of the Fighting McCooks.

Spring Grove Cemetery in Cincinnati, Ohio, is the final resting place for most of Daniel's family. The graceful Grecian monument, containing two turns and twelve columns, was designed by Martha.

Union Cemetery in Steubenville, Ohio, is the final resting place for many members of Dr. John's family. Also, McCook Walk is where George and Margaret lie.

The town of McCook, Nebraska, is named in honor of Major General Alexander McDowell McCook. The village of McCook, Illinois, is named in honor of Colonel John James McCook. McCook County and McCook Lake in South Dakota are named in honor of Major General Edwin Stanton McCook.

At Kenyon College in Gambier, Ohio, the largest bell in the tower of the Church of the Holy Spirit rings in memory of Private Charles Morris McCook, who refused to surrender at Bull Run. Inscribed on it are his dying words: "Dulce decorum est pro patria mori."

And whatever became of the little brass cannon?

It remained in New Lisbon as the artillery piece of the Democrat Party. In 1884, when Grover Cleveland became the first Democrat in twenty-four years to be elected president, an overzealous partisan packed it with too much powder.

It blew itself up!

— THE END —

Acknowledgments

There is a certain ring to historic truth. Hearing its clarion call, after 125 years of silence, is a reward in itself. Many fine people at many fine institutions helped us in this quest. We are deeply grateful to them all.

This book was born in 1986 when we discovered the McCook Family Papers in the Manuscript Reading Room of the Library of Congress, Washington, D.C. Bringing it to maturity took many years of research and writing, during which we had the enthusiastic encouragement of the late Mary Wolfskill, head of the Manuscript Reading Room. Our only regret is that she is no longer with us to enjoy the fruits of her labors. She organized the letters, diaries, photographs, and newspaper clippings of the McCook Family Papers when they were given to the Library of Congress in 1954 by Mrs. Katherine McCook Knox, daughter of Civil War Brigadier General Anson G. McCook.

Researching the Civil War records of the Fighting McCooks took us to forty-six battlefields where they fought to save the Union. These fields of battle are in the eleven states of Alabama, Georgia, Kentucky, Maryland, Mississippi, North Carolina, Ohio, South Carolina, Tennessee, Virginia, and West Virginia. We benefited greatly from the knowledge of the fine officials of the National Park Service, U.S. Department of the Interior, at the battlefield parks of Perryville, Chickamauga, Kennesaw Mountain, Fredericksburg, Spotsylvania, and Manassas. We are especially grateful to James Burgess, Manassas National Battlefield Park, for sending us the reminiscences of former

Virginia State Senator John Taylor, which furnished many eyewitness details about the first Battle of Bull Run.

Historical societies were invaluable. In Ohio our thanks go to the tireless researchers at the Ohio Historical Society, Columbus; the historical societies of Cincinnati and Lisbon; as well as those in the counties of Carroll, Hamilton, Jefferson, and Montgomery; the Western Reserve Historical Society, Cleveland; and the Rutherford B. Hayes Presidential Center, Fremont, Ohio. Thanks also to the Illinois State Historical Society, Springfield; Kansas State Historical Society, Topeka; Missouri Historical Society, St. Louis; South Dakota State Historical Society, Pierre; Colorado Historical Society, Denver; and the Historical Society of Western Pennsylvania, Pittsburgh.

Libraries provided great assistance. We are indebted to the excellent staffs at the Library of Congress and those at the U.S. Military Academy, West Point, New York; the U.S. Naval Academy Museum, Annapolis, Maryland; the University of Chicago; Kenyon College, Gambier, Ohio; Miami University, Oxford, Ohio; Duke University, Durham, North Carolina; Washington and Jefferson College, Washington, Pennsylvania; Southern Illinois University, Carbondale, Illinois; Hobart College, Geneva, New York; and the University of Maryland, College Park. The Ohio public libraries in Cincinnati, Dayton, Lorain, and Steubenville were of great help, as well as those in Canonsburg, Pennsylvania, and Leesburg, Virginia.

Invaluable assistance was given to us in Washington, D.C., by the Office of the Curator, the White House; the Medical Museum and Military Archives Division, Department of the Army; the National Archives and Records Administration; the Library of Congress; the National Archives; and the National Portrait Gallery, Smithsonian Institution. In Pennsylvania the U.S. Army Institute, Carlisle, and the Jefferson Medical College, Philadelphia, also were helpful, as was the Hardin County Clerk's Office, Elizabethtown, Illinois; and the McCook Area Chamber of Commerce, McCook, Nebraska.

The descendants of the Fighting McCooks generously shared their memories and memoirs. These included the unpublished memoirs of Brigadier General Anson G. McCook, given to us by his granddaughter, Mrs. Richard A. Smith; and the Genealogical Study of Kate Phillips McCook, given to us by her descendants. The Civil War letters from Dr.

John McCook's sons to their cousin, Mary Sheldon, were made available by the Antiquarian and Landmarks Society, Hartford, Connecticut.

Many thanks to Robert Younger, Morningside Press, Dayton, Ohio, for loaning us his collection of regimental histories; to Steven Wood, who shared with us the Civil War collection of his grandfather, Major General Thomas J. Wood; to Joseph H. Ewing, great-grandson of U.S. Senator Thomas Ewing Sr.; to Dr. James Herron, Jefferson College Historical Society, Canonsburg, Pennsylvania, for providing the history of the little brass cannon; and to historian, author, and Lincoln scholar Michael A. Burlingame, who kindly read our manuscript and offered suggestions.

Deep debts of gratitude go to Martha Jones, former manager of the McCook House in Carrollton, Ohio, and to Shirley Anderson, current manager. We appreciate their cheerful patience during the long years when this book was being researched and written. Wise counsel was provided by our former publisher at Seven Locks Press, Calvin Kytle. The fine editorial pen of Mac Secrest guided the book toward its final form. Book designer Jill Dible and copyeditor Bob Land gave us a finished product of which we are proud. Last but not least, our daughter Anne spent countless hours reviewing the book and making suggestions, and to her we are very grateful.

To all our six wonderful children we give thanks for their enthusiasm and love. If they had not insisted on getting married, having babies, and making us grandparents, this book would have been finished a long time ago!

SOURCE NOTES

ABBREVIATED TITLES

Battles and Leaders	*Battles and Leaders of the Civil War*
Butler-McCook Papers	Letters and journals of the McCooks, Butler-McCook Homestead, Antiquarian and Landmarks Society, Hartford, Connecticut
McCook Papers	Letters, diaries, and newspaper clippings of the McCooks, Manuscript Division, Library of Congress, Washington. D.C.
Memoirs	Unpublished memoirs of Anson McCook
U.S.A.M.I.	U.S. Army Military Institute, Carlisle Barracks, Carlisle, Pennsylvania
N.A.R.A.	National Archives and Records Administration
O.R.	Official Records of the War of the Rebellion
O.R. Navy	Official Naval Records of the War of the Rebellion

CHAPTER 1: JUDGE DANIEL MCCOOK AT THE WHITE HOUSE

2　　"Is this the 'irrepressible'"　question to himself, mentioned in letter from Daniel McCook to Richard H. Phelps, May 4, 1861, McCook Papers. Reference to a speech given by Senator William H. Seward of New York at Rochester on October 25, 1858. Carl Sandburg, *Abraham Lincoln: The Prairie Years and the War Years*, 167.

3　　*My Dear Sir*　letter from Daniel McCook to Richard Phelps, January 12, 1861, McCook Papers.

3　　*Politically*　Ibid., January 15, 1861.

3　　. . . *many thought*　Ibid., January 16, 1861.

3　　*Politically*　Ibid., January 27, 1861.

4　　. . . it is not　Ibid., February 21, 1861.

6　　. . . *the terms*　Ibid., April 3, 1861.

6　　*My Dear Sir*　Ibid., April 15, 1861.

9　　"Password?"　*Washington Evening Star*, April 19, 1861, 2.

10   "Why don't they come?" John G. Nicolay and John Hay, *Abraham Lincoln, A History*, 4:152.

12   *My Dear Sir*   letter from Daniel McCook to Richard Phelps, May 4, 1861, McCook Papers.

CHAPTER 2: THE WHISKEY BOY AND HIS CLAN IN THE OHIO RIVER VALLEY

15   "'A' thought A' was a-comin'"   McCook family history. Quoted by George McCook's grandson, Reverend Henry C. McCook, D.D., in *The Latimers*, his narrative of the Whiskey Rebellion, 330. Attribution made in letter from Henry McCook to his niece Fanny, February 23, 1905. McCook Papers.

20   *$5 reward* and subsequent articles in *The Washington Reporter*   James T. Herron Jr., *Canonsburgh's Cannon Caper, Jefferson College Times* 14, October 1981, Jefferson College Historical Society, Canonsburg, Pennsylvania. (Note: The spelling of the town of Canonsburg[h] has changed over time. The contemporary is Canonsburg.)

22   *A deal was struck*   Ibid.

23   "If this bill becomes law"   Velma Griffin and Lynn R. Fox, *Early History of Carroll County*, 7, Carroll County Historical Society, Carrollton, Ohio.

25   "in strict accordance with the facts"   William Johnston, *Trial of Daniel McCook, Esq. on Articles of Impeachment for Good Behavior in Office*, 15.

25   *falsely and corruptly*   Ibid., 7.

26   *Dear Sir*   letter from Chaplain Charles Henry Alden to Daniel McCook, April 2, 1842, McCook Papers.

27   *Apr. 1st*   David G. Farragut, *Some Reminiscences of Early Life by D. G. Farragut of the U.S. Navy*, 184, William W. Jeffries Memorial Archives, U.S. Naval Academy, Annapolis, Maryland.

27   *. . . the unchristian*   Carrollton Presbyterian Church Records, vol. 2, Carrollton, Ohio.

29   *Margaret*   letter from Edwin Stanton to Margaret Beatty, undated, McCook Papers.

30   *My dearest*   letter from George McCook to Margaret Beatty, undated, McCook Papers.

35   *Dear Father and Mother*   letter from George McCook to his parents, June 29, 1858, McCook Papers.

35   "A house divided"   speech made by Abraham Lincoln on June 16, 1858, Henry Horner Lincoln Collection, Illinois State Historical Library, Springfield.

36   *Dear Judge*   letter from Daniel McCook to Stephen A. Douglas, January 20, 1859, Stephen A. Douglas Papers, University of Chicago Library.

37   *Dear Sir*   letter from Edwin Stanton to George McCook, February 4, 1861, McCook Papers.

38   "Listen old fellow"   Henry Howe, *A Brief Historical Sketch of the Fighting McCooks*, reprinted from the proceedings of the Scotch-Irish Society of America, McCook Papers. Also *In the Company of Heroes*, Jim Schottelkotte, *Cincinnati Enquirer*, May 30, 1983.

38   "Young man"   Ibid.

CHAPTER 3: LIEUTENANT JOHN MCCOOK IN THE FIRST LAND BATTLE OF THE CIVIL WAR

41   *was never exceeded*   New York Times, June 7, 1861, 1.

43   *the end of justice*   letter from President Alden to Dr. H. G. Commings, October 21, 1860, Butler-McCook Papers.

44   "our friends over there"   Rev. John J. McCook, D.D., *Pictures from Memory*, 18, Butler-McCook Papers.

44   "let the wayward sisters go in peace"   Gideon Welles, *Diary*, 1:172.

44   "Extra! Extra!"   Charlotte Reeve Conover, *Dayton and Montgomery County*, 1:83.

44   *What portion*   telegram from Governor Dennison to President Lincoln, April 15, 1861, O.R. Series III, 1:73.

44   *Thirteen regiments*   Ibid.

45   *Love of mine*   letter from George to Margaret, October 18, 1860, McCook Papers.

46   *My dearest Margaret*   letter from George to Margaret, April 25, 1861, McCook Papers.

47   *Dear John*   letter from Dr. John McCook to his son, Lieutenant John J. McCook, May 30, 1861, Butler-McCook Papers.

48   *Dear John*   Ibid., July 6, 1861.

50   *We have annihilated*   O.R. Series I, 2:204.

50   *Soldiers of the Army*   O.R. Series I, 2:236.

51   *I cannot*   letter from Dr. John McCook to his son John, May 30, 1861, Butler-McCook Papers.

51   *Dear Father and Mother*   letter from John McCook to his parents, August 10, 1861, Butler-McCook Papers.

CHAPTER 4: PRIVATE CHARLES MCCOOK AT THE BATTLE OF BULL RUN

54   *Forward to Richmond*   *New York Tribune*, June 26, 1861, 1.

56   "I shall never go with McCook"   letter from Daniel McCook to his son Robert, July 26, 1861, McCook Papers.

58   "Victory! Victory!"   William C. Davis, *Battle at Bull Run*, 187.

59   "Victory!"   *Washington Evening Star*, July 22, 1861, 2.

61   "The cannonade"   letter from Daniel McCook to his son Robert, July 26, 1861, McCook Papers.

62   "Surrender"   Ibid.

62   "No"   Ibid.

62   "Now, damn you"   Ibid.

63   "No, never"   Ibid.

64   "I can die"   Ibid.

64   "Tell her that I refused"   Henry Howe, *A Brief Historical Sketch of the Fighting McCooks*, 18, Scotch-Irish Society of America, McCook Papers.

64   "Dulce et decorum est"   Ibid.

64   *This was the most gloomy*   letter from Daniel McCook to his son Robert, July 26, 1861, McCook Papers.

66   *I leave on tomorrow*   letter from Daniel McCook to Owen Steed, October 10, 1861, McCook Papers.

CHAPTER 5: COLONEL ALEXANDER MCCOOK AND THE WAR IN THE WEST

69   "Father, get down"   letter from Daniel McCook to his son George, August 2, 1861, McCook Papers.

69   "There's going to be a war"   McCook, *Pictures from Memory*, p. 20.

70   "the happiest man alive"   letter from Dan McCook Jr. to his father, May 29, 1858, McCook Papers.

70   *Dear Father*   letter from Alex McCook to his father, January 3, 1855, McCook Papers.

72   *So McCook . . . saw you off*   letter from Colonel Hardee to Clara Paige, Clara K. Paige Papers, New York Public Library, cited by Nathaniel C. Hughes, *General William J. Hardee: Old Reliable*, 62.

74   "Schenck," asked Lincoln   James R. Therry, *The Life of General Robert Cumming Schenck*, 190, Schenck Papers, Miami University, Oxford, Ohio.

74   "I don't know, sir"   Ibid.

74   "Well," said Lincoln   Ibid.

75   *. . . incompetent commanders*   *New York Times*, June 19, 1861, 4.

76   "We deem it"   Donald Eugene Day, *Military Career of Robert Cumming Schenck*, 60, Schenck Papers, Miami University, Oxford, Ohio.

76   "That you shall never do"   Ibid.

77   *. . . a piece of affectation*   letter from Sarah Howard Forrer to her daughter, January 24, 1858, Forrer-Pierce-Wood Collection, Dayton Public Library, Dayton, Ohio.

78   *We hated to part with McCook*   Levi Wagner, *Reminiscences*, 14, U.S.A.M.I.

78   *Kentucky will furnish*   telegram from Kentucky Governor Magoffin to Lincoln, Benjamin P. Thomas, *Abraham Lincoln*, 260.

78   *If Kentucky will not*   Stephen Z. Starr, *The Union Cavalry in the Civil War*, 3:2.

78   *I think to lose Kentucky*   letter from Lincoln to Senator Orville Browning, September 22, 1861, Henry Horner Lincoln Collection, Illinois State Historical Library.

79   *...awaits us*   O.R. Series I, 4:307.

80   *. . . an overgrown schoolboy*   William F. G. Shanks, *Personal Recollections of Distinguished Generals*, 248.

81   "has the power"   John F. Marszalek, *Sherman: A Soldier's Passion for Order*, 166.

81   *It affords me pleasure*   O.R. Series I, 5:242 (chap. 14).

CHAPTER 6: CHAPLAIN HENRY MCCOOK AND THE HOLY WAR

85   *Dear Johnny*   letter from Henry McCook to his brother Johnny, January 13, 1860, Butler-McCook Papers.

88   "who shall take up arms"   O.R. Series I, 3:467.

90   *My dear Cousin*   letter from Henry McCook to cousin Mary Sheldon, November 12, 1861, Butler-McCook Papers.

92   *The laws of the United States*   O.R. Series I, 4:307.

93   *Dear Johnny*   letter from Henry to Johnny, November 29, 1861, Butler-McCook Papers.

94   *I hereby*   letter from Henry McCook to J. C. Kelton, December 21, 1861, Personal Records, N.A.R.A.

CHAPTER 7: COLONEL ROBERT MCCOOK AT THE BATTLE OF MILL SPRINGS

97   "Charge, my bully Dutchmen"   Constantin Grebner, *We Were the Ninth,* ed. Frederic Trautmann, 71.

98   "An old-fashioned child"   *Steubenville Herald*, August 24, 1877, McCook Papers.

100   "I have just found out"   *Cincinnati Daily Times*, August 24, 1877, McCook Papers.

100   "to hell itself"   Grebner, *We Were the Ninth*, 13.

100   "We came to fight"   *Harper's Weekly*, August 30, 1862, McCook Papers.

100   *My advance guard*   O.R. Series I, 2:200.

103   *Dear L*   letter from Rutherford B. Hayes to his wife Lucy, September 27, 1861, Rutherford B. Hayes Presidential Center.

103   *McCook can feed*   Ibid., October 19, 1861.

106   "Charge, my bully Dutchmen"   Grebner, *We Were the Ninth*, 71.

106 "Hurrah" Ibid., 91.

106 *. . . like chaff before the wind* O.R. Series I, 7:87.

107 *I am delighted* letter from Rutherford B. Hayes to his wife Lucy, January 28, 1862, Hayes Presidential Center.

107 *Robert is painfully* letter from George McCook to his father, January 22, 1862, reported in the *New York Times*, January 25, 1862, 2.

108 "If that giraffe" Donn Piatt, *Memories of the Men Who Saved the Union*, 56.

108 "painful imbecility" Benjamin P. Thomas and Harold M. Hyman, *Stanton, the Life and Times of Lincoln's Secretary of War*, 124.

108 "original gorilla" Thomas, *Abraham Lincoln*, 295.

108 "Illinois ape" Ibid.

108 "low cunning clown" Thomas and Hyman, *Stanton*, 116.

110 "Yes," crowed Stanton Piatt, *Memories of the Men Who Saved the Union*, 57.

110 "What will you do?" Ibid.

110 "Do?" Ibid.

111 *. . . while men are striving* Charles A. Dana, *Recollections of the Civil War*, 5.

CHAPTER 8: CAPTAIN EDWIN STANTON MCCOOK AT FORTS HENRY AND DONELSON

115 *Edwin S. McCook is* Roy P. Basler, ed., *The Collected Works of Abraham Lincoln*, 4:392.

117 "Well, we cut our way" Ulysses Simpson Grant, *Personal Memoirs of U.S. Grant*, 1:224.

117 "Die with it" O.R. Series I, 3:289 (chap. 10).

118 *Fort Henry is ours* James M. McPherson, *Battle Cry of Freedom*, 397.

119 "Gentlemen" Lew Wallace, *Battles and Leaders*, 1:422.

120 *If all the gunboats* O.R. Series I, 7:618 (chap. 17).

121 "No flinching now" Wallace, *Battles and Leaders*, 1:423.

121   *No terms*   O.R. Series I, 7:161.

122   "I propose to move"   Dana, *Recollections*, 7.

122   "He's got the slows"   Sandburg, *Abraham Lincoln: The Prairie Years and the War Years*, 296.

123   "We may be obliged"   Thomas, *Abraham Lincoln*, 296.

124   *As we move southward*   Letter from Alex to Kate, March 24, 1862, McCook Papers.

125   *I have scarcely*   O.R. Series I, 10:89 (part 1).

Chapter 9: Brigadier General Alexander McCook at the Battle of Shiloh

128   "For God's sake"   Wagner, *Reminiscences*, 28.

128   "I will blow my brains out"   Ibid.

128   "Ready. Aim. Fire."   *Harper's New Monthly Magazine*, May 1864, 830.

129   "Captain McCook"   *Boston Evening Transcript*, June 13, 1903, McCook Papers.

130   "Good-bye, Dan"   Ibid.

130   "No"   Ulysses S. Grant, *Century Magazine*, February 1885, 593.

131   *I concede*   O.R. Series I, 10:252 (part 1).

134   "The secessionists"   Grebner, *We Were the Ninth*, 104.

134   "If the boys"   Ibid.

135   "Let's move out of the way," and subsequent quotes until Captain Hunter Brooke is taken prisoner   *National Republican*, undated, McCook Papers.

137   "What has become of Colonel McCook?"   *Cincinnati Daily Times*, August 24, 1877, McCook Papers.

137   *The murderers*   letter from Amos Fleagle to his brother and sister, August 24, 1862, Harrisburg Civil War Round Table Collection, U.S.A.M.I.

137   "Andy," and subsequent quotes of General McCook   *Cincinnati Daily Times*, August 23, 1877, McCook Papers.

138   *This wanton murder*   *Harper's Weekly*, August 23, 1862, 530.

138   *The rebel assassination*   *New York Times*, August 9, 1862, 4.

140   *The sad news*   letter from Rutherford B. Hayes to his wife Lucy, August 10, 1862, Hayes Presidential Center.

140   *Sad news*   entry in Rutherford B. Hayes diary, August 9, 1862, Hayes Presidential Center.

CHAPTER 10: LIEUTENANT JOHN McCOOK AND McCOOK'S AVENGERS

144   *A profuse allowance*   *Triennial Catalogue of the Theological Seminary of the Diocese of Ohio and Kenyon College*, 47.

145   *My army has promised*   letter from General Braxton Bragg to General John C. Breckinridge, O.R. Series I, 16:995 (part 2).

147   "Rally 'round the flag, boys"   *The Re-Union, 52nd Ohio Regiment*, Barnesville, Ohio, September 19–20, 1877, McCook Papers.

148   *Drill in morning*   letter from Thomas J. Frazee to his brother, September 25, 1862, Thomas J. Frazee Collection, Illinois State Historical Library.

148   *We have got Bully*   Ibid.

151   "that Yankee rifle"   *150th Anniversary of McCook House 1837–1987*, 26, Carroll County Historical Society.

CHAPTER 11: MAJOR GENERAL ALEXANDER McCOOK AT THE BATTLE OF PERRYVILLE

155   "would not hold dress parade"   James B. Shaw, *History of the Tenth Indiana Volunteer Infantry*, 171–72, cited by Kenneth A. Hafendorfer, *Perryville*, 96.

156   *Please keep me advised*   O.R. Series I, 16:575 (part 2).

157   "There will be fun"   O.R. Series I, 16:71 (part 1).

158   "Who is down in Perryville?"   Ibid., 90.

158   "Hardee, with two divisions"   Ibid.

158   "I am going down to drink"   Ibid.

158   "There is a great waste"   Ibid., 11.

158   *Stop that useless waste*   Ibid.

160   "Colonel McCook"   Julius Birney Work, *McCook's Brigade: Reunion of Col. Dan McCook's Third Brigade*, 115.

160   *There is one rule*   Hughes, *General William J. Hardee*, 127.

161   "If General Buell supposes"   Shanks, *Personal Recollections*, 250.

161   *Strike with your whole strength*   Hughes, *General William J. Hardee*, 127.

162   "Let me go to Alex's help"   Anson McCook, *Memoirs*, 219.

162   "The orders are"   Ibid.

163   "God help our poor boys"   L. G. Bennett and William H. Haigh, *History of the 36th Regiment Illinois Volunteers during the War of the Rebellion*, 259.

163   "Minutes are terribly important"   Horace C. Fisher, *A Staff Officer's Story: The Personal Experiences of Horace Newton Fisher in the Civil War*, 44.

163   "General McCook's entire command"   O.R. Series I, 16:1040 (part 1).

163   "I'll think about it"   James Harrison Wilson, *Alexander McDowell McCook*, Thirty-fifth Annual Reunion of the Association Graduates of the United States Military Academy at West Point, New York, 58.

164   "astonished"   Don Carlos Buell, *Battles and Leaders*, III, 48.

164   "Captain, you must be mistaken"   Henry Villard, *Memoirs of Henry Villard*, I, 321.

165   "We are just back there"   McCook, *Memoirs*, 213.

165   "Hold your ground"   O.R. Series I, 16:1025 (part 1).

167   "You shall not have"   Ibid., 102.

168   *Have you commenced*   Ibid., 536.

168   *For the time engaged*   Ibid., 1087.

169   . . . *the enemy's batteries*   Ibid., 1084.

169   *I was not apprised*   Ibid., 1031.

170   . . . *a brave man*   *New York Times*, October 19, 1862, 2.

170   *I was badly whipped*   O.R. Series I, 16:99 (part 1).

170 "I'll send you to hell"   letter from Rev. G. W. Chandler to his brother, October 17, 1862, U.S. Army Archives, Miscellany, Officers and Soldiers Miscellaneous Letters 1847–1961, William R. Perkins Library, Duke University, Durham, North Carolina.

CHAPTER 12: MAJOR GENERAL ALEXANDER MCCOOK AT THE BATTLE OF STONES RIVER

173 "We move tomorrow"   William D. Bickham, *Rosecrans' Campaign with the Fourteenth Army Corps, Army of the Cumberland*, 134–39.

174 "We move tomorrow"   Ibid.

175 "Well," Stanton muttered   Piatt, *Memories of the Men Who Saved the Union*, 81.

177 "Spread out your skirmishers"   Bickham, *Rosecrans' Campaign*, 134–39.

177 "Good night, general"   Ibid., 162.

178 "Give me more cavalry"   William M. Lamers, *The Edge of Glory*, 210.

179 "Tell General McCook"   Ibid., 211.

179 "It is looking better"   Ibid.

179 *Take a strong position*   O.R. Series I, 20:255 (part 1).

180 "You know the ground"   Ibid., 192.

180 "Yes, I think I can"   Ibid.

180 "His attack"   James H. Woodward, *Gen. A. McD. McCook at Stone's River*, War Paper No. 9, Commandery of the State of California, 13.

181 "McCook seemed"   Memoirs of David S. Stanley, West-Stanley-Wright Family Papers, U.S.A.M.I., Carlisle, Pennsylvania.

181 "That is contrary"   Frank Moore, ed., *The Rebellion Record: A History of American Events*, Vol. 6, *Doc. 174, Chattanooga Daily Rebel*, January 2, 1863.

181 "Who is opposing"   Ibid.

181 "Major General Cheatham"   Ibid.

181 "Is it possible"   Ibid.

183 "The right wing is broken"   Bickham, *Rosecrans' Campaign*, 208.

183 "Tell General McCook"   Ibid., 209.

183   "It is working right"   Ibid.

183   "So soon?"   Lamers, *The Edge of Glory*, 220.

183   . . . *brave to a fault*   *New York Times*, January 4, 1863, 1.

186   "Hello Yank"   McCook, *Memoirs*, 261.

186   "I would like Bragg"   Shelby Foote, *The Civil War, A Narrative: Fredericksburg to Meridian*, 94.

186   "Gentlemen"   Bickham, *Rosecrans' Campaign*, 290.

187   *What terrible sights*   John A. Duncan Civil War Diary, January 3, 1863, *Civil War Times, Illustrated Collections*, 12, U.S.A.M.I.

187   "There goes poor"   Luther F. Bradley letter, January 5, 1863, Luther F. Bradley Papers, U.S.A.M.I.

187   *God has crowned*   O.R. Series I, 20:185 (part 1).

187   *God bless you*   Ibid., 186.

188   . . . *partially surprised*   Ibid., 184.

188   *At one o'clock*   Moore, *The Rebellion Record*, 9:480.

188   *At present*   *New York Times*, January 8, 1863, 1.

188   . . . *the city is electrified*   *Dayton Daily Empire*, January 29, 1863, McCook Papers.

189   . . . *the most brilliant*   *Dayton Daily Empire*, February 6, 1863, McCook Papers.

189   *A very brilliant*   *Cincinnati Daily Times*, January 30, 1863, McCook Papers.

189   "I hate to injure"   Whitelaw Reid, *Ohio in the War*, 752.

191   . . . *finely*   Frederick D. Williams, *The Wild Life of the Army: Civil War Letters of James A. Garfield*, 254.

191   *My dear Mama Phillips*   letter from Alex to Mrs. Jonathan D. Phillips, April 1, 1863, McCook Papers.

192   . . . *degraded at such*   Henry M. Cist, *The Army of the Cumberland*, 150.

193   "stepchild army"   Glenn Tucker, *Chickamauga: Bloody Battle in the West*, 8.

194   "Stanton is a natural"   Lamers, *The Edge of Glory*, 265.

CHAPTER 13: DR. LATIMER MCCOOK AT VICKSBURG

201 "modest," "honest," and "disinterested" Dana, *Recollections of the Civil War*, 61.

202 . . . *for a soldier* William S. McFeely, *Grant*, 120.

202 "I can't spare this man" T. Harry Williams, *Lincoln and His Generals*, 86.

206 "good night" McFeely, *Grant*, 134.

207 "My God" Earl S. Miers, *The Web of Victory*, 283.

208 During battle Grant did not see dead men *Personal Memoirs of U.S. Grant*, 1:307–8, cited by McFeely, *Grant*, 100.

208 *For God's sake* Piatt, *Memories of the Men Who Saved the Union*, 297.

209 "its annual excursion" Thomas, *Abraham Lincoln*, 368.

209 "My God, my God" Ibid., 370.

210 *I beg in behalf* O.R. Series I, 23:518 (part 2).

210 "He shall not have" Lamers, *The Edge of Glory*, 295.

213 *This community* *Cincinnati Daily Commercial*, July 23, 1863, McCook Papers.

CHAPTER 14: MAJOR GENERAL ALEXANDER MCCOOK AT THE BATTLE OF CHICKAMAUGA

217 "My God, we are doomed" newspaper clipping from *Cleveland Herald*, undated, McCook Papers.

218 . . . *the patience of* O.R. Series I, 23:552 (part 2).

219 *All goes on swimmingly* O.R. Series I, 30:326 (part 3).

220 *I am not desirous* Ibid., 569.

221 "lies" Daniel H. Hill, *Battles and Leaders III*, 645.

221 *Major-General Grant* O.R. Series I, 30:694 (part 3).

222 "I was sent here" Dana, *Recollections*, 107.

223 "about a mile" Shanks, *Personal Recollections*, 266.

224 "You Yanks" Henry J. Aten, *History of the Eighty-Fifth Regiment, Illinois Volunteer Infantry*, 103.

225 *We have just* O.R. Series I, 30:136 (part 1).

225 "I would strengthen" Dana, *Recollections*, 114.

225 "Where are we" Ibid.

225 "You will defend" O.R. Series I, 30:69 (part 1).

225 "Her father's God" Hymn of the Hebrew Maiden, Dana, *Recollections*, 114.

226 "Good morning Wood" George K. Shaffer to Captain George H. Wood, January 20, 1905, Thomas J. Wood Collection.

226 "General, why didn't" General Thomas J. Wood to the editor of the *New York Times*, November 4, 1882, Wood Collection.

226 "I moved" Ibid.

226 "damnable negligence" Tucker, *Chickamauga*, 33.

227 "Hurry up" General Wood to the *New York Times*, November 4, 1882, Wood Collection.

227 *General Thomas* O.R. Series I, 30:70 (part 1).

227 *The general commanding* Ibid.

228 "Brannan is out" Gates P. Thruston, *Battles and Leaders III*, 663.

228 *The general commanding* O.R. Series I, 30:635 (part 1).

228 "My God" George K. Shaffer letter, October 29, 1883, Wood Collection.

228 "The only thing" Ibid.

228 "I am glad" Oral history, General Alexander McCook to his grandson, Alexander Craighead.

228 "I will have Sheridan" George Shaffer letter, October 29, 1883, Wood Collection.

229 "Charge them once" William Robertson, *An Account of the Battle*, Civil War 125th Anniversary booklet, American Civil War Commemorative Committee, 30.

230 "I will send in" Cist, *Army of the Cumberland*, 970.

230 "We'll talk to you" Thruston, *Battles and Leaders III*, 665.

230 *. . . in case our army* O.R. Series I, 30:69 (part 1).

230   *My report today*   Ibid., 192.

231   *I am happy to report*   Ibid., 193.

231   *The disaster*   Ibid., 194.

231   *The battle of the 20th*   O.R. Series I, 30:57.

231   "I know the reasons"   John Hay, *Letters of John Hay and Extracts from Diary, I*, 104.

231   "No, they need not"   Ibid., 105.

232   . . . *that dangerous blunderhead*   O.R. Series I, 30:194 (part 1).

232   *This feeling is universal*   Ibid., 201.

233   *Headquarters 20th Army Corps*   O.R. Series I, 30:126 (part 4).

CHAPTER 15: COLONEL ANSON MCCOOK AT THE BATTLE OF CHATTANOOGA

237   *Dear George*   letter from Anson McCook to his cousin George, October 8, 1863, McCook Papers.

237   *The whole thing*   Ibid.

237   *I scarcely know*   Ibid.

239   "Go west, young man"   McPherson, *Battle Cry of Freedom*, 42.

240   *Dear Father*   letter from Anson to his father, June 10, 1854, McCook Papers.

240   *Dear Cousin*   letter from Anson to Mary Sheldon, July 10, 1861, Butler-McCook Papers.

242   "Well, what do you say?"   McCook, *Memoirs*, 154.

242   "You might spoil"   Ibid.

242   "I will risk it"   Ibid.

242   *Dear Coz*   letter from Anson to Mary, December 1, 1861, Butler-McCook Papers.

243   *Dear Coz*   Ibid., February 4, 1862.

243   *Dear Coz*   Ibid., March 7, 1862.

244   *Dear Cousin*   Ibid., August 7, 1862.

244   "Oh, we are all right"   McCook, *Memoirs*, 249.

245   "McCook, if anything happens"   Ibid., 247.

245   "Did you hear me?"   Ibid.

245   "Certainly I heard you"   *New York Evening Journal*, undated, McCook Papers.

245   *Dear Mary*   letter from Anson to Mary, January 10, 1863, Butler-McCook Papers.

246   *Dear Mary*   Ibid., April 5, 1863.

247   *Dear Mary*   Ibid., June 6, 1863.

247   *But for the imbecility*   Ibid.

248   *If we maintain*   Lamers, *The Edge of Glory*, 379.

248   *I intend doing something*   Ibid.

248   "throwing water on a duck's back"   Gideon Welles, *Diary of Gideon Welles*, I, 102.

249   *the soldiers have lost*   O.R. Series I, 30:204 (part 1).

249   "Like a duck"   Hay, *Letters and Extracts from Diary*, I, 112.

249   "The tycoon of the War Department"   Thomas and Hyman, *Stanton*, 290.

250   "How do you do"   Peter Cozzens, *The Shipwreck of Their Hopes*, 3.

250   "This is to be expected"   Villard, *Memoirs*, II, 209.

250   *Dear Mary*   letter from Anson to Mary, October 24, 1863, Butler-McCook Papers.

252   "Hello, Yank"   McCook, *Memoirs*, 335.

252   "Only sixty"   Ibid.

252   "There, damn you"   Ibid.

252   "I fear they cannot"   Cist, *Army of the Cumberland*, 259.

253   "Boys"   Wagner, *Reminiscences*, 102.

253   "Thomas, who ordered," and subsequent conversation between Grant, Thomas, and Granger   Joseph S. Fullerton, *Battles and Leaders, III*, 725.

254   "Chickamauga!"   McPherson, *Battle Cry of Freedom*, 680.

254   "Here is your commander"   James Lee McDonough, *Chattanooga, A Death Grip on the Confederacy*, 211.

255   "It is a shame"   McCook, *Memoirs*, 346.

255   "Oh, Lieutenant"   Ibid.

CHAPTER 16: COLONEL DANIEL MCCOOK JR. AT THE
BATTLE OF KENNESAW MOUNTAIN

258   "Here's for a general's star"   *Ohio Archaeological and Historical Publications*, 23:310, Ohio Historical Society, Columbus.

259   *His speech*   *The Tazewell Register*, May 12, 1859, Tazewell County Genealogical Society newsletter, October 1987, Pekin, Illinois.

259   *My dear Father*   letter from Dan to his father, August 20, 1859, Stephen A. Douglas Papers, University of Chicago Library.

260   *Did you ever see Julia?*   letter from Thomas Ewing to his sister, Ellen Ewing Sherman, June 6, 1860, Thomas Ewing Jr. Papers, Kansas State Historical Society, Topeka.

260   *Hon. Joseph Holt*   O.R. Series III, 1:64.

261   *My dear Brother*   letter from Dan to George, March 10, 1861, Butler-McCook Papers.

261   *We are yours to command*   newspaper clipping, unattributed and undated, McCook Papers.

262   *The Gen. commanding*   letter from Private Levi Ross to his father, September 16, 1862, Levi Adolphus Ross Collection, Illinois State Historical Library.

263   "It is the duty"   O.R. Series I, 16:505.

264   "I know you're a Union man"   Lamers, *The Edge of Glory*, 241.

264   "Oh, no"   Ibid.

264   "I reckon"   Ibid.

264   "my boys"   Work, *McCook's Brigade*, 81.

264   *Col. D. McCook from the officers*   Carroll County Historical Society, Carrollton, Ohio, Vol. 16, no. 3: 7.

264   "Make it an utter"   Work, *McCook's Brigade*, 80.

265   *Withdraw McCook and Mitchell*   Peter Cozzens, *The Battle of Chickamauga: This Terrible Sound*, 122.

265   "Which brigade"   Freeman Cleaves, *Rock of Chickamauga*, 158.

266   "Tell General Granger"   Cozzens, *This Terrible Sound*, 441.

266   *I saw Dan*   letter from Anson to George, November 15, 1863, McCook Papers.

268   *. . . to be sure*   letter from Margaret to Jane H. Dick, August 16, 1843, McCook Papers.

268   *The small force*   O.R. Series I, 30:961 (part 1).

269   *The Court are of the opinion*   Ibid.

269   "The particulars of your plans"   Thomas, *Abraham Lincoln*, 420.

270   *THE SECOND DIVISION AT SHILOH*   *Harper's New Monthly Magazine*, May 1864, 828–33.

272   "He is a butcher"   David Herbert Donald, *Lincoln*, 515.

274   "Officers"   J. R. Kinnear, *History of the 86th Regiment, Illinois Volunteer Infantry, 4th Reunion*, 16.

274   "Don't be rash"   Work, *McCook's Brigade*, 84.

274   "No"   Ibid., 30.

275   "Tis an easy matter"   Ibid., 34.

275   "Then out spoke brave Horatius"   Lucy Harmon McPherson, *Life and Letters of Oscar Fitzalan Harmon*, 42.

275   "Attention battalions"   Robert M. Rogers, *The One Hundred Twenty-fifth Regiment Illinois Volunteer*, 91.

276   "Stop, Joe"   James T. Holmes, *52nd O.V.I. Then and Now*, 179.

276   "Come on, boys"   Rev. Nixon B. Stewart, *Dan McCook's Regiment, Fifty-Second O.V.I. A History of the Regiment*, 118.

276   "Bring up those colors"   Work, *McCook's Brigade*, 40.

276   "Colonel Dan"   Ibid.

276   "Goddamn you"   Ibid.

277   "Surrender"   Ibid., 85.

277   "Stick to them"   Ibid.

277   "Come on, boys"   Stewart, *Dan McCook's Regiment*, 119.

277   "Forward"   Ibid.

277   "Soldier, throw that gun"   Work, *McCook's Brigade*, 41.

277   "Boys, what regiment"   Ibid., 34.

277   "Go on up"   Ibid.

278   "This is to be my last"   Ibid., 42.

278   "Oh, let us hope not"   Ibid.

278   *. . . and for which*   O.R. Series I, 38:69 (part 1).

278   *I regret beyond measure*   O.R. Series I, 30:611 (part 4).

278   "Ans"   McCook, *Memoirs*, 370.

279   "Break step"   Work, *McCook's Brigade*, 83.

280   *He lives best*   letter from Daniel Gale to President Rutherford B. Hayes, May 12, 1879, Hayes Presidential Center.

284   *The enemy is advancing*   O.R. Series I, 37:197 (part 2).

284   "Get down, you damn fool"   Thomas, *Abraham Lincoln*, 434.

285   *The Sixth Corps*   O.R. Series I, 37:232 (part 1).

285   *Everything is quiet*   O.R. Series I, 37:229 (part 2).

285   *. . . unless you direct*   O.R. Series I, 37:223 (part 2).

286   *. . . if possible*   John Y. Simon, *The Papers of Ulysses S. Grant*, 11:231.

287   "The promotion is too late"   Stewart, *Dan McCook's Regiment*, 123.

287   "Return it with my compliments"   Ibid.

CHAPTER 17: BRIGADIER GENERAL EDWARD McCOOK IN THE BATTLE FOR ATLANTA

290   *They would have got more*   O.R. Series I, 38:761 (part 2).

290   *. . . dashing officer*   newspaper clipping, unattributed and undated, McCook Papers.

290   "Good morning"   McCook, *Memoirs*, 25.

292   *My Dear Cousin*   letter from Ed McCook to Mary Sheldon, May 10, 1861, Butler-McCook Papers.

293   *My Dear Cousin*   Ibid., June 3, 1861.

293   *Dear Cousin*   Ibid., July 2, 1861.

294   *Dear Cousin Mary*   Ibid., August 28, 1861.

294   *Dear Cousin Mary*   Ibid., September 29, 1861.

295   *Dear Little Cousin*   Ibid., March 29, 1862.

296   *Dear Cousin Mary*   Ibid., April 13, 1862.

296   *Dear Cousin Mary*   Ibid., August 17, 1862.

297   *Dear Mary*   Ibid., February 24, 1863.

298   "Give me more cavalry"   Lamers, *The Edge of Glory*, 210.

298   *They are almost*   O.R. Series III, 3:249–50 (part 3).

300   *The rebel loss*   O.R. Series I, 30:69 (part 4).

300   *Dear Cousin*   letter from Ed to Mary, November 28, 1863, Butler-McCook Papers.

301   *Dear Cousin Mary*   Ibid., January 31, 1864.

302   *The request*   General Edward McCook's compiled military service records, 4-F, N.A.R.A.

304   *I am so tired*   O.R. Series I, 38:575 (part 4).

304   *I send by the right*   O.R. Series I, 38:260 (part 3).

305   *The railroad*   Ibid., 255.

307   "Surrender"   Granville C. West, *McCook's Raid in the Rear of Atlanta and Hood's Army, August 1864*, 18–21. War Papers No. 29, District of Columbia Commandery, 1898.

307   "Go to hell!"   Ibid.

307   "The Yankees"   Fannie A. Beers, *Memories: A Record of Personal Experience and Adventure*, 180.

308   "Save yourselves"   O.R. Series I, 8:774 (part 2).

308   *General McCook is safe*   Ibid., 340.

308   *I regard the raid*   O.R. Series I, 38:77 (part 1).

309   *General McCook is entitled*   Ibid.

309   *STOP THE WAR!*   McPherson, *Battle Cry of Freedom*, 76.

310   *So Atlanta is ours*   O.R. Series I, 38:777 (part 5).

311   *I can make this march*   Thomas, *Abraham Lincoln*, 487.

311   *I beg to present you*   O.R. Series I, 44:783.

CHAPTER 18: NAVAL LIEUTENANT RODERICK McCOOK FIGHTS
THE CIVIL WAR AT SEA

313   *My dearest Lizzie*   letter from Shed to Lizzie, December 23, 1864, McCook Papers.

314   *Capt. Goldsborough*   letter from Roderick McCook to Captain L. M. Goldsborough, December 14, 1856, William W. Jeffries Archives, U.S. Naval Academy, Annapolis, Maryland.

315   *Commander Goldsborough*   letter from James C. Dobbin to Goldsborough, December 19, 1856, Ibid.

315   *. . . a most promising*   report from William Armstrong, Captain, U.S. San Jacinto, to Naval Board of Examiners, November 30, 1859, McCook Papers.

316   "When will they wake up?"   McCook, *Pictures from Memory*, 22.

317   *Dear Friend Lizzie*   letter from Shed to Lizzie, May 26, 1861, McCook Papers.

318   *My Dear Cousin*   letter from Shed to Mary Sheldon, June 25, 1861, Butler-McCook Papers.

319   *Dear Lizzie*   letter from Shed to Lizzie, September 7, 1861, McCook Papers.

319   *My Dear Cousin*   letter from Shed to Mary, November 28, 1861, Butler-McCook Papers.

320   *My dearest Lizzie*   letter from Shed to Lizzie, February 9, 1862, McCook Papers.

321   *Dear Lizzie*   Ibid., March 15, 1862.

321   *Dearest Lizzie*   Ibid., March 28, 1862.

322   *Dearest Lizzie*   Ibid., April 25, 1862.

322 *Sir, I want you to be off* message from Goldsborough to McCook, June 9, 1862, McCook Papers.

323 *My dear Cousin* letter from Shed to Mary, August 26, 1862, Butler-McCook Papers.

325 "look of incredulity" Welles, *Diary*, 1:64.

325 "A cheesebox on a raft" Sandburg, *Abraham Lincoln*, 292.

327 *My own dear wife* letter from Shed to Lizzie, December 20, 1864, McCook Papers.

329 *My darling Lizzie* Ibid., December 25, 1864.

330 *My own dear Lizzie* Ibid., December 26, 1864.

331 *Dearest Lizzie* Ibid., January 16, 1865.

332 *Riding out heavy gales* O.R. Navy, Series I, 2:259.

332 *My own darling* letter from Shed to Lizzie, February 19, 1865, McCook Papers.

333 *I am anxious* Ibid.

Chapter 19: "Horse Ed" Sweeps through the South

336 *Dear Mary* letter from Anson to Mary Sheldon, March 8, 1865, Butler-McCook Papers.

336 *Dear Mary* letter from Ed to Mary, March 10, 1865, Butler-McCook Papers.

339 *I occupied the city* O.R. Series I, 49:331 (part 2).

340 "With malice toward none" Thomas, *Abraham Lincoln*, 504.

341 "Did Grant surrender to Lee?" Ibid., 515.

342 "No bloody work" Ibid., 517.

342 "continued through the night" Sandburg, *Abraham Lincoln*, 715.

343 *I regard the war as over* O.R. Series I, 49:486 (part 2).

344 *With the exception of* Ibid., 663.

345 *When the big wars* letter from Ed to Mary, May 10, 1861, Butler-McCook Papers.

345 "'A' thought" McCook, *The Latimers*, 330.

EPILOGUE

348   "two-faced scoundrel"   Thomas and Hyman, *Stanton*, 290.

349   *This useless*   letter from Dr. John to Mary Sheldon, April 24, 1861, Butler-McCook Papers.

350   "Well," his father replied   McCook, *Memoirs*, 394.

350   "I told you"   Ibid.

350   "Yes," Anson laughed   Ibid.

350   "I saw Mother"   Ibid., 397.

350   "How did Mother look?"   Ibid.

350   "As young and beautiful"   Ibid.

352   "If I can't whip"   Clark J. Pahlas, "Wintermute and McCook," *The WI-IYOHI Monthly*, South Dakota State Historical Society (Pierre), Vol. 11, No. 8: 1-4.

352   "be a good boy"   Ibid.

353   "His name and fortune"   Thomas and Hyman, *Stanton*, 634.

353   "The man will fight"   Piatt, *Memories of the Men Who Saved the Union*, 85.

354   *The true story of the late war*   Ibid., 77.

355   "He is my son"   McCook family oral history, as related by Helen Jordan to Barbara Whalen.

355   "You can punish"   Ibid.

356   . . . *was a splendid*   letter from Captain George E. Belknap to Mrs. Roderick McCook, May 15, 1888, McCook Papers.

357   *Dear McCook*   letter from Sherman to McCook, August 23, 1884, McCook Papers.

358   *My Dear Lady*   letter from Sherman to Annie Colt, August 23, 1884. McCook Papers.

359   *In closing*   Villard, *Memoirs*, 1:325.

359   *I saw troops*   Grant, *Century Magazine*, February 1885, 593.

360   *I did General McCook injustice*   Grant, *Battles and Leaders*, I, 479.

360   *There can be*   letter from Lew Wallace to President Benjamin Harrison, July 5, 1890, Benjamin Harrison Collection, Vol. 109, Manuscript Division, Library of Congress, Washington, D.C.

362   *. . . to add interest*   letter from Ed to cousin Mary, November 28, 1863, Butler-McCook Papers.

363   *. . . beautiful, brilliant*   Frank Hall, *History of the State of Colorado, II*, 172.

364   *It has long been*   newspaper clipping, unattributed and undated, McCook Papers.

365   *Mr. McCook would*   *New York Express*, undated, McCook Papers.

366   *You perhaps know*   letter from Anson to Hetty, undated, McCook Papers.

367   *Dear Katherine and George*   McCook, *Memoirs*, 1.

368   *I am aware*   McCook, *Pictures from Memory*, 1.

369   On Fame's Eternal Camping Ground   *New York Tribune*, June 13, 1903, editorial page.

BIBLIOGRAPHY

Government Documents

Official Records (O.R.) of the Union and Confederate Armies in the War of the Rebellion, 130 volumes. Washington, D.C.: U.S. Government Printing Office, 1880–1900.

Official Records (O.R. Navy) of the Union and Confederate Navies in the War of the Rebellion, 31 volumes. Washington, D.C.: U.S. Government Printing Office, 1894–1922.

National Archives and Records Administration, (N.A.R.A.), Washington, D.C. Pension Records, Personal Records.

United States Naval Department, Naval History Division, *Civil War Naval Chronology*, 6 vols. Washington D.C.: U.S. Government Printing Office, 1961–1965.

Diaries, Letters, and Manuscripts

Butler-McCook Homestead, Hartford, Connecticut.
    Butler-McCook Papers
    Rev. John J. McCook, D.D., Memoirs, *Pictures from Memory*
Carroll County Historical Society, Carrollton, Ohio.
    Carroll County Historical Society Newsletter, Published quarterly.
    150th Anniversary McCook House 1837–1987, Velma Griffin, ed.
    Early History of Carroll County, Velma Griffin and Lynn R. Fox.
Carrollton Presbyterian Church, Carrollton, Ohio.
    Church records, Vol. 2.
Dayton Public Library, Dayton, Ohio.
    Forrer-Pierce-Wood Collection, Sarah Howard Forrer Letters.
Duke University, Durham, North Carolina
    William R. Perkins Library, U.S. Army Archives, Miscellany, Officers and Soldiers Miscellaneous Letters, 1847–1961.
        Rev. G. W. Chandler Letters.
        John Wesley Timmons, Sr. Papers.
Franklin College, Wheeling, West Virginia.
    College Register–Biographical and Historical.
Rutherford B. Hayes Presidential Center, Fremont, Ohio.
    Hayes Letters and Diaries.
    Letter from Daniel Gale to President Hayes.
Illinois State Historical Library, Springfield, Ill.
    Thomas J. Frazee Collection.
    Henry Horner Lincoln Collection.
    Levi Adolphus Ross Collection.

Jefferson College Historical Society, Canonsburg, Pennsylvania.

> *Jefferson College Times*, Vol. 14.

Kansas State Historical Society, Topeka.

> Thomas Ewing Jr. Papers.
>
> Daniel McCook Jr. Certificate of Election, Leavenworth County, December 17, 1859.

Kenyon College, Episcopal Office, Gambier, Ohio.

> *Triennial Catalogue of the Theological Seminary of the Diocese of Ohio and Kenyon College*, 1861.

Library of Congress, Manuscript Division, Washington, D.C.

> Benjamin Harrison Collection.
>
> McCook Papers.

Miami University, Oxford, Ohio.

> Schenck Papers.
>
> > Day, Donald Eugene, *Military Career of Robert Cumming Schenck*, 1963.
> >
> > Therry, James R., *The Life of General Robert Cumming Schenck*, 1968.

Ohio State Archaeological and Historical Society, Columbus, Ohio.

> Ohio Archaeological and Historical Publications, Vol. 23.

Private Collections

> Dunlop, Alexander McCook, *A Genealogical Study of the Descendants and Ancestors of Horatio Gates Phillips and Some Collateral Families*, owned by family of A. M. Dunlop.
>
> McCook, Anson, *Memoirs*, owned by the family of Mrs. Richard A. Smith, Noank, Connecticut.
>
> Thomas J. Wood Collection, owned by Stephen Wood, Washington, D.C.

Scotch-Irish Society of America, Bryn Mawr, Pennsylvania.

> Howe, Henry, *A Brief Historical Sketch of the Fighting McCooks*, reprinted from the proceedings of the Society, undated, McCook Papers.

South Dakota State Historical Society, Pierre.

> The *WI-IYOHI Monthly*, vol. 11, no. 8.

Tazewell County Genealogical Society, Pekin, Illinois.

> Society newsletter, October 1987.

Topeka Public Library, Topeka, Kansas.

> Paxton, W. N. *Annals of Platte County, Missouri and Historical Publications*, Vol. 23.

Trinity College, *The Tripod*, undergraduate publication, Vol. 23, No. 13, Hartford, Connecticut, 1927.

U.S. Army Military Institute (U.S.A.M.I), Carlisle Barracks, Carlisle, Pennsylvania.

> Luther F. Bradley Papers.
>
> > *Civil War Times Illustrated Collection.*
> >
> > > John A. Duncan Diary.
> > >
> > > Levi Wagner, *Reminiscences.*

Harrisburg Civil War Round Table Collection.
   Amos Fleagle Letters.
  West-Stanley-Wright Papers.
   Maj. Gen. David S. Stanley Memoirs.
United States Naval Academy, William W. Jeffries Memorial Archives, Annapolis, Maryland.
  Farragut, David Glasgow, *Some Reminiscences of Early Life.*
  Louis M. Goldsborough Letters.
University of Chicago Library, Chicago, Illinois.
  Stephen A. Douglas Papers.
   Letter from Daniel McCook Sr. to Douglas.
   Letter from Dan McCook Jr. to his father.

Addresses and Articles

Grant, Ulysses S. "Shiloh" *Century Magazine*, February 1885.

McCook, Daniel, Jr. "The Second Division at Shiloh." *Harper's New Monthly Magazine*, May 1864.

Robertson, William. "An Account of the Battle." Civil War 125th Anniversary booklet. Chattahoochee County, GA: American Civil War Commemorative Committee, 1988.

Taylor, John. "The Story of a Battle." Addressed to the Young Men's Catholic Club, Trenton, NJ, December 11, 1893. J. A. Cresfe & Co., Trenton, NJ. Virginia State Library, Richmond.

West, Granville C. "McCook's Raid in the Rear of Atlanta and Hood's Army, August 1864." War Papers No. 29, District of Columbia Commandery, 1898.

Wilson, James Harrison. "Alexander McDowell McCook." Thirty-fifth Annual Reunion of the Association Graduates of the United States Military Academy at West Point, NY; Saginaw, MI, Sherman and Peters, Printers and Binders, 1904.

Woodward, James H. "Gen. A. McD. McCook at Stone's River." Commandery of the State of California, Military Order of the Loyal Legion of the United States, War Paper No. 9, Times-Mirror Printing and Binding House, 1892.

Oral Histories

George McCook's quotes during the Whiskey Rebellion, related by his daughter Fanny to her nephew Henry and used by him in *The Latimers: A Tale of the Western Insurrection of 1794.*

General Alexander McCook's quote to his grandson, Alexander McCook Craighead, that General Thomas J. Wood said of General William S. Rosecrans during the battle of Chickamauga, "I'm glad that Catholic son of a bitch put it in writing."

Martha McCook's quotes to her son George, "You can punish your son and I can punish mine. There will be no dinner tonight," told by her great-granddaughter, Mrs. Helen Jordan, to Barbara Whalen.

Unit Histories
Aten, Henry J. *History of the Eighty-fifth Regiment, Illinois Volunteer Infantry.* Hiawatha, KS: The Regimental Association, 1901.

Bennett, L. G., and William H. Haigh. *History of the 36th Regiment Illinois Volunteers during the War of the Rebellion.* Aurora, IL: Nickerbocker and Hodder Printers and Binders, 1876.

Grebner, Constantin. *We Were the Ninth, A History of the Ninth Regiment Ohio Volunteer Infantry, April 17, 1861 to June 7, 1864.* Frederic Trautmann, ed. Kent, OH, and London: Kent State University Press, 1987.

Holmes, James T. *52nd Ohio O.V.I. Then and Now.* Columbus, OH: Berlin Print Company, 1898.

Kinnear, J. R. *History of the 86th Regiment, Illinois Volunteer Infantry.* Chicago: Tribune Company's Book and Job Printing Office, 1890.

Morris, William S. *History of the 31st Regiment Illinois Volunteers, Organized by John A. Logan.* Evansville, IN: Keller Printing and Publishing Co., 1902.

Rogers, Robert M. *The One Hundred Twenty-fifth Regiment Illinois Volunteer.* Champagne, IL: Gazette Steam Print, 1882.

Stewart, Nixon B. *Dan McCook's Regiment, Fifty-second O.V.I., A History of the Regiment.* Alliance, OH: Review Print, 1900.

Work, Julius Birney. *McCook's Brigade: Reunion of Col. Dan McCook's Third Brigade, Second Division, Fourteenth Army Corps, Army of the Cumberland, August, 1900.* Chicago: Allied Trades Printing Council, 1901.

Newspapers and Magazines
Boston Evening Transcript
Century Magazine
Chattanooga Daily Rebel
Cincinnati Daily Commercial
Cincinnati Daily Times
Cincinnati Enquirer
Cincinnati Gazette
Cincinnati Times Star
Cleveland Herald
Dayton Daily Empire
Harper's New Monthly Magazine
Harper's Weekly
National Republican

New York Evening Journal
New York Express
New York Law Journal (formerly the *Daily Register*)
New York Times
New York Tribune
Pittsburgh Gazette Times
Steubenville Daily Herald
Tazewell Register (Pekin, IL)
Washington Evening Star
Washington (PA) *Reporter*

Books

Andrews, J. Cutler. *The North Reports the Civil War.* Pittsburgh: University of Pittsburgh Press, 1955.

Basler, Roy P., ed. The Abraham Lincoln Associates. *The Collected Works of Abraham Lincoln.* 8 vols. New Brunswick, NJ: Rutgers University Press, 1953.

Beers, Fannie A. *Memories: A Record of Personal Experience and Adventure.* Philadelphia: Press of J. B. Lippincott Co., 1889.

Bickham, William D. *Rosecrans' Campaign with the Fourteenth Army Corps, Army of the Cumberland: A Narrative of Personal Observations.* Cincinnati: Moore, Wilstach, Keyes & Co., 1863.

Bowers, John. *Chickamauga and Chattanooga.* New York: Harper Collins, 1994.

Cadwallader, Sylvanus. *Three Years with Grant.* Edited by Benjamin Thomas. New York: Alfred A. Knopf, 1955.

Castel, Albert. *Decision in the West: The Atlanta Campaign of 1864.* Lawrence: University Press of Kansas, 1992.

Catton, Bruce. *This Hallowed Ground.* New York: Pocket Books, a Division of Simon & Schuster, Inc., 1961.

Cist, Henry M. *The Army of the Cumberland.* Army in the Civil War Series. Vol. 8. New York: Charles Scribner's Sons, 1885.

Cleaves, Freeman. *Rock of Chickamauga: The Life of General George H. Thomas.* Norman: University of Oklahoma Press, 1948.

Conover, Charlotte Reeve. *Dayton and Montgomery County.* Vol. 1. New York: Lewis Historical Publishing Company, 1932.

Cooling, Benjamin Franklin. *Forts Henry and Donelson: The Key to the Confederate Heartland.* Knoxville: University of Tennessee Press, 1987.

———. *Jubal Early's Raid on Washington 1864.* Baltimore: The Nautical & Aviation Publishing Company of America, 1989.

———. *Symbol, Sword, and Shield: Defending Washington During the Civil War.* Shippensburg, PA: The White Mane Publishing Co., 1991.

Cozzens, Peter. *The Battle for Stones River: No Better Place to Die.* Urbana: The University of Illinois Press, 1990.

————. *The Battle of Chickamauga: This Terrible Sound.* Urbana: The University of Illinois Press, 1992.

————. *The Shipwreck of their Hopes: The Battles for Chattanooga.* Urbana and Chicago: The University of Illinois Press, 1994.

Dana, Charles A. *Recollections of the Civil War.* New York: Collier Books, 1963.

Daniel, Larry J. *Shiloh, the Battle That Changed the Civil War.* New York: Simon and Schuster, 1997.

Davis, William C. *Battle at Bull Run: A History of the First Major Campaign of the Civil War.* Baton Rouge and London: Louisiana State University Press, 1977.

Dawson, George F. *Life and Service of Gen. John A. Logan As Soldier and Statesman.* Chicago: Belford, Clarke & Company, 1887.

Donald, David Herbert. *Lincoln.* New York: Simon & Schuster, 1995.

Dupuy, R. Ernest, and Trevor N. Dupuy. *The Compact History of the Civil War.* New York: Warner Books, 1960.

Dyer, John P. *From Shiloh to San Juan: The Life of "Fightin' Joe" Wheeler.* Baton Rouge: Louisiana State University Press, 1941.

Eisenschiml, Otto. *Why Was Lincoln Murdered?* Boston: Little, Brown and Company, 1937.

Evans, David. *Sherman's Horsemen: Union Cavalry Operations in the Atlanta Campaign.* Bloomington and Indianapolis: Indiana University Press, 1996.

Ewing, Joseph H. *Sherman at War.* Dayton, OH: Morningside House, Inc. 1992.

Fisher, Horace C. *A Staff Officer's Story: The Personal Experiences of Horace Newton Fisher in the Civil War.* Boston: Thomas Todd Company, 1960.

Foote, Shelby. *The Civil War, A Narrative: Fort Sumter to Perryville.* New York: Random House, 1958.

————. *The Civil War, A Narrative: Fredericksburg to Meridian.* New York: Random House, 1963.

————. *The Civil War, A Narrative: Red River to Appomattox.* New York: Random House, 1974.

Fowler, William M., Jr. *Under Two Flags: The American Navy in the Civil War.* New York: Avon Books, 1990.

Gracie, Archibald. *The Truth about Chickamauga.* Boston and New York: Houghton Mifflin Company, 1911.

Grant, Ulysses Simpson. *Personal Memoirs of U. S. Grant.* 2 vols. New York: Charles L. Webster & Co., 1885.

Hafendorfer, Kenneth A. *Perryville: Battle for Kentucky.* Louisville, KY: Kenneth A. Hafendorfer, 1981.

Hall, Frank. *History of the State of Colorado.* 4 vols. Chicago: Blakely Printing Company, 1889–1895.

Hay, John. *Letters of John Hay and Extracts from Diary.* 3 vols. *New York: Gordian Press, 1969.*

Herald, Peter. *Early History of Carroll County, 1883–1884.* Edited by Velma Griffin. Strasburg, OH: Gordon Printing, Inc. 1988.

Horn, Stanley F. *The Decisive Battle of Nashville.* Baton Rouge and London: Louisiana State University Press, 1956.

Howe, Henry. *Howe's Historical Collections of Ohio.* Cincinnati: Derby, Bradley & Co., 1847.

Hughes, Nathaniel C. *General William J. Hardee: Old Reliable.* Baton Rouge: Louisiana State University Press, 1965.

Johnson, Robert Underwood, and Clarence Clough Buel, eds. *Battles and Leaders of the Civil War.* 4 vols., 1887–1888. New York: Thomas Yoseloff, Inc. 1956.

Johnston, William. *Trial of Daniel McCook, Esq., on Articles of Impeachment for Good Behavior in Office.* Cincinnati: Hefly, Hubbel and Co., 1839.

Jones, James B. *"Black Jack": John A. Logan and Southern Illinois in the Civil War Era.* Tallahassee: Florida State University Press, 1967.

Jones, James Pickett. *Yankee Blitzkrieg: Wilson's Raid through Alabama and Georgia.* Athens and London: University of Georgia Press, 1976.

Jordan, David M. *Winfield Scott Hancock.* Bloomington and Indianapolis: Indiana University Press, 1988.

Kerksis, Sydney C., ed. *The Atlanta Papers.* Dayton, OH: Morningside Bookshop Press, 1980.

Klement, Frank L. *The Limits of Dissent: Clement L. Vallandigham & the Civil War.* Lexington: University Press of Kentucky, 1970.

Lamers, William M. *The Edge of Glory: A Biography of General William S. Rosecrans, U.S.A.* New York: Harcourt, Brace and World, 1961.

Leech, Margaret. *Reveille in Washington.* New York: Carroll & Graf Publishers, Inc., 1941.

Leyburn, James G. *The Scotch-Irish, A Social History.* Chapel Hill: University of North Carolina Press, 1962.

Logan, John A. *Uncle Daniel's Story of "Tom Anderson" and Twenty Great Battles.* New York: A. R. Hart & Company Publishers, 1886.

Longacre, Edward G. *Mounted Raids of the Civil War.* South Brunswick and New York: A. S. Barnes & Company, 1975.

Lowry, Terry. *September Blood: The Battle of Carnifex Ferry.* Charleston, WV: Pictorial Histories Publishing Co., 1985.

Macdonald, John. *Great Battles of the Civil War.* New York: Macmillan Publishing Company, 1988.

Marszalek, John F. *Sherman: A Soldier's Passion for Order.* New York: Free Press, Division of Macmillan, Inc., 1993.

McClellan, George B. *McClellan's Own Story: The War for the Union.* New York: Charles L. Webster and Company, 1887.

McCook, Henry Christopher. *The Latimers: A Tale of the Western Insurrection of 1794.* Philadelphia: George W. Jacobs and Company, 1898.

McDonough, James Lee. *Stones River: Bloody River in Tennessee.* Knoxville: University of Tennessee Press, 1980.

———. *Chattanooga, A Death Grip on the Confederacy.* Knoxville: University of Tennessee Press, 1984.

———. *War in Kentucky—From Shiloh to Perryville.* Knoxville: University of Tennessee Press, 1994.

McFeely, William S. *Grant: A Biography.* New York: W. W. Norton & Company, 1981.

McPherson, James M. *Battle Cry of Freedom: The Civil War Era.* New York: Oxford University Press, 1988.

McPherson, Lucy Harmon. *Life and Letters of Oscar Fitzalan Harmon.* Trenton, NJ: MacRillish & Quigley Company, Printers, 1914.

Miers, Earl Schenck. *The General Who Marched to Hell.* New York: Dorset Press, 1951.

———. *The Web of Victory: Grant at Vicksburg.* New York: Alfred A. Knopf, 1955.

Mitchell, Joseph B. *Decisive Battles of the Civil War.* New York: Fawcett Premier, 1955.

Moore, Frank, ed. *The Rebellion Record: A History of American Events.* 11 vols. New York: G. P. Putnam, published between 1861 and 1869.

Morris, Ray, Jr. *Sheridan: The Life and Wars of General Phil Sheridan.* New York: Crown Publishers, Inc., 1992.

Nicolay, John G., and John Hay. *Abraham Lincoln, A History.* 10 vols. New York: The Century Co., 1917.

O'Connor, Richard. *Sheridan: The Inevitable.* New York: Konecky & Konecky, 1953.

Parks, Joseph H. *General Leonidas Polk, C.S.A.: The Fighting Bishop.* Baton Rouge: Louisiana State University Press, 1962.

Piatt, Donn. *Memories of the Men Who Saved the Union.* New York: Belford, Clarke and Company, 1887.

Prokopowicz, Gerald J. *All for the Regiment: The Army of the Ohio, 1861–62.* Chapel Hill and London: University of North Carolina Press, 2001.

Reid, Whitelaw. *Ohio in the War: Her Statesmen, Her Generals and Soldiers.* Cincinnati: Moore, Wilstach and Baldwin, 1868.

Royster, Charles. *The Destructive War.* New York: Alfred A. Knopf, 1991.

Sandburg, Carl. *Abraham Lincoln: The Prairie Years and the War Years.* New York: Harcourt, Brace & World, Inc., 1954.

Seale, William. *The President's House: A History.* Washington, DC: White House Historical Association, 1986.

ABOUT THE AUTHORS

Charles Whalen, a native of Dayton, Ohio, graduated from the University of Dayton and Harvard Business School. A professor of economics at the University of Dayton, he served for twelve years in the Ohio General Assembly. Elected to the U.S. Congress in 1966, he represented Ohio's Third District until retiring in 1978.

Barbara Whalen was born in Detroit, Michigan, and graduated from Marymount College, Tarrytown, New York. She is a former newspaper columnist, radio and television writer, and advertising executive.

The Whalens are the authors, collectively, of four nonfiction books. They coauthored *The Longest Debate: A Legislative History of the 1964 Civil Rights Act*. Charles Whalen also wrote *The House and Foreign Policy: The Irony of Congressional Reform* and *Your Right to Know: How the Free Flow of News Depends on the Journalist's Right to Protect His Sources*. With former Congressmen Robert T. Stafford, Frank J. Horton, Richard S. Schweiker, and Garner E. Shriver, Charles Whalen wrote *How to End the Draft: The Case for an All-Volunteer Army*.

Charles and Barbara Whalen have six children and six grandchildren, and live in Bethesda, Maryland.